Everything's an Argument

Andrea A. Lunsford and John J. Ruszkiewicz

with WRITING RESPONSIBLY

edited by Sherrie Weller

2017–2018

macmillan learning
curriculum solutions

Manufactured in the United States of America

2 1 0 9 8 7

f e d c b a

Macmillan Learning Curriculum Solutions
14903 Pilot Drive
Plymouth, MI 48170
www.macmillanlearning.com

978-1-319-14714-3

Acknowledgements

Text acknowledgements and copyrights appear at the back of the book on pages 625–628, which constitute an extension of the copyright page. It is a violation of the law to reproduce these selections by any means whatsoever without the written permission of the copyright holder.

bedford/st. martin's • hayden-mcneil
w.h. freeman • worth publishers

TABLE OF CONTENTS

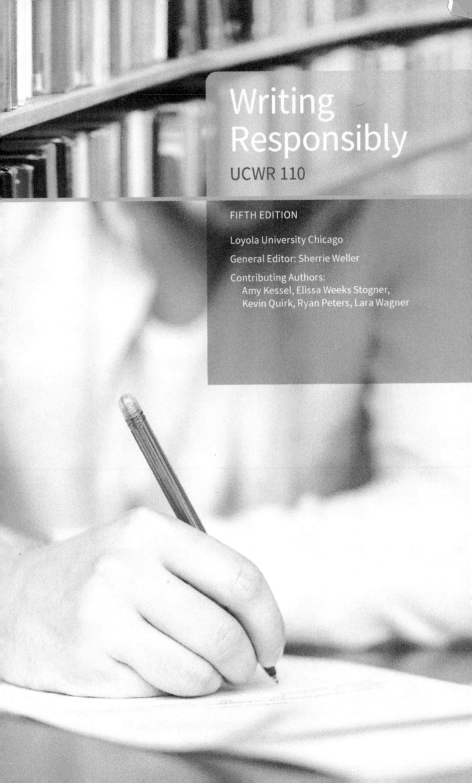

Writing Responsibly

UCWR 110

FIFTH EDITION

Loyola University Chicago

General Editor: Sherrie Weller

Contributing Authors:
Amy Kessel, Elissa Weeks Stogner,
Kevin Quirk, Ryan Peters, Lara Wagner

1

Writing
Responsibly

UCWR 110

Writing Responsibly

General Editor, Sherrie Weller

Copyright © 2017 by the Writing Program, Loyola University Chicago

F. Scott Fitzgerald once quipped that "the test of a first-rate intelligence is the ability to hold two opposed ideas in mind at the same time and still retain the ability to function" (41). As an author, Fitzgerald understood that the ability to navigate contradictory viewpoints—to summarize, analyze, synthesize, and develop arguments about a variety of texts—is an essential part of the manner in which writing asks us to interact with a topic from multiple perspectives. As you enter the first phase of your higher education, you'll need to practice and sharpen those analytical and argumentative writing skills you have already developed and begin to understand their importance in dealing with diverse points of view both in and outside the classroom.

The single most misleading myth about writing is that it is an inherent skill: that some have it, others don't, and while the former pursue a life of novel-writing, letters, and memoirs, the rest of us are left with nothing but text messages and tweets of 140 characters or less. Yes, writing comes more intuitively to some students, but it is also a process with identifiable patterns, elements, and stages. The four genres of writing mentioned above—summary, analysis, synthesis, and researched argument—can all be broken down into manageable steps, and with practice, those steps help to create a better and more persuasive piece of writing. In your high school classes, you no doubt studied summary, analysis, synthesis, and argumentation to some degree, but your college classes (and your life beyond that) will require more complexity and sophistication than have been asked of your writing in the past. A thorough understanding of the writing process will allow you to expand your writing capabilities on multiple fronts—from the topics you discuss to the complexity with which you approach them.

And as the range of your writing increases, so will the breadth of what you study. In college, the definition of the term "text" expands exponentially. In addition to the works of classic literature, poetry, history, and the heavy textbooks you are probably accustomed to, your courses at Loyola University Chicago will ask you to analyze graphic novels, newspaper articles, advertisements, political campaigns, speeches, film, music, art, and research studies in psychology, economics, mathematics, science, and medicine. University courses view nearly any document that conveys information or a position about a topic as having intellectual and sociological value, and college level writing asks you to adeptly compose and respond to this diverse array of texts.

This writing guide is designed to help you anticipate and navigate the sophistication and diversity of writing you will engage in at Loyola. It is organized around the four forms we have already briefly discussed—summary, analysis, synthesis, and argument—and encourages you to view these elements as foundations upon which you can build and develop the skills you already possess. We view college writing as a contribution to ongoing academic discussions; the topics and texts you will study belong to a long history of conversation and debate among scholars, intellectuals, and professionals, and the writing techniques you hone here will allow you to enter those conversations with confidence and complexity.

2 Summary

As you probably already know, a summary is a sentence, paragraph, or paper that gives an overview of another text. A summary is significantly shorter than its source text, but it still covers the source text's main ideas. The idea behind a summary is that it allows a reader to understand the point or "gist" of the source text without actually reading it.

According to linguists and educators, summary writing is a sophisticated cognitive task. First of all, it demands that the writer read and fully understand the source text. Then, it requires the writer to select information based on its importance in the source text, to condense details by incorporating them into more general statements, and to integrate all of the selected, condensed materials into an organized structure. In other words, summary writing is more than just deleting insignificant material from the source text; it transforms the source text's details and ideas into a new, more condensed piece (Hidi and Anderson). Research has also shown that knowing how to summarize is crucial for students. Not only is summary writing a common assignment at all levels of education, but it also improves reading comprehension, content-area learning, and information retention (Maclellan; Hidi and Anderson 473; Yu 116-7).

No doubt you have already written a summary at some point in your schooling, and the situations in which you will need to write a summary will only become more frequent at the university level. Across disciplines, university instructors assign summaries in many ways. In class, they might ask for an "overview" of a reading or the "point" of a particular argument. They might require that you write a summary of a text as an introduction to a paper that **analyzes** that text or **synthesizes** it with another text. Also, summary questions often appear on final exams because they not only effectively test reading comprehension, but they also require students to identify and prioritize important ideas within a reading. Furthermore, as you progress to upper-division classes, you will be asked to write **research papers** in which you will want to summarize the work of another scholar in order to use it as evidence. In that case, a summary of another person's research will function as part of your own argument.

The Basics of Summary Writing

Summaries share certain basic characteristics or *conventions*. Most importantly, a summary re-presents or reproduces the content of a source text. A summary is always written in the writer's own words and is shorter than the source text. The following summary of Malcolm X's "A Homemade

Education" was written by student Teyana Morgan and conforms to these conventions of summary writing:

> In Malcolm X's "A Homemade Education," he details how creating a self-educational system while in prison allowed him to gain a love for education and new knowledge. While in prison, he explains how he felt incapable of expressing his thoughts and emotions through writing due to his limited vocabulary. This limitation compelled Malcolm X to begin teaching himself. He tells how after teaching himself how to read and write, he began spending a vast amount of time consumed in his newfound literature. Malcolm X describes how studying mostly history and philosophical readings gave him fresh feelings about the knowledge and action of the black race in America. In closing he tells how his homemade education system was more valuable than if he had chosen or had the fate of being anywhere else. Malcolm X gained a freedom in the captivity of prison through immersing himself in new knowledge.

Notice how this summary of "A Homemade Education" demonstrates some of the key characteristics of a well-written summary. To begin with, it does not include any of the student writer's ideas; it focuses on the material in "A Homemade Education." In addition, it is composed entirely in the writer's own words; none of the phrases or sentence structures is taken from Malcolm X's piece. Also, it is much shorter than the source text; Malcolm X's essay is forty-four paragraphs long whereas the summary is only around 150 words. Note as well that the student's summary is a well-constructed paragraph: it contains a topic sentence—in this case, the paragraph's first sentence—that identifies the main idea of "A Homemade Education" and supporting sentences that cover the source text's main points.

The first step in writing a strong summary is knowing when a summary is being asked for by an assignment. The following are essay prompts from various disciplines that ask for some kind of summary:

- What is Vaida's opinion about the importance of water cluster mediated atmospheric chemistry?

- Give an overview of Hanson's and Mohn's discussions on educational assessment trends.

- Summarize Piaget's stages of cognitive development.

- What is Caroline Bird's argument concerning college education?

When looking for key words or phrases that indicate that a prompt is asking for a summary, look for instructions that somehow ask you to re-state what you read in a source. You might see words like "overview," "point," "identify," or "describe." These words, and words like them, ask you to re-encapsulate, but not interpret or analyze, what is in a source text. When this happens, you should examine the prompt more carefully to see if you are being asked to summarize a source. Be aware, too, that sometimes an instructor will ask for a summary and then ask for an interpretation in the same prompt; summaries are frequently used as introductions to arguments and response essays.

In order to write a strong, efficient summary, you will need to understand your source text hierarchically. In other words, you will need to identify the text's main idea, or the idea that encapsulates all the other ideas in the text. Then, you will need to prioritize the main points that support or explain the main idea, understanding that all of the details in the text can be generalized into these main points. In source texts that are already well structured by the author, this task will be relatively easy. However, not all source texts are well organized; often, you will need to analyze the text and infer the hierarchy of ideas. It might help for you to think of a source text in terms of a tree diagram like the one below. Each level encapsulates the levels that are underneath it.

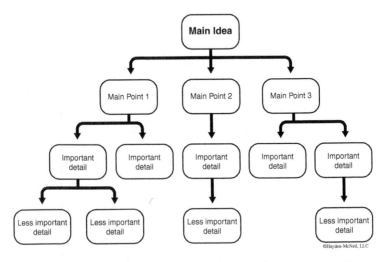

©Hayden-McNeil, LLC

Thinking about a text in this way and ordering information according to importance will help you with many aspects of summary writing. Most importantly, it will help you to eliminate unnecessary information from your summary, and it will help you group details under more general main points. For example, in the summary above, the writer does not, like Malcolm X, list the books from the prison library that he checked out and read, nor does she tell us exactly what information these books contained. These are details that are generalized in the statement that Malcolm X studied "history and philosophical readings."

Although brevity is a defining feature of a summary, different assignments require different lengths for summaries. Again, thinking of your source text in terms of a tree diagram can help you decide how much information to include in your summary. If you are asked for a single-sentence summary, you will only want to include the first, broadest level of the diagram, the source text's main idea. If you are asked to write a paragraph-length summary (and this is the most common kind of summary), you will probably include only the first two levels of the diagram, the source's main ideas and main points. Although it is rare, you might be asked to summarize a text over several pages; in this case, you might (if there are not too many main points to cover) include the third level of information, some important details.

As you compose your summary, you should be aware that conventions of strong academic writing are still relevant. In other words, your paragraphs should be well organized with a main idea and corresponding topic sentence. Fortunately, your tree chart will provide you with a ready-made structure. For paragraph-length summaries, simply turn the main idea identified in your chart into a topic sentence, and use the main points to fill in the paragraph. If your summary is longer than a single paragraph, decide how to logically divide the main points into several paragraphs, each with its own topic sentence. Usually, you will still state the main idea of the source text at the beginning of the first paragraph.

As we have discussed, a lot of cognitive work goes into writing a strong summary. When students do not fully understand how to write a summary or do not want to do the cognitive work, they often make two crucial mistakes. The first should be obvious from the discussion above: it is the mistake of including too much detail or unimportant information. The second is what is called "patchwriting" or "copy-delete" summarizing. This happens when students copy chunks of the source text, possibly changing some grammar or vocabulary, and stitch these chunks into a single paragraph (Howard 264; Maclellan). Not only does patchwriting fail to accomplish the goals of summarizing, but also, when quotation marks are not used to indicate original phrasing and word choice, it is a form of plagiarism. Below is a summary that exemplifies patchwriting:

While Malcolm X was in prison, he was jealous of Bimbi and other inmates who could take charge of conversations. He decided to get hold of a dictionary. He copied the first page and read it aloud to himself over and over again. Once his word-base broadened, Malcolm X checked out books from the prison library and joined weekly debates between inmate teams. He loved to read so much that he read at night in his prison cell in the glow from the hallway. Not even Elijah Muhammad could have guessed what a new world opened up to Malcolm X as he learned that the collective white man had acted like the devil by oppressing black people. When people asked Malcolm X where he went to college, he said that prison enabled him to study more than college where there are too many distractions.

If you refer back to Malcolm X's essay, you will see that the writer of this summary has copied much phrasing and vocabulary, not to mention sentence structure, from the source text. In addition, this summary does not generalize details but instead includes an unbalanced sampling of them (with a few misreadings) from different parts of "A Homemade Education." This summary does not show that the writer has understood the source text, processed and prioritized the information in it, and reproduced it in an organized way for her readers.

Strategies for Writing Strong Summaries

It is important to reflect the source text's genre in your summary. If you don't, your reader will not get a full understanding of your source text. Your job as the summary writer is to give your reader an understanding of not only the content of the source text but also the source text's form—its purpose and structure. For example, if you summarized Malcolm X's essay, which is a narrative, by emphasizing his argument about the "whitening" of history, you would not be giving your readers an accurate idea of what the source text is. "A Homemade Education" tells the story of Malcolm X's education, and it is important that your summary offers a shortened, condensed version of that story not an analysis of his ideas or an outline of his underlying argument.

Although, in your university classes, you will encounter and be asked to summarize many different kinds of source texts, three of the most common genres you will see are narrative, expository, and argumentative. These three genres not only have very different structures, but the hierarchies of ideas are different as well. In a source text that is an argument, the main idea is—predictably—the author's thesis or position. Usually, the main points are the author's major reasons that support his or her thesis. Concrete evidence makes up the details that correspond to the author's major reasons. A tree diagram for an argument, then, would look something like this:

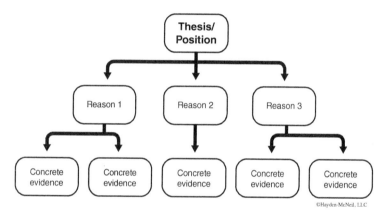

©Hayden-McNeil, LLC

Here, the tree diagram reflects the structure of an argument, which is the source text's genre. A tree diagram for another genre would likely look very different. For example, if we constructed a tree diagram for a narrative, the main idea would not be the thesis of an argument but a statement of the main action in the narrative. The second level of the diagram, the main points, would be the main plot points in the narrative. On the other hand, an expository text, which is a text that explains something and the purpose of which is to inform the reader, would have as its main idea an overview of the information provided in the source text and more specific statements of fact as the main points. Understanding a source text hierarchically means understanding what kind of hierarchy is in place. That way, your summary will accurately represent the source text's content and form.

At the beginning of this section, you read a summary of a narrative, Malcolm X's "A Homemade Education." Below are a few more examples. Consider, first, this summary of an argument, Caroline Bird's "The Case Against College," which was written by a student in a first-year composition course. As with the other summaries you have read in this section, the first sentence states the main idea of the source text, in this case, the source text's thesis or position, and the following sentences explain the source text's main points, in this case, the argument that supports the thesis:

Evaluating higher education in "The Case Against College," Caroline Bird questions the effectiveness of such an institution. She argues that the expectations of the value of college may not actually be assessed in college. For example, some expectations people have of what they will derive from college are supposed to be acquired during earlier stages in life. Caroline Bird also discusses how education can be learned elsewhere, such as through books or television, and does not need to be learned in a school setting. Another point that Bird asserts in her argument is that putting the weight of the future of mankind on university students is quite unrealistic. She explains that most students do not know or are too young to have determined their wants for the future. Caroline Bird closes by suggesting that college be closely critiqued by potential students for its possible worth before they make the decision to attend (Morgan).

Following the structure of Bird's own argument, this student begins and closes by stating Bird's position. In the middle of the paragraph, she lists some of the main reasons that Bird uses to justify her position.

The next example is a summary written of an expository text, "On the Breeds of Cattle—Historic and Current Classifications." Notice the differences between this summary and those of "A Homemade Education" and "The Case Against College":

In "On the Breeds of Cattle—Historic and Current Classifications," the authors list, sort, and discuss the various systems used to classify cattle breeds over the last several hundred years. In doing so, they report the difficulties scientists have faced in classifying cattle because of the long, largely undocumented history of cross-breeding. However, they also detail the reasons why classifying cattle is important and why many scientists over the years have attempted to establish a classification system. According to this article, classification systems of the past were based on head/horn shape and size, coat color, or geographic origin. More modern classification systems have been founded upon modern scientific advances; these systems use biochemical traits—often in conjunction with previous systems—to classify cattle. The most recent developments in cattle classification are DNA-based; the article implies that scientists believe that the DNA-based classification system is the most accurate and useful.

You can see that, in this summary, the writer focuses on what information is provided by the source text and how that information is presented. The topic sentence, which states the source text's main idea, gives an overview of the information covered in the source. The following sentences break that information down into parts; these sentences discuss exactly how the authors list, sort, and discuss cattle classification systems. Notice that, unlike a summary of an argument, which reproduces the logical framework of an argument, a summary of an expository text reports a set of facts.

Once you have an idea of what you want to say in your summary—that is, once you have identified the main idea and main points—you will move on to thinking about how you want to say it. There are specific writing strategies, or composition "moves," that effective summary writers use in order to indicate to their readers that the piece they are reading is a summary. Below are some of the common moves summary writers make in their summaries:

- They introduce a written summary by orienting their readers to the author and title of the source text. Here are two different ways of introducing the source text at the beginning of a summary:

    a. "In Malcolm X's 'A Homemade Education,' he tells the story..."

    b. "Malcolm X's 'A Homemade Education' tells the story of..."

- They refer often to their source as a way of reminding their readers that the information is coming from a source text. Notice below how the writer intentionally refers back to the source text in the phrases, "the narrative" and "Malcolm X":

    a. "The narrative begins by describing his frustration."

    b. "Malcolm X details the many books he encountered in prison."

- They use verbs that are appropriate to the genre of the source text. Below are examples and lists of verbs that correspond to narrative, expository, and argumentative source texts:

    a. Narrative

        - Example: "Malcolm X *recounts* his experiences learning to read and write."

        - Verbs: *recounts, tells, narrates, describes, remembers*

b. Expository

- Example: "The authors *detail* the many classification systems used over the last 100 years."

- Verbs: *explains, lists, reports, expands upon, details*

c. Argumentative

- Example: "Bird *defends* her position by providing specific examples as evidence."

- Verbs: *asserts, argues, affirms, reasons, defends, justifies*

To see how these moves work to produce a coherent, clear summary, see the examples provided earlier in this section.

For additional resources on writing summaries, please see Purdue OWL at https://owl.english.purdue.edu/, and search for "Writing Summaries."

Sample Student Summary/Response Essay

Annesley Clark
Professor Weller
UCWR 110
9 September 2014

iNeed: A Reflection on Technology Today

People today often find it impossible to fathom living without technology. When an iPhone breaks or the Internet goes down, people of all ages feel anything from annoyance to panic, frustration to rage. In their essays, "A Reunion with Boredom," and "Is Google Making Us Stupid," Charles Simic and Nicholas Carr explore the idea that technology is changing the way people think and live. Both men are suspicious of our clear reliance on technology, and their essays serve as grains of salt to take with our unbending love of electronics. I agree with Carr and Simic that technology is changing the way we live our lives, and that we need to be wary of our dependence on and use of technology.

In "A Reunion with Boredom," Simic explains how his 72 hours without power (and thus, without technology) in the wake of a hurricane allowed him to reflect on how our increased use of technology has changed our lives. He notes that those who are constantly on their phones miss chances to connect with people and surroundings because they are glued to their screens (Simic 374). In the frequent, technology-free boredom of Simic's youth, he discovered himself. He describes coming "face-to-face" with himself and becoming a "spectator of [his] own existence" (Simic 375). Simic used this time with himself to discover who he was and laments that today "we are only puppets jerked this way and that by whatever device we think we are operating" (376). Simic believes that we are losing our uniqueness and our very personalities to our obsession with electronic devices.

While still focused on how we interact with our devices, Carr takes a slightly different approach. He explores how advances in technology, particularly the advent of the Internet, have changed the way we read and how we think in his essay "Is Google Making Us Stupid?" He first looks at how reading patterns have changed, describing how, ever since he began reading primarily online, his brain "expects to take in information the way the Net distributes it: in a swiftly moving stream of particles" (Carr 92). A scientific study out of the University College London showed that people researching online "power browse" though many different articles, looking at a page or two before "bouncing" to the next article to skim (Carr 93–94). Carr says that when we read in the "power browse," style we've adopted, "Our ability to interpret text…remains largely disengaged" (94). When we read online, we don't process the material the same way we do when we read an actual book.

The Internet is pervasive and powerful. It layers multiple types of media on top of one another, so engaging with only one source of information at a time is rare. The addition of advertisements, games, and accessories also divert our attention, contributing to our inability to engage with longer texts. Carr goes on to describe Google's agenda and the idea that, "The human brain is just an outdated processor that needs a faster processor and a bigger hard drive." (99). The financial backers of the Internet need our brains to function this way—the faster we go, the more money they make off of advertisements, the more they can learn about their target audience, and persuade us to purchase their products and services. (Carr 99–100). After all, Carr recognizes that technological advances have historically been met with opposition. At the same time, however, he is wary of the way the Internet has changed our brains and memories. Carr concludes his powerful essay by reminding the reader about a scene from *2001: A Space Odyssey*. In the world of the film, "People have become so machinelike that the most human character is a machine" (Carr 101). Carr wonders if this is the way we are headed as well.

After taking the time to look at my daily life, I have to agree with both Simic and Carr that constant attachment to our devices has changed us. I can't go an hour without checking my phone, logging on to Facebook or sending a SnapChat. I absolutely feel addicted to my technology. Most of my social interaction now takes place in the cyber world, and I often find that I would rather text friends than make the effort to see them in person. This scares me, and it should. Seeing my friends should not feel like a chore, but with technology being so easy and readily available, anything that requires more effort seems that much more difficult.

My social life is not the only affected area—my memory and attention span have been impacted as well. Carr describes how the Internet seems to be "chipping away at my capacity for concentration and contemplation," which is an idea I can relate to completely (92). While watching a show online, I often have several other tabs open to check social media, all while playing a game on my phone. I feel that I no longer have the capacity to dedicate all of my attention to one incoming channel, except for when settling down to read. When I am sucked into a good book, the world around me blurs. Nothing is more real than what is contained in the pages of my reading. That, in my opinion, is powerful. If none of these new technologies can captivate me the same way a book can, then I need to explore whether they are truly as helpful and important as I think. Luckily, I haven't lost my passion for reading. I try to read at least one non-required book per week, and I still get a rush from reading a great novel, a fascinating memoir, or interesting nonfiction. I don't think I will ever lose my love of books.

At the same time, however, I notice that my ability to read for long spans of time has gone down. Just a few years ago I was reading at least 2-3 books a week. I could curl up in a chair and devour a book in hours. Today this is rare for me because reading requires physical and mental attention. In order to reap the benefits of reading, I have to hold the book, turn the pages, and keep my eyes on the text. With television, the Internet, social media, or Netflix, I can go back and forth between multiple different things at once, providing so many different sources of incoming stimulation that I don't truly have to pay attention to any one of them to feel occupied or to escape boredom.

Simic and Carr's essays provide an important warning—we need to slow down and carefully examine our relationship with technology. We rarely have time to get to know ourselves, because any "down time" we come across makes us uncomfortable.

Even one moment without incoming information makes us nervous—we pull out our phones or turn on some music to take the discomfort of doing nothing away. And the brain-changing style of the Internet has reached incredibly far, even hitting those of us who, like me, consider ourselves avid readers. Even though I love to read, at this point I'm so trained to multitask and synthesize data coming in from all angles that to narrow it down to just words on a page can feel boring. My younger self, the middle school Annesley whose favorite activity was browsing the library and who only asked for books for Christmas, would be appalled to hear that. I can only assume, as Carr and Simic do, that the prevalence of the Internet and Google have changed my brain, and possibly made me a little more stupid.

Works Cited

Carr, Nicholas. "Is Google Making Us Stupid?" *50 Essays: A Portable Anthology*, edited by Samuel S. Cohen, 4th ed., Bedford/St. Martin's, 2014, pp. 91–102.

Simic, Charles. "A Reunion with Boredom." *50 Essays: A Portable Anthology*, edited by Samuel S. Cohen, 4th ed., Bedford/St. Martin's, 2014, pp. 374–77.

OR

Works Cited

Cohen, Samuel, editor, *50 Essays: A Portable Anthology*, 4th ed., Bedford/St. Martin's, 2014.

Carr, Nicholas. "Is Google Making Us Stupid?" Cohen, pp. 91–102.

Simic, Charles, "A Reunion with Boredom." Cohen, pp. 374–77.

Other Kinds of Summaries

Before concluding, there are a few variations on the standard form of summary, which you should know about. The first is the directed summary, which is a summary of a particular aspect of a text rather than the whole text (Strahan, Moore, and Heumann 19–20). So, for example, in a literature class, you might be asked to summarize Jay Gatsby's long romance with Daisy Buchanan in *The Great Gatsby* instead of summarizing the entire novel. Or, on a psychology exam, you might be asked to summarize the censoring function of the conscious mind rather than the entire text of Freud's *Interpretation of Dreams*. A directed summary is written just like a standard summary, but the hierarchy of main ideas and main points is more specific. This is why it is important to carefully read the prompt or question before you begin writing your summary.

Another variation on the standard form of summary is the annotated bibliography entry. Typically, an annotated bibliography is formatted like a normal bibliography, but it also includes a brief summary-like entry, or annotation, after each source's information. Below is an excerpt from an annotated bibliography:

> Bird, Caroline. "The Case Against College." *Writing Responsibly*, edited by Victoria Anderson, Fountainhead Press, 2012, pp. 80–84.

> In "The Case Against College," Caroline Bird argues that potential college students should consider options other than attending college. She provides many reasons that suggest that college has been overvalued in American culture. While Bird's argument is compelling, much of her evidence is anecdotal and undermines the strength of her position. However, the essay is helpful in that it gathers many of the most reasonable arguments offered against attending college. For my paper, which is an academic essay on why attending college is the best option for high school seniors, I can use Bird's essay when constructing my counterarguments.

What you include in an annotation always depends on what your instructor asks for. However, usually, the annotation includes at least one, but sometimes all three, of the following elements:

1. A one- to two-sentence summary of the source text;

2. An evaluation of the credibility or general usefulness of the source text and/or how it compares to other sources on the list; and/or,

3. A reflection on the source as to its relevance to or usefulness for your specific project (Bisignani and Brizee).

While, technically speaking, an annotated bibliography entry is not a summary, it almost always includes a summary of the source text. As you can see in the example above, the annotation opens with a summary of Caroline Bird's essay and then continues on to evaluate it and reflect on its usefulness.

For additional resources on annotated bibliographies, please see Purdue OWL.

Sample Student Annotated Bibliography

Emily Wagner
UCWR 110
23 March 2014

Annotated Bibliography

"Abuse by Men 'Not Considered a Crime' in Many Countries."
Women's International Network News, vol. 25, no. 4, 1999,
p. 37. *Academic Search Complete*, http://flagship.luc.edu/
login?url=http://search.ebscohost.com/login.aspx?direct=tru
e&db=ulh&AN=2436859&site=ehost-live.

This source is an informative article written for a scholarly
journal. The intended audience is activists and scholars interested
in human rights, specifically gender based violence, and the bias
is towards the prevention of such crimes, given the nature of the
statistics reported. The content of the source features statistics of
the number of women and girls subjected to domestic and sexual
violence in a number of countries worldwide, as well as outlining the negative impact of such crimes. This source is valuable to
me because it helps place a devastating number on the injustices
experienced globally by women. It will be useful in constructing
my argument because the shocking figures featured in the article
will help provide the pathos needed to persuade my audience that
violence against women is truly a global issue that needs to be
eradicated.

Elakkary, Sally, et al. "Honor Crimes: Review and Proposed
Definition." *Forensic Science, Medicine & Pathology*, vol. 10,

no. 1, 2014, pp. 76-82. *Academic Search* Complete, http://
flagship.luc.edu/login?url=http://search.ebscohost.com/
login.aspx?direct=true&db=a9h&AN=94005402&site
=ehost-live.

This source is an essay written for an academic journal.
The intended audience is legislators looking for information on
"honor crimes" and how to redefine the term. The bias is towards
persecuting those who kill in the name of "family honor." The
content of the source features a review of honor crimes, who en-
gages in such acts, the role they play in patriarchal societies, and
the reasoning behind their existence. It also discusses the low
conviction rate in honor killings, and ways to prevent femicide in
the name of honor. This source is valuable to me because not only
does it outline in detail the motives behind honor killings and
an accepted definition, but it also recommends some solutions in
stopping this violence. I plan on using the source to describe one
out of the many facets of gender-based violence, as well as support
the claim that there are solutions to the problems women face.

*Half the Sky: Turning Oppression into Opportunity for Women
Worldwide.* Directed by Maro Chermayeff, Independent
Lens, 2012.

This source is an educational documentary. The intended audience is the general public because it aired on PBS, a public TV
channel, as well as human rights activists due to the content and
charity work demonstrated in the film. It is clearly biased towards
helping women become equals in their respective cultures. The
source features the stories of women and girls in 10 developing

countries, their experience with violence and discrimination, and their efforts to fight injustice through education and activism. This source is valuable to me because it provides real-life examples of women fighting their oppression, preventative measures to stop the violence, and benefits of eliminating it. I plan on using this source as an appeal to logic; it will be used to back up my thesis with hard evidence of what good can be done in the world when violence against women is prevented or decreased.

Sharma, Monica. "Twenty-First Century Pink or Blue: How Sex Selection Technology Facilitates Gendercide and What We Can Do about It." *Family Court Review*, vol. 46, no. 1, 2008, pp. 198-215. *Academic Search Complete*, http://flagship.luc.edu/login?url=http://search.ebscohost.com/login.aspx?direct=true&db=a9h&AN=27968188&site=ehost-live.

This source is an essay written for an academic journal. The intended audience is those who are concerned with the family court system, including judges, attorneys, mediators & professionals in mental health & human services. The bias is against sex selection in the cases of gendercide. The source contains a description of different sex selection technologies, and how they are being abused in order for families in cultures where boys are valued more highly, to have male children. It also discusses many of the negative implications of gendercide and female infanticide, as well as the cultural ideologies behind this phenomenon. This source is valuable to me because it directly discusses the negative impacts in the world relating to gendercide and what is being done to stop it. I plan on using this source as an appeal to logic;

it gives hard evidence and facts in order to prove to the reader that the world will benefit when gender based violence is stopped.

Smith, Cristine, et al. "A Model of Women's Educational

Factors Related to Delaying Girls' Marriage." *International Review of Education*, vol. 58, no. 4, 2012, pp. 533-555. *Academic Search Complete*, http://flagship.luc.edu/ login?url=http://search.ebscohost.com/login.aspx?direct=tru e&db=a9h&AN=78305221&site=ehost-live.

This source is an essay written for an academic journal. The intended audience is those who are interested in scholarly information on major educational innovations, research projects, and trends. The bias is towards educating girls and women in order to prevent them from marrying so young. This source contains a review of all of the problems associated both economically and socially with early marriage and a description of what factors can prevent marriage. It also outlines many of the benefits of educating young women and girls. This source is valuable to me because it clearly discusses many of the benefits of preventing girls from marrying so young, which directly supports my argument of stopping crimes against women can only benefit society.

Ulltveit-Moe, Tracy. *Lives Blown Apart: Crimes against Women in Times of Conflict: Stop Violence against Women*. Amnesty International, 2004.

This source is a non-fiction book printed by Amnesty International, a leader in protecting human rights. The intended audience is those who are interested in the role of women in wartime and what is being done to prevent the serious breach of human rights in times of violence. The bias is towards preventing gender-based violence used in wartime, and encouraging peaceful measures instead. This source contains many firsthand accounts of survivors of armed conflicts, an analysis of a woman's role in war, both as a civilian and a soldier, and numerous recommendations on how to prevent gender-based violence as an act of war. This source is valuable to me because it provides copious amounts of first hand experiences and anecdotes, which can be used as an appeal to emotion in my argument in order to persuade the reader that gender-based violence is a human rights violation and not just an act of war.

UN Women. United Nations, 2011. http://www.un-
women.org/en.

This source is a website run by the United Nations, a leader in protecting human rights. This website provides information about gender based violence in the world and what the UN is doing to stop it. The intended audience is anyone curious about activism and the oppression women face around the world. The site is biased towards women, and helping other countries form legislation and other policies in order to prevent gender based violence and oppression. This source is valuable to me because it gives great background information on the injustices against women globally, and outlines many of the procedures that are being implemented by other countries and activist groups in order to stop the injustice. I plan on using this source to discuss the techniques used to raise women's status, as well as to provide context for the rest of my argument.

3

Analysis

UCWR 110

Simply put, analysis is a detailed examination and investigation of the elements of a text, often a piece of writing, literature, art, film, or music. As students, you engage in analysis in nearly every facet of your daily academic lives: in classroom discussions about economic policy, literary theory, or history; in biology labs; in law practicums or in pre-med study groups. Analysis occurs in the form of engaged study, discussion, and dissection that leads to a deep understanding of a subject and its importance, effects, and implications for the future.

In the previous section, we discussed how an effective **summary** condenses a text to its core elements and arguments and re-presents them in a way that is concise and clear. While summarizing, writers need to search for the main points that comprise a text and then separate important details that support these core points from the other secondary elements in the text. In a way, the process of summarizing a text involves analysis; determining the main arguments of a text and prioritizing the evidence and detail that an author gives in support of these points requires a writer to think critically about which elements are most important to a novel, film, essay, or work of art. More than a rote memorization of facts, analysis is the ability to critically evaluate a work and come to a conclusion about it.

As noted, analysis is a central part of a student's academic work, and it is a requirement in essays, discussions, and assignments in most (if not all) classes you will take in college. It is also important to grasp that analysis can be applied to any imaginable text. Students are probably accustomed to being asked to analyze written stories in your high school English classes, but consider how in film studies courses students analyze the themes, lighting, plot, shot construction, cinematography, and dozens of other components of a movie. In history courses, professors ask students to evaluate the factors that lead to and surround an event and perhaps to analyze the outcomes or the solutions proposed by historical figures. In nursing and pre-med courses, the patients are the texts, and the students determine the best course of treatment using facts or inferences gleaned from a patient's condition and the student's own knowledge of medical treatment. Advertisements, cartoons, news stories, business meetings, works of music, or political speeches are all texts that you can analyze.

While analysis relies on some of the same skills that you use when summarizing, remember that analysis extends beyond summarization. Good analysis implicitly *makes an argument* about the text—for example, its subject matter, its format, its rhetorical strategies, its origin—and so the most effective analyses do not simply restate what the original text says.

A compelling piece of analysis examines specific elements of a text and then evaluates them for meaning or effectiveness. The following example of analysis is a paragraph drawn from an actual student's response to Alan Moore's graphic novel *Watchmen*. In it, this student analyzes the nature of the character Rorschach:

> The character Rorschach elicits varied, yet strong, responses from readers. Throughout the novel, Rorschach reacts to events with an absolute, black-and-white manner. He is guided by a conservative, fundamental set or morals from which he never wavers. For example, when Rorschach and Nite Owl II learn about Veidt's scheme, and the deceit and murder involved, Rorschach reacts by saying "No. Not even in the face of Armageddon. Never Compromise" (20). Although Veidt argues he is acting for the greater good, Rorschach cannot see past the use of Veidt's amoral means to an end. This scene in particular is an instance where the reader identifies with Rorschach; we are just as surprised and disgusted at the turn of events as he is, and therefore, we identify with him. Rorschach is perhaps attractive to the reader because he is a concrete viewpoint in a story where right and wrong are hazy.

This student's analysis is effective for a number of reasons. To start, the student begins with a claim about the role of the character Rorschach in *Watchmen*, suggesting with a claim that he is an uncompromising character with a clear moral code (that he "reacts to events with an absolute, black-and-white manner").

Then, the student supports that claim with a quote from the text as evidence of how Rorschach responds to a complex situation with unwavering certainty. The last portion of the paragraph is the most significant; in it, the student contends that the Rorschach character, despite holding some extreme views, is nonetheless appealing to the reader because his "concrete viewpoint" represents moral certitude in a story where good and bad always seem to be in flux. This student's analysis is stylish and perceptive and attempts to draw larger conclusions about the text from the smaller element being analyzed in this particular paragraph.

Approaching Analysis Assignments

Instructors approach analysis in a variety of ways. While many will ask you to analyze the work and ideas of others, you also will be asked to turn the lens of analysis back on yourself and your own work. In the following sample assignment, drawn from an actual course, the instructor asks students to analyze the impact of their disciplinary background on a difficult or controversial issue.

> **Assignment:** This project asks you to analyze an issue of public importance from the context of your disciplinary background or interests. The project will have two parts, detailed below:
>
> You will choose a single issue of public significance and produce an analysis of the issue, its current stakes, and its importance or future implications. For example, you might explore how the current public debate about the balance between government spending and the need to reduce the deficits affects public employees in Chicago. Or, you might examine issues of environmental awareness, public health, or union funding. Whichever issue you choose, you need to analyze its parameters, stakes, and implications.
>
> You will then turn to an analysis of your topic from the perspective of your disciplinary field (if you have not declared a major, simply pick a subject area that you might like to study in the future). What does your field of study/interest have to contribute to the larger public debate about the issue? Are there specific concerns for your field in regards to this topic? Are there certain elements, theories, or practices from your field that will help illuminate the issue or more effectively work toward a solution?

Through the assignment, the instructor is encouraging students to draw numerous connections between their class and a real-world issue and between that issue and their disciplinary background. Requiring a disciplinary reflection means the student must analyze their own work and begin to think critically about the ways in which their individual studies will intersect with the world outside the classroom. Below is a brief excerpt from a student response to this assignment:

> The English discipline plays a huge role in the issue of immigration and immigration laws, not only when it comes to the immigrants and aspiring US citizens, but the people who are trying to change and rectify this issue through rhetoric, argumentation, and persuasion. These are all skills learned in the English discipline and can be used when trying to sway a certain group a certain way. Many news stations such as FOX News and MSNBC constantly talk about the issue of immigration and what it means to this country, but both networks have very different viewpoints when it comes to this issue.

This student is attempting to connect the discipline of English to the issue of immigration reform. In this paragraph, she notes that English is important, not only because literacy and language fluency is a central component of the immigration debate, but also because the skills that English students practice are needed to navigate the public debate over immigration reform. Processing the arguments made in different outlets—from FoxNews, MSNBC, and many places elsewhere—and determining their persuasiveness requires critical thinking. In essence, she is suggesting that navigating a public debate demands analysis skills. In connecting the skills of English majors to a contemporary public controversy, this student uses the same skills of analysis that she suggests the discipline of English provides.

A Methodology for Analysis

Though there are many ways to approach analysis—and we encourage you to develop your own, specific to your preferences, the context of your writing, and your discipline—here are a few critical steps to get started with analysis:

1. **Begin with the text.** Strong analysis begins by being exceptionally familiar with the text. You can't analyze a text successfully unless you have identified its main points and clarified for yourself any moments of confusion. For example, are there any vocabulary terms that you do not understand? Look them up. Are there any references to outside events and information that you do not know—for example, historical figures or movements? Again, research these subjects until you are comfortable with the ins-and-outs of the text. Not only will this research make you more familiar with the text, it will it will make your analysis more insightful, and ensure your credibility as an informed authority on the topic.

2. **Start small.** Because analysis requires that you define and defend an arguable claim, the best way to find this claim is by using the text(s). Think of yourself as a lawyer in a courtroom, and the text is your best and most persuasive piece of evidence! Identify the pieces of the text(s) you are interested in and then ask yourself these questions: What do these things tell me? What is the effect of these pieces of evidence have on the text overall, or in comparison to other texts, or on how I understand the subject matter? Are there any pieces of evidence available that contradict each other or my assumptions?

Notice that we are advocating that you start with your evidence and only then build a claim. You are more likely to achieve a defendable claim when you *work from* the text than if you *look for* specific moments to defend a pre-existing assumption. Why? Because you end up plundering the text for only those facts or moments that support your idea, which makes it easy to overlook evidence that doesn't fit or may even overrule your claim.

3. **Define your claim.** Analytical claims can be as big as the whole thesis for a dissertation or as small as a simple, conversational declarative sentence like, "Brian Urlacher was the most consistent middle line-backer in the NFL." Regardless of whether they require ten pages or ten seconds to defend, claims need to be **specific**. Spend time identifying just what you want to argue and how. In the same way that summary requires that you to make clear all the parameters of another person's argument, analysis requires that you make clear all the parameters of your own argument.

Be incredibly intentional with your word choice; generalizations always hurt an argument and make it harder for your reader to anticipate the steps you will take to defend your claim. For example, in the statement made above, it matters whether the writer argues that Brian Urlacher is the *best* middle linebacker or the *most consistent*. A reader can anticipate how the writer will defend the claim that Urlacher is the "most consistent" middle linebacker by using statistics and comparisons with other middle linebackers in the NFL. It would be much harder to anticipate, and to argue, that he is simply the "best" without relying too much on opinion. If you are thoughtful about the words you choose to define your claim, it should provide you with a blueprint for the rest of your analysis.

4. **Quote, summarize, and paraphrase selectively to guide your interpretation. As we mentioned above, the text is your best piece of evidence.** Use it carefully and constructively to advance your claim. Remember, though, that evidence—particularly quotations—don't speak for themselves; your analysis should indicate *how* you want your reader to understand the textual evidence. It is your responsibility as a writer to drive the conversation with your insights. Phrases such as "this demonstrates," "which results in," or "revealing that" can provide helpful clues to your reader and will force you to make strong choices about how the evidence should be interpreted.

5. **Work outward.** The most effective pieces of analysis consider a range of implications beyond the specific text being analyzed. It's not enough to simply make a claim when analyzing for the sake of making a claim; your audience should understand why your claim matters, and you should be able to answer the age-old question, "So what?" There are a number of different ways to work outward when analyzing. In the immigration and disciplinary reflection example we looked at before, the student considers the impact of the field of English on the public debate over immigration. While her narrow conclusion is that the skills of analysis taught in an English classroom will help a person navigate the contentious arguments related to immigration reform, her work also implies that those analytical skills can serve a person in processing nearly any controversial public debate. Your analysis does not necessarily need to be connected to national or international issues like immigration reform, but working outward from the text can be valuable.

Once you have made an argument about a text, consider how your conclusions relate to other texts you have read or watched. Are there parallels or differences? You should also consider the larger themes or discussions that you have studied in your course. Does this particular text have something new or significant to say about a topic of interest to your class? Does it bring you any closer to fully understanding a subject? Knowledge is found in the fissures and overlaps of ideas, and you can illuminate yourself (and your fellow students and instructor) as to how the thoughts and arguments in one text relate to the bigger picture.

Consider the following example of student work as a model of the methodology we proposed. The student was asked to write a brief analysis of a play, Henrik Ibsen's *The Wild Duck*, specifically examining its themes of illness and blindness:

> Ibsen's *The Wild Duck* connects Gregers's inability to understand what is really happening with himself to blindness and physical sickness. Gregers is driven by guilt from not helping his friend Hjalmar Ekdal's family at a critical time in the past. By revealing the lies within Hjalmar's marriage, Gregers convinces himself that he has saved his friend from living a life that is not his own. However, his help actually is very poisonous to the Ekdal family, because Gregers himself, according to the doctor Relling, is "a sick man, too,"

whose main problem is that he is "forever going around in a delirium of adoration—forever butting in where [he doesn't] belong, looking for something to admire" (54-57). Reling wants Gregers to realize that because he is "blind" to his own motivations, he cannot possibly help Hjalmar and in fact is making everything much worse for the Ekdal family.

You'll notice that the student begins by identifying the text in question and then proceeds to state her claim (that the play connects the character "Gregers's inability to understand what is really happening within himself to blindness and physical sickness."). She demonstrates her familiarity with the text by summarizing concisely and quoting intelligently; as an audience, we have the sense that the author is guiding the analysis and not simply dropping in quotes to fill space. Finally, she works outward from claim, not merely proving that Gregers is physically ill but suggesting that Ibsen, the play's author, is using Gregers's physical illness to symbolize his "blind[ness]" to his internal inadequacies. This analysis is effective, then, because it is concise, demonstrates the author's familiarity with the text, and uses the evidence from the text to advance her thoughts and perceptions.

For additional resources on analysis, please see Purdue Owl at https://owl.english.purdue.edu/, and search for *analysis essay*.

Jacob Dumbauld
Professor Lahey
UCWR 110
6 February 2015

How to Tame Institutionalized Prejudice

While the human race has come a long way from enslaving each other and slaughtering their own for causes of race and religion, institutionalized racism and oppression are far from gone. Battles are fought every day for the right to free press, freedom of religion, and equal rights among minorities and women. While the prejudices might not be as pronounced as they were just a couple of decades ago, they are still a very real problem. In the battleground of gender and cultural oppression, intelligent and educated authors like Gloria Anzaldúa have pushed for changes through their writing. In her essay "How to Tame a Wild Tongue," Anzaldúa particularly showcases her native Chicano tongue not only to emphasize an inclination towards her cultural roots, but also to provide the non-Spanish-speaking reader a glimpse into the difficult and traumatic experience of not being accepted.

Anzaldúa makes use of powerful anecdotal evidence to help prove this point at the beginning of her essay. She was caught speaking Spanish at recess and her "Anglo" (her word for white American) teacher said, "If you want to be American, speak 'American.' If you don't like it, go back to Mexico where you belong" (34). This kind of blatant racism would be grounds to fire a teacher in the modern day, and Andzaldúa capitalizes on this to deliver her point with maximum effect. Americans, particularly white Americans, born and raised in the United States, will most likely never experience this degree of prejudice and disrespect towards their roots. In addition to all of this, Anzaldúa was just a little girl being told this by a woman three or more times her age. One can only imagine how she felt after being scolded by her teacher, and Anzaldúa fully intends to provoke this kind of thought.

Not long before the rise of 1970s women's rights movements, a young Anzaldúa was told, "*En Boca cerrada no entran moscas.* 'Flies don't enter a closed mouth'" (34). Whether it was from her parents, teachers, or other adults in her life, Anzaldúa makes an important point here. In the time period of Anzaldúa's childhood, it was still common for women to be taught to be polite, and never to voice their own ideas. Commonly held belief stated that women played the role of homemaker, and that the man functioned as the breadwinner. In this kind of role, Anzaldúa was doubly suppressed: firstly on account of her gender and secondly on account of her culture. She was not allowed to speak her mind, especially not in her native tongue. But in quoting this snippet of a point in her life where she could not speak freely, she fights back against the oppressive nature of this advice. In writing her essay, Anzaldúa not only speaks her mind, but also does so in the language that she sees fit.

However, that is not to say that Anzaldúa never struggled emotionally with the oppression and alienation that came with being of a different culture. She voices her pains when she says, "I have so internalized the borderland conflict that sometimes I feel like one cancels out the other and we are zero, nothing, no one. *A veces no soy nada ni nadie. Per hasta cuando no lo soy, lo soy*" (43). Roughly translated, she initially says that at times she feels like nothing to nobody. But Anzaldúa's second claim in Spanish shows her resolve to keep fighting oppression. She says that "when I wasn't, I was." Her sense of belonging to something greater because of her cultural roots—even when she felt like nothing and nobody—should strike the reader. However, a reader unable to understand Spanish would completely miss out on the power of this quote (which is an exceedingly important part of her reasoning behind putting it in Spanish). This sense of togetherness belongs to her and to those of the same cultural and linguistic background, and that is not something she is willing to give up. She hides that connection in plain view behind the barrier of a different language in order to recreate the effect of isolation and neglect she experienced because of linguistic difference.

Anzaldúa keeps this barrier alive by peppering the rest of her work with Spanish words and phrases. She does this enough that her overall message will not be lost in translation, but those who cannot speak Spanish will be at the very least frustrated. For her, alternating languages serves as a tool to show the reader what it was like to grow up in a world where people did not accommodate her native tongue. She even goes on to say that as long as she feels like she has to accommodate the English speakers, her tongue will be illegitimate (39). These are simply not things that the average American has to deal with on a day-to-day basis. Anzaldúa knows this and takes full advantage of it. She makes any Anglo reader feel guilty by association about the way she has been treated, dispersing the blame for cultural oppression amid a large group.

A final point Anzaldúa makes is the sense of togetherness she feels with those who share her struggles. She uses the example of her experiences watching movies about Mexican culture to further the sense of exclusive community that Chicanos share. She sets the scene by saying, "'*Vámanos a las vistas,*' my mother would call out and we'd all—grandmother, brothers, sister and cousins—squeeze into the car" (Anzaldúa 40). In this example, she gives the trip to the movies a strong sense of belonging by describing a situation where her whole family, her whole community, is crammed together in a single car. Yet, to the reader who can't speak Spanish, they don't understand her mother's request, and hence the reason behind her family's closeness is lost in translation. It instills a sense of exclusion from that community for those who can't speak the language, and Anzaldúa intentionally does this. It is not that she is being selfish, but rather she is trying to recreate the feeling of living in a world where all of the movies celebrated American culture and ignored her own.

In a war against racial stereotypes and oppression, Anzaldúa bombards her oppressors with stories of her frustration and suffering. Anzaldúa's struggle is apparent throughout her essay, but it is seen most powerfully through her use of Chicano Spanish. Nevertheless, through all of the pain came something beautiful: a Chicano culture of which she could be proud. With suffering came a strong sense of community that bore her through her most difficult times. While the reader should feel her frustration and pain through the words on the page, it is just as important that they see what good has come of it. Anzaldúa does not want to make the same mistakes as those who berated her endlessly for being herself. Rather, she wants to give them a glimpse of the pain they've caused, in order to give future Chicanos a fighting chance in a world slowly becoming more accepting of differences.

Works Cited

Anzaldúa, Gloria. "How to Tame a Wild Tongue." *50 Essays: A Portable Anthology*, 4th ed., edited by Samuel Cohen, Bedford/St. Martin's, 2014, pp. 33–45.

Synthesis

UCWR 110

The term "synthesis" has a number of specific meanings, depending on the disciplinary context of the term. In chemistry, synthesis is the process of combining two or more simple substances to make a more complex one. In psychology, synthesis is the integration of attitudes, traits, and responses into a personality. In philosophy, synthesis reconciles two propositions, the thesis and the antithesis, into a new configuration of meaning. In college writing, synthesis involves combining and integrating ideas from two or more sources to develop a new idea. Synthesis writing is sometimes called *discourse synthesis* or *dialectical thinking*, because the task is to put source texts into dialogue, or conversation, with one another (McGinley 227). In a synthesis paper, the writer discusses how two or more texts can be viewed in the light of an organizing theme, structure, or idea and integrates these perspectives to form a complex conclusion or develop a starting point for further inquiry. Synthesis is one of the most effective operations of learning because it requires a constructive thought process. Through synthesis, new ideas are generated; not only our thoughts but also our thought processes are transformed (McGinley 234).

As a university student, you will be required to synthesize in a variety of assignments. For example, in a paper prompt or an exam question, your instructor might ask you to consider the position of theorist C in relation to the views of theorists A and B. In a research paper, you might discuss several arguments about possible causes of the 2008 financial meltdown and use the evidence and viewpoints in these papers to come to your own conclusions about the cause. You might be asked to consider how two authors from the same literary period exemplify the characteristics of that period and how their works have influenced each other. You could be expected to consolidate and explain data from several experiment results. Here are some prompts that ask for a synthesis response:

Discuss Martin Luther King's notion of an "unjust law" in the light of the Dalai Lama's criteria for "great compassion."

Compare and contrast what Helen Keller, Malcolm X, and Richard Rodriguez have to say about education and identity.

How do you think Robert Reich, Gregory Mantsios, and Fatema Mernissi affect your thinking about class and choice?

Successful synthesis requires mastery of two other writing/thinking processes that we have already described in this text: **summary** and **analysis**. First, the writer must be able to demonstrate an understanding of the source texts by objectively restating those ideas in her own words (summary). The writer must also demonstrate an understanding of the component parts of the source text arguments and how these components work together as a whole (analysis). Synthesis completes the process of transformation begun by summary (transforming another's ideas into one's own words) and analysis (selecting, organizing, and interpreting the components of another's ideas) by connecting and integrating the ideas of several texts under a common structure to create a new set of ideas. If the synthesis writer does not have a clear sense of the source texts' meaning, structure, and context, she will have difficulty relating those texts to each other or to her own ideas and experience. The synthesis will fail, and no complex understanding will emerge, if the writer lacks the ability to think *about* and to think *with* source texts.

The Process of Synthesis

We might consider the process of synthesis as a journey, a thought excursion on which we lead our readers. Think of Dorothy and her journey through the Land of Oz. She begins with a question that is of interest to her (How can I get home?) and a hypothesis (The Wizard can get me home.). Her experiences in Kansas give her a certain perspective about how to address her problem. Along the way to the Emerald City, Dorothy encounters a variety of characters, each with a different perspective. She learns the story of the Scarecrow and alters the goal of her journey to include his point of view. Together, they meet the Tin Man and connect his knowledge, experience, and goals to their own. The Cowardly Lion's take adds a new dimension. The integration of these perspectives alters the hypothesis about the Wizard's capabilities as the journey moves forward. Just as every argument meets with opposition, Dorothy and company must deal with the counter-objectives of the Wicked Witch of the West as well as those of the Wizard. The travelers take unexpected detours. Each character has a talent or skill that responds to these challenges, just as each text in a synthesis can provide elements of a counterargument or different strategies for pursuing a question. Dorothy's journey culminates in a new thought configuration, one quite different from the original hypothesis (There's no place like home—I was home all along).

Synthesis writing is a complex process, and research and experience tell us that students struggle with this kind of writing. While synthesis may seem to be the result of a linear procedure (reading → summarizing → analyzing → synthesis), such an understanding of synthesizing would be misleading. Research has shown that writers who think of synthesis as the last step

in a linear process tend to produce papers that are strung-together summaries and analyses rather than true integrations and connections of ideas (Mateos and Solé 448; McGinley 235).

In order to put texts into conversation with each other, the synthesis writer plays several roles. First, she is a careful reader of texts, placing herself in the position of each text's ideas in order to fully comprehend them. Next, she is a careful summarizer and analyzer, selecting significant ideas from the texts, integrating and connecting them in accordance with an overarching idea that begins as a hypothesis and emerges as a thesis from interaction with the texts. This second role requires note-taking and draft writing, as well as revisiting the texts in order to develop and support a thesis. Then she must become the reader of her own draft, ensuring that she leads the reader clearly through the thought processes that connect the texts she is synthesizing. Successful synthesis writers engage in a recursive process, moving back and forth between reading and writing. Likewise, the structure of the synthesis reflects this recursive process, considering each text in light of both the controlling idea (thesis) and the texts that have already been discussed so far.

Strategies for Synthesis Writing

When you write a synthesis, much of your thought journeying will take place before you begin to write the paper that will be the final product—in reading, note-taking, pre-writing, drafting, and especially *thinking* about the texts you are synthesizing. Careful reading (or viewing, if it is a visual text) and annotation of each source text is a good way to begin. You may find it useful to write a brief summary of each text to consolidate the main and subordinate points of the argument or information firmly in your mind. In note-taking or free-writing, analyze elements of each text such as context, structure, strategy, and tone. As you progress through your note-taking and annotations, you will already be comparing sources in your mind, revisiting the first text in the light of subsequent texts.

A synthesis paper can begin with a question to be explored through multiple source texts. An instructor may ask you to generate your own *issue question* about the texts, or you may be asked to respond to a prompt question. Working with source texts through summary and analysis will lead to the refinement of a controlling idea: the thesis. The synthesis writer will bring the texts into dialogue with each other by asking questions: What do these texts have in common? In what ways to they disagree? Do they differ in the presentation or interpretation of evidence? Do they disagree about underlying beliefs or important assumptions? How do I, as the writer, respond to these texts and the subject or issue under discussion? How do the texts bring my own knowledge and assumptions into question? What insights come out of this interaction among source texts and my own ideas? After considering such questions, you should be able to formulate a tentative thesis or at least an issue question (Ramage, Bean, and Johnson 4-45).

This writer, student Lisa Regganie, begins an exploratory argument by introducing an issue question that she will use as a controlling idea in the synthesis of three texts:

> Growing up in a small farming town, I have witnessed many of the townspeople not continue on to college after high school. They instead go into trades and work blue collar jobs. I am the daughter of parents who did not go to college. My father just did not want to go; he wanted to be a blue collar worker. My mother, on the other hand wanted to go, but her parents could not afford it. My father does not regret not going to college, but my mother regrets it every day that she steps into her dead end job. Both of my parents did not even question sending me to college, and I knew that going to college would be the only way out of the tentative lifestyle I grew up in. Luckily my parents knew this from the day I was born, so they started a college fund early and told me I could go wherever I wanted to go, be whatever I want to be, and they would bask in the glow of success. My background leads me to the question: *Does education really open up a whole new world to students?* I explored this idea in three essays by Helen Keller, Richard Rodriguez, and Malcolm X.

The author develops her argument by exploring the three essays with the aim of answer her question. She arrives at her conclusion by considering how each text relates to her issue question:

> Helen Keller, Richard Rodriguez, and Malcolm X experience the awakening of different kinds of opportunity through very different modes of education. *In all three cases, opportunity lies within the learner; the opportunity of education is not something I passively receive, but is mine to take, as these students did.* The new outlook on the world I will gain after college will be worth the hard classes, homework, and stress.

In the example above, the author began with a question and answered it in her conclusion. In the following introduction, writer Gabrielle Caputo answers a prompt question (What do Robert Reich and Colin Beavan say about the relationship between happiness and material success, and how to these authors affect your view of this relationship?) in a thesis that synthesizes the views of two authors and her own view:

> People are distracted from what is truly important in life because they fixate on making decisions concerning insignificant things and believing that possessions will bring happiness. Robert B. Reich in his article "The Choice Fetish: Blessings and Curses of a Market Idol," and Colin Bevan in his book *No Impact Man* insist upon this, and while they are right, each fails to address how the lack of popular examples of people who are successful without money makes us think having money and items is the sole way to achieve success.

Methods of Organization

There are two common methods for organizing a synthesis: around the source texts (*block method*) or around the points of connection (*alternating method*).

1. Block Method:

    *   **Introduction** with claim or issue question

    *   Text 1

        *   Introduce this source with a brief summary of its ideas, providing its rhetorical context. (Some relevant points for context might include the following: Who is the author(s)? Why should the reader pay attention to what the author(s) has to say about this subject? What is the source's place in the conversation about the claim or issue?) Apply the methods and conventions of good **summary** writing.

        *   Analyze this source's ideas in relation to the points of connection you have discovered among the source texts and the controlling idea that has emerged from these connections. Respond with your own ideas about the source's position on these points. For example, if your main idea is that knowledge

of language opens the door to human relationship and you are discussing Helen Keller's "Everything Has a Name," you will consider how her account of acquiring language demonstrates a new connection to the people in her life.

- Text 2

    - Introduce this source as well, by giving a summary of its main ideas and putting it in context. The difference between this introduction and the first one is that you will transition from the first text to this one by pointing out some similarity of dissimilarity (or both) between the first source text and this one. This connection you establish between texts is crucial and should be discussed in clear, specific fashion. Don't expect your reader to see or make the connection herself. For example, let's say you are introducing Richard Rodriguez's "Private and Public Language" into a conversation about language and human relationship. You might open the summary by pointing out that while Keller's account tells of how language leads to a discovery of relationships in her immediate family circle, Rodriguez's knowledge of language opens the possibility of public relationships.

    - Analyze this source's ideas in relation to the controlling idea, but do so by putting this source in conversation with the previous text as well as your own ideas. How is Rodriguez's experience similar to Keller's, and how is it different?

- Text 3

    - Repeat this process with the third text and with any subsequent texts you discuss. Avoid isolating the texts into a string of separate summaries/analyses. Keep the texts in conversation with each other by discussing points of connection.

- **Conclude** by telling the reader how the conversation among these texts has changed our understanding of the subject under discussion.

2. Alternating Method:

    - **Introduction** with claim or issue question. Let's say that in your essay you want to discuss three components of happiness: choice, wealth, and community. You will be considering these ideas in the light of essays by Robert Reich ("The Choice Fetish,")

and Gregory Mantsios ("Class in America—2006") and Colin Beavan's book *No Impact Man*.

- **First point of connection** among the source texts. Describe one of the ideas that these texts have in common. The texts may agree or disagree or take differently nuanced positions on this point.

  - Introduce Text 1 by briefly placing it in its rhetorical context (see questions relevant to rhetorical context in "Text 1" above). Discuss this text's position on this point of connection. For example, Robert Reich sees the overabundance of trivial choices as a nuisance that distracts us from issues that are more important to our ultimate happiness.

  - Add Text 2 to the conversation, also briefly placing it in context. Colin Beavan would agree with Reich, in that he believes that most of the choices we make concerning material objects are unnecessary and even destructive.

  - Add Text 3 and any subsequent texts in the same way. Include your own ideas in the conversation. Gregory Mantsios would point out that many Americans are too poor to have *enough* choice and would appreciate having some of the choices that Reich and Beavan are complaining about.

- **Second point of connection.** Repeat the process described above, putting the texts in conversation about this point. In the discussion of this and subsequent points, you obviously will not need to introduce the texts and put them in context.

- Continue discussion with connecting point 3.

- **Conclude** by telling the reader how the conversation among these texts has changed our understanding of the subject under discussion.

You can combine these methods by beginning with the block method and then putting sources in conversation with each other using the alternating method. Notice that decisions about the order in which you discuss texts or connecting points will be very important to your argument. You may decide, during the drafting process, to change the order of these elements to enhance the effectiveness of your argument.

Dorothy and friends follow the yellow brick road and signs along the way of the journey. In synthesis writing, you must use *transitional language* to guide readers on the thought journey, helping readers identify the various "speakers" in the conversation and their positions. Use words and phrases to introduce a new perspective and to signal a shift in thought. To introduce the ideas of one text, use active verbs. Don't merely tell us that an author or work "says" something. Try:

> Jones *demonstrates, argues, asserts, or reminds…*
>
> This film *portrays, represents*, or *tells the story of…*
>
> Use transitions to signal the relations of source ideas to each other:
>
> While Jones believes _____, Smith takes the opposite view.
>
> Jones and Smith hold similar positions in all but _____. (Graff, Birkenstein, and Durst 71–75)

Note in the following paragraphs how student writer Judith Howard uses transitional language to put the ideas of her sources in a conversation about the individual and community responsibility:

> **Both Beavan and the Dalai Lama** see individual action as having a powerful impact on more than just the individual. At various places in *No Impact Man*, **Beavan expresses** the idea that individual actions are what constitute collective action. He values the influence of small, individual actions as being critical to the formation of larger movements. **The Dalai Lama speaks** about the impact of one person's actions on another person. He calls for compassion in action, arguing that if our actions lack compassion, they can become dangerous. He makes the point that if we are not considerate of how our individual actions affect the welfare of other people, "inevitably we end up hurting them" (261). **Beavan makes a similar point** concerning the environment: that if we are careless about our impact on the environment, we will cause great harm to it and all other people as a result.

> When discussing the individual, **Reich maintains** a position that supports the value of individual choice for the individual's sake **while the Dalai Lama, in contrast**, considers individuals almost entirely as part of a collective. **Reich, despite supporting community**, puts more emphasis on personal desires. After dismissing the smaller, less significant choices that people are able to make, he calls for us to make the more relevant choices, "Such as what we

stand for, to what and whom we're going to commit our lives, and what we want by way of a community and a society" (Reich 66). The focus in this sentence is on the important aspects of life from an individual's perspective. **When the Dalai Lama focuses** on the desires of people, he uses the same phrase various times to describe the most basic desire of humanity: "to be happy and not to suffer" (258). He uses this shared wish to connect all of mankind and to therefore emphasize the responsibility that we have toward each and every other human being.

Remember that the conventions of acknowledging sources apply in this kind of writing. Cite sources in text whenever you summarize, paraphrase, or quote another author's ideas. Provide a Works Cited page that fully and accurately cites all your sources.

For additional resources on writing synthesis essays, please see Purdue OWL at https://owl.english.purdue.edu/, and search for "Synthesis Essays."

Sample Student Synthesis Essays

Emmylou Ford
Professor Weller
UCWR 110
Synthesis Essay
3 March 2015

From Emmylou to Ami Gaye: A Perspective on Multicultural Identity

"*Ey, Ami Gaye!*" It was a name I often heard while walking down the sandy pathways of my village in rural Senegal, but it took months before I felt like it was my identity. Upon arriving in my new home, I was given a new name and a new way of life. For months, I resisted when told to eat with my hands, attend Muslim prayer, and correct the pronunciation of my distorted Wolof words. I struggled to balance a new culture with my old identity while still wanting to be accepted by this new community despite my blatant differences. Bhatia Mukherjee's essay "Two Ways to Belong to America" and Amy Tan's essay "Mother Tongue" touch on these struggles of multiculturalism. In Mukherjee's essay, she explores the differences between herself and her sister as they navigate immigration and identity. Tan, in her essay, describes the effect her mother has had on her perception of her environment. By means of these relationships, Tan and Mukherjee explore how language and assimilation have impacted their multicultural identity.

Tan's ability to oscillate between Chinese and American culture allows her to observe how language can be a barrier when trying to be accepted in a new culture. Tan's use of anecdotes is

powerful in demonstrating the sharp contrast between the treatment that she and her mother receive due to language. Tan builds
the reader's vicarious frustration as she progresses from her previously ashamed view of her mother, to the anecdote of the baffled
stockbroker, and then to the incident with the last CAT scan.
In the latter anecdote, Tan portrays the staff at the hospital as
uncompassionate when Tan's mother states her anxiety over the
scan in light of her husband and son's death due to brain tumors;
however, the staff "did not seem to have any sympathy" that compelled them to find her results (420). This treatment ceases when
a staff member communicates directly to Tan, who speaks "perfect English" (420). This demonstrates the mentality of disregard
toward those who speak English with an accent or with incorrect grammar.

Mukherjee's narrative also showcases the barriers immigrants face; however, she addresses the struggles they face when
confronted with the choice of assimilation. Mukherjee portrays
her sister, Mira's, anger over the law reform that discriminates
against resident non-citizens. After years of dedicating her "professional skills into the improvement of [America]," she states that
she "feel[s] used...manipulated and discarded" (292). However,
by comparing Mira's situation to a similar one Mukherjee faced
in Canada, Mukherjee implies that Mira is responsible for her
struggles since she did not decide to simply obtain American citizenship. Muhkerjee chose to be in a place that allowed her to be
"a part of the community [she] adopted," arguing that the only
way to be accepted and appreciated by society is to assimilate,
culturally and legally, to the new country (293). Mira's aversion

to assimilation is a choice that distances her from her new country, whereas Tan's mother's struggles in her new country are arbitrated by others.

Despite the barriers immigrants face, Tan's capability to navigate language has allowed her to build connections, especially with her mother. Tan's ability to understand her mother's "broken" or "limited" English is imperative in establishing the dynamic of their relationship (419). The transcription of her mother's dialogue is a powerful tool to showcase the apparent challenges in understanding her speech. Tan's later description of her attachment to her mother and this style of speech, despite its difficulty, produces a sense of respect from the reader. This is further developed when Tan describes the protective ways in which she caters to her mother, mainly through speaking on her mother's behalf. Tan needs to defend her mother since her speech has "helped shape the way [she] saw things, expressed things, [and] made sense of the world" (419).

Like Tan, Mukherjee can also compare herself to familial relationships and come to a better understanding of her multicultural identity. Using Mira as a calibration for assimilation, Mukherjee is able to look at her own sense of belonging with satisfaction. Looking at their immigrant journey, Mukherjee comments that "there could not be a wider divergence" (292). While Mira clings to her "saris [and] delightfully accented English," Mukherjee "surrender[ed] those" for the "trauma of self-transformation" (292, 293). Mukherjee's diction elicits negative and painful connotations, but she also states that she "married" America and "embraced" her immigrant status (292). Willing

to undergo the arduous pursuit of citizenship and cultural assimilation, Mukherjee, unlike her sister, also gained acceptance.
Unfortunately, unlike Tan's multicultural relationship with her
mother, Mukherjee distanced herself from her sister through this
assimilation.

Due to my experience abroad, I can empathize with both
Mukherjee's and Tan's perspective on multicultural identity.
Seeing how language is our primary means of communication
and understanding, it's fitting that Tan argues that it drives our
perception of the world. I can attest that when I speak Wolof
because I very much embody Ami Gaye, a girl who tends to relationships differently than Emmylou Ford. This is partly due to
how culture drives the language but is also in response to how
others treat me when I speak "broken" Wolof. As much as I tried
to straddle the multicultural line, I was never fully accepted,
which is imperative to assimilation, as we saw with Tan's mother
and both the Mukherjee sisters. Bharati Mukherjee was able to
overcome some of her flagrant differences, unlike Tan's mother,
and assimilate. The Mukherjee sisters and I understand that assimilation comes at a great cost: giving up parts of oneself. As
trivial as it may seem, I was never willing to neglect the comfort of pants and don a wrap-around *pagne*, a traditional garment
made from a rectangular strip of fabric fashioned into a loincloth
or wrapped on the body to form a short skirt. For this reason I
could never be looked at as an accepted equal. While language
and physicality hinder acceptance, as in my own case as well as
Tan's mother and the Mukherjee sisters, so does the choice to
surrender one's own traditions and identity, a decision Mira and
I struggled with.

Mukhurjee and Tan's relationships help them better understand their personal identity, but also their identity within the cultures they navigate. Tan's unique communication with her mother is a form of intimacy that defines her perception of self, which contributes to her interpretation of the world. Tan is able to transcend both American and Chinese culture, while Mukherjee stakes her identity firmly in American culture. By comparing herself to her sister, these choices are affirmed. The struggles of immigrants, second-generation children, and even travelers spawn from how we interact with the world. My name, whether it's Ami Gaye, Emily, or Emmylou, is how I identify myself but also how the world recognizes me. This is why relationships are so central to identity, as with Tan and Mukherjee; it is an understanding of self that is affirmed by those around us.

Works Cited

Mukherjee, Bharati. "Two Ways to Belong in America." *50 Essays: A Portable Anthology*, 4th ed., edited by Samuel Cohen, Bedford/St. Martin's, 2014, pp. 290–293.

Tan, Amy. "Mother Tongue." *50 Essays: A Portable Anthology*, 4th ed., edited by Samuel Cohen, Bedford/St. Martin's, 2014, pp. 417–423.

OR

Works Cited

Cohen, Samuel, editor. *50 Essays: A Portable Anthology*, 4th ed., Bedford/St. Martin's, 2014.

Mukherjee, Bharati, "Two Ways to Belong in America." Cohen, pp. 290–293.

Tan, Amy. "Mother Tongue," Cohen, pp. 417–423.

Olivia Oeff
Professor Johnstone
UCWR 110-601
27 October 2015

The No-Name Life of Willa Shakespeare

It is said that everyone has skeletons in their closets, but what
about ghosts on their shoulders? As children, we all believed in
ghosts, and perhaps we were not wrong to do so; we carry around
the ghosts of our past in our bones, and by knowing them we can
have a fuller idea of our own identity. My search to illuminate the
ghosts on my shoulder, as well as my journey in discovering how
these ghosts impact my personal identity as a woman artist, led
me to the essays "No Name Woman" by Maxine Hong Kingston
and "What If Shakespeare Had Had A Sister?" by Virginia Woolf.
These essays, written by and about women who experienced some
sort of creative oppression, guided me in my examination of my
role as a legacy of the female "ghosts" who were not allowed to
live or create as I do. In order to find my own place in this line
of succession, I asked of the essays and of myself: what were the
means of women's oppression, and how did this oppression contribute to their roles as the ghosts that haunted Woolf, Kingston,
and, through them, me?

"No Name Woman" discusses Chinese culture in the 1930s
and one socially ostracized, nameless woman, who eventually
takes her own life rather than live in a world where she is universally hated. A modern reader like myself immediately wonders
how her own self-worth became lower in her estimation than
honoring her family and community. The short answer seems to

be that she was indoctrinated into a culture that conditioned her to have this belief. One way this was manifested was denying women education and other opportunities that their male relatives were able to enjoy. Kingston discusses the inherent disadvantage that Chinese women inherited by contrasting her father and uncle's educations and travels to America while "they expected her alone to keep the traditional ways, which her brothers... could fumble without detection" (231) That she took her own life is also a sign of her deep indoctrination; her culture's disapproval of her and her upbringing, which taught her the utmost important of honoring one's family, led her to her death without the community members ever laying a hand on her. In this way, it is apparent that the no-name woman was conditioned socially to place less value on her life than on the lives of those around her.

These same means of oppressing women can be seen in Woolf's "What If Shakespeare Had Had a Sister?" because it also discusses the ways women were conditioned to be devoid of creativity. As in "No Name Woman," women were intellectually and emotionally manipulated at a young age so that their ambitions of being anything but faithful wives and mothers would dry up. Like the nameless aunt who was forced to stick to housewivery while her brother went to America, one way this was put into practice was the lack of meaningful education, the education that was offered to boys like William Shakespeare. The sixteenth-century woman, as Woolf points out, was given neither the education nor the creative freedom that begets genius. Despite being "as adventurous, as imaginative, as agog to see the world as he was" (470), Shakespeare's hypothetical sister "was not sent to school. She had no chance of learning grammar or logic, let alone of reading Horace or Virgil" (470). Just as Kingston depicts the gruesome scene of the nameless aunt's suicide, Woolf predicts that the creative woman "would certainly have gone crazed, shot herself, or ended her days in some lonely cottage outside the village" (472). In these ways, "No Name Woman" and "What If Shakespeare Had Had a Sister?" present the social conditioning that women underwent that led them to abhor their own rebellious minds and the shame they would bring on themselves by being unladylike enough to have a child or write a book.

Both of these essays focus on society's outrage at women's potency, the creative ability of female minds and wombs. Babies and ideas are, after all, both *conceptual* in the strictest of senses, and society resented Kingston's aunt and Shakespeare's hypothetical sister for their conceiving minds and bodies. In Kingston's essay, society rejected her aunt's physical conception of a child, though if women conceive, who can be blamed in the first place but a man? In Kingston's essay, the man who was her rapist was "not, after all, much different from her husband. They both gave orders: she followed" (231). This homogenizing of men reveals their status as a class above women, a class that seemed to be made up more of drill officers than of fellow human beings. While women were socially and politically on a class beneath men, the cultural mystique raised the expected ideal of femininity to almost an astral plane. Women were expected to fulfill the social ideal of a chaste, graceful, attractive, godlike woman so pure that she seemed to operate on some angelic realm entirely parallel to reality. The no-name aunt was punished for breaking this image of the cultural ideal of womanly perfection by disillusioning the village with the blatant humanity of her not-so-immaculate conception.

Woolf's essay deals with a parallel issue in that the hypothetical female Shakespeares were scorned for their mental conceptions as a result of being simultaneously idolized and oppressed. Again, men play an important role in this subjection of women. Woolf expresses this idea by discussing the ways men used women as vehicles in their own art without allowing women the freedom to make art themselves. Masculine artists placed women on the same pedestal that the ideally chaste Chinese woman occupies in "No Name Woman"; Woolf's summation of the situation is that a woman in real life compared to artistic renderings of woman was "a worm winged like an eagle; the spirit of life and beauty in a kitchen chopping up suet" (468). This emphasizes the contrast between the heavenly ideal of women and their lack of artistic allowance in real life. These images signify men's appropriating women's power by rendering them pretty...and powerless. Kingston recognizes that without men, women would never conceive babies; Woolf reminds us that without women as subjects, men could never conceive the art that they do. These women's creations end up sharing the same fate as their conceivers. The no-name aunt dies clutching her newborn baby, as nameless as the titleless books that the Shakespearean sister died without articulating when "she died young. She never wrote a word" (475). The difference between the two essays lies in society's response to the conceptions of mind and body. Ironically, Kingston's no-name aunt, who is persecuted for her physical conception, is mentally beaten down and driven to suicide by her community;

Shakespeare's hypothetical sister would have experienced the reverse situation, being physically "severely beaten" (470) as punishment for the mental conception her book represented.

Shakespeare's sister is indeed hypothetical; Shakespeare himself had no sisters. In this way Woolf's essay and Kingston's are also more interrelated than originally meets the eye. Both essays are mixes of facts, fiction, history, biography, and supposition. Woolf and Kingston devote their attentions not to the proud family histories or the books actually written, but to the lack of female writers, the aunt-shaped holes in history. This is especially shown in Kingston's essay when she emphasizes the no-name aunt as silent, nameless, purposefully forgotten by her family and by history. This silence was a form of punishment; Kingston states that "the real punishment was not the raid swiftly inflicted by the villagers, but the family's deliberately forgetting her" (238). This form of oppressive silence lasts for decades until Kingston's mother tells her daughter the story to scare her and shame her into submission to the culture. Kingston's mother's instruction for her to not "tell this story to anyone" sets the theme of silencing women and their stories for the remainder of the essay. Kingston, in the very writing of the essay, breaks the stigma around her aunt and the decades-long silence. Ghosts are nothing if not silent, and perhaps that is Kingston's purpose in writing, to speak for the ghost without words.

Woolf seems to share this goal by writing for the thousands of women who weren't able to write for themselves. Woolf indicated that she is haunted in the same was as Kingston by stating that "this poet who never wrote a word and was buried at the cross-roads still lives. She lives in you and me" (475). The ghosts of the Chinese woman whose lives were scapegoats for their culture and the ghosts of a million female Shakespeares who were never encouraged to write are also similar in their namelessness. Just as Kingston's aunt's name has been erased by history, so are names of the millions of writers who never got to write. In Woolf's essay too, silence plays an important role. Maxine Hong Kingston's mother's instruction to not "tell this story to anyone" is directly tied to Victorian women's inability to speak for themselves through art. The distinction between the two essays lies, perhaps, in the ghosts' dispositions. While Kingston suggests that her aunt's ghost might be mad at her for "telling on her", all indications suggest that Woolf believes that Shakespeare's hypothetical sister would want to live on through future women artists.

It is strange for me to realize that, in perspective of the time these essays were written, I am one of these women artists of the future that Woolf puts her faith in. As a woman today, and in particular a woman artist today, I can't imagine the weight of repression that the women depicted in these essays had to bear. In fact, I can't picture myself growing up in such a world and being able to have become the person I am at all. My life is also very affected by my family's history and ghosts, as I presume all families are. I grew up with anecdotes about relatives who died before I ever met them, and I wonder if one day I will be summed up in a quick story to someone's children. I wonder which corner of my life they will choose, which tiny anecdote will become the whole story to some future generation. Not all ghosts are as pleasant as family heirlooms, of course, and some haven't even gotten around to dying yet. My last name is a ghost of my great-grandfather, a man who left his family, but not before switching the "o" and the "e" of my German last name to help people pronounce it more easily (it didn't help). Though no one was sad to see him go and no one talks much of him, I still carry around the ghost of the violent man every time I introduce myself or sign my name.

The junction of these two articles allows me to not only appreciate my artistic freedom, my ability to conceive ideas and create, but also gives me a greater peace with the idea of ghosts like my great grandfather. Our pasts enrich us, and the death and destruction that ghosts are associated with also hold the deepest possibility of conception and birth. The past can never be relived, but it can be retold, and perhaps even reborn. When I was reading Maya Angelou's book *A Letter to My Daughter* several years ago, a quote struck a chord with me that I have remembered since: "I believe that one carries the shadows, the dreams, the fears and dragons of home under one's skin, at the extreme corners of one's eyes and possibly in the gristle of the earlobe." This quote is applicable to Woolf's essay and Kingston's because both speak of the past in terms of the present; both bring legacies from the past forward to haunt us and to fulfill their lost destinies. Home is less of a place than we believe it to be, and while I think "home is where the heart is" is too broadly encompassing to fit the bill, I do believe that our legacies, the family and national histories that form our identities, and our homes are one and the same. The "fears and dragons of home" that Woolf and Kingston reveal do not lurk in their earlobes, but in their hands, as they write words and pass them on to us, the readers. Their words—sometimes gentle, sometimes violent—pass from their hands to ours, and from their shoulders, ghosts silent as death find speech once again.

Works Cited

Kingston, Maxine Hong. "No Name Woman." *50 Essays: A Portable Anthology,* 4th ed., edited by Samuel Cohen, Bedford/St. Martin's, 2014, pp. 227–39.

Woolf, Virginia. "What if Shakespeare Had Had a Sister?" *50 Essays: A Portable Anthology,* 4th ed., edited by Samuel Cohen, Bedford/St. Martin's, 2014, pp. 466–76.

OR

Works Cited

Cohen, Samuel, editor. *50 Essays: A Portable Anthology,* 4th ed., Bedford/St. Martin's, 2014.

Kingston, Maxine Hong. "No Name Woman," Cohen, pp. 227–39.

Woolf, Virginia. "What if Shakespeare Had Had a Sister?" Cohen, pp. 446–76.

5

Researched Argument

UCWR 110

Types of Research Assignments

A Research-Based Argument vs. An Informational Research Project

In UCWR 110, you will be required to compose a research paper that makes an argument. This requirement may be different from research projects that you have done in the past.

In high school, students are often asked to do research projects for the purpose of gathering information and presenting that information to the reader. This type of project is akin to creating an encyclopedia entry or Wikipedia page.

However, the purpose of the research assignment is different in UCWR 110. Most often, the main purpose is to develop an argument based on the research you have done. While the project will of course require you to do substantial information gathering, in your paper you will be expected to develop an argument and shape the paper around a thesis. Students sometimes struggle with this argumentative aspect of the assignment because they see research as strictly collecting information about a topic. As you conduct your research, you should therefore not only gather information but also identify the different debates your sources are engaged in. These debates can point you toward a more specific issue around which you can structure your argument.

Here is an illustration of the difference between an informational project and a research-based argument: Suppose you are interested in the protest movement against the Vietnam War in the 1960s and 1970s. For an informational project you would gather material about the leading anti-war figures and the major anti-war organizations, their reasons for opposing the war, and the methods of protest they employed. Indeed, your paper itself might be organized around these sub-topics. However, for a research-based argument, you would gather the same information but would also investigate the various debates among historians about the antiwar movement. There are a number of these, but one prominent debate focuses on the effectiveness of the movement in helping bring the war to an end.

As a researcher, you could enter this conversation about the movement by researching and analyzing the different interpretations of its effectiveness. In your paper, you would frame the debate in your introduction, present your broad stance on the issue of the movement's effectiveness, and then structure your paper around the reasons that support your argument. Be sure to make your argument throughout the paper. Each paragraph should advance your argument in some way. Beware of the misguided perception that a research-based argument is just an informational paper with your personal opinion tacked on in the introduction and conclusion.

Writing as Inquiry or Exploratory Research

While some instructors may require a researched argument, others require a paper in which you conduct research as a means to explore or inquire into an issue you find compelling. As discussed above, in order to produce a research-based argument, you need to gather information, identify key questions related to your issue, and consider different views on the subject. Then you structure your paper around a thesis on the issue. But in an exploratory essay the focus and content of your paper will be the very type of research and thinking you do before writing a thesis-driven research paper. Rather than making an argument about a specific issue and developing that argument throughout your paper as you would in a researched-based argument, an exploratory essay offers a sort of analytical overview of your process of discovery.

Although it does not present an overarching argument, an exploratory essay does nevertheless involve a great deal of **analysis, synthesis,** and evaluation of the sources and their views on the topic. This is the major distinction between an exploratory essay and an informational one. Informational essays tend to focus primarily on summary and contain only minimal analysis, synthesis, and evaluation. An exploratory essay on the antiwar movement of the 1960s, for example, would not only summarize the information you have gathered but would also lay out the main debates or differences in interpretation that historians have offered on the issue. In addition, and perhaps most importantly, it would offer some analysis of the strengths and weaknesses of different views and point the reader toward the more convincing ones, even though it might not necessarily come to definitive conclusions about the debates it has reviewed.

Planning and Time Management

One of the greatest challenges of writing a successful research paper involves planning the various stages of your project and setting aside sufficient time for each. One reason a research paper can seem so daunting is that we tend to see it as one huge task. This can make us feel overwhelmed and lead to a deadly pattern of procrastination. However, effective planning and time-management can reduce the stress of a big project and help you produce a more successful research paper.

Your instructor will likely break down parts of the project into various stages. Typically, an instructor may require you to submit a proposal, do an annotated bibliography, write a draft for peer review, and revise that draft for submission. However, you should break those tasks down as well. Instead of seeing the project as a series of deadlines and assignments (a sort of "teacher-centered" or "assignment-centered" view), approach it from a writer's point of view. This means trying to see it as a set of discrete yet related tasks that can be tackled at various stages and even re-visited as you proceed.

As a writer, in order to meet the deadlines and do the assignments, you are faced with the following: choosing a topic, finding sources, making notes, drafting a thesis, planning and organizing your paper, writing a draft, revising, and editing. This is quite a bit, but by tackling the various tasks in stages and seeing how they relate to one another, you can keep the project manageable.

Here are some suggestions for planning and time management:

- Start exploring topics after you've received the assignment. You will likely have to narrow, refine, and even discard topics before you settle on one. This takes time, so don't put it off.

- Set aside ample time to find sources. Plan for multiple research sessions, and consider asking for help from your instructor or a research librarian.

- Avoid doing your research in one big push before a deadline. You should regularly re-examine the sources you have in order to consider what kinds of sources you still need to find.

- Adopt an effective and organized note-taking system. There's nothing worse than scrambling to find that great quotation you want to plug in but have lost track of.

- Develop a tentative thesis early on. Your argument will likely change, but having a thesis will help you focus and manage your research more efficiently.

- Create an outline before drafting, ideally one organized around your argument, i.e., its thesis, the reasons supporting that thesis, and/or the major counter-arguments you will be addressing. Elaborating on your argument is crucial to your success, so structuring your outline around its key components, rather than broad topics or sources, will streamline the drafting process and help you produce a draft that is focused and convincing.

- Set aside extensive time for drafting. Unlike other assignments, with a research paper you are juggling large amounts of material. Even with a strong outline, synthesizing this material on the page can be challenging and time-consuming.

- Draft in stages. Consider beginning with a section you feel comfortable with. We often assume that drafting is a linear process. It rarely is. Starting with the parts you find easier to write can build confidence and momentum for those more challenging aspects of the project.

- Revise in stages as well. Just like with research and drafting, trying to revise in one big push is generally ineffective. Identify two to four priorities for revision, begin with one or two of those, proceed methodically, and then move on to new priorities in later revision sessions.

- Edit for continuity and coherence as well as grammar and style. Because this is a longer paper that you will have drafted and revised in stages, it will often need continuity editing that ensures that the various parts are unified and connected. Make sure you have developed your main argument and asserted your voice in each section.

The Recursive Nature of the Research Process

The suggestions above might make the writing of the research paper seem like a straightforward, step-by-step procedure; however, writing an effective research paper, like almost all writing, is a more recursive than linear process. Keep in mind that many of these seemingly discrete tasks are overlapping. When executing a new stage of the process, you may need to return to previous tasks.

Take, for example, doing research and finding sources. Chances are that once you've chosen a topic, your instructor will require you to submit an annotated bibliography in which you document and summarize your sources, often a specific number of them. At this stage, it can feel like the research process is complete, and if you are lucky, it may be. However, producing the annotated bibliography often highlights gaps in your research or points to further questions that need to be addressed before you start drafting. This will require more research. Even as you are drafting or after peer review, you may continue to identify gaps in your knowledge. As a result, you will have to do additional research to shore up your paper.

For additional information and ideas, see *Pearson Writer*. On the Purdue Owl website at https://owl.english.purdue.edu/owl, search for "How do you develop a research project?," "How do you schedule a research project?," and "How do you organize a writing project?"

Choosing and Narrowing a Topic

The process of choosing a topic is another highly challenging part of the research process. While occasionally a writer quickly comes up with a viable, engaging focus, the process of choosing a topic and narrowing its focus can be complex, time-consuming, and—let's admit it—frustrating. Yet producing a successful paper depends greatly on choosing a topic that is clearly defined and engaging. Moreover, having a well-defined topic can make the subsequent stages of the process more focused and efficient.

Here are some guidelines for choosing and narrowing your topic:

- To get started, use whatever idea-generating techniques you find valuable. These can include brainstorming, free-writing, talking to others, or perusing newspapers and magazines.

- Find a topic that truly interests you. Working on something that you are genuinely curious about will make the process far more engaging and rewarding.

- Beware of stale, hand-me-down topics like abortion or capital punishment. While these can be approached in interesting ways, they are overdone and broad, and students often choose them simply because they seem familiar and easy rather than genuinely interesting.

- Revise your topic as you proceed. As you research and acquire knowledge of your subject, your interest and focus will likely shift and narrow. Follow your interests.

- Consider focusing on a sub-topic within your larger topic. This is related to the suggestion above. Often in the process of researching, planning, and even drafting, we discover our topic is too broad.

Rather than finding an entirely new topic, the more effective strategy is to focus on a sub-topic, i.e., a topic within your original topic. While students are often reluctant to narrow in this way because they feel they may not have enough to say, the truth is that focusing on a sub-topic often allows the writer to develop a more interesting and complex argument.

- Use sources to identify specific issues or questions. Your topic should be a debatable one, so your sources will, in one form or another, be framing the debatable issues within that topic. You as a writer are entering the conversation these sources are engaged in, so look for the questions and issues the sources are addressing, and feel free to focus on a specific issue that they have identified.

As the above suggestions indicate, finalizing a topic usually involves research, often substantial amounts of it. While it is useful to brainstorm and reflect on your interests in order to generate possible topics, you will likely need to do some preliminary research before you can settle comfortably into a topic. Later in the process, as your research becomes more thorough and your knowledge of the subject matter increases, you may have to refine your topic to reflect your greater understanding.

The process of refining your topic can continue right up to the submission of your final draft. As you draft, go through peer review, and revise your paper, you may realize that you want to focus more on one specific aspect of the topic and will need to re-work your paper accordingly.

A Topic vs. An Issue

While we have thus far spoken primarily of choosing a topic, the term "topic" can be misleading because it is so general. Since you are developing an argument, it might be more helpful to think of addressing an issue or, perhaps even better, answering a question. Looking at the process as choosing a topic can lead us to rather broad and ultimately unmanageable topics. But if we think about addressing an issue or answering a question, we can give our work focus and ensure that we are producing an argumentative essay.

But what's the difference between a topic and an issue? A topic is typically rather general and doesn't necessarily point to a debate, while an issue points to a debate or a debatable question. Here's an example that illustrates the distinction between a topic and an issue and also delineates the process of moving from a topic to a specific issue and question:

Suppose after reading essays by Malcolm X and Carolyn Bird you decide you are interested in the topic of college education. However, writing about "college education" is obviously too broad, so you have to narrow your focus. What has intrigued you perhaps is the suggestion that college education is not necessary or valuable for most people. Now you are moving toward an issue.

This is still somewhat broad, however. Now you might consider why you have asked yourself this question. You realize that you have been challenged by Malcolm X's claim that college life, with its parties and panty raids, is actually a distraction from genuine learning. In addition, Malcolm X demonstrates that he has educated himself better than any college could have, while Bird claims that, because we have such wide access to materials now, pretty much anyone can educate himself or herself in the way colleges promise to. You are torn because you recognize some truth in Malcolm X's and Bird's arguments but also value your own college experience. You know that so much of college life is distracting yet so much is rewarding as well. Now you are refining the issue even further. You might arrive at the following question: "Given the problems and value present in college life, how can colleges create an environment that better fosters the kind of education Malcolm achieved on his own?" This question would point you toward research on the goals of college education, the main problems in student achievement, and the ways these problems have been addressed.

Pragmatic Issues vs. Conceptual Issues

Determining whether you want to approach your topic from a pragmatic or a conceptual angle can help you narrow your focus.

Almost every paper will address both pragmatic and conceptual issues, but most successful ones tend to focus primarily on one or the other. The difference between the two is this: a pragmatic focus will ask readers to do something or adopt a specific action to solve a problem while a conceptual focus will ask readers to gain understanding or adopt a belief regarding an issue or problem.

Conceptual and pragmatic problems of course overlap; you can't solve a problem without some conceptual understanding of the issue, and conceptual thinking can point you to pragmatic solutions. However, it is best to identify whether your main purpose is to create understanding (conceptual) or if it is to urge a solution or action (pragmatic) (Williams and Colomb 70).

Let's return to the topic of college education mentioned earlier in this section. Suppose that in addition to having read Malcolm X and Carolyn Bird on education, you have read articles about the failure of universities to adequately prepare students for the world of work. You've found general agreement about this. If you were to adopt a *conceptual* approach to the topic, you might research the reasons for this failure: Why are college graduates consistently under-prepared for professional careers? This might involve debates over issues of curriculum, standards, student attitudes, or employer needs.

You would focus your research on finding material that addresses these conceptual issues. In your conclusion, you might briefly address the implications of your conceptual analysis for pragmatic solutions, but this would not be the main focus on the paper.

However, you could also tackle this topic from a *pragmatic* angle by examining solutions to the problem: How can colleges better prepare students for careers and the world of work? While this approach would have to address some conceptual issues about the causes of the problem, your main focus—and the overwhelming proportion of your paper—would analyze possible solutions in order to propose the best course of action. What are colleges doing to better prepare students? What seems to be working or not working? Based on your research, what would you recommend as an effective approach or set of approaches to solving this problem?

For addtional resources on research essays, please see Purdue OWL at https://owl.english.purdue.edu/, and search for "How do you find a research topic?", "How to refine your topic," and "How to write research essays."

Sample Student Researched Argument

Ross Carpino
Professor Quirk
UCWR 110
05 Dec 2014

Plan B: The Only Plan

After many years of age restrictions, the emergency contraceptive Plan B One-Step was recently made available to women
universally. Many find that this change in policy regarding the
emergency contraceptive pill will increase promiscuity among
teenagers. Others feel that there was not substantial medical and
scientific evidence to implement an age restriction in the first
place. Ultimately, the debate boils down to whether or not adolescent females are capable of understanding the pill's use and being
able to use such a medication correctly. However, females who
are old enough to ovulate are old enough to make the decision
to use Plan B One-Step responsibly. Therefore, Plan B One-Step
should be available to females of all ages without a prescription
or an age requirement. What is at stake here is providing females
the right to choose whether having a child is right for them or
not, regardless of age.

A recent court ruling from Judge Edward R. Korman, an
appointed United States District Judge for the Eastern District
of New York, ordered that the most common emergency contraceptive medication, Plan B One-Step, be made available over the
counter without any age restrictions (Belluck). The judge's main
argument for his ruling was politics. By accusing the Obama

administration of "putting politics ahead of science" Korman deduced that the decision to only sell Plan B One-Step behind the counter to females over the age of 18 was not made on scientific evidence (Belluck). Instead the decision was made based on political moves for Obama's reelection. In 2011, prime campaigning time for reelection, the Health and Human Services secretary, Kathleen Sebelius countermanded the F.D.A.'s decision to make Plan B One-Step universally available. Judge Korman comments on this decision, declaring "the secretary's action was politically motivated...and scientifically unjustified" (Belluck). In 2011, the F.D.A. found no scientific reasoning to prohibit selling Plan B One-Step universally, yet Sebelius saw an opportunity to make a political move to help Obama's reelection. If the Food and Drug Administration saw no reason in 2011 to prohibit the pill's sale, and no scientific evidence has come to show any chronic medical consequences, then there is no reason that the pill should be regulated.

The Center for Drug Evaluation and Research, or CDER, also did a review for Plan B One-Step's application and found its own scientific solution. As they worked to find its solution, the CDER experimented to determine whether younger females were able to understand the use of Plan B One-Step (Bailey). Based on their results, they found that the emergency contraceptive was "safe and effective for adolescents" and that "adolescent females understood the product was not for routine use...and would not protect them against sexually transmitted diseases" (Bailey). One of the few points in this argument which is supported by the CDER's research is that young females are capable of understanding what Plan B One-Step is used for as well as what it does not protect against. As the government continues to put politics ahead of science, it is the young women who fail to meet the legislated age requirements who suffer the consequences.

The main opposition to selling Plan B One-Step without any age restrictions is that it causes abortions of developing fetuses. However, this is a complete misconception. Plan B One-Step is not an abortifacient medication, meaning that the medication will not prohibit the growth and development of a fetus, nor will it stop pregnancy (Stangl). Plan B One-Step is the most commonly sold emergency contraceptive in the United States, which works only hormonally (Stangl). Through the medical lens, the purpose of taking this emergency contraceptive is to inhibit either ovulation or fertilization by making the endometrium an inhospitable environment (Stangl). In the words of Rebecca Stangl, an assistant professor of philosophy at the University of Virginia, "The longstanding consensus in the medical community is that pregnancy begins when a fertilized egg implants itself in the uterus...and everyone agrees that emergency contraction cannot cause the termination of a fertilized egg that has already implanted itself in the uterus" (Stangl).

Therefore, the argument that Plan B One-Step is an abortifacient medication is invalid. Those who oppose the sale of this emergency contraceptive on the grounds that it causes abortions ignore the clear scientific evidence stating that Plan B One-Step cannot be classified as an abortifacient medication. How can a pill such as Plan B One-Step cause abortions if a life was never conceived to begin with? It can't, proving the common misconception that Plan B One-Step is an abortifacient medication invalid.

Carpino   4

Even if we overlook the scientific facts which prove that Plan B One-Step is not an abortifacient medication, we can still permit its use using Thomas Aquinas's doctrine of double effect. Within the field of philosophy the doctrine of double effect is often "invoked to explain the permissibility of an action that causes a serious harm...as a side effect of promoting some good end" (McIntyre). If we evaluate the use of Plan B One-Step through a moral lens, the doctrine of double effect enables its use. In the words of Rebecca Stangl, "If one accepts the doctrine of double effect, there are circumstances that still permit its [Plan B One-Step] use" (Stangl). When a female takes Plan B One-Step as an emergency contraceptive, the serious harm would hypothetically come from aborting the life of a developing fetus. Yet the "good end" would be the female does not conceive a child. By using the doctrine of double effect, philosophy has proved that even if Plan B One-Step was an abortifacient drug, which it is not, then its use would still be permitted. By allowing females everywhere to make the choice of what outcome will provide their life with a "good end", we permit the use of the emergency contraceptive.

A second opposition that many agree with is for Plan A, also known as abstinence. *The Washington Times* in their editorial *Shelving Plan B* discusses the benefits of choosing Plan A over Plan B. *The Washington Times* states that "By slowly rolling back the age at which Plan B is available...Congress can't build the momentum needed to ditch Plan B in favor of Plan A...which works every time ("Shelving Plan B"). While their argument that "Plan A works every time" is a valid one, it is unrealistic to expect all adolescents to abstain from engaging in sexual activities.

Statistics regarding the sexual activity among American adolescents show that 48% of American adolescents have engaged in sexual intercourse by the age of 17 ("American Teens' Sexual and Reproductive Health"). The previous age restriction for purchasing Plan B One-Step was 17. If we put that into context, 48% of American adolescents have engaged in sexual intercourse by the age of 17, and are theoretically at risk of pregnancy. These adolescents who are younger than the age restriction still need to have access to this emergency contraceptive if they are engaging in sexual intercourse. If Plan A fails, females should not be punished with the possibility of having a child solely because Plan B One-Step has a scientifically unjustified age restriction. Plan A is a good plan; however, when Plan A fails, females of all ages should have Plan B One-Step available to them if they need it.

As Plan B One-Step has continued to have scientifically unjustified age restriction, it is also in violation of the Fourteenth Amendment. Vanessa Lu, a legal extern at the U.S. Securities & Exchange Commission and a research assistant to Professor Neil Williams of Loyola University Chicago School of Law, clarifies that "Under the Due Process Clause of the Fourteenth Amendment, the Supreme Court has stated that each person is entitled to 'a right of personal privacy'" (Lu). She continues to explain how the constitution never plainly states what a "right of privacy" is, but it does however guarantee an individual "the interest in independence in making certain kinds of important decisions" (Lu). What this means is that the government cannot interfere with important choices which are protected as a "right of privacy." One of these "rights of privacy" is the choice to use contraceptives or to not use contraceptives. The Fourteenth Amendment protects against the government imposing their views on important decisions such as who should be able to use emergency contraceptives. Therefore, without scientific evidence, denying someone access to an emergency contraceptive, such as Plan B One-Step, due to age restrictions is a direct violation of the Fourteenth Amendment. Denying a female under the age of 17 access to Plan B One-Step without a prescription from a physician violates that woman's "right of privacy" and is a direct violation of the Fourteenth Amendment.

A third opposition which opposes the sale of Plan B One-Step without age restrictions is that it will increase promiscuity among minors. This unvalidated argument is commonly viewed as an endeavor by the government to control sexual behavior among minors (Lu). In the words of Vanessa Lu, "The FDA has not presented evidence to show that over-the-counter access to Plan B [One-Step] will increase unprotected sex among minors nor has it shown that minors will use more common reliable forms of contraceptives any less" (Lu). Increased promiscuity among minors is an assumption made by the FDA which ignores "conclusive scientific evidence that proves access to Plan B [One-Step] without a prescription does not increase health-related risks to minors" (Lu). This is more than just another unjustified argument, as it is also another example of how politics is being put ahead of science on the topic of emergency contraceptives.

Judge Edward R. Korman's decision to order the FDA to revoke its age restriction on Plan B One-Step brought justice to this controversy. The FDA must allow the emergency contraceptive to be sold without age restrictions; otherwise they are limiting a minor's right to access emergency contraceptives and in a direct violation of the Fourteenth Amendment. Until the FDA finds evidence to prove medical side effects for females under the age of 17 or 18 who take Plan B One-Step, they have no reason to limit the sale of the emergency contraceptive. Since Plan B One-Step is not an abortifacient medication, Plan A only works around 50% of the time, and promiscuity will not be increased among minors, the only conceivable conclusion is to permit the sale of the emergency contraceptive without age restrictions. After all, the age restriction is a violation of the Fourteenth Amendment.

Ultimately, the argument over Plan B One-Step comes down to the freedom for females everywhere, regardless of age, to be able to choose what is right for them. Without scientific evidence to demonstrate any reason why Plan B One-Step shouldn't be available universally, there is no reason why people should disapprove of the emergency contraceptive. Also, as it is medically proven that the emergency contraceptive in no way causes abortions, the main counterargument is invalid. Without scientific evidence to support the restrictions that are implemented on the emergency contraceptive, there is no logical reason to have them. Judge Edward R. Korman clearly made the long overdue decision to make Plan B One-Step universally available to females, finally putting science ahead of politics.

Works Cited

"American Teens' Sexual and Reproductive Health." *Guttmacher Institute*, Guttmacher Institute, 2 Nov. 2016, www.guttmacher.org/fact-sheet/american-teens-sexual-and-reproductive-health. Accessed 10 May 2017.

Bailey, Ronald. "Obama, Plan B, Fear of Promiscuity, Sex and the Single Teen." *Reason.com*, Reason Foundation, 9 Apr. 2013, reason.com/blog/2013/04/09/obama-plan-b-fear-of-promiscuity-sex-and. Accessed 10 May 2017.

Belluck, Pam. "Access Increases for Emergency Contraception." *The New York Times,* 1 June 2013, www.nytimes.com/2013/04/06/health/judge-orders-fda-to-make-morning-after-pill-available-over-the-counter-for-all-ages.html. Accessed 10 Apr. 2017.

Lu, Vanessa. "The Plan B Age Restriction Violates a Minor's Right to Access Contraceptives." *Family Law Quarterly*, vol. 44, no. 3, 2010, pp. 398–401. Accessed 31 Oct. 2017

McIntyre, Alison. "Doctrine of Double Effect." *Stanford Encyclopedia of Philosophy*, Metaphysics Research Lab, 2014.

"Shelving Plan B; Pssst! A Government Pusher's Got Abortion Pills for Children." *The Washington Times (Washington, DC)*, 3 May 2013, www.highbeam.com/doc/1G1-328507664.html?refid=easy_hf. Accessed 26 Oct. 2017.

Stangl, Rebecca. "Plan B and the Doctrine of Double Effect." *The Hastings Center Report,* Hastings Center, 1 July 2009, www.questia.com/library/journal/1G1-220561133/plan-b-and-the-doctrine-of-double-effect. Accessed 31 Oct. 2017.

Amanda Friedlander
Position Essay
Professor Foss
UCWR 110-200

Stop the Madness: The Negative Impacts of Solitary
Confinement on Inmates, Society, and the United States
Government

Tens of thousands of Americans currently live in concrete boxes, which are empty except for cold, concrete cots, rusty metal sinks, paint-chipped desks chained to the wall, and a small hole in the floor. It is in this miniscule box that many will slowly descend into madness, either from withdrawal symptoms, loneliness, or untreated mental health issues. Some people will even die here. This punishment, called solitary confinement, has been a controversial topic within the U.S. prison system since its birth in the mid-1800s. Despite experts and inmates alike agreeing that it's a form of inexcusable torture, there are still over 25,000 adult inmates currently housed in Supermax facilities—also known as solitary confinement facilities—across the country (Casella and Ridgeway). With so many people sentenced to such an extreme punishment, it's hard to imagine why so few have questioned how so many people have come to deserve such endless torture. Due to expensive, inefficient, and unconstitutional nature of solitary confinement, the United States government should outlaw all uses of solitary confinement as a form of punishment for inmates in prisons.

In 1829, Eastern State Penitentiary opened in Pennsylvania. Its mission was to become a spectacle of penitence and regret, a divine sanctuary to bridge between punishment and repentance.

Isolation and deprivation were the main methods used to facilitate this labyrinth of self-condemnation and remorse. Inmates, whose crimes ranged from first-degree murder to horse-stealing (Hazard 89), were confined to an eight-by-ten cell and were given a cot, a bible, and the opportunity to beg for holy forgiveness. Their only exposure to the outside world was a slim window in the ceiling called an "Eye of God," named so because it was theorized that, in their deprivation, these inmates would find God (Farrell). However, extreme separation from socialization with other humans and a severe lack of understanding of mental health led many prisoners to become violent, unstable, even suicidal. In fact, Al Capone, who was jailed for tax evasion, was the most famous inmate at Eastern State. Though he was allowed furniture and other luxuries, he too eventually began to exhibit signs of serious mental illness. He claimed he was being haunted by the ghost of the man he killed in the St Valentine's Day Massacre. He would stay up all night, screaming and wailing (Anderson, 6). Amid controversy that accused the prison's deprivation-based system of being inhumane, Eastern State realigned its practices with mercy and rehabilitation rather than punishment, and eventually closed down in 1971 due to the high costs of necessary repairs.

The practice of solitary confinement did not die with it, however. In 1983, two correctional officers fell victim to the debilitating effects at the hands of several inmates at a prison in Marion, Illinois (Sullivan). Six years later, Pelican Bay was opened and represented the beginning of Supermax facilities—prisons that only house inmates in solitary confinement. Within just a couple of years, Supermax facilities had popped up across the country, despite a Supreme Court case that condemned solitary confinement, particularly at Pelican Bay. However, the benchmark case—Madrid v Gomez—ruled that the federal government could not constitutionally close down Supermax facilities; the court must "defer to the states about how best to incarcerate offenders" (Sullivan). The lack of Supreme Court interference would prove to be one of the greatest obstacles anti-solitary protesters would face; such little regulation led to dramatic overpopulation of solitary confinement housing, and today there are over 80,000 inmates currently locked in solitary cells across the country.

Conditions have hardly improved from Eastern State's so-called theological methods of punishment. For instance, in most Supermax facilities, inmates are not allowed to work or take classes. Inmates are fed through a slot in the door twice a day, and may occasionally be allowed outside for only 90 minutes a day in a caged exercise pen under the watchful eye of prison personnel (Gordon). If they are deemed a threat to themselves, they are not allowed to wear prison uniforms. Instead, they must wear padding as a type of robe and sleep without sheets so they do not find a way to strangle themselves with any form of fabric. In the meantime, prisoners are told to reflect upon their actions and behave for the next day, week, month or any number of years that they could be contained in solitary (Edge). In extreme cases, like the federal Supermax facility ADX Florence, even visitation is restricted to an inmate's immediate family and legal team (Sanchez and Field). Only the worst of the worst end up in ADX Florence, also referred to as the 'Alcatraz of the Rockies', which houses the Unabomber, the accomplice to the Oklahoma City Bombing, a

9/11 conspirator, and other violent criminals, but it is not just violent inmates who wind up in solitary confinement.

Many proponents of solitary confinement argue that locking violent inmates in solitary will prevent other, more impressionable inmates from following their lead and inciting riots and chaos within the prison; however, non-violent inmates are also placed in solitary housing, countering the idea that solitary confinement is simply a preventative measure. For example, Charles E. Samuels, Jr, director of the Federal Bureau of prisons, insists that solitary confinement sequesters violent inmates to a controlled location where they can be of less harm to themselves, others inmates, and correctional officers (Goode). It may be true that locking away truly malicious inmates who pose a significant threat to general population inmates would be a noble effort to increase the safety of prisons, but in reality, it is not just those violent inmates who were getting sentenced to the "SHU", i.e. the solitary housing unit. Senator Richard Durbin of Illinois has vehemently condemned solitary confinement, saying that "solitary confinement isn't just used for the worst of the worst. Instead, we're seeing an alarming increase in isolation for those who don't really need to be there, and for many, many vulnerable groups like immigrants, children, LGBT inmates, supposedly there for their own protection" (Friedmann). Inmates are often held in solitary for religious or political beliefs rather than posing a legitimate danger to others within the prison. For instance, Rastafarian inmates have been historically targeted by correctional officers due to a religious inclination to growing out body hair (Grilo). In certain facilities, inmates are required to shave regularly and keep hair short, so Rastafarian inmates who refuse to sacrifice their religious obligations are sentenced to solitary confinement. In adhering to their religious beliefs, those inmates are putting themselves at risk for punishment; this is the exact opposite of what solitary confinement originally aimed to achieve. Even violent inmates who are put in solitary confinement as a means of preventing chaos within the prison do not require the extreme destitution that most solitary housing units provide. If correctional officers claim that solitary confinement is used as a means of protection against unruly inmates, then the solitary cells need not be paired with deprivation. Separating inmates does not have to mean indirectly torturing them as well.

Furthermore, solitary confinement does not do anything to solve the underlying issues that often lead inmates to act in irrational or dangerous ways. The drug trade within prison contributes to prison violence that only increases with inmates' tolerance levels for various illegal substances. The higher the demand, the more dangerous the drug trade becomes, since inmates who are high on narcotics are more likely to be paranoid, irritable, and prone to bouts of inconsolable rage. In this manner especially, rehabilitation should be what prisons focus on, not punishment. Prisoners are often sentenced to solitary confinement for possession of illegal contraband, which may consist of illegal drugs or weapons. In an environment where possession of such items represent status and authority, inmates often find themselves sentenced to months in solitary confinement after an unannounced prison raid; however, the presence of drugs in prisons is too often viewed through the lens of punishment, rather than identifying the underlying issues of substance abuse that only perpetuate prison violence and gang activity. Since 2006, over 150 inmates in California have overdosed on drugs, and 69 have died of Hepatitis C from sharing intravenous needles ("Overdose Deaths in California"). The secretary of Corrections in California has claimed that without serious prison reform, "we're going to have people keep dying, we're going to have continued violence in the prisons" ("Overdose Deaths in California"). Solitary confinement does not fix the issue of substance abuse within prisons, an offense that could send inmates to the SHU for months. Instead, it puts inmates at risk of withdrawal poisoning. After a certain period of time without a given drug, substance abusers begin to go through withdrawal. The length and severity of the withdrawal depends on how often and how much the abuser has been using the drug, but in extreme cases, it can lead to agonizing pain that lasts for hours and may even eventually lead to death. Even inmates who have not yet been sentenced are often kept in solitary confinement cells, left to the mercy of the detoxification process. In 2003, a young woman was arrested for petty theft and died in her cell after three days of being denied proper medical treatment for her detoxification. When a nurse was made aware of the woman's unconscious, desperately ill state, she replied, "What do you want me to do about it?" (Greenberg and Coutts). Despite clearly written standards for prison health care, defined by the National Commission of Correctional Health Care, over a million inmates still risk succumbing to drug and alcohol withdrawal in prison (Fiscella). The drug issues within prison simply cannot be solved by punishing drug-addicted inmates, just as prison violence cannot be solved by locking away especially dangerous inmates.

Though it seems reasonable to confine historically violent inmates in order to protect correctional officers, the safety of guards has been only further compromised by the use of long-term solitary confinement. Female guards are often targeted by male inmates with a history of rape and gender-based violence convictions. After an inmate has attacked a correctional officer, it seems fitting that they would be sentenced to time in the "SHU", but the overarching dangers of long-term solitary confinement only perpetuate violent behavior, or worse, cause inmates to project that violence upon themselves. In studies conducted upon lab rats subjected to Supermax-like conditions, neurologists have found that connections in the cerebral cortex of the brain—the part that determines functions like emotional responsiveness—are thinner than rats who had been exposed to "normal" conditions (Willigan). In addition, inmates subjected to long-term solitary confinement, particularly those with preexisting mental illnesses, are at least 50% more likely to engage in self-harm than inmates in general population (Fatos et al, Solitary Confinement and Risk of Self-Harm). Craig Haney, a psychology professor at University of California, has studied the psychological effects of solitary confinement on inmates and found that prolonged confinement leads to "'intolerable levels of frustration" in some prisoners, which can lead to "uncontrollable and sudden outbursts of rage'" (Gordon 506). An increase of paranoia and rage is clearly not the desired effect of solitary confinement, which is so often used to punish inmates who have engaged in paranoid, raging behaviors in general population. Fortunately, due to studies that have consistently proven that solitary confinement worsens inmate behavior, states like New York and Illinois have made changes to some prisons, even shutting down an entire Supermax facility in 2013 (Fetting).

The investment in solitary confinement is not a cheap one. Not only does it often cost inmates their sanity and dignity, it also costs the country about 80 billion dollars per year (Kearney, Melissa et al.). Between the high costs of healthcare for inmates who have attempted suicide or self-harmed, lawsuits from inmates who believe they've been tortured at the hands of the state, costs of meals and long-term housing, and piling fees that stack up with each new offense, solitary confinement has proven to be detrimental even to those living on the other side of those concrete walls. Construction costs alone can reach up to $60 million, as it did for ADX Florence. Staffing and dining requirements for inmates hike the cost of solitary confinement up to $75,000 a year in some states, which is twice as high as the cost for general population units. In California, citizens pay 175 million dollars in taxes per year just to keep inmates housed at the infamous Supermax facility, Pelican Bay ("Paying the Price for Solitary Confinement"). Within the prison, inmates are not allowed money as it is considered illegal contraband; if they are lucky enough to be allowed to work, their reward is usually virtual currency put into their commissary accounts (*Commissary Cart*). As a result, their families are left to pay their various fines, which can be up to $200 each time the inmate is sent back to the solitary unit. But it's all too easy to be sent to solitary; Glenn Martin, founder of JustLeadershipUSA and former prison inmate, says that "you don't really have to do anything wrong to find yourself getting a disciplinary ticket" (Eichelberger), and with each ticket costing at least $25, fees add up. As inmates' mental health begins to decline with each passing day in solitary confinement, violent and "unwanted" behavior only increases. While families are grieving over incarcerated loved ones, they must also pay for suicide attempts, phone calls, clothing, food, and more. Once a prisoner is released, it is much more difficult for them to get jobs, especially after having served time in prison, so their families must take them back in and continue to pay their rent. Families find themselves burdened by solitary confinement even if they believe that they are physically safer with their loved ones locked up within it. Already impoverished families are unlikely to be able to pay for another mouth to feed, causing a need to steal food and other necessary resources in order to simply survive. Theft and petty crimes committed by inmates desperate for food and clothing are part of the reason that the rate of recidivism for inmates who've spent a substantial amount of time in solitary confinement is about 60%, compared to 50% for general population inmates (Butler, Burke, et al.). It is because of the severe lack of rehabilitation and concern for the source of the motivation to commit violent crimes that the prison system is one of the most expensive institutions in the United States today. There is no reasonable way to justify using taxpayers' dollars for the cruel and unusual treatment of human beings.

Solitary confinement is neither constitutional nor ethical in its practices. The eighth amendment of the Constitution of the

United States protects all citizens against cruel and unusual punishment; several court cases like Madrid v. Gomez, Coleman v. Wilson, and Casey v. Lewis have already ruled that solitary confinement of mentally ill inmates is unconstitutional, yet inmates with mental illness are among those most often sentenced to solitary confinement due to their aggressive or self-harming behaviors (Gordon 503). In fact, according to the American Psychiatric Association, 20% of inmates in solitary confinement are classified as mentally ill (Kayatekin). Despite the clearly inhumane conditions of solitary confinement, the Supreme Court has refused to rule it as an overall violation of the constitution for non-mentally ill inmates, however, the effects of solitary confinement are enough to unravel any inmate's mind and turn a perfectly well-functioning human into a paranoid, violent, unstable victim of the system. According to a former solitary confinement inmate, the isolation is akin to "stewing in nothing-ness...The lethargy of months that add up to years in a cell, alone, entwines (sic) itself about every 'physical' activity of the living body and strangles it slowly to death...Time descends in your cell like the lid of a coffin'" (Haney, Craig, and Monica Lynch). Suicide and self-harm attempts are extremely common in solitary housing units, which only leads to inmates losing privileges to clothes and bedsheets, items that could potentially be used for hanging and self-strangulation. The very nature of solitary confinement disregards the natural human need for connection; it starves the brain of meaningful interactions so that inmates "quickly become withdrawn, hypersensitive to sights and sounds, paranoid, and more prone to violence and hallucinations" ("Solitary Is Cruel and Unusual").

Inmates have been known to throw human waste, blood, even semen at correctional officers through slots in the door just to get attention. Like a child who's been in "time-out" too long, inmates become desperate to hear a voice that's not from their own head, and "in the face of the monotony, deprivation, and punitive environment of segregation units...resort[ed] to feigning illness or engaging in self-harm in an attempt to be removed to a medical setting" (Cloud, Drucker, et al.). Unfortunately, engaging in these behaviors is completely disregarded by correctional officers and other proponents of solitary confinement, and the vicious cycle of isolation continues.

Even though thousands of inmates are still subjected to the suffering and agony that solitary confinement causes, the silver lining is that their suffering is being heard around the country. For the first time in centuries, prisoners are being recognized as human beings worthy of the same decency that society provides for all its citizens. Supermax facilities are closing down, prison reform is being pushed through Congress, and some inmates are being heard in court and awarded money in lawsuits against the state governments that betrayed them. With a renewed focus on rehabilitation rather than punishment, mental health care instead of condemnation, and inmate education rather than isolation, there is finally hope for those living behind bars in the United States. Though it is understandable that victims of violent criminals feel avenged by knowing that their attacker is locked up and is potentially experiencing pain, fear, and hopelessness, there must be standards of decency in the way humans treat other humans. Whether it's the belief that God will make the final

Friedlander   12

call or that the criminal him/herself will be the ultimate judge, there is no human being on Earth who is capable of administering universally fitting standards of a proper punishment to even the worst offenders. Abolishing solitary confinement would abolish the indiscriminate torture of not just those who, in the eyes of the majority, "deserve" it, but also those who have been sentenced to such a punishment for petty offenses, like refusing to shave their beard or giving a correctional officer the "wrong look" on a bad day. Abolishing solitary confinement may not stop all crimes from happening, but it would stop one: the exorbitantly expensive, inhumane, and inexcusable mistreatment of American citizens.

Works Cited

Anderson, Annie. "Al Capone: Approved Source for Tour Content." *Eastern State Penitentiary Historic Site*, May 2013, http://www.pdessay.info/pars_docs/refs/1/85/85.pdf.

Butler, Burke, et al. "A Solitary Failure: The Waste, Cost, and Harm of Solitary Confinement." *ACLU of Texas*, edited by Rebecca Robertson, 5 Feb. 2015, https://www.aclutx.org/en/report/a-solitary-failure.

Castella, Jean, and James Ridgeway. "How Many Prisoners are in Solitary Confinement in the United States?" *Solitary Watch*, 1 Feb. 2012, http://solitarywatch.com/2012/02/01/how-many-prisoners-are-in-solitary-confinement-in-the-united-states/.

Cloud, David H., et al. "Public Health and Solitary Confinement in the United States." *American Journal of Public Health*, vol. 105, no.1, 2015, pp. 18–26. *Academic Search Complete*, DOI: 10.2105/AJPH.2014.302205.

Commissary Cart. Prod. Caller-Times. *YouTube* 6 May 2011, https://www.youtube.com/watch?v=-w7x_IEOgnU.

Edge, Dan, dir. "Locked Up in America." *PBS Frontline*, 2014. PBS, http://www.pbs.org/wgbh/frontline/investigation/locked-up-in-america/.

Eichelberger, Erika. "The Literal Cost of Solitary Confinement." *New Republic*, 15 Sept. 2015, https://newrepublic.com/.../prisons-use-solitary-confinement-empty-inmates-wallets.

Farrell, Brenna. "Shattering Silence and an Eye of God." Audio blog post. RadioLab, 10 July 2014, http://www.radiolab.org/story/eastern-state-penitentiary/.

Fatos, Kaba, et al. "Solitary Confinement and the Risk of Self-Harm among Jail Inmates." *American Journal of Public Health*, 2014, vol. 104, no. 3, pp. 442–447. *Academic Search Complete*, DOI: 10.2105/AJPH.2013.301742.

Fetting, Amy. "Tamms 'Supermax' Prison, with Its Inhumane and Ridiculously Expensive Solitary Confinement Practices, Is Officially a Thing of the Past!" *American Civil Liberties Union*, 4 Jan. 2013. *ACLU*, https://www.aclu.org/blog/tamms-supermax-prison-its-inhumane-and-ridiculously-expensive-solitary-confinement-practices.

Fiscella, Kevin, et al. "Alcohol and Opiate Withdrawal in US Jails." *American Journal of Public Health*, vol. 94, no. 9, pp. 1522–1524, 2004.

Friedmann, Alex. "Solitary Confinement Subject of Unprecedented Congressional Hearing." *Prison Legal News*, 15 Oct. 2012, https://www.prisonlegalnews.org/news/2012/oct/15/solitary-confinement-subject-of-unprecedented-congressional-hearing/

Goode, Erica. "Senators Start a Review of Solitary Confinement." *The New York Times*, 19 June 2012. *ProQuest*, http://search.proquest.com/docview/1705895273/fulltextPDF/79A63DFD712F4D71PQ/1?accountid=12163.

Gordon, Shira E. "Solitary Confinement, Public Safety, and Recidivism." *University of Michigan Journal of Law Reform*, vol. 47, no. 2, pp. 497–506, 2014, http://repository.law.umich.edu/mjlr/vol47/iss2/6/.

Greenberg, Zoe, and Sharona Coutts. "Punished for Addiction: Women Prisoners Dying from Lack of Treatment." *Rewire*. 1 Apr. 2015, https://rewire.news/article/2015/04/01/punished-addiction-women-prisoners-dying-lack-treatment/

Grilo, Carlos. "Behind Bars II: Substance Use and America's Prison Population." *IN Slide Share*, Casacolumbia/ The National Center on Addiction and Substance Abuse, 18 Dec. 2013, www.slideshare.net/centeronaddiction/behind-bars-ii-final. Accessed 20 Nov. 2015.

Haney, Craig, and Monica Lynch. "REGULATING PRISONS OF THE FUTURE: A PSYCHOLOGICAL ANALYSIS OF SUPERMAX AND SOLITARY CONFINEMENT." N.Y.U. Rev. L. & Soc. Change 23 (1997): 477–558. Heinonline. Accessed 7 Nov. 2015.

Hazard, Samuel. The Register of Pennsylvania: Devoted to the Preservation of Facts and Documents and Every Other Kind of Useful Information Respecting the State of Pennsylvania. Philadelphia: Printed by W.F. Geddes, 1828. 89.

Kayatekin, Zerrin Emel. "Psychiatric Services in Jails and Prisons: A Task Force Report of the American Psychiatric Association, second edition." Psychiatric Services, vol.52, no.8, p. 1114, http://ps.psychiatryonline.org/doi/full/10.1176/appi.ps.52.8.1114

Kearney, Melissa, Benjamin Harris, Elisa Jacome, and Lucie Parker. "Ten Economic Facts about Crime and Incarceration in the United States." Choice Reviews Online. Vol. 40, no. 2 (2002): Brookings.edu. The Hamilton Project, May 2014. Accessed 30 Nov. 2015, http://www.hamiltonproject.org/papers/ten_economic_facts_about_crime_and_incarceration_in_the_united_states

"Overdose Deaths in California Prisons Persist despite Tougher Regulations.'" *The Guardian*, 21 June 2015, www.theguardian.com/us-news/2015/jun/21/drug-overdoses-california-inmates-strip-searches-dogs. Accessed 20 Nov. 2015.

"Paying the Price for Solitary Confinement." *Prison Legal News*, Prison Legal News, 2015, www.prisonlegalnews.org/news/publications/paying-price-solitary-confinement-aclu-factsheet-2015/. Accessed 30 Nov. 2015.

Sanchez, Ray, and Alexandra Field. "What's Life like in Supermax Prison?" CNN.com. CNN. Cable News Network, 25 June 2015. Accessed 30 Nov. 2015, http://www.cnn.com/2015/06/25/us/dzhokhar-tsarnaev-supermax-prison/

"Solitary Is Cruel and Unusual." *Scientific American*, vol. 309, no. 2, ser. 10, 2013. 10.

Sullivan, Laura. "Timeline: Solitary Confinement in U.S. Prisons." NPR. NPR, 26 July 2006. Accessed 30 Nov. 2015., http://www.npr.org/templates/story/story.php?storyId=5579901

Willigan, Mclyn. "What Solitary Confinement Does to the Human Brain." *Solitary Watch*, Solitary Watch, 16 Oct. 2015, solitarywatch.com/2014/08/04/what-solitary-confinement-does-to-the-human-brain/. Accessed 30 Nov. 2015.

Julie Malewicz
UCWR 110
Professor Kevin Quirk
23 November 2015

What Do We Really Know About "Giftedness"?

Above-level. Precocious. Brainy, whiz kid. So many words we tend to use to qualify intellectually gifted young individuals. The definition of "gifted" itself is plural and readily prone to debate even among the educational community. The confusion around it is also symptomatic of the lack of interest we usually have for the problems those children are used to facing every day, as we might think that they must be smart enough to handle themselves. But it nonetheless does not justify our disdain. Actually, if there is a single consensus amongst this same educational community, it is that "gifted" and "with special needs" are definitely not two mutually exclusive labels. And although the area of giftedness is one of the most neglected ones in education, it makes no doubt that their difficult adaptability to social and strict academical expectations is a cause of frustration for kids. *Every child must be proposed alternatives that help him develop his potential. And despite any common preconceptions, gifted children are no exception.* A claim supported by years of research and studies from specialists all over the world is that because of their nonconformity to the classic educational track, those children tend to suffer on a deep emotional level. They are not supported enough in the classical educational environment they are not adapted to, and it is therefore crucial to solve this problem to acknowledge their difference and needs, and help offering efficient solutions, thus making a tremendous step towards a better education for all.

The thing is, gifted children are inherently different from their classmates, and the classical educational track is more often than not profoundly unadapted to their eagerness for learning and understanding. To begin with, if there is something that really needs to be understood, it is that this crucial difference between a gifted individual and a child within the commonly accepted norm is not a matter of degree, but "of a different quality of experiencing: vivid, absorbing, penetrating, encompassing, complex, commanding" (Pietchowski qtd. by Gross, "The Saddest Sound"). And this is expressed through an intense need for intellectual challenge, the burning desire to acquire new knowledge and the longing for the ecstatic experience of the meeting of like minds through passionate discussions ("The Saddest Sound"). To take a concrete example, this is the reason for which it has been observed that they often know how to read before school, teaching themselves avidly with what they find within their reach, from street signs to magazines and television. Author Miraca U.M. Gross, doctor in psychology specialized in giftedness in children, indeed reminds us that at least half of the moderately gifted children (IQ range 130-144) and at least 80% of the highly gifted (IQ of 145+) enter the school "already reading" ("The 'Me' Behind the Mask").

Take for example Akash, a 5-year-old Atlanta native, labeled as profoundly gifted (which is the highest degree of giftedness according to specialists) and featured in one of FOX 5's TV report last year. The small boy who is said to "love playing outside" like any child of his age proudly considers that his favorite element of the periodic table is Krypton and can recite anything from its atomic number to the capital cities of South Africa, China and the exact spelling of "participant". With his book on atoms in his hands, he softly explains to the reporter how uranium was thought to be the last element of the periodic table at the time it was discovered.

This striking difference between Akash and other children of the same age has a very profound cognitive basis. As mentioned earlier, being gifted does not have anything to do with being seemingly "smarter", but lies on a difference in the way the brain treats information on a deep level. We can consider their brains as being wired differently actually. And while it is true that they learn more easily, quicker and at a younger age, their way to process external information is the crucial variable at a cognitive level that may explain it: specific studies have shown that the very speed of information processing is indeed significantly greater than their same-age peers'. Chinese psychologists have demonstrated that in children from 9 to 13 years old, gifted children performed notably better than the others in exercises involving their speed of reaction (Duan, Xiaoju et al). Their attention span is as well greater, as shown by Dr. Shi in an analogous study (Shi et al. 29), as young gifted children are able to stay focused on a single task longer than their peers and perform better on tests requiring a great attention span. But these elements come hand in hand with a higher sensitivity to an important numbers of parameters. Michelle Barmazel is the mother of a profoundly gifted young boy, and in her keynote about why the term "gifted" might not refer to what you think, she evokes his great difficulty to cope with everyday elements. Those variables gifted children are highly sensitive to are referred as Dabrowski's over-excitabilities and go from psycho-motor sensations to imaginational, intellectual and emotional perceptions. So yes, again, being gifted is being susceptible to a more intense way of digesting information. It is not uncommon either that they present a type of asynchrony of development: which means that they can achieve outstanding feats in a particular field such as mathematics, while being unable to comprehend very basic other types of tasks; or do very well in an area and start doing poorly when the method of teaching is altered.

These elementary differences have profound repercussions on how the kid will feel and behave in a classroom that is not adapted to his rhythm and eagerness for knowledge. At a very young age, gifted children are fascinated by moral dilemmas their peers won't care about for a couple more years. They have a high sensitivity to any type of injustice, and their great lucidity about themselves and their environment is often more painful than appreciated in a classroom. On the other hand, we indeed often talk about how intellectually gifted children might obviously feel bored in under-level classes. Dr. Gross puts the issue in very simple words. Simply imagine yourself being stuck in a class with an IQ 40 points inferior to yours, for the entirety of your school years ("From the 'saddest sound' to the D Major chord"). Would that have any impact on you? Michelle Barmazel also mentions this example in her talk about the common misconceptions of giftedness in children: it is undeniable that the teacher is not going to adapt their entire teaching for a single individual and she reminds her audience that it is actually not unusual that highly gifted individuals simply fail at school. Being a great achiever in a domain doesn't shield the child from lacking other basic abilities and how are we supposed to treat the "8-year-old kids who master middle-school level maths but whose handwriting are still barely legible"? The schools feel already overwhelmed by the important diversity of ability in their classrooms so the easy answer is to let the smart kid take care of himself.

However, even worse as young children are still in social development, gifted pupils can simply face a wall of incomprehension from both their classmates and teachers. From the easiness they have to learn completely new concepts stems not only a sentiment that they should not need any kind of help, but also a certain kind of jealousy from their classmates. It is to be recognized that this type of resentment can also come from teachers, who do not understand that the difference may lie on a profound cognitive basis and that those kids may not necessarily have been taught by incredibly competitive parents. As mentioned before, it is not uncommon that children teach themselves how to read before school to entertain themselves, and Dr. Gross brings up her own experience on this field to remind us that there are still teachers who refuse to see the child as gifted, making comments, sometimes cruel ones, to the parents such as "there's no point in pushing her like that; the others will catch up anyway", and disturbingly enough, often in presence of the kid himself. Conversely, Dr. Barbara Kerr in her book addressed to education counselors warns her readers that over-the-top admiration is likewise harmful to the child. The same way that there is a possibility for the said counselor to feel threatened by the young child's abilities, the "awestruck counselor may feel overwhelmed by the verbally brilliant student [...] allowing the counseling session to be sidetracked" (Kerr 152). None of those attitudes can have a beneficial impact on the child who sees himself denied as an independent individual, but the reality is that few teachers have the training to handle the unique needs of the gifted children.

From all this stems a real need for crucial alternatives that needs to be acknowledged by teachers and counselors. Solutions worth considering that have been greatly fostered in other countries but not yet in the American school system are grade-skipping as well as acceleration. Dr. Gross presents in "From the 'Saddest Sound' to the D Major Chord" an important variety of possibilities as well as their benefits on children she had already worked with. The first one being grade-skipping, which merely consists of moving a certain kid in a higher grade, with older classmates whose abilities match more easily those of the said kid. Transferring an 8th-grader to a 11th-grade maths class is also absolutely a possibility for those who may be afraid of a full grade-skipping. Both are mostly solutions worth considering in a school that doesn't necessarily provide special resources, but acceleration is also another process that has been proven to be profoundly beneficial for the child's well-being in special schools ("The Saddest Sound"). It would consist of a special classroom in which the program of several school years would be compacted in two or less. In Australia, for example, it is not so rare that a class of 11-year-old gifted students study the program of both the 6th and 7th grade during the same year.

However, there is some reluctance from different individuals concerning first and foremost the social well-being of such children that might be impacted by a specific treatment. Jessica Lahey, in an editorial of the New York Times, expresses her concern that grade-skipping may have harmful consequences on the child's socio-affective development, as he no longer has same age peers to play and develop bonds with. Eventually, the child becomes not only the smart kid, but also the small one who gets picked on by his older, bigger, stronger classmates. If the young years with hardly judgmental children overall can become unbearable, then what could happen during the high-school years? Highly gifted children might skip several grades at a time because of their important intellectual gap from their classmates, and both the physical—and even hormonal—difference between a 12-year-old and a 15-year-old cannot be ignored.

Notwithstanding, it is to be reminded that a child put in a more advanced program was inherently more mature than his peers, and thus suffered from the fact that they couldn't understand him. Dr. Gross in her research on the gifted individuals' handling of their identity mentions the "forced choice dilemma" as having a great impact on the young gifted child, whose desire to master an area of talent commonly undervalued by his classmates is confronted, not without pain, to his craving need to be accepted by the peer culture ("The 'Me' Behind the Mask"). That explains why they tend to seek the company of older children, who they can more easily interact with and who they know will surely have similar games as they do. And actually, grade-skipping consists—in the greatest majority of cases—of just one year.

In a typical French senior high-school class, at least 20% of the students have skipped one or more classes.

But it has to be recognized that other arguments can be put forward concerning possible drawbacks of solutions such as grade-skipping. Those claims that those solutions can directly affect the child can be refuted each time by individuals who, by their training or experience tend to know a bit more about the issue. It is easy to argue that a sense of superiority may grow in the child that sees himself put in the big kids' playground. Or that children put in special programs may develop a tendency for elitism. But the thing is, this has never been proven to be true. Besides, Dr. Barbara Kerr, who extensively worked herself with several moderately to highly gifted children has a rather clear stance on that matter: she argues firstly that it is very often not in the personality of such children to express self-contempt like this. On the contrary, they have very often low self-concepts: it is in their nature to expect much of themselves, and are therefore not prone to arrogant character. Moreover, leaving them in grades where they blatantly see their academical superiority without having had their special gifts formally acknowledged, may lead them into thinking that if they succeed so easily, it is because they put work and interest in their accomplishments. Therefore, if they are not explicitly explained that such innate ability is not necessarily common, they may come to think that their classmates are simply lazy and do not care as much about school as themselves do.

In primary school, a close friend of mine once won a mathematical contest with flying colors, competing against his whole class. When he received his prize, he was genuinely surprised, and told me that he was absolutely certain he had failed it. Embarrassed, he then added that for him to win even though, the others must have had really done poorly. His mother heard him, and made a remark about it, reproaching his arrogance. But that wasn't arrogance at all to my friend. He was later diagnosed as being gifted by the school psychologist. His parents had believed he indeed was since early childhood, but never told anything by fear "he might grow pretentious". When they finally had a talk, he remembered that remark years earlier and was hurt as he felt that his mother had preferred to lie to him fearing arrogance than help him handle his difference for the best.

The thing is, he was indeed radically different from all the children he had ever really known. Gifted children are intrinsically highly sensitive to a great number of different parameters, as a result of their great intellectual potential. The classic educational track is far from being adapted to their needs and expectations, and they suffer from the denial of those very same needs. And if there is something that puts everyone on the same page, it is the claim that every child should be offered an education that fulfills their needs. Rebecca Walsh, in her paper praising the benefits of special education in prior-to-school setting, notes very justly that "all children deserve to have their individual needs met and therefore, as a matter of equity, we should not ignore the unique needs of the gifted." Even more, she reminds that "reinforcement for this argument comes from the United Nations Declaration of the Rights of the Child: '[The child] shall be given an education which will…enable him, on a basis of equal opportunity, to develop his abilities'. Thus, logically, a child with different needs must be offered different solutions" (Walsh 45)

Apart from acceleration—which is a purely administrative procedure—there are numerous ways to help the child to indeed develop his potential and blossom at his own rhythm, preventing in-achievement to grow into frustration. According to Francoys Gagné's *Differentiated Model of Talent and Giftedness*, the only barrier between giftedness (potential) and talent (achievement) is related to knowing how to foster the child. Gagné is a professor at the University of Montreal who developed a sociologically based theory according to which the child's environment is a crucial variable—a catalysis—in the development of his talents. In an environment sufficiently controlled and cleverly managed, the child can find space to express himself. Not only can he lift off pressure on his shoulders, but the study that showed earlier how gifted children perform better than their same-age peers when it comes to attention span have proven in the very same experiment that if they are taught in "enriched" environment, their results are even better (Shi et al). The term is simply scientific jargon for adapted classes, with intense but comprehensive rhythm, and fostering from the entourage, from parents to teachers and friends.

The key element is indeed knowing how to foster the child: by leaving him space and constantly stimulating his intellect and creativity, we can bring a response to his craving need of understanding. The parents of the young Akash mentioned earlier are both working in the advanced scientific field, and know how to provide him with resources. He is part of a program called Mensa helping him transform his potential into the striking talent that was depicted in the TV report. Likewise, acknowledging both the child's capacities as well as his needs—which are intrinsically related—can help him understand his position, build realizable expectations and truly blossom. In fact, Dr. Gross concludes her speech on the beneficial outcomes of accelerated progression by telling the story of a highly gifted young girl, who after several years of social isolation found herself at 10 years old in a special class, where she could interact with girls who understood her to an extent no one else ever did. Profoundly happy of her class, she wrote to Dr. Gross: "we are like totally different music notes, but I feel like that at us three, we come to form a chord: the D major chord". Beethoven composed the choral movement of his exulting 9th symphony with this chord as key: it is widely depicted as the chord of pure joy ("From the 'Saddest Sound' to the D Major Chord").

To conclude with, it is undeniable that there exists a profound misunderstanding of what it means to be gifted. We are easily prone to assume elements about them and their needs based on our own perception, inevitably biased because we don't experience this difference. Every single child deserve support and help for the best, and 'gifted' is still a very large concept, encompassing a great variety of individuals whose crucial similarity is that they possess characteristics deeply different from the rest of their peers. Gifted is sort of an umbrella term for a number of children who happen to perform considerably well in specific fields while being inherently different from their classmates from a very profound level. They have the potential to become incredible adults, they indeed have this deep wish, and our responsibility is to provide them with resources that will direct them to the path of success.

Works Cited

Barmazel, Michelle. "Why Gifted May Not Be What You Think." TedxHGSE, 5 May 2014, www.youtube.com/watch?v=W4Gj2UC8gYI. Accessed 7 Nov. 2015.

Duan, Xiaoju, et al. "*The Speed of Information Processing of 9- to 13-Year-Old Intellectually Gifted Children.*" Psychology Reports, 2013, "*The Speed of Information Processing of 9- to 13-Year-Old Intellectually Gifted Children.*," www.readbyqxmd.com/read/23654024/the-speed-of-information-processing-of-9-to-13-year-old-intellectually-gifted-children. Accessed 8 Nov. 2015.

Fox 5 Atlanta. "*Akash: a 'Profoundly Gifted' Child.*" Youtube.com, 28 July 2014, www.youtube.com/watch?v=4K2D6ZF4M6E. Accessed 8 Nov. 2015.

Gagne, Francoys. "Transforming Gifts into Talents: the DMGT as a Developmental theory1." *High Ability Studies*, vol. 15, no. 2, 2004, pp. 119–147., doi:10.1080/1359813042000314682. Accessed 30 Oct. 2015.

Gross, Miraca U.M. "The 'Me' Behind the Mask:Intellectually Gifted Students and the Search for Identity." *Roeper Review*, vol. 20, no. 3, 1998, pp. 167–174. *Academic Search Complete [EBSCO]*, doi:10.1080/02783199809553885. Accessed 26 Oct. 2015.

Gross, Miraca U.M. "From 'the saddest sound' to the D Major chord: the gift of accelerated progression." 3rd Biennial Australasian International Conference on the Education of Gifted Students. Melbourne. 15 Aug 1999. Keynote. Accessed 1 Nov 2015.

Kerr, Barbara, Kirk Hallowell, and Stephen Schroeder-Davis. *A Handbook for Counseling the Gifted and Talented*. American Association for Counseling and Development, 1991.

Lahey, Jessica. "Against Accelerating the Gifted Child." *The New York Times*, 14 Oct. 2012, nytimes.com. Accessed 7 Nov. 2015.

Shi, Jiannong, et al. "Sustained Attention in Intellectually Gifted Children Assessed Using a Continuous Performance Test." *PubMed Central*, vol. 8, no. 2, 2013, journals.plos.org/plosone/article?id=10.1371/journal.pone.0057417. Accessed 30 Oct. 2015.

Walsh, Rosalind L. "Same Age, Different Page: Overcoming the Barriers to Catering for Young Gifted Children in Prior-to-School Settings.'" *International Journal of Early Childhood*, vol. 41, no. 1, 2010, pp. 43–58. *Education Research Complete [EBSCO]*, Accessed 2 Nov. 2015.

6

Library Services at Loyola

UCWR 110

Writing a research paper can be a daunting task, even for experienced researchers. Fortunately, dedicated help and effective research resources are always available at Loyola libraries. A librarian will be part of your UCWR class this semester, and librarians might participate in other classes you take. Librarians and other library staff are committed to helping students do their best work. For them, no question is too small or silly, so do not hesitate to ask for assistance.

Library Reference Desk

Librarians assist students on the second floor of the Information Commons on the Lakeshore Campus and in Lewis Library at the Water Tower Campus. You can drop by or schedule an appointment in advance. There is also online help; you can access assistance through a chat connection or by sending questions to librarians as text messages. Details about all of these services are available through the library's website.

Library Circulation Desk

Library staff at the circulation desk in Cudahy and Lewis Libraries will help you check out books, pick up materials on hold or requested through Interlibrary Loan, and check out course reserve materials.

Library Information Resources

A well-written, research-based argument is supported by quality information resources. Locating these resources, especially those from scholarly sources, requires learning about library catalogs and research databases.

Before you are ready to delve into scholarly sources on an unfamiliar topic, you will usually need to consult reference sources, or sources of background information. Many reference sources are available online, but some classic ones still exist only in print. Reference sources may be found using a library catalog or other search aids, but often the best method is simply asking a librarian for a referral. A librarian will suggest at least one reference source to your UCWR class during class with you this semester.

Once you have basic knowledge about a topic, you will be ready to begin searching a library catalog or research database. Our library supports various catalogs which may be accessed through the library's website. These catalogs help locate books, both print and electronic, in the library's collections. A librarian will introduce the catalogs to your class, but you are encouraged to experiment and contact librarians with your questions.

The library also provides students with access to hundreds of databases, most of them tied to research in specific subject areas. In UCWR classes, librarians will focus on one general database that can be used for nearly any topic. Databases are linked from the library's website, both by title and by subject area through our Research Guides.

Your instructor and the research librarian who works with your class will be eager to help you navigate through the college-level research project. Make good use of these individuals and their expertise. But successful research requires perhaps more independent work than any other type of writing assignment. Because of this, Loyola libraries have created a number of useful web pages that can help facilitate the research project. On the library web page (libraries.luc.edu), you can access "Research Guides" that are organized by disciplines such as Anthropology, Environmental Studies, and Physics. Among these, moreover, is a guide designed especially for UCWR. This guide may be your most useful electronic link.

The Research Guide for UCWR (libguides.luc.edu/UCWR?hs=a) contains a number of extremely useful tabs that address various areas of research. Some of these, such as "Types of Academic Sources," provide helpful overviews. Others, such as "Evaluating Sources" and "The Research Question," reinforce information and skill sets you will need to compose a successful research paper. Perhaps most importantly, other tabs provide links to the most used and most useful databases, as well as the catalogs. Consider opening this page and working from there whenever you are conducting your research. Make it your home base for each research session, and you should be able to navigate swiftly among the various tabs and links the library has designed to serve your research needs.

7

Works Cited

UCWR 110

Caputo, Gabrielle. "The Lies We Waste Our Lives On." *Communities in Conversation: Environmental Issues and Green Activism.* Eds. Sherrie Weller, et al. Loyola University Chicago, 2011. 50–51. Print.

Fitzgerald, F. Scott. *The Crack-Up.* New York: New Directions Press, 1945. 41. Print.

Felius, Marleen, et al. "On the Breeds of Cattle—Historic and Current Classifications." *Diversity 3* (2011): 660–692. *Academic Search Premier.* Web. 26 Sept. 2012.

Graff, Gerald, Cathy Birkenstein, and Russel Durst. *They Say/I Say: The Moves That Matter in Academic Writing with Readings.* 2nd ed. New York: W. W. Norton, 2012.

Hidi, Suzanne, and Valerie Anderson. "Producing Written Summaries: Task Demands, Cognitive Operations, and Implications for Instruction." *Review of Educational Research* 56.4 (Winter 1986): 473–493. JSTOR. Web. 25 June 2012.

Howard, Judith. "The Need for Connection." *Communities in Conversation: Environmental Issues and Green Activism.* Eds. Sherrie Weller, et al. Loyola University Chicago, 2011. 47–49. Print.

Howard, Rebecca Moore. *Writing Matters.* New York: McGraw-Hill, 2011. Print.

Maclellan, Effie. "Reading to Learn." *Studies in Higher Education* 22.3 (Oct. 1997): 277–289. *Academic Search Premier.* Web. 28 June 2012.

Mateos, Mar, and Isabel Sol. "Synthesising Information from Various Texts: A Study of Procedures and Products at Different Educational Levels." *European Journal of Psychology of Education* 24.1 (2009) 435–451. Print.

McGinley, William. "The Role of Reading and Writing While Composing from Sources." *International Reading Association* 27.3 (1992) 227–248.

Morgan, Teyana. "Summary Assignment." 27 February 2012. MS.

Ramage, John D., John C. Bean, and June Johnson. *Writing Arguments: A Rhetoric with Readings.* Brief 9th Ed. Boston: Pearson, 2011.

Regannie, Lisa. "A Whole New World." 27 Oct. 2012. MS.

Strahan, Linda, Kathleen Moore, and Michael Heumann. *Write It: A Process Approach to College Essays.* Dubuque: Kendall Hunt, 2011. Print.

Williams, Joseph M., and Gregory G. Colomb. *The Craft of Argument.* 2nd ed. New York: Longman, 2003. Print.

Yu, Guoxing. "The Shifting Sands in the Effects of Source Text Summarizability on Summary Writing." *Assessing Writing* 14 (2009): 116–137. *ScienceDirect.* Web. 25 June 2012.

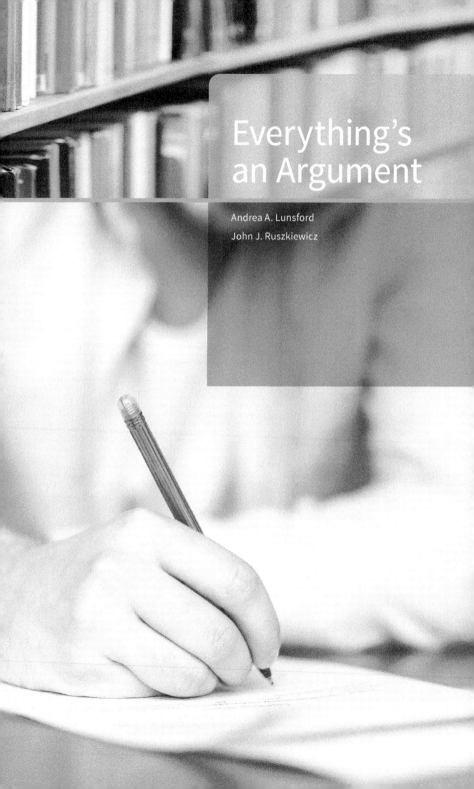

Everything's an Argument

Andrea A. Lunsford

John J. Ruszkiewicz

PART 1

READING AND UNDERSTANDING ARGUMENTS

8

Everything
Is an Argument

Reading and Understanding Arguments

Chapter 8, "Everything Is an Argument," from *Everything's an Argument*, Seventh Edition,
by Andrea A. Lunsford and John J. Ruszkiewicz, pp. 1–27 (Chapter 1).
Copyright © 2016 by Bedford/St. Martin's.

Left: Pacific Press/Getty Images; right: © Akintunde Akinleye/Corbis

On May 7, 2014, First Lady of the United States Michelle Obama turned to new media to express her concern over the kidnapping of more than 200 young Nigerian girls by the terrorist group Boko Haram. Her tweet, along with an accompanying photo highlighting the trending hashtag #BringBackOurGirls, ramped up an argument over what the international community could do to stop an organization responsible for thousands of deaths in northeastern Nigeria. In bringing her appeal to Twitter, the First Lady acknowledged the persuasive power of social media like Facebook, YouTube, Instagram, and innumerable political and social blogs. The hashtag itself, it would appear, had become a potent tool for rallying audiences around the globe to support specific ideas or causes. But to what ends?

The First Lady ⊘
@FLOTUS
⬩ Follow

Our prayers are with the missing Nigerian girls and their families. It's time to #BringBackOurGirls. -mo

Just weeks before Obama's notable appeal, a U.S. State Department spokesperson Jen Psaki drew attention with a tweet of her own aimed at countering attempts by Russian social media to co-opt the U.S. State Department's #UnitedforUkraine hashtag:

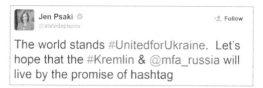

Jen Psaki ⊘
@statedeptspox
⬩ Follow

The world stands #UnitedforUkraine. Let's hope that the #Kremlin & @mfa_russia will live by the promise of hashtag

The Russian government, it seems, having just annexed the Crimea region and threatening all of Ukraine, was showing more skill than Western nations at using Twitter and other social media to win propaganda points

in the diplomatic crisis. Yet Psaki's response via Twitter earned her disapproval from those who interpreted her social media riposte as further evidence of U.S. weakness. For instance, Texas senator Ted Cruz tweeted in reply to Psaki:

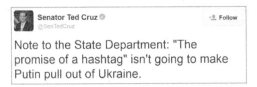

> **Senator Ted Cruz** ⊘   ⁺⚑ Follow
> @SenTedCruz
>
> Note to the State Department: "The promise of a hashtag" isn't going to make Putin pull out of Ukraine.

Even Michelle Obama took heat for her earnest appeal on behalf of kidnapped girls the same age as her own daughters. While celebrities such as Amy Poehler and Mary J. Blige posted supportive items, Obama's tweet got quick international pushback from those who argued (in 140 characters) that the anti-terrorist use of drones by the U.S. military was no less reprehensible than the tactics of Boko Haram. And domestic critics saw Obama's message as a substitute for real action, with columnist Jeffrey Goldberg chiding well-intentioned activists with a dose of reality:

> **Jeffrey Goldberg** ⊘   ⁺⚑ Follow
> @JeffreyGoldberg
>
> All the charity bicycle rides in the world won't get those girls back from Boko Haram. Marines, however, might work.

Clearly, social media play out on crowded, two-way channels, with claims and counterclaims whizzing by, fast and furious. Such tools reach audiences and they also create them, offering an innovative way to make and share arguments. Just as important, anyone, anywhere, with access to a phone, tablet, or other electronic device, can launch arguments that circle the globe in seconds. Social networking and digital tools are increasingly available to all.

We've opened this chapter with dramatic, perhaps troubling, examples of Twitter controversies to introduce our claim that arguments are all around us, in every medium, in every genre, in everything we do. There may be an argument on the T-shirt you put on in the morning, in the sports column you read on the bus, in the prayers you utter before an exam, in the off-the-cuff political remarks of a teacher lecturing, in the assurances of a health center nurse that "This won't hurt one bit."

The clothes you wear, the foods you eat, and the groups you join make nuanced, sometimes unspoken assertions about who you are and what you value. So an argument can be any text—written, spoken, aural, or visual—that expresses a point of view. In fact, some theorists claim that language is inherently persuasive. When you say, "Hi, how's it going?" in one sense you're arguing that your hello deserves a response. Even humor makes an argument when it causes readers to recognize—through bursts of laughter or just a faint smile—how things are and how they might be different.

More obvious as arguments are those that make direct claims based on or drawn from evidence. Such writing often moves readers to recognize problems and to consider solutions. Persuasion of this kind is usually easy to recognize:

> The National Minimum Drinking Age Act, passed by Congress 30 years ago this July, is a gross violation of civil liberties and must be repealed. It is absurd and unjust that young Americans can vote, marry, enter contracts, and serve in the military at 18 but cannot buy an alcoholic drink in a bar or restaurant.
>
> —Camille Paglia, "The Drinking Age Is Past Its Prime"

> We will become a society of a million pictures without much memory, a society that looks forward every second to an immediate replication of what it has just done, but one that does not sustain the difficult labor of transmitting culture from one generation to the next.
>
> —Christine Rosen, "The Image Culture"

RESPOND

Can an argument really be any text that expresses a point of view? What kinds of arguments—if any—might be made by the following items?

- a Boston Red Sox cap
- a Livestrong bracelet
- the "explicit lyrics" label on a best-selling rap CD
- the health warnings on a package of cigarettes
- a Tesla Model S electric car
- a pair of Ray-Ban sunglasses

Why We Make Arguments

In the politically divided and entertainment-driven culture of the United States today, the word *argument* may well call up negative images: the hostile scowl or shaking fist of a politician or news "opinionator" who wants to drown out other voices and prevail at all costs. This winner-take-all view turns many citizens off to the whole process of using reasoned conversation to identify, explore, and solve problems. Hoping to avoid personal conflict, many people now sidestep opportunities to speak their mind on issues shaping their lives and work. We want to counter this attitude throughout this book.

Some arguments, of course, *are* aimed at winning, especially those related to politics, business, and law. Two candidates for office, for example, vie for a majority of votes; the makers of one smartphone try to outsell their competitors by offering more features at a lower price; and two lawyers try to outwit each other in pleading to a judge and jury. In your college writing, you may also be called on to make arguments that appeal to a "judge" and "jury" (perhaps your instructor and classmates). You might, for instance, argue that students in every field should be required to engage in service learning projects. In doing so, you will need to offer better arguments or more convincing evidence than potential opponents—such as those who might regard service learning as a politicized or coercive form of education. You can do so reasonably and responsibly, no name-calling required.

There are many reasons to argue and principled ways to do so. We explore some of them in this section.

Arguments to Convince and Inform

We're stepping into an argument ourselves in drawing what we hope is a useful distinction between *convincing* and—in the next section—*persuading*. (Feel free to disagree with us.) Arguments to convince lead audiences to accept a claim as true or reasonable—based on information or evidence that seems factual and reliable; arguments to persuade then seek to move people beyond conviction to *action*. Academic arguments often combine both elements.

Many news reports and analyses, white papers, and academic articles aim to convince audiences by broadening what they know about a subject. Such fact-based arguments might have no motives beyond laying out what the facts are. Here's an opening paragraph from a 2014 news story by

Anahad O'Connor in the *New York Times* that itself launched a thousand arguments (and lots of huzzahs) simply by reporting the results of a recent scientific study:

> Many of us have long been told that saturated fat, the type found in meat, butter and cheese, causes heart disease. But a large and exhaustive new analysis by a team of international scientists found no evidence that eating saturated fat increased heart attacks and other cardiac events.
>
> —Anahad O'Connor, "Study Questions Fat and Heart Disease Link"

Wow. You can imagine how carefully the reporter walked through the scientific data, knowing how this new information might be understood and repurposed by his readers.

Similarly, in a college paper on viability of nuclear power as an alternative source of energy, you might compare the health and safety record of a nuclear plant to that of other forms of energy. Depending upon your findings and your interpretation of the data, the result of your fact-based presentation might be to raise or alleviate concerns readers have about nuclear energy. Of course, your decision to write the argument might be driven by your conviction that nuclear power is much safer than most people believe.

Even an image can offer an argument designed both to inform and to convince. On the following page, for example, editorial cartoonist Bob Englehart finds a way to frame an issue on the minds of many students today, the burden of crushing debt. As Englehart presents it, the problem is impossible to ignore.

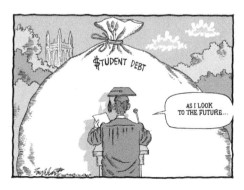

© Bob Englehart/Cagle Cartoons, Inc.

Arguments to Persuade

Today, climate change may be the public issue that best illustrates the chasm that sometimes separates conviction from persuasion. The weight of scientific research may convince people that the earth is warming, but persuading them to act on that knowledge doesn't follow easily. How then does change occur? Some theorists suggest that persuasion—understood as moving people to do more than nod in agreement—is best achieved via appeals to emotions such as fear, anger, envy, pride, sympathy, or hope. We think that's an oversimplification. The fact is that persuasive arguments, whether in advertisements, political blogs, YouTube videos, or newspaper editorials, draw upon *all* the appeals of rhetoric (see p. 178) to motivate people to act—whether it be to buy a product, pull a lever for a candidate, or volunteer for a civic organization. Here, once again, is Camille Paglia driving home her argument that the 1984 federal law raising the drinking age in the United States to 21 was a catastrophic decision in need of reversal:

> What this cruel 1984 law did is deprive young people of safe spaces where they could happily drink cheap beer, socialize, chat, and flirt in a free but controlled public environment. Hence in the 1980s we immediately got the scourge of crude binge drinking at campus fraternity keg parties, cut off from the adult world. Women in that boorish free-for-all were suddenly fighting off date rape. Club drugs—Ecstasy, methamphetamine, ketamine (a veterinary tranquilizer)—surged at raves for teenagers and on the gay male circuit scene.

Paglia chooses to dramatize her argument by sharply contrasting a safer, more supportive past with a vastly more dangerous present when drinking was forced underground and young people turned to highly risky behaviors. She doesn't hesitate to name them either: binge drinking, club drugs, raves, and, most seriously, date rape. This highly rhetorical, one might say *emotional*, argument pushes readers hard to endorse a call for serious action—the repeal of the current drinking age law.

Admit it, Duchess of Cornwall. You *knew* abandoned dogs need homes, but it was heartrending photos on the Battersea Dogs & Cats Home Web site that *persuaded* you to visit the shelter.

WPA Pool/Getty Images

RESPOND

Apply the distinction made here between convincing and persuading to the way people respond to two or three current political or social issues. Is there a useful distinction between being convinced and being persuaded? Explain your position.

Arguments to Make Decisions

Closely allied to arguments to convince and persuade are arguments to examine the options in important matters, both civil and personal—from managing out-of-control deficits to choosing careers. Arguments to make decisions occur all the time in the public arena, where they are often slow to evolve, caught up in electoral or legal squabbles, and yet driven by a genuine desire to find consensus. In recent years, for instance, Americans have argued hard to make decisions about health care, the civil rights of same-sex couples, and the status of more than 11 million immigrants in the country. Subjects so complex aren't debated in straight lines. They get haggled over in every imaginable medium by thousands of writers, politicians, and ordinary citizens working alone or via political organizations to have their ideas considered.

For college students, choosing a major can be an especially momentous personal decision, and one way to go about making that decision is to argue your way through several alternatives. By the time you've explored the pros and cons of each alternative, you should be a little closer to a reasonable and defensible decision.

Sometimes decisions, however, are not so easy to make.

www.CartoonStock.com

Arguments to Understand and Explore

Arguments to make decisions often begin as choices between opposing positions already set in stone. But is it possible to examine important issues in more open-ended ways? Many situations, again in civil or personal arenas, seem to call for arguments that genuinely explore possibilities without constraints or prejudices. If there's an "opponent" in such situations at all (often there is not), it's likely to be the status quo or a current trend which, for one reason or another, puzzles just about everyone. For example, in trying to sort through the extraordinary complexities of the 2011 budget debate, philosophy professor Gary Gutting was able to show how two distinguished economists—John Taylor and Paul Krugman—draw completely different conclusions from the exact same sets of facts. Exploring how such a thing could occur led Gutting to conclude that the two economists were arguing from the same facts, all right, but that they did not have *all* the facts possible. Those missing or unknown facts allowed them to fill in the blanks as they could, thus leading them to different conclusions. By discovering the source of a paradox, Gutting potentially opened new avenues for understanding.

Exploratory arguments can also be personal, such as Zora Neale Hurston's ironic exploration of racism and of her own identity in the essay "How It Feels to Be Colored Me." If you keep a journal or blog, you have no doubt found yourself making arguments to explore issues near and dear to you. Perhaps the essential argument in any such piece is the writer's realization that a problem exists—and that the writer or reader needs to understand it and respond constructively to it if possible.

Explorations of ideas that begin by trying to understand another's perspective have been described as **invitational arguments** by researchers Sonja Foss, Cindy Griffin, and Josina Makau. Such arguments are interested in inviting others to join in mutual explorations of ideas based on discovery and respect. Another kind of argument, called **Rogerian argument** (after psychotherapist Carl Rogers), approaches audiences in similarly nonthreatening ways, finding common ground and establishing trust among those who disagree about issues. Writers who take a Rogerian approach try to see where the other person is coming from, looking for "both/and" or "win/win" solutions whenever possible. (For more on Rogerian strategies, see Chapter 14.)

"You say it's a win-win, but what if you're wrong-wrong and it all goes bad-bad?"

The risks of Rogerian argument

What are your reasons for making arguments? Keep notes for two days about every single argument you make, using our broad definition to guide you. Then identify your reasons: How many times did you aim to convince? To inform? To persuade? To explore? To understand?

Occasions for Argument

In a fifth-century BCE textbook of **rhetoric** (the art of persuasion), the philosopher Aristotle provides an ingenious strategy for classifying arguments based on their perspective on time—past, future, and present. His ideas still help us to appreciate the role arguments play in society in the twenty-first century. As you consider Aristotle's occasions for argument, remember that all such classifications overlap (to a certain extent) and that we live in a world much different than his.

Arguments about the Past

Debates about what has happened in the past, what Aristotle called **forensic arguments**, are the red meat of government, courts, businesses, and academia. People want to know who did what in the past, for what reasons, and with what liability. When you argue a speeding ticket in court, you are making a forensic argument, claiming perhaps that you weren't over the limit or that the officer's radar was faulty. A judge will have to decide what exactly happened in the past in the unlikely case you push the issue that far.

More consequentially, in 2014 the federal government and General Motors found themselves deeply involved in arguments about the past as investigators sought to determine just exactly how the massive auto company had allowed a serious defect in the ignition switches of its cars to go undisclosed and uncorrected for a decade. Drivers and passengers died or were injured as engines shut down and airbags failed to go off in subsequent collisions. Who at General Motors was responsible for not diagnosing the fault? Were any engineers or executives liable for covering up the problem? And how should victims of this product defect or their families be compensated? These were all forensic questions to be thoroughly investigated, argued, and answered by regulatory panels and courts.

From an academic perspective, consider the lingering forensic arguments over Christopher Columbus's "discovery" of America. Are his expeditions cause for celebration or notably unhappy chapters in human history? Or some of both? Such arguments about past actions—heated enough to spill over into the public realm—are common in disciplines such as history, philosophy, and ethics.

Mary Barra, the chief executive officer of General Motors, testifies before a congressional panel looking into problems with ignition switches in the company's cars.

AP Photo/Ron Sachs/picture-alliance/dpa/AP Images

Arguments about the Future

Debates about what will or should happen in the future—**deliberative arguments**—often influence policies or legislation for the future. *Should local or state governments allow or even encourage the use of self-driving cars on public roads? Should colleges and universities lend support to more dual-credit programs so that students can earn college credits while still in high school? Should coal-fired power plants be phased out of our energy grid?* These are the sorts of deliberative questions that legislatures, committees, or school boards routinely address when making laws or establishing policies.

But arguments about the future can also be speculative, advancing by means of projections and reasoned guesses, as shown in the following passage from an essay by media maven Marc Prensky. He is arguing that it is time for some college or university to be the first to ban physical, that is to say *paper*, books on its campus, a controversial proposal to say the least:

> Colleges and professors exist, in great measure, to help "liberate" and connect the knowledge and ideas in books. We should certainly pass on to our students the ability to do this. But in the future those

liberated ideas—the ones in the books (the author's words), and the ones about the books (the reader's own notes, all readers' thoughts and commentaries)—should be available with a few keystrokes. So, as counterintuitive as it may sound, eliminating physical books from college campuses would be a positive step for our 21st-century students, and, I believe, for 21st-century scholarship as well. Academics, researchers, and particularly teachers need to move to the tools of the future. Artifacts belong in museums, not in our institutions of higher learning.

—Marc Prensky, "In the 21st-Century University, Let's Ban Books"

Arguments about the Present

Arguments about the present—what Aristotle terms **epideictic** or **ceremonial arguments**—explore the current values of a society, affirming or challenging its widely shared beliefs and core assumptions. Epideictic arguments are often made at public and formal events such as inaugural addresses, sermons, eulogies, memorials, and graduation speeches. Members of the audience listen carefully as credible speakers share their wisdom. For example, as the selection of college commencement speakers has grown increasingly contentious, Ruth J. Simmons, the first African American woman to head an Ivy League college, used the opportunity of such an address (herself standing in for a rejected speaker) to offer a timely and ringing endorsement of free speech. Her words perfectly illustrate epideictic rhetoric:

> Universities have a special obligation to protect free speech, open discourse and the value of protest. The collision of views and ideologies is in the DNA of the academic enterprise. No collision avoidance technology is needed here. The noise from this discord may cause others to criticize the legitimacy of the academic enterprise, but how can knowledge advance without the questions that overturn misconceptions, push further into previously impenetrable areas of inquiry and assure us stunning breakthroughs in human knowledge? If there is anything that colleges must encourage and protect it is the persistent questioning of the status quo. Our health as a nation, our health as women, our health as an industry requires it.

—Ruth J. Simmons, Smith College, 2014

Perhaps more common than Smith's impassioned address are values arguments that examine contemporary culture, praising what's admirable and blaming what's not. In the following argument, student Latisha Chisholm looks at the state of rap music after Tupac Shakur:

> With the death of Tupac, not only did one of the most intriguing rap rivalries of all time die, but the motivation for rapping seems to have changed. Where money had always been a plus, now it is obviously more important than wanting to express the hardships of Black communities. With current rappers, the positive power that came from the desire to represent Black people is lost. One of the biggest rappers now got his big break while talking about sneakers. Others announce retirement without really having done much for the soul or for Black people's morale. I equate new rappers to NFL players that don't love the game anymore. They're only in it for the money. . . . It looks like the voice of a people has lost its heart.
>
> —Latisha Chisholm, "Has Rap Lost Its Soul?"

As in many ceremonial arguments, Chisholm here reinforces common values such as representing one's community honorably and fairly.

Are rappers since Tupac — like Jay Z — only in it for the money?
Many epideictic arguments either praise or blame contemporary culture in this way.

Michael N. Todaro/FilmMagic/Getty Images

In a recent magazine, newspaper, or blog, find three editorials—one that makes a forensic argument, one a deliberative argument, and one a ceremonial argument. Analyze the arguments by asking these questions: Who is arguing? What purposes are the writers trying to achieve? To whom are they directing their arguments? Then decide whether the arguments' purposes have been achieved and how you know.

Occasions for Argument

	Past	**Future**	**Present**
What is it called?	Forensic	Deliberative	Epideictic
What are its concerns?	What happened in the past?	What should be done in the future?	Who or what deserves praise or blame?
What does it look like?	Court decisions, legal briefs, legislative hearings, investigative reports, academic studies	White papers, proposals, bills, regulations, mandates	Eulogies, graduation speeches, inaugural addresses, roasts

Kinds of Argument

Yet another way of categorizing arguments is to consider their status or stasis—that is, the specific *kinds of issues they address*. This approach, called **stasis theory**, was used in ancient Greek and Roman civilizations to provide questions designed to help citizens and lawyers work their way through legal cases. The status questions were posed in sequence because each depended on answers from the preceding ones. Together, the queries helped determine the point of contention in an argument—where the parties disagreed or what exactly had to be proven. A modern version of those questions might look like the following:

- Did something happen?

- What is its nature?

- What is its quality or cause?

- What actions should be taken?

Each stasis question explores a different aspect of a problem and uses different evidence or techniques to reach conclusions. You can use these questions to explore the aspects of any topic you're considering. You'll discover that we use the stasis issues to define key types of argument in Part 2.

Did Something Happen? Arguments of Fact

There's no point in arguing a case until its basic facts are established. So an **argument of fact** usually involves a statement that can be proved or disproved with specific evidence or testimony. For example, the question of pollution of the oceans—is it really occurring?—might seem relatively easy to settle. Either scientific data prove that the oceans are being dirtied as a result of human activity, or they don't. But to settle the matter, writers and readers need to ask a number of other questions about the "facts":

- Where did the facts come from?

- Are they reliable?

- Is there a problem with the facts?

- Where did the problem begin and what caused it?

For more on arguments based on facts, see Chapters 11 and 15.

What Is the Nature of the Thing? Arguments of Definition

Some of the most hotly debated issues in American life today involve questions of definition: we argue over the nature of the human fetus, the meaning of "amnesty" for immigrants, the boundaries of sexual assault. As you might guess, issues of definition have mighty consequences, and decades of debate may nonetheless leave the matter unresolved. Here, for example, is how one type of sexual assault is defined in an important 2007 report submitted to the U.S. Department of Justice by the National Institute of Justice:

> We consider as incapacitated sexual assault any unwanted sexual contact occurring when a victim is unable to provide consent or stop what is happening because she is passed out, drugged, drunk, incapacitated, or asleep, regardless of whether the perpetrator was responsible for her substance use or whether substances were administered without her knowledge. We break down incapacitated sexual assault into four subtypes. . . .
>
> —"The Campus Sexual Assault (CSA) Study: Final Report"

The specifications of the definition go on for another two hundred words, each of consequence in determining how sexual assault on college campuses might be understood, measured, and addressed.

Of course many **arguments of definition** are less weighty than this, though still hotly contested: Is playing video games a sport? Can Batman be a tragic figure? Is Hillary Clinton a moderate or a progressive? (For more about arguments of definition, see Chapter 16.)

What Is the Quality or Cause of the Thing? Arguments of Evaluation

Arguments of evaluation present criteria and then measure individual people, ideas, or things against those standards. For instance, a *Washington Post* story examining long-term trend lines in SAT reading scores opened with this qualitative assessment of the results:

> Reading scores on the SAT for the high school class of 2012 reached a four-decade low, putting a punctuation mark on a gradual decline in the ability of college-bound teens to read passages and answer questions about sentence structure, vocabulary and meaning on the college entrance exam. . . . Scores among every racial group except for those of Asian descent declined from 2006 levels. A majority of test takers—57 percent—did not score high enough to indicate likely success in college, according to the College Board, the organization that administers the test.
>
> —Lyndsey Layton and Emma Brown, "SAT Reading Scores Hit a Four-Decade Low"

The final sentence is particularly telling, putting the test results in context. More than half the high school test-takers may not be ready for college-level readings.

In examining a circumstance or situation like this, we are often led to wonder what accounts for it: *Why are the test scores declining? Why are some groups underperforming?* And, in fact, the authors of the brief *Post* story do follow up on some questions of cause and effect:

> The 2012 SAT scores come after a decade of efforts to raise test scores under the No Child Left Behind law, the federal education initiative crafted by President George W. Bush. Critics say the law failed to address the barriers faced by many test takers.

"Some kids are coming to school hungry, some without the health care they need, without the vocabulary that middle-class kids come to school with, even in kindergarten," said Helen F. Ladd, a professor of public policy and economics at Duke University.

Although evaluations differ from causal analyses, in practice the boundaries between stasis questions are often porous: particular arguments have a way of defining their own issues.

For much more about arguments of evaluation, see Chapter 17; for causal arguments, see Chapter 18.

What Actions Should Be Taken? Proposal Arguments

After facts in a controversy have been confirmed, definitions agreed on, evaluations made, and causes traced, it may be time for a **proposal argument** answering the question *Now, what do we do about all this?* For example, in developing an argument about out-of-control student fees at your college, you might use all the prior stasis questions to study the issue and determine exactly how much and for what reasons these costs are escalating. Only then will you be prepared to offer knowledgeable suggestions for action. In examining a nationwide move to eliminate remedial education in four-year colleges, John Cloud offers a notably moderate proposal to address the problem:

STASIS QUESTIONS AT WORK

Suppose you have an opportunity to speak at a student conference on the impact of climate change. You are tentatively in favor of strengthening industrial pollution standards aimed at reducing global warming trends. But to learn more about the issue, you use the stasis questions to get started.

- **Did something happen?** Does global warming exist? *Maybe not*, say many in the oil and gas industry; at best, evidence for global warming is inconclusive. *Yes*, say most scientists and governments; climate change is real and even seems to be accelerating. To come to your conclusion, you'll weigh the facts carefully and identify problems with opposing arguments.

- **What is the nature of the thing?** Skeptics define climate change

as a naturally occurring event; most scientists base their definitions on change due to human causes. You look at each definition carefully: *How do the definitions foster the goals of each group? What's at stake for each group in defining it that way?*

- **What is the quality or cause of the thing?** Exploring the differing assessments of damage done by climate change leads you to ask who will gain from such analysis: *Do oil executives want to protect their investments? Do scientists want government money for grants? Where does evidence for the dangers of global warming come from? Who benefits if the dangers are accepted as real and present, and who loses?*

- **What actions should be taken?** If climate change is occurring naturally or causing little harm, then arguably *nothing* needs to be or can be done. But if it is caused mainly by human activity and dangers, action is definitely called for (although not everyone may agree on what such action should be). As you investigate the proposals being made and the reasons behind them, you come closer to developing your own argument.

The No Child Left Behind Act was signed in 2002 with great hopes and bipartisan support.

AFP/Getty Images

Students age twenty-two and over account for 43 percent of those in remedial classrooms, according to the National Center for Developmental Education. . . . [But] 55 percent of those needing remediation must take just one course. Is it too much to ask them to pay extra for that class or take it at a community college?

—John Cloud, "Who's Ready for College?"

For more about proposal arguments, see Chapter 19.

Appealing to Audiences

Exploring all the occasions and kinds of arguments available will lead you to think about the audience(s) you are addressing and the specific ways you can appeal to them. Audiences for arguments today are amazingly diverse, from the flesh-and-blood person sitting across a desk when you negotiate a student loan to your "friends" on social media, to the "ideal" reader you imagine for whatever you are writing. The figure below suggests just how many dimensions an audience can have as writers and readers negotiate their relationships with a text, whether it be oral, written, or digital.

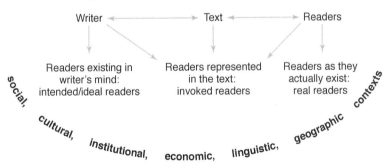

Readers and writers in context

As you see there, texts usually have **intended readers**, the people writers hope and expect to address—let's say, routine browsers of a newspaper's op-ed page. But writers also shape the responses of these actual readers in ways they imagine as appropriate or desirable—for example, maneuvering readers of editorials into making focused and knowledgeable judgments about politics and culture. Such audiences, as imagined and fashioned by writers within their texts, are called **invoked readers**.

Making matters even more complicated, readers can respond to writers' maneuvers by choosing to join the invoked audiences, to resist them, or maybe even to ignore them. Arguments may also attract "real" readers from groups not among those that writers originally imagined or expected to reach. You may post something on the Web, for instance, and discover that people you did not intend to address are commenting on it. (For them, the experience may be like reading private email intended for someone else: they find themselves drawn to and fascinated by your ideas!) As authors of this book, we think about students like you whenever we write: you are our intended readers. But notice how in dozens of ways, from the images we choose to the tone of our language, we also invoke an audience of people who take writing arguments seriously. We want you to become that kind of reader.

So audiences are *very* complicated and subtle and challenging, and yet you somehow have to attract and even persuade them. As always, Aristotle offers an answer. He identified three time-tested appeals that speakers and writers can use to reach almost any audience, labeling them *pathos, ethos,* and *logos*—strategies as effective today as they were in ancient times, though we usually think of them in slightly different terms. Used in the right way and deployed at the right moment, emotional, ethical, and logical appeals have enormous power, as we'll see in subsequent chapters.

RESPOND

You can probably provide concise descriptions of the intended audience for most textbooks you have encountered. But can you detect their invoked audiences—that is, the way their authors are imagining (and perhaps shaping) the readers they would like to have? Carefully review this entire chapter, looking for signals and strategies that might identify the audience and readers invoked by the authors of *Everything's an Argument*.

Emotional Appeals: Pathos

Emotional appeals, or **pathos**, generate emotions (fear, pity, love, anger, jealousy) that the writer hopes will lead the audience to accept a claim. Here is an alarming sentence from a book by Barry B. LePatner arguing that Americans need to make hard decisions about repairing the country's failing infrastructure:

When the I-35W Bridge in Minneapolis shuddered, buckled, and collapsed during the evening rush hour on Wednesday, August 1, 2007, plunging 111 vehicles into the Mississippi River and sending thirteen people to their deaths, the sudden, apparently inexplicable nature of the event at first gave the appearance of an act of God.

—*Too Big to Fall: America's Failing Infrastructure and the Way Forward*

If you ever drive across a bridge, LePatner has probably gotten your attention. His sober and yet descriptive language helps readers imagine the dire consequence of neglected road maintenance and bad design decisions. Making an emotional appeal like this can dramatize an issue and sometimes even create a bond between writer and readers. (For more about emotional appeals, see Chapter 9.)

Ethical Appeals: Ethos

When writers or speakers come across as trustworthy, audiences are likely to listen to and accept their arguments. That trustworthiness (along with fairness and respect) is a mark of **ethos**, or credibility. Showing that you know what you are talking about exerts an ethical appeal, as does emphasizing that you share values with and respect your audience. Once again, here's Barry LePatner from *Too Big to Fall*, shoring up his authority for writing about problems with America's roads and bridges by invoking the ethos of people even more credible:

> For those who would seek to dismiss the facts that support the thesis of this book, I ask them to consult the many professional engineers in state transportation departments who face these problems on a daily basis. These professionals understand the physics of bridge and road design, and the real problems of ignoring what happens to steel and concrete when they are exposed to the elements without a strict regimen of ongoing maintenance.

It's a sound rhetorical move to enhance credibility this way. For more about ethical appeals, see Chapter 10.

Logical Appeals: Logos

Appeals to logic, or **logos**, are often given prominence and authority in U.S. culture: "Just the facts, ma'am," a famous early TV detective on *Dragnet* used to say. Indeed, audiences respond well to the use of reasons and evidence—to the presentation of facts, statistics, credible testimony, cogent examples, or even a narrative or story that embodies a sound reason in support of an argument. Following almost two hundred pages of facts, statistics, case studies, and arguments about the sad state of American bridges, LePatner can offer this sober, logical, and inevitable conclusion:

> We can no longer afford to ignore the fact that we are in the midst of a transportation funding crisis, which has been exacerbated by an even larger and longer-term problem: how we choose to invest in our infrastructure. It is not difficult to imagine the serious consequences that will unfold if we fail to address the deplorable conditions of our bridges and roads, including the increasingly higher costs we will pay for goods and services that rely on that transportation network, and a concomitant reduction in our standard of living.

For more about logical appeals, see Chapter 11.

Bringing It Home: Kairos *and the Rhetorical Situation*

In Greek mythology, Kairos—the youngest son of Zeus—was the god of opportunity. In images, he is most often depicted as running, and his most unusual characteristic is a shock of hair on his forehead. As Kairos dashes by, you have a chance to seize that lock of hair, thereby seizing the opportune moment; once he passes you by, however, you have missed that chance.

Kairos is also a term used to describe the most suitable time and place for making an argument and the most opportune ways of expressing it. It is easy to point to shimmering rhetorical moments, when speakers find exactly the right words to stir an audience: Franklin Roosevelt's "We have nothing to fear but fear itself," Ronald Reagan's "Mr. Gorbachev, tear down this wall," and of course Martin Luther King Jr.'s "I have a dream . . ." But *kairos* matters just as much in less dramatic situations, whenever speakers or writers must size up the core elements of a rhetorical situation to decide how best to make their expertise and ethos work for a particular message aimed at a specific audience. The diagram below hints at the dynamic complexity of the rhetorical situation.

But rhetorical situations are embedded in contexts of enormous social complexity. The moment you find a subject, you inherit all the knowledge, history, culture, and technological significations that surround it. To lesser and greater degrees (depending on the subject), you also bring personal circumstances into the field—perhaps your gender, your race, your religion, your economic class, your habits of language. And all those issues weigh also upon the people you write to and for.

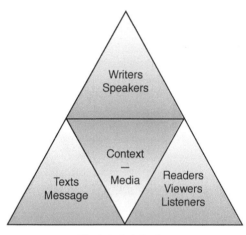

The rhetorical situation

Ronald Reagan at the Berlin Wall, June 12, 1987: "Mr. Gorbachev, tear down this wall!"

© Dennis Brack/PhotoShot

So considering your rhetorical situation calls on you to think hard about the notion of *kairos*. Being aware of your rhetorical moment means being

able to understand and take advantage of dynamic, shifting circumstances and to choose the best (most timely) proofs and evidence for a particular place, situation, and audience. It means seizing moments and enjoying opportunities, not being overwhelmed by them. Doing so might even lead you to challenge the title of this text: *is* everything an argument?

That's what makes writing arguments exciting.

RESPOND

Take a look at the bumper sticker below, and then analyze it. What is its purpose? What kind of argument is it? Which of the stasis questions does it most appropriately respond to? To what audiences does it appeal? What appeals does it make and how?

© Kevin Lamarque/Reuters/Corbis

CULTURAL CONTEXTS FOR ARGUMENT

Considering What's "Normal"

If you want to communicate effectively with people across cultures, then learn about the traditions in those cultures and examine the norms guiding your own behavior:

- Explore your assumptions! Most of us regard our ways of thinking as "normal" or "right." Such assumptions guide our judgments about what works in persuasive situations. But just because it may seem natural to speak bluntly in arguments, consider that others may find such aggression startling or even alarming.

- Remember: ways of arguing differ widely across cultures. Pay attention to how people from groups or cultures other than your own argue, and be sensitive to different paths of thinking you'll encounter as well as to differences in language.

- Don't assume that all people share your cultural values, ethical principles, or political assumptions. People across the world have different ways of defining *family*, *work*, or *happiness*. As you present arguments to them, consider that they may be content with their different ways of organizing their lives and societies.

- Respect the differences among individuals *within* a given group. Don't expect that every member of a community behaves—or argues—in the same way or shares the same beliefs. Avoid thinking, for instance, that there is a single Asian, African, or Hispanic culture or that Europeans are any less diverse or more predictable than Americans or Canadians in their thinking. In other words, be skeptical of stereotypes.

9

Arguments Based on Emotion: Pathos

Reading and Understanding Arguments

Emotional appeals (*appeals to pathos*) are powerful tools for influencing what people think and believe. We all make decisions—even including the most important ones—based on our feelings. That's what the Food and Drug Administration hoped to capitalize on when it introduced nine tough warning labels for cigarettes, one of which you see above. One look at the stained, rotting teeth and the lip sore may arouse emotions of fear strong enough to convince people not to smoke.

In the second panel, Bob Dorigo Jones, an opponent of lawsuit abuse, takes concerns about product liability in a different direction, publishing a book entitled *Remove Child before Folding: The 101 Stupidest, Silliest, and Wackiest Warning Labels Ever* to make us laugh and thereby, perhaps, to wonder why common sense seems in such short supply. In the third panel, editorial cartoonist for the *Indianapolis Star* Gary Varvel uses the anti-smoking meme to point out a potent irony in burgeoning campaigns to legalize marijuana.

The arguments packed into these three images all appeal to emotion, and research has shown us that we often make decisions based on just such appeals. So when you hear that formal or academic arguments should rely solely on facts to convince us, remember that facts alone often won't carry the day, even for a worthy cause. The largely successful case made this decade for same-sex marriage provides a notable example of a movement that persuaded people equally by virtue of the reasonableness and the passion of its claims. Like many political and social debates, though, the issue provoked powerful emotions on every side—feelings that sometimes led to extreme words and tactics.

Of course, we don't have to look hard for arguments fueled with emotions such as hatred, envy, and greed, or for campaigns intended to drive wedges between economic or social groups, making them fearful or resentful. For

that reason alone, writers should not use emotional appeals rashly or casually. (For more about emotional fallacies, see p. 206.)

Reading Critically for Pathos

On February 24, 2014, Senator Tom Harkin of Iowa, fresh from two "fact-finding" trips to Cuba, described his experiences on the Senate floor in a rambling, forty-minute speech, praising that island nation's accomplishments in health care and education and urging a normalization of Cuban–American relationships. Later that day, Florida senator Marco Rubio, expecting to speak about growing repression in Venezuela, found it impossible to ignore Harkin's rosy view of the "fascinating" socialist experiment ninety miles from the coast of the United States. Seizing a kairotic moment, the first-term senator delivered a passionate fifteen-minute rejoinder to Harkin without a script or teleprompter—though Rubio did use posters prepared originally for the Venezuelan talk. After a sarcastic taunt ("Sounded like he had a wonderful trip visiting what he described as a real paradise"), Rubio quickly turned serious, even angry, as he offered his take on the country Harkin had toured:

> I heard him also talk about these great doctors that they have in Cuba. I have no doubt they're very talented. I've met a bunch of them. You know where I met them? In the United States because they defected. Because in Cuba, doctors would rather drive a taxi cab or work in a hotel than be a doctor. I wonder if they spoke to him about the outbreak of cholera that they've been unable to control, or about the three-tiered system of health care that exists where foreigners and government officials get health care much better than that that's available to the general population.

The speech thereafter settles into a rhythm of patterned inquiries designed to raise doubts about what Senator Harkin had seen, Rubio's informal language rippling with contempt for his colleague's naïveté:

> I heard about their [the Cubans'] wonderful literacy rate, how everyone in Cuba knows how to read. That's fantastic. Here's the problem: they can only read censored stuff. They're not allowed access to the Internet. The only newspapers they're allowed to read are *Granma* or the ones produced by the government. . . .

> He talked about these great baseball players that are coming from Cuba—and they are. But I wonder if they informed him [that] every single one of those guys playing in the Major Leagues defected. They left Cuba to play here. . . .
>
> So it's great to have literacy, but if you don't have access to the information, what's the point of it? So I wish somebody would have asked about that on that trip. . . .
>
> I wonder if anybody asked about terrorism, because Cuba is a state sponsor of terrorism. . . .

Language this heated and pointed has risks, especially when a young legislator is taking on a genial and far more experienced colleague. But Rubio, the son of Cuban immigrants, isn't shy about allowing his feelings to show. Segueing to his original topic—growing political repression in socialist Venezuela—he uses the kind of verbal repetition common in oratory to drive home his major concern about Cuba, its influence on other nations:

> Let me tell you what the Cubans are really good at, because they don't know how to run their economy, they don't know how to build, they don't know how to govern a people. What they are really good at is repression. What they are really good at is shutting off information to the Internet and to radio and television and social media. That's what they're really good at. And they're not just good at it domestically, they're good exporters of these things.

Rubio's actual audience in the U.S. Senate was very small, but today all speeches from that chamber are carried nationwide and archived by C-SPAN, and in the age of YouTube, bits and pieces of political addresses reach many listeners. Former speechwriter and *Wall Street Journal* columnist Peggy Noonan was among those who caught Rubio's remarks and blogged about them: "We have pressed in these parts for American political figures to speak clearly and with moral confidence about American sympathies in various international disputes. Rubio's speech is honest political indignation successfully deployed." You can watch the entire speech on C-SPAN's Web site (listed as "Rubio Speech on Venezuela") to see if you agree. And though Cuba and the United States did re-establish diplomatic relationships roughly ten months after the Harkin/Rubio exchange, issues raised by both senators—from health care to the immigration status of Cuban baseball players—will likely be argued for years to come.

As originally aired on C-SPAN2 on February 24 2014

RESPOND

Working with a classmate, make a list of reasons why speakers in highly charged situations might need to use emotional appeals cautiously, even sparingly. What consequences might heightened emotional appeals lead to? What is at stake for the speaker in such situations, in terms of credibility and ethos? What are the advantages of evoking emotions in support of your claims or ideas?

Using Emotions to Build Bridges

You may sometimes want to use emotions to connect with readers to assure them that you understand their experiences or "feel their pain," to borrow a sentiment popularized by President Bill Clinton. Such a bridge is especially important when you're writing about matters that readers regard as sensitive. Before they'll trust you, they'll want assurances that you understand the issues in depth. If you strike the right emotional note, you'll establish an important connection. That's what Apple founder Steve Jobs does in a much-admired 2005 commencement address in which he tells the audience that he doesn't have a fancy speech, just three stories from his life:

> My second story is about love and loss. I was lucky. I found what I loved to do early in life. Woz [Steve Wozniak] and I started Apple in my parents' garage when I was twenty. We worked hard and in ten years, Apple had grown from just the two of us in a garage into a $2 billion company with over four thousand employees. We'd just

released our finest creation, the Macintosh, a year earlier, and I'd just turned thirty, and then I got fired. How can you get fired from a company you started? Well, as Apple grew, we hired someone who I thought was very talented to run the company with me, and for the first year or so, things went well. But then our visions of the future began to diverge, and eventually we had a falling out. When we did, our board of directors sided with him, and so at thirty, I was out, and very publicly out. . . .

I didn't see it then, but it turned out that getting fired from Apple was the best thing that could have ever happened to me. The heaviness of being successful was replaced by the lightness of being a beginner again, less sure about everything. It freed me to enter one of the most creative periods in my life. During the next five years I started a company named NeXT, another company named Pixar and fell in love with an amazing woman who would become my wife. Pixar went on to create the world's first computer-animated feature film, *Toy Story*, and is now the most successful animation studio in the world.

> —Steve Jobs, "You've Got to Find What You Love, Jobs Says"

In no obvious way is Jobs's recollection a formal argument. But it prepares his audience to accept the advice he'll give later in his speech, at least partly because he's speaking from meaningful personal experiences.

A more obvious way to build an emotional tie is simply to help readers identify with your experiences. If, like Georgina Kleege, you were blind and wanted to argue for more sensible attitudes toward blind people, you might ask readers in the first paragraph of your argument to confront their prejudices. Here Kleege, a writer and college instructor, makes an emotional point by telling a story:

I tell the class, "I am legally blind." There is a pause, a collective intake of breath. I feel them look away uncertainly and then look back. After all, I just said I couldn't see. Or did I? I had managed to get there on my own—no cane, no dog, none of the usual trappings of blindness. Eyeing me askance now, they might detect that my gaze is not quite focused. . . . They watch me glance down, or towards the door where someone's coming in late. I'm just like anyone else.

> —Georgina Kleege, "Call It Blindness"

Given the way she narrates the first day of class, readers are as likely to identify with the students as with Kleege, imagining themselves sitting in a classroom, facing a sightless instructor, confronting their own prejudices about the blind. Kleege wants to put her audience on the edge emotionally.

Let's consider another rhetorical situation: how do you win over an audience when the logical claims that you're making are likely to go against what many in the audience believe? Once again, a slightly risky appeal to emotions on a personal level may work. That's the tack that Michael Pollan takes in bringing readers to consider that "the great moral struggle of our time will be for the rights of animals." In introducing his lengthy exploratory argument, Pollan uses personal experience to appeal to his audience:

> The first time I opened Peter Singer's *Animal Liberation*, I was dining alone at the Palm, trying to enjoy a rib-eye steak cooked medium-rare.

THE BIRTH OF A VEGETARIAN

A visual version of Michael Pollan's rhetorical situation.

© Robert Mankoff/The New Yorker Collection/The Cartoon Bank

> If this sounds like a good recipe for cognitive dissonance (if not indigestion), that was sort of the idea. Preposterous as it might seem to supporters of animal rights, what I was doing was tantamount to reading *Uncle Tom's Cabin* on a plantation in the Deep South in 1852.

—Michael Pollan, "An Animal's Place"

In creating a vivid image of his first encounter with Singer's book, Pollan's opening builds a bridge between himself as a person trying to enter into the animal rights debate in a fair and open-minded, if still skeptical, way and readers who might be passionate about either side of this argument.

Using Emotions to Sustain an Argument

You can also use emotional appeals to make logical claims stronger or more memorable. That is the way that photographs and other images add power to arguments. In a TV attack ad, the scowling cell phone video of a disheveled political opponent may do as much damage as the insinuation that he bought his home on the cheap from a financier convicted of fraud. In contrast, a human face smiling or showing honest emotion can sell just about any product—that's why indicted political figures now routinely smile for their mug shots. Using emotion is tricky, however. Lay on too much feeling—especially sentiments like outrage, pity, or shame, which make people uncomfortable—and you may offend the very audiences you hoped to convince.

Still, strong emotions can add energy to a passage or an entire argument, as they do when Walter Russell Mead, editor-at-large of the *American Interest*, argues about what *really* motivates Americans to donate lavishly to many colleges and universities. As you read the following excerpt, notice how the author paints vivid pictures of people at college sporting events, describes the emotions at those games, and then argues what schools really need to do to win contributions:

> But if you want to understand why so many generations of Americans have sent so much dough back to the campuses where they wasted some of the happiest years of their lives, watch the intensity of the tens of thousands of fans who attend these events. Look at the shirtless boys with faces and torsos painted in the school colors; look at the cheerleaders on the fields, the "waves" surging through the stands.

> American universities, those temples of reason (at their best), are tribes. The kids bond to each other and to their schools in the heat of the intense emotions that these contests generate. Those shirtless kids covered in paint, shivering in the November weather as they cheer their team on, will be prosperous, middle-aged alumni one day—and when they are, they will still be stirred by the memory

of the emotions and the loyalty that brought them out to the field.

If you want your alumni to give, you first have to make them fall in love with your school. This is not about having better chemistry programs or more faculty with higher name recognition than the school up the road. It is not about scoring higher on world indices of university quality. It is about competition, drama, intensity, about hope and fear, collective celebrations or collective disasters, seared into young and impressionable hearts where they will never be forgotten—and where they will be annually renewed as each sport in its season produces new highs and lows, new hopes and fears. Alumni watching their schools' games on TV, or celebrating or mourning their schools' results each week with friends, family and colleagues, are renewing their ties with their alma maters affirming that being an "Aggie" or a "Tar Heel" is an *identity*, not a line on the resume.

This is why most of them give. It is irrational and tribal love. It is intense emotion, not a vague sense of obligation or philanthropy. They want to beat State.

—Walter Russell Mead and *The American Interest* staff,
"It All Begins with Football"

Mead's claim, emotional in itself, may not be exactly what college and university administrators and faculty want to hear. But in using language this evocative, he makes his argument memorable, hoping perhaps to make general readers admit how they have felt and acted themselves.

Kevin C. Cox/Getty Images

It's difficult to gauge how much emotion will work in a given argument. Some issues—such as racism, immigration, abortion, and gun control—provoke strong feelings and, as a result, are often argued on emotional terms. But even issues that seem deadly dull—such as reform of federal student loan programs—can be argued passionately when proposed changes in these programs are set in human terms: reduce support for college loans and Kai, Riley, and Jayden end up in dead-end, low-paying jobs; don't reform the program and we're looking at another Wall Street–sized loan bailout and subsequent recession. Both alternatives might scare people into paying enough attention to take political action.

Using Humor

Humor has always played an important role in argument, sometimes as the sugar that makes the medicine go down. You can slip humor into an argument to put readers at ease, thereby making them more open to a proposal you have to offer. It's hard to say *no* when you're laughing. Humor also makes otherwise sober people suspend their judgment and even their prejudices, perhaps because the surprise and naughtiness of wit are combustive: they provoke laughter or smiles, not reflection. Who can resist a no-holds-barred attack on a famous personality, such as this assessment of *Twilight* star Kristen Stewart:

> The original scoffing, scowling, stammering, stuttering, gaping open mouth, temper-tantrum throwing, lip-biting, hair-flipping, plank of wood moody actress . . . A tape recorder in a mannequin could do her job.

Humor deployed cleverly may be why TV shows like *South Park* and *Modern Family* became popular with mainstream audiences, despite their willingness to explore controversial themes. Similarly, it's possible to make a point through humor that might not work in more sober writing. People argue endlessly about eating the right foods, typically defined by diet gurus who favor locally sourced, organically grown, and profoundly dull vegetables. *Wall Street Journal* columnist Ron Rosenbaum will have none of that. With new research suggesting that fatty diets may have unanticipated health benefits, Rosenbaum deploys some high-calorie humor to argue for the pleasures of dining lavishly:

> Preventing obesity is a laudable goal, but it has become the rationale for indiscriminate fat hunters. It can shade into a kind of bullying of the overweight, a badgering of anyone who likes butter or heavy

cream. To the antifat crusaders, I say: Attack fatty junk food all you want. I'm with you. But you can deny me my roasted marrow bones when you pry them from my cold, dead hands.

I'm not suggesting that we embrace these life-changing food experiences just on grounds of pure pleasure (though there's much to be said for pure pleasure). As it turns out, the science on the matter is changing as well. We are discovering that fatty delights can actually be good for you: They allow Spaniards, Italians and Greeks to live longer, and they make us satisfied with eating less. I'm speaking up not for obesity-generating fat, then, but for the kind of fatty food that leads to swooning sensual satiety.

Roast goose, for instance, is a supremely succulent, mind-alteringly flavorful fatty food. In most of America, roast goose would be viewed as the raven of cardiac mortality, hoarsely honking "never more." And listening to the doctors on cable TV, you might think that it's better to cook up a batch of meth than to cook with butter.

Eating fatty foods has become the culinary version of *Breaking Bad*: a dangerous walk on the wild side for the otherwise timid consumers of tasteless butter substitutes and Lean Cuisine.

—Ron Rosenbaum, "Let Them Eat Fat"

Our laughter testifies to what some people have thought all along: people who want us to eat tofu are the real problem. Note the pleasure Rosenbaum takes in the emotive power of words themselves: *swooning sensual satiety*; *the raven of cardiac mortality, hoarsely honking "never more."*

A writer or speaker can even use humor to deal with sensitive issues. For example, sports commentator Bob Costas, given the honor of eulogizing the great baseball player Mickey Mantle, couldn't ignore problems in Mantle's life. So he argues for Mantle's greatness by admitting the man's weaknesses indirectly through humor:

It brings to mind a story Mickey liked to tell on himself and maybe some of you have heard it. He pictured himself at the pearly gates, met by St. Peter, who shook his head and said, "Mick, we checked the record. We know some of what went on. Sorry, we can't let you in. But before you go, God wants to know if you'd sign these six dozen baseballs."

—Bob Costas, "Eulogy for Mickey Mantle"

Similarly, politicians may use humor to deal with issues they couldn't acknowledge in any other way. Here, for example, is former president George W. Bush at the 2004 Radio and TV Correspondents' Dinner discussing his much-mocked intellect:

> Those stories about my intellectual capacity do get under my skin. You know, for a while I even thought my staff believed it. There on my schedule first thing every morning it said, "Intelligence briefing."
>
> —George W. Bush

Not all humor is well-intentioned or barb-free. In fact, among the most powerful forms of emotional argument is ridicule—humor aimed at a particular target. Eighteenth-century poet and critic Samuel Johnson was known for his stinging and humorous put-downs, such as this comment to an aspiring writer: "Your manuscript is both good and original, but the part that is good is not original and the part that is original is not good." (Expect your own writing teachers to be kinder.) In our own time, the *Onion* has earned a reputation for its mastery of both ridicule and satire, the art of using over-the-top humor to making a serious point.

But because ridicule is a double-edged sword, it requires a deft hand to wield it. Humor that reflects bad taste discredits a writer completely, as does satire that misses its mark. Unless your target deserves riposte and you can be very funny, it's usually better to steer clear of such humor.

Using Arguments Based on Emotion

You don't want to play puppet master with people's emotions when you write arguments, but it's a good idea to spend some time early in your work thinking about how you want readers to feel as they consider your persuasive claims. For example, would readers of your editorial about campus traffic policies be more inclined to agree with you if you made them envy faculty privileges, or would arousing their sense of fairness work better? What emotional appeals might persuade meat eaters to consider a vegan diet—or vice versa? Would sketches of stage props on a Web site persuade people to buy a season ticket to the theater, or would you spark more interest by featuring pictures of costumed performers?

Consider, too, the effect that a story can have on readers. Writers and journalists routinely use what are called *human-interest stories* to give presence

to issues or arguments. You can do the same, using a particular incident to evoke sympathy, understanding, outrage, or amusement. Take care, though, to tell an honest story.

RESPOND

1. To what specific emotions do the following slogans, sales pitches, and maxims appeal?

   "Just do it." (ad for Nike)

   "Think different." (ad for Apple computers)

   "Reach out and touch someone." (ad for AT&T)

   "By any means necessary." (rallying cry from Malcolm X)

   "Have it your way." (slogan for Burger King)

   "The ultimate driving machine." (slogan for BMW)

   "It's everywhere you want to be." (slogan for Visa)

   "Know what comes between me and my Calvins? Nothing!" (tag line for Calvin Klein jeans)

   "Don't mess with Texas!" (anti-litter campaign slogan)

   "American by Birth. Rebel by Choice." (slogan for Harley-Davidson)

2. Bring a magazine to class, and analyze the emotional appeals in as many full-page ads as you can. Then classify those ads by types of emotional appeal, and see whether you can connect the appeals to the subject or target audience of the magazine. Compare your results with those of your classmates, and discuss your findings. For instance, how exactly are the ads in publications such as *Cosmopolitan, Wired, Sports Illustrated, Motor Trend,* and *Smithsonian* adapted to their specific audiences?

3. How do arguments based on emotion work in different media? Are such arguments more or less effective in books, articles, television (both news and entertainment shows), films, brochures, magazines, email, Web sites, the theater, street protests, and so on? You might explore how a single medium handles emotional appeals or compare different media. For example, why do the comments pages of blogs seem to encourage angry outbursts? Are newspapers an emotionally colder source of information than television news programs? If so, why?

4. Spend some time looking for arguments that use ridicule or humor to make their point: check out your favorite Twitter feeds or blogs; watch for bumper stickers, posters, or advertisements; and listen to popular song lyrics. Bring one or two examples to class, and be ready to explain how the humor makes an emotional appeal and whether it's effective.

10

Arguments Based on Character: Ethos

Reading and Understanding Arguments

Chapter 10, "Arguments Based on Character: Ethos," from *Everything's an Argument*, Seventh Edition, by Andrea A. Lunsford and John J. Ruszkiewicz, pp. 40–50 (Chapter 3). Copyright © 2016 by Bedford/St. Martin's.

Left to right: © Jon Arnold Images Ltd./Alamy; © Bernhard Classen/age fotostock;
Richard Shotwell/Invision/AP

Whenever you read anything—whether it's a news article, an advertisement, a speech, or a text message—you no doubt subconsciously analyze the message for a sense of the character and credibility of the sender: *Is this someone I know and trust? Does the PBS reporter seem biased? Why should I believe an IRS official? Is this scholar really an authority on the subject?* Our culture teaches us to be skeptical of most messages, especially those that bombard us with slogans, and such reasonable doubt is a crucial skill in reading and evaluating arguments.

For that reason, people and institutions that hope to influence us do everything they can to establish their character and credibility, what ancient rhetors referred to as *ethos*. And sometimes slogans such as "All the News That's Fit to Print," "Fair & Balanced," or "Lean Forward" can be effective. At the very least, if a phrase is repeated often enough, it begins to sound plausible. Maybe CNN *is* the most trusted name in news!

But establishing character usually takes more than repetition, as marketers of all kinds know. It arises from credentials actually earned in some way. In the auto industry, for instance, companies such as Toyota, General Motors, and Nissan are hustling to present themselves as environmentally responsible producers of fuel-efficient, low-emission cars—the Prius, Volt, and Leaf. BMW, maker of "the ultimate driving machine," points to its fuel-sipping i3 and i8 cars as evidence of its commitment to "sustainable mobility." And Elon Musk (who builds rockets as well as Tesla cars) polishes his good-citizenship bona fides by sharing his electric vehicle patents with other manufacturers. All of these companies realize that their future success is linked to an ability to project a convincing ethos for themselves and their products.

If corporations and institutions can establish an ethos, consider how much character matters when we think about people in the public arena. Perhaps no individual managed a more exceptional assertion of personal ethos than Jorge Mario Bergoglio did after he became Pope Francis on March 13, 2013, following the abdication of Benedict XVI—a man many found scholarly, cold, and out of touch with the modern world. James Carroll, writing for the *New Yorker*, identifies the precise moment when the world realized that it was dealing with a new sort of pope:

> "Who am I to judge?" With those five words, spoken in late July [2013] in reply to a reporter's question about the status of gay priests in the Church, Pope Francis stepped away from the disapproving tone, the explicit moralizing typical of popes and bishops.
>
> —James Carroll, "Who Am I to Judge?"

Carroll goes on to explain that Francis quickly established his ethos with a series of specific actions, decisions, and moments of identification with ordinary people, marking him as someone even nonbelievers might listen to and respect:

> As pope, Francis has simplified the Renaissance regalia of the papacy by abandoning fur-trimmed velvet capes, choosing to live in a two-room apartment instead of the Apostolic Palace, and replacing the papal Mercedes with a Ford Focus. Instead of the traditional red slip-ons, Francis wears ordinary black shoes. . . . Yet Francis didn't criticize the choices of other prelates. "He makes changes without attacking people," a Jesuit official told me. In his interview with *La Civiltà Cattolica*, Francis said, "My choices, including those related to the day-to-day aspects of life, like the use of a modest car, are related to a spiritual discernment that responds to a need that arises from looking at things, at people, and from reading the signs of the times."

In that last sentence, Francis acknowledges that ethos is gained, in part, through identification with one's audience and era. And this man, movingly photographed embracing the sick and disfigured, also posed for selfies!

AP Photo/L'Osservatore Romano, Riccardo Aguiari

You can see, then, why Aristotle treats ethos as a powerful argumentative appeal. Ethos creates quick and sometimes almost irresistible connections between readers and arguments. We observe people, groups, or institutions making and defending claims all the time and inevitably ask ourselves, *Should we pay attention to them? Can we rely on them? Do we dare to trust them?* Consider, though, that the same questions will be asked about you and your work, especially in academic settings.

Thinking Critically about Arguments Based on Character

Put simply, arguments based on character (ethos) depend on *trust*. We tend to accept arguments from those we trust, and we trust them (whether individuals, groups, or institutions) in good part because of their reputations. Three main elements—credibility, authority, and unselfish or clear motives—add up to *ethos*.

To answer serious and important questions, we often turn to professionals (doctors, lawyers, engineers, teachers, pastors) or to experts (those with knowledge and experience) for good advice. Based on their backgrounds, such people come with their ethos already established. Thus, appeals or arguments about character often turn on claims like these:

- A person (or group or institution) is or is not trustworthy or credible on this issue.

- A person (or group or institution) does or does not have the authority to speak to this issue.

- A person (or group or institution) does or does not have unselfish or clear motives for addressing this subject.

Establishing Trustworthiness and Credibility

Trustworthiness and credibility speak to a writer's honesty, respect for an audience and its values, and plain old likability. Sometimes a sense of humor can play an important role in getting an audience to listen to or "like" you. It's no accident that all but the most serious speeches begin with a joke or funny story: the humor puts listeners at ease and helps them identify with the speaker. Writer J. K. Rowling, for example, puts her audience (and herself) at ease early in the commencement address she delivered at Harvard in 2008 by getting real about such speeches:

> Delivering a commencement address is a great responsibility; or so I thought until I cast my mind back to my own graduation. The commencement speaker that day was the distinguished British philosopher Baroness Mary Warnock. Reflecting on her speech has helped me enormously in writing this one, because it turns out that I can't remember a single word she said. This liberating discovery enables me to proceed without any fear that I might inadvertently influence you to abandon promising careers in business, the law, or politics for the giddy delights of becoming a gay wizard.
>
> You see? If all you remember in years to come is the "gay wizard" joke, I've come out ahead of Baroness Mary Warnock. Achievable goals: the first step to self improvement.
>
> —J. K. Rowling, "The Fringe Benefits of Failure,
> and the Importance of Imagination"

In just a few sentences, Rowling pokes fun at herself, undercuts the expectation that graduation addresses change people's lives, slides in an allusion from her Harry Potter series, and then even offers a smidgen of advice. For an audience well disposed toward her already, Rowling has likely lived up to expectations.

But using humor to enhance your credibility may be more common in oratory than in the kind of writing you'll do in school. Fortunately, you have many options, one being simply to make plausible claims and then back them up with evidence. Academic audiences appreciate a reasonable disposition; we will discuss this approach at greater length in the next chapter.

You can also establish trustworthiness by connecting your own beliefs to core principles that are well established and widely respected. This strategy is particularly effective when your position seems to be—at first glance, at least—a threat to traditional values. For example, when former Smith College president Ruth J. Simmons describes her professional self to a commencement audience she is addressing (see Chapter 8), she presents her acquired reputation in terms that align perfectly with contemporary values:

> For my part, I was cast as a troublemaker in my early career and accepted the disapproval that accompanies the expression of unpopular views: unpopular views about disparate pay for women and minorities; unpopular views about sexual harassment; unpopular views about exclusionary practices in our universities.
>
> —Ruth J. Simmons

It's fine to be a rebel when you are on the right side of history.

Writers who establish their credibility seem trustworthy. But sometimes, to be credible, you have to admit limitations, too, as *New York Times* columnist David Brooks does as he wrestles with a problem common in our time, an inability to focus on things that matter:

> Like everyone else, I am losing the attention war. I toggle over to my emails when I should be working. I text when I should be paying attention to the people in front of me. I spend hours looking at mildly diverting stuff on YouTube. ("Look, there's a bunch of guys who can play 'Billie Jean' on beer bottles!")
>
> And, like everyone else, I've nodded along with the prohibition sermons imploring me to limit my information diet. Stop multitasking! Turn off the devices at least once a week!
>
> And, like everyone else, these sermons have had no effect. Many of us lead lives of distraction, unable to focus on what we know we should focus on.
>
> —David Brooks, "The Art of Focus"

Making such concessions to readers sends a strong signal that you've looked critically at your own position and can therefore be trusted when you turn to arguing its merits. Speaking to readers directly, using *I* or *you* or *us*, can also help you connect with them, as can using contractions and everyday or colloquial language—both strategies employed by Brooks. In other situations, you may find that a more formal tone gives your claims greater credibility. You'll be making such choices as you search for the ethos that represents you best.

In fact, whenever you write a paper or present an idea, you are sending signals about your credibility, whether you intend to or not. If your ideas are reasonable, your sources are reliable, and your language is appropriate to the project, you suggest to academic readers that you're someone whose ideas *might* deserve attention. Details matter: helpful graphs, tables, charts, or illustrations may carry weight with readers, as will the visual attractiveness of your text, whether in print or digital form. Obviously, correct spelling, grammar, and mechanics are important too. And though you might not worry about it now, at some point you may need letters of recommendation from instructors or supervisors. How will they remember you? Often chiefly from the ethos you have established in your work. Think about that.

Claiming Authority

When you read or listen to an argument, you have every right to ask about the writer's authority: *What does he know about the subject? What experiences does she have that make her especially knowledgeable? Why should I pay attention to this person?* When you offer an argument yourself, you have to anticipate and be prepared to answer questions like these, either directly or indirectly.

How does someone construct an authoritative ethos? In examining what he describes as "the fundamental problem with President Obama's communications ethos," Ron Fournier, editorial director of *National Journal*, explains that authority cannot be taken for granted:

> He and his advisers are so certain about their moral and political standing that they believe it's enough to make a declaration. *If we say it, the public should believe it.*
>
> That's not how it works. A president must earn the public's trust. He must teach and persuade; speak clearly, and follow word with

action; show empathy toward his rivals, and acknowledge the merits of a critique. A successful president pays careful attention to how his image is projected both to U.S. voters and to the people of the world. He knows that to be strong, a leader must look strong. Image matters, especially in an era so dominated by them.

> —Ron Fournier, "Is the White House Lying,
> or Just Bad at Crisis Communications?"

Of course, writers establish their authority in various ways. Sometimes the assertion of ethos will be bold and personal, as it is when writer and activist Terry Tempest Williams attacks those who poisoned the Utah deserts with nuclear radiation. What gives her the right to speak on this subject? Not scientific expertise, but gut-wrenching personal experience:

> I belong to the Clan of One-Breasted Women. My mother, my grandmothers, and six aunts have all had mastectomies. Seven are dead. The two who survive have just completed rounds of chemotherapy and radiation.

> I've had my own problems: two biopsies for breast cancer and a small tumor between my ribs diagnosed as a "borderline malignancy."

> —Terry Tempest Williams, "The Clan of One-Breasted Women"

We are willing to listen to Williams because she has lived with the nuclear peril she will deal with in the remainder of her essay.

Other means of claiming authority are less dramatic. By simply attaching titles to their names, writers assert that they hold medical or legal or engineering degrees, or some other important credentials. Or they may mention the number of years they've worked in a given field or the distinguished positions they have held. As a reader, you'll pay more attention to an argument about global warming offered by a professor of atmospheric and oceanic science at the University of Minnesota than one by your Uncle Sid, who sells tools. But you'll prefer your uncle to the professor when you need advice about a reliable rotary saw.

When readers might be skeptical of both you and your claims, you may have to be even more specific about your credentials. That's exactly the strategy Richard Bernstein uses to establish his right to speak on the subject of "Asian culture." What gives a New York writer named Bernstein the authority to write about Asian peoples? Bernstein tells us in a sparkling example of an argument based on character:

The Asian culture, as it happens, is something I know a bit about, having spent five years at Harvard striving for a Ph.D. in a joint program called History and East Asian Languages and, after that, living either as a student (for one year) or a journalist (six years) in China and Southeast Asia. At least I know enough to know there is no such thing as the "Asian culture."

—Richard Bernstein, ***Dictatorship of Virtue***

When you write for readers who trust you and your work, you may not have to make such an open claim to authority. But making this type of appeal is always an option.

Coming Clean about Motives

When people are trying to convince you of something, it's important (and natural) to ask: *Whose interests are they serving? How will they profit from their proposal?* Such suspicions go to the heart of ethical arguments.

In a hugely controversial essay published in the *Princeton Tory*, Tal Fortgang, a first-year student at the Ivy League school, argues that those on campus who used the phrase "Check your privilege" to berate white male students like him for the advantages they enjoy are, in fact, judging him according to gender and race, and not for "all the hard work I have done in my life." To challenge stereotypical assumptions about the "racist patriarchy" that supposedly paved his way to Princeton, Fortgang writes about the experiences of his ancestors, opening the paragraphs with a striking parallel structure:

> Perhaps it's the privilege my grandfather and his brother had to flee their home as teenagers when the Nazis invaded Poland, leaving their mother and five younger siblings behind, running and running. . . .

> Or maybe it's the privilege my grandmother had of spending weeks upon weeks on a death march through Polish forests in subzero temperatures, one of just a handful to survive. . . .

> Perhaps my privilege is that those two resilient individuals came to America with no money and no English, obtained citizenship, learned the language and met each other. . . .

Perhaps it was my privilege that my own father worked hard enough in City College to earn a spot at a top graduate school, got a good job, and for 25 years got up well before the crack of dawn, sacrificing precious time he wanted to spend with those he valued most—his wife and kids—to earn that living.

—Tal Fortgang, "Checking My Privilege:
Character as the Basis of Privilege"

Fortgang thus attempts to establish his own ethos and win the argument against those who make assumptions about his roots by dramatizing the ethos of his ancestors:

That's the problem with calling someone out for the "privilege" which you assume has defined their narrative. You don't know what their struggles have been, what they may have gone through to be where they are. Assuming they've benefitted from "power systems" or other conspiratorial imaginary institutions denies them credit for all they've done, things of which you may not even conceive. You don't know whose father died defending your freedom. You don't know whose mother escaped oppression. You don't know who conquered their demons, or may still [be] conquering them now.

As you might imagine, the pushback to "Checking My Privilege" was enormous, some of the hundreds of comments posted to an online version accusing Fortgang himself of assuming the very ethos of victimhood against which he inveighs. Peter Finocchiaro, a reviewer on *Slate*, is especially brutal: "Only a few short months ago he was living at home with his parents. His life experience, one presumes, is fairly limited. So in that sense, he doesn't really know any better. . . . He is an ignorant 19-year-old white guy from Westchester." You can see in this debate how ethos quickly raises issues of knowledge and motives. Fortgang tries to resist the stereotype others would impose on his character, but others regard the very ethos he fashions in his essay as evidence of his naïveté about race, discrimination, and, yes, privilege.

We all, of course, have connections and interests that bind us to other human beings. It makes sense that a young man would explore his social identity, that a woman might be concerned with women's issues, that members of minority groups might define social and cultural conditions on their own terms—or even that investors might look out for their investments. It's simply good strategy to let your audiences know where your loyalties lie when such information does, in fact, shape your work.

Using Ethos in Your Own Writing

•   Establish your credibility by acknowledging your audience's values, showing respect for them, and establishing common ground where (and if) possible. How will you convince your audience you are trustworthy? What will you admit about your own limitations?

•   Establish your authority by showing you have done your homework and know your topic well. How will you show that you know your topic well? What appropriate personal experience can you draw on?

•   Examine your motives for writing. What, if anything, do you stand to gain from your argument? How can you explain those advantages to your audience?

CULTURAL CONTEXTS FOR ARGUMENT

Ethos

In the United States, students are often asked to establish authority by drawing on personal experiences, by reporting on research they or others have conducted, and by taking a position for which they can offer strong evidence. But this expectation about student authority is by no means universal.

Some cultures regard student writers as novices who can most effectively make arguments by reflecting on what they've learned from their teachers and elders — those who hold the most important knowledge and, hence, authority. When you're arguing a point with people from cultures other than your own, ask questions like:

• Whom are you addressing, and what is your relationship with that person?

• What knowledge are you expected to have? Is it appropriate or expected for you to demonstrate that knowledge — and if so, how?

• What tone is appropriate? And remember: politeness is rarely, if ever, inappropriate.

RESPOND

1. Consider the ethos of these public figures. Then describe one or two products that might benefit from their endorsements as well as several that would not.

   Edward Snowden—whistleblower
   Kaley Cuoco-Sweeting—actress
   James Earl Jones—actor
   Michael Sam—athlete
   Megyn Kelly—TV news commentator
   Miley Cyrus—singer
   Seth Meyers—late-night TV host
   Cristiano Ronaldo—soccer player

2. Opponents of Richard Nixon, the thirty-seventh president of the United States, once raised doubts about his integrity by asking a single ruinous question: *Would you buy a used car from this man?* Create your own version of the argument of character. Begin by choosing an intriguing or controversial person or group and finding an image online. Then download the image into a word-processing file. Create a caption for the photo that is modeled after the question asked about Nixon: *Would you give this woman your email password? Would you share a campsite with this couple? Would you eat lasagna that this guy fixed?* Finally, write a serious 300-word argument that explores the character flaws or strengths of your subject(s).

3. Take a close look at your Facebook page (or your page on any other social media site). What are some aspects of your character, true or not, that might be conveyed by the photos, videos, and messages you have posted online? Analyze the ethos or character you see projected there, using the advice in this chapter to guide your analysis.

11

Arguments Based on Facts and Reason: Logos

Reading and Understanding Arguments

Chapter 11, "Arguments Based on Facts and Reason: Logos,"
from *Everything's an Argument*, Seventh Edition,
by Andrea A. Lunsford and John J. Ruszkiewicz, pp. 51–70 (Chapter 4).
Copyright © 2016 by Bedford/St. Martin's.

"And it's recommended by nine out of ten people we believe to be doctors."

Left to right: Yui Mok/Press Association via AP Images; © NBC/Photofest, Inc.; © Frank Cotham/The New Yorker/The Cartoon Bank

These three images say a lot about the use and place of logic (*logos*) in Western and American culture. The first shows Benedict Cumberbatch from the BBC TV series *Sherlock*, just one of many actors to play Arthur Conan Doyle's much-loved fictional detective Sherlock Holmes, who solves perplexing crimes by using precise observation and impeccable logic. The second refers to an equally popular TV (and film) series character, Spock, the Vulcan officer in *Star Trek* who tries to live a life guided by reason alone—his most predicable observation being some version of "that would not be logical." The third is a cartoon spoofing a pseudo-logical argument (nine out of ten prefer X) made so often in advertising that it has become something of a joke.

These images attest to the prominent place that logic holds for most people: like Holmes, we want to know the facts on the assumption that they will help us make sound judgments. We admire those whose logic is, like Spock's, impeccable. So when arguments begin, "Nine out of ten authorities recommend," we respond favorably: those are good odds. But the three images also challenge reliance on logic alone: Sherlock Holmes and Spock are characters drawn in broad and often parodic strokes; the "nine out of ten" cartoon itself spoofs abuses of reason. Given a choice, however, most of us profess to respect and even prefer *appeals* to *logos*—that is, claims based on facts, evidence, and reason—but we're also inclined to read factual arguments within the context of our feelings and the ethos of people making the appeals.

Thinking Critically about Hard Evidence

Aristotle helps us out in classifying arguments by distinguishing two kinds:

Artistic Proofs	Arguments the writer/speaker creates	Constructed arguments	Appeals to reason; common sense
Inartistic Proofs	Arguments the writer/speaker is given	Hard evidence	Facts, statistics, testimonies, witnesses, contracts, documents

We can see these different kinds of logical appeals at work in a single paragraph from President Barack Obama's 2014 State of the Union address. Typically in such speeches—nationally televised and closely reviewed—the president assesses the current condition of the United States and then lays out an agenda for the coming years, a laundry list of commitments and goals. One of those items mentioned about halfway through the 2014 address focuses on the admirable objective of improving the conditions of working women:

> Today, women make up about half our workforce. But they still make 77 cents for every dollar a man earns. That is wrong, and in 2014, it's an embarrassment. A woman deserves equal pay for equal work. She deserves to have a baby without sacrificing her job. A mother deserves a day off to care for a sick child or sick parent without running into hardship—and you know what, a father does, too. It's time to do away with workplace policies that belong in a *Mad Men* episode. This year, let's all come together—Congress, the White House, and businesses from Wall Street to Main Street—to give every woman the opportunity she deserves. Because I firmly believe when women succeed, America succeeds.
>
> —Barack Obama, State of the Union address

As you see, Obama opens the paragraph with an important "inartistic" proof, that ratio of just 77 cents to a dollar representing what women earn in the United States compared to men. Beginning with that fact, he then offers a series of reasonable "artistic" appeals phrased as applause lines: *that is wrong; a woman deserves equal pay; a mother deserves a day off . . . a father does, too.*" Obama then concludes the paragraph by stating the core principle behind all these claims, what we'll later describe as the *warrant* in an argument (see Chapter 14): *when women succeed, America succeeds.*

Note, then, the importance of that single number the president puts forward. It is evidence that, despite decades of political commitment to pay equity and even federal laws banning gender discrimination in employment and compensation, much work remains to be done. Who can be satisfied with the status quo in the face of that damning number? But where did that statistic come from, and *what if it is wrong*?

Now, no one expects footnotes and documentation in a presidential address. The ethos of the office itself makes the public (at least some portion of it) willing to accept a president's factual claims, if only because his remarks have surely been vetted by legions of staffers. Yet some statistics and claims assume a life of their own, repeated so often that most people— even presidents and their speechwriters—assume that they are true. Add the problem of "confirmation bias," the tendency of most people to believe evidence that confirms their views of the world, and you have numbers that will not die.

We live, however, in an age of critics and fact-checkers. Writing for the *Daily Beast*, Christina Hoff Sommers, a former professor of philosophy and no fan of contemporary feminism, complains that the president is perpetuating an error: "What is wrong and embarrassing is the President of the United States reciting a massively discredited factoid." And in case you won't believe Sommers (and most feminists and those in the president's camp wouldn't), she directs skeptics to a more objective source, the *Washington Post*, which routinely fact-checks the State of the Union and other major addresses.

Like Sommers, that paper does raise questions about the 77/100 earnings ratio, and its detailed analysis of that number suggests just how complicated evidential claims can be. Here's a shortened version of the *Post*'s statement, which you'll note cites several government sources:

> There is clearly a wage gap, but differences in the life choices of men and women—such as women tending to leave the workforce when they have children—make it difficult to make simple comparisons.

> Obama is using a figure (annual wages, from the Census Bureau) that makes the disparity appear the greatest. The Bureau of Labor Statistics, for instance, shows that the gap is 19 cents when looking at weekly wages. The gap is even smaller when you look at hourly

wages—it is 14 cents—but then not every wage earner is paid on an hourly basis, so that statistic excludes salaried workers. . . .

Factual arguments are often made or enhanced by charts, graphs, and infographics.
Here PayScale, an online salary and wage information site, presents numbers to explain the pay
equity issue: "Yes, men do earn more than women on average, but not that much more when
they work the same job and they have similar experience and abilities."
We reproduce here just a portion of the full infographic.

PayScale, Inc., by permission

Economists at the Federal Reserve Bank of St. Louis surveyed economic literature and concluded that "research suggests that the actual gender wage gap (when female workers are compared with male workers who have similar characteristics) is much lower than the raw wage gap." They cited one survey, prepared for the Labor Department, which concluded that when such differences are accounted for, much of the hourly wage gap dwindled, to about 5 cents on the dollar.

Is the entire paragraph of the president's address discredited because his hard evidence seems overstated or oversimplified? Not if we accept the *constructed* arguments he makes on the general principle of fairness for offering women—and men—more support as laborers in the job force. But he might have been more convincing at this point in a very lengthy speech if someone in the White House had taken a moment to check the government's own numbers, as the *Washington Post* did. This ongoing controversy over wage equity does, however, illustrate how closely logical arguments—whether artistic or inartistic—will be read and criticized. And so the connections between them matter.

RESPOND

Discuss whether the following statements are examples of hard evidence or constructed arguments. Not all cases are clear-cut.

1. Drunk drivers are involved in more than 50 percent of traffic deaths.

2. DNA tests of skin found under the victim's fingernails suggest that the defendant was responsible for the assault.

3. A psychologist testified that teenage violence could not be blamed on video games.

4. An apple a day keeps the doctor away.

5. "The only thing we have to fear is fear itself."

6. Air bags ought to be removed from vehicles because they can kill young children and small-framed adults.

Facts

Gathering factual information and transmitting it faithfully practically define what we mean by professional journalism and scholarship. We'll even listen to people we don't agree with if their evidence is really good. Below, a reviewer for the conservative *National Review* praises William Julius Wilson, a liberal sociologist, because of how well he presents his case:

> In his eagerly awaited new book, Wilson argues that ghetto blacks are worse off than ever, victimized by a near-total loss of low-skill jobs in and around inner-city neighborhoods. In support of this thesis, he *musters mountains of data, plus excerpts from some of the thousands of surveys and face-to-face interviews that he and his research team conducted among inner-city Chicagoans.* It is a book that deserves a wide audience among thinking conservatives.
>
> —John J. DiIulio Jr., "When Decency Disappears" (emphasis added)

When your facts are compelling, they may stand on their own in a low-stakes argument, supported by little more than saying where they come from. Consider the power of phrases such as "reported by the *Wall Street*

Journal" or "according to FactCheck.org." Such sources gain credibility if they have reported facts accurately and reliably over time. Using such credible sources in an argument can also reflect positively on you.

In scholarly arguments, which have higher expectations for accuracy, what counts is drawing sober conclusions from the evidence turned up through detailed research or empirical studies. The language of such material may seem dryly factual to you, even when the content is inherently interesting. But presenting new knowledge dispassionately is (ideally at least) the whole point of scholarly writing, marking a contrast between it and the kind of intellectual warfare that occurs in many media forums, especially news programs and blogs. Here for example is a portion of a lengthy opening paragraph in the "Discussion and Conclusions" section of a scholarly paper arguing that people who spend a great deal of time on Facebook often frame their lives by what they observe there:

> The results of this research support the argument that using Facebook affects people's perceptions of others. For those that have used Facebook longer, it is easier to remember positive messages and happy pictures posted on Facebook; these readily available examples give users an impression that others are happier. As expected in the first hypothesis, the results show that the longer people have used Facebook, the stronger was their belief that others were happier than themselves, and the less they agreed that life is fair. Furthermore, as predicted in the second hypothesis, this research found that the more "friends" people included on their Facebook whom they did not know personally, the stronger they believed that others had better lives than themselves. In other words, looking at happy pictures of others on Facebook gives people an impression that others are "always" happy and having good lives, as evident from these pictures of happy moments. In contrast to their own experiences of life events, which are not always positive, people are very likely to conclude that others have better lives than themselves and that life is not fair.
>
> —Hui-Tzu Grace Chou, PhD, and Nicholas Edge, BS,
> "'They Are Happier and Having Better Lives Than I Am':
> The Impact of Using Facebook on Perceptions of Others' Lives"

There are no fireworks in this conclusion, no slanted or hot language, no unfair or selective reporting of data, just a faithful attention to the facts and behaviors uncovered by the study. But one can easily imagine these facts being subsequently used to support overdramatized claims about the dangers of social networks. That's often what happens to scholarly studies when they are read and interpreted in the popular media.

Of course, arguing with facts can involve challenging even the most reputable sources if they lead to unfair or selective reporting or if the stories are presented or "framed" unfairly.

In an ideal world, good information—no matter where it comes from—would always drive out bad. But you already know that we don't live in an ideal world, so sometimes bad information gets repeated in an echo chamber that amplifies the errors.

Statistics

You've probably heard the old saying "There are three kinds of lies: lies, damned lies, and statistics," and, to be sure, it is possible to lie with numbers, even those that are accurate, because numbers rarely speak for themselves. They need to be interpreted by writers—and writers almost always have agendas that shape the interpretations.

Of course, just because they are often misused doesn't mean that statistics are meaningless, but it does suggest that you need to use them carefully and to remember that your careful reading of numbers is essential. Consider the attention-grabbing map on the next page that went viral in June 2014. Created by Mark Gongloff of the *Huffington Post* in the wake of a school shooting in Oregon, it plotted the location of all seventy-four school shootings that had occurred in the United States since the Sandy Hook tragedy in December 2012, when twenty elementary school children and six adults were gunned down by a rifle-wielding killer. For the graphic, Gongloff drew on a list assembled by the group Everytown for Gun Safety, an organization formed by former New York City mayor and billionaire Michael Bloomberg to counter the influence of the National Rifle Association (NRA). Both the map and Everytown's sobering list of shootings received wide attention in the media, given the startling number of incidents it recorded.

It didn't take long before questions were raised about their accuracy. Were American elementary and secondary school children under such frequent assault as the map based on Everytown's list suggested? Well, yes and no. Guns were going off on and around school campuses, but the firearms weren't always aimed at children. The *Washington Post*, CNN, and other news outlets soon found themselves pulling back on their initial reporting, offering a more nuanced view of the controversial number. To do that, the *Washington Post* began by posing an important question:

Everytown for Gun Safety Action

What constitutes a school shooting?

That five-word question has no simple answer, a fact underscored by the backlash to an advocacy group's recent list of school shootings. The list, maintained by Everytown, a group that backs policies to limit gun violence, was updated last week to reflect what it identified as the 74 school shootings since the massacre in Newtown, Conn., a massacre that sparked a national debate over gun control.

Multiple news outlets, including this one, reported on Everytown's data, prompting a backlash over the broad methodology used. As we wrote in our original post, the group considered any instance of a firearm discharging on school property as a shooting—thus casting a broad net that includes homicides, suicides, accidental discharges and, in a handful of cases, shootings that had no relation to the schools themselves and occurred with no students apparently present.

—Niraj Chokshi, "Fight over School Shooting List Underscores Difficulty in Quantifying Gun Violence"

CNN followed the same path, re-evaluating its original reporting in light of criticism from groups not on the same page as Everytown for Gun Safety:

Without a doubt, that number is startling.

So . . . CNN took a closer look at the list, delving into the circumstances of each incident Everytown included. . . .

CNN determined that 15 of the incidents Everytown included were situations similar to the violence in Newtown or Oregon—a minor or adult actively shooting inside or near a school. That works out to about one such shooting every five weeks, a startling figure in its own right.

Some of the other incidents on Everytown's list included personal arguments, accidents and alleged gang activities and drug deals.

> —Ashley Fantz, Lindsey Knight, and Kevin Wang,
> "A Closer Look: How Many Newtown-like
> School Shootings since Sandy Hook?"

Other news organizations came up with their own revised numbers, but clearly the interpretation of a number can be as important as the statistic itself. And what were Mark Gongloff's Twitter reactions to these reassessments? They made an argument as well:

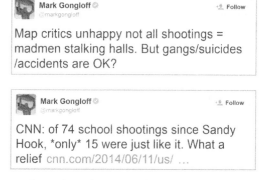

One lesson, surely, is that when you rely on statistics in your arguments, make sure you understand where they come from, what they mean, and what their limitations might be. Check and double-check them or get help in doing so: you don't want to be accused of using fictitious data based on questionable assumptions.

RESPOND

Statistical evidence becomes useful only when interpreted fairly and reasonably. Go to the *USA Today* Web site and look for the daily graph,

chart, or table called the "USA Today Snapshot." Pick a snapshot, and use the information in it to support three different claims, at least two of which make very different points. Share your claims with classmates. (The point is not to learn to use data dishonestly but to see firsthand how the same statistics can serve a variety of arguments.)

Surveys and Polls

When they verify the popularity of an idea or a proposal, surveys and polls provide strong persuasive appeals because they come as close to expressing the will of the people as anything short of an election—the most decisive poll of all. However, surveys and polls can do much more than help politicians make decisions. They can be important elements in scientific research, documenting the complexities of human behavior. They can also provide persuasive reasons for action or intervention. When surveys show, for example, that most American sixth-graders can't locate France or Wyoming on a map—not to mention Ukraine or Afghanistan—that's an appeal for better instruction in geography. It always makes sense, however, to question poll numbers, especially when they support your own point of view. Ask who commissioned the poll, who is publishing its outcome, who was surveyed (and in what proportions), and what stakes these parties might have in its outcome.

Are we being too suspicious? No. In fact, this sort of scrutiny is exactly what you might anticipate from your readers whenever you use (or create) surveys to explore an issue. You should be confident that enough subjects have been surveyed to be accurate, that the people chosen for the study were representative of the selected population as a whole, and that they were chosen randomly—not selected because of what they are likely to say. In a splendid article on how women can make research-based choices during their pregnancy, economist Emily Oster explores, for example, whether an expectant mother might in fact be able to drink responsibly. She researches not only the results of the data, but also who was surveyed, and how their participation might have influenced the results:

> It is possible to unearth research that points to light drinking as a problem, but this work is deeply flawed. One frequently cited study from the journal *Pediatrics*, published in 2001, interviewed women about their drinking while they were pregnant and then contacted them for a child behavior assessment when their children were about 6. The researchers found some evidence that lighter drinking

had an impact on behavior and concluded that even one drink a day could cause behavior problems.

So what's wrong with this finding?

In the study, 18% of the women who didn't drink at all and 45% of the women who had one drink a day reported using cocaine during pregnancy. Presumably your first thought is, really? Cocaine? Perhaps the problem is that cocaine, not the occasional glass of Chardonnay, makes your child more likely to have behavior problems.

—Emily Oster, "Take Back Your Pregnancy"

Clearly, polls, surveys, and studies need to be examined critically. You can't take even academic research at face value until you have explored its details.

The meaning of polls and surveys is also affected by the way that questions are posed. In the recent past, research revealed, for example, that polling about same-sex unions got differing responses according to how questions are worded. When people were asked whether gay and lesbian couples should be eligible for the same inheritance and partner health benefits that heterosexual couples receive, a majority of those polled said yes—unless the word *marriage* appeared in the question; then the responses are primarily negative. If anything, the differences here reveal how conflicted people may have been about the issue and how quickly opinions might shift—as they did. Remember, then, to be very careful in reviewing the wording of survey or poll questions.

Finally, always keep in mind that the date of a poll may strongly affect the results—and their usefulness in an argument. In 2010, for example, nearly 50 percent of California voters supported building more nuclear power plants. Less than a year later, that percentage had dropped to 37 percent after the meltdown of Japanese nuclear power plants in the wake of the March 2011 earthquake and tsunami. On public and political issues, you need to be sure that you are using timely information.

RESPOND

Choose an important issue and design a series of questions to evoke a range of responses in a poll. Try to design a question that would make people strongly inclined to agree, another question that would lead them to oppose the same proposition, and a third that tries to be more neutral. Then try out your questions on your classmates.

Testimonies and Narratives

Writers can support arguments by presenting human experiences in the form of narrative or testimony—particularly if those experiences are their own. In courts, judges and juries often take into consideration detailed descriptions and narratives of exactly what occurred. Look at this reporter's account of a court case in which a panel of judges decided, based on the testimony presented, that a man had been sexually harassed by another man. The narrative, in this case, supplies the evidence:

> The Seventh Circuit, in a 1997 case known as *Doe v. City of Belleville*, drew a sweeping conclusion allowing for same-sex harassment cases of many kinds. . . . This case, for example, centered on teenage twin brothers working a summer job cutting grass in the city cemetery of Belleville, Ill. One boy wore an earring, which caused him no end of grief that particular summer—including a lot of menacing talk among his coworkers about sexually assaulting him in the woods and sending him "back to San Francisco." One of his harassers, identified in court documents as a large former marine, culminated a verbal campaign by backing the earring-wearer against a wall and grabbing him by the testicles to see "if he was a girl or a guy." The teenager had been "singled out for this abuse," the court ruled, "because the way in which he projected the sexual aspect of his personality"—meaning his gender—"did not conform to his coworkers' view of appropriate masculine behavior."
>
> —Margaret Talbot, "Men Behaving Badly"

Personal perspectives can support a claim convincingly and logically, especially if a writer has earned the trust of readers. In arguing that Tea Party supporters of a government shutdown in 2011 had no business being offended when some opponents described them as "terrorists," Froma Harrop, one of the writers who used the term, argued logically and from experience why the characterization was appropriate:

> [T]he hurt the tea party writers most complained of was to their feelings. I had engaged in name-calling, they kept saying. One professing to want more civility in our national conversation, as I do, should not be flinging around the *terrorist* word.
>
> May I presume to disagree? Civility is a subjective concept, to be sure, but hurting people's feelings in the course of making solid ar-

guments is fair and square. The decline in the quality of our public discourse results not so much from an excess of spleen, but a deficit of well-constructed arguments. Few things upset partisans more than when the other side makes a case that bats home.

"Most of us know that effectively scoring on a point of argument opens us to the accusation of mean-spiritedness," writes Frank Partsch, who leads the National Conference of Editorial Writers' Civility Project. "It comes with the territory, and a commitment to civility should not suggest that punches will be pulled in order to avoid such accusations."

—Froma Harrop, "Hurt Feelings Can
Be a Consequence of Strong Arguments"

This narrative introduction gives a rationale for supporting the claim Harrop is making: we can expect consequences when we argue ineffectively. (For more on establishing credibility with readers, see Chapter 10.)

RESPOND

Bring to class a full review of a recent film that you either enjoyed or did not enjoy. Using testimony from that review, write a brief argument to your classmates explaining why they should see that movie (or why they should avoid it), being sure to use evidence from the review fairly and reasonably. Then exchange arguments with a classmate, and decide whether the evidence in your peer's argument helps to change your opinion about the movie. What's convincing about the evidence? If it doesn't convince you, why doesn't it?

Using Reason and Common Sense

If you don't have "hard facts," you can turn to those arguments Aristotle describes as "constructed" from reason and common sense. The formal study of such reasoning is called *logic*, and you probably recognize a famous example of deductive reasoning, called a **syllogism**:

All human beings are mortal.

Socrates is a human being.

Therefore, Socrates is mortal.

Logic: another thing that penguins aren't very good at.

© Randy Glasbergen/glasbergen.com

In valid syllogisms, the conclusion follows logically—and technically—
from the premises that lead up to it. Many have criticized syllogistic reasoning for being limited, and others have poked fun at it, as in the cartoon above.

But we routinely see something like syllogistic reasoning operating in public arguments, particularly when writers take the time to explain key principles. Consider the step-by-step reasoning Michael Gerson uses to explain
why exactly it was wrong for the Internal Revenue Service in 2010–2011
to target specific political groups, making it more difficult for them to
organize politically:

> Why does this matter deserve heightened scrutiny from the rest of
> us? Because crimes against democracy are particularly insidious.
> Representative government involves a type of trade. As citizens, we
> cede power to public officials for important purposes that require
> centralized power: defending the country, imposing order, collect-
> ing taxes to promote the common good. In exchange, we expect
> public institutions to be evenhanded and disinterested. When the
> stewards of power—biased judges or corrupt policemen or politi-
> cally motivated IRS officials—act unfairly, it undermines trust in
> the whole system.
>
> —Michael Gerson, "An Arrogant and Lawless IRS"

Gerson's criticism of the IRS actions might be mapped out by the following sequence of statements.

> Crimes against democracy undermine trust in the system.

> Treating taxpayers differently because of their political beliefs is a crime against democracy.

> Therefore, IRS actions that target political groups undermine the American system.

Few writers, of course, think about formal deductive reasoning when they support their claims. Even Aristotle recognized that most people argue perfectly well using informal logic. To do so, they rely mostly on habits of mind and assumptions that they share with their readers or listeners—as Gerson essentially does in his paragraph.

In Chapter 14, we describe a system of informal logic that you may find useful in shaping credible appeals to reason—Toulmin argument. Here, we briefly examine some ways that people use informal logic in their everyday lives. Once again, we begin with Aristotle, who used the term **enthymeme** to describe an ordinary kind of sentence that includes both a claim and a reason but depends on the audience's agreement with an assumption that is left implicit rather than spelled out. Enthymemes can be very persuasive when most people agree with the assumptions they rest on. The following sentences are all enthymemes:

> We'd better cancel the picnic because it's going to rain.

> Flat taxes are fair because they treat everyone the same.

> I'll buy a PC instead of a Mac because it's cheaper.

Sometimes enthymemes seem so obvious that readers don't realize that they're drawing inferences when they agree with them. Consider the first example:

> We'd better cancel the picnic because it's going to rain.

Let's expand the enthymeme a bit to say more of what the speaker may mean:

> We'd better cancel the picnic this afternoon because the weather bureau is predicting a 70 percent chance of rain for the remainder of the day.

Embedded in this brief argument are all sorts of assumptions and fragments of cultural information that are left implicit but that help to make it persuasive:

> Picnics are ordinarily held outdoors.

> When the weather is bad, it's best to cancel picnics.

> Rain is bad weather for picnics.

> A 70 percent chance of rain means that rain is more likely to occur than not.

> When rain is more likely to occur than not, it makes sense to cancel picnics.

For most people, the original statement carries all this information on its own; the enthymeme is a compressed argument, based on what audiences know and will accept.

CULTURAL CONTEXTS FOR ARGUMENT

Logos

In the United States, student writers are expected to draw on "hard facts" and evidence as often as possible in supporting their claims: while ethical and emotional appeals are important, logical appeals tend to hold sway in academic writing. So statistics and facts speak volumes, as does reasoning based on time-honored values such as fairness and equity. In writing to global audiences, you need to remember that not all cultures value the same kinds of appeals. If you want to write to audiences across cultures, you need to know about the norms and values in those cultures. Chinese culture, for example, values authority and often indirect allusion over "facts" alone. Some African cultures value cooperation and community over individualism, and still other cultures value religious texts as providing compelling evidence. So think carefully about what you consider strong evidence, and pay attention to what counts as evidence to others. You can begin by asking yourself questions like:

- What evidence is most valued by your audience: Facts? Concrete examples? Firsthand experience? Religious or philosophical texts? Something else?

- Will analogies count as support? How about precedents?

- Will the testimony of experts count? If so, what kinds of experts are valued most?

But sometimes enthymemes aren't self-evident:

> Be wary of environmentalism because it's religion disguised as science.

> iPhones are undermining civil society by making us even more focused on ourselves.

> It's time to make all public toilets unisex because to do otherwise is discriminatory.

In these cases, you'll have to work much harder to defend both the claim and the implicit assumptions that it's based on by drawing out the inferences that seem self-evident in other enthymemes. And you'll likely also have to supply credible evidence; a simple declaration of fact won't suffice.

Providing Logical Structures for Argument

Some arguments depend on particular logical structures to make their points. In the following pages, we identify a few of these logical structures.

Degree

Arguments based on degree are so common that people barely notice them, nor do they pay much attention to how they work because they seem self-evident. Most audiences will readily accept that *more of a good thing* or *less of a bad thing* is good. In her novel *The Fountainhead*, Ayn Rand asks: "If physical slavery is repulsive, how much more repulsive is the concept of servility of the spirit?" Most readers immediately comprehend the point Rand intends to make about slavery of the spirit because they already know that physical slavery is cruel and would reject any forms of slavery that were even crueler on the principle that *more of a bad thing is bad*. Rand still needs to offer evidence that "servility of the spirit" is, in fact, worse than bodily servitude, but she has begun with a logical structure readers can grasp. Here are other arguments that work similarly:

If I can get a ten-year warranty on an inexpensive Kia, shouldn't I get the same or better warranty from a more expensive Lexus?

The health benefits from using stem cells in research will surely outweigh the ethical risks.

Better a conventional war now than a nuclear confrontation later.

Analogies

Analogies, typically complex or extended comparisons, explain one idea or concept by comparing it to something else.

Here, writer and founder of literacy project 826 Valencia, Dave Eggers, uses an analogy in arguing that we do not value teachers as much as we should:

When we don't get the results we want in our military endeavors, we don't blame the soldiers. We don't say, "It's these lazy soldiers and their bloated benefits plans! That's why we haven't done better in

Afghanistan!" No, if the results aren't there, we blame the planners. . . . No one contemplates blaming the men and women fighting every day in the trenches for little pay and scant recognition. And yet in education we do just that. When we don't like the way our students score on international standardized tests, we blame the teachers.

—Dave Eggers and Nínive Calegari, "The High Cost of Low Teacher Salaries"

Precedent

Arguments from **precedent** and arguments of analogy both involve comparisons. Consider an assertion like this one, which uses a comparison as a precedent:

If motorists in most other states can pump their own gas safely, surely the state of Oregon can trust its own drivers to be as capable. It's time for Oregon to permit self-service gas stations.

You could tease out several inferences from this claim to explain its reasonableness: people in Oregon are as capable as people in other states; people with equivalent capabilities can do the same thing; pumping gas is not hard; and so forth. But you don't have to because most readers get the argument simply because of the way it is put together.

Here is an excerpt from an extended argument by blogger Abby Phillip, in which she argues that the Ebola outbreak that began in 2014 may not follow the same pattern as past outbreaks:

An idea long viewed as an unlikely possibility is now becoming increasingly real: Ebola might not go away for a very long time.

It has never happened before in the thirty-eight-year history of the virus. Every other time Ebola has made the unlikely jump from the animal world to the human one, it has been snuffed out within days, weeks or, at most, months.

This time, though, in Guinea, Sierra Leone and Liberia, the Ebola virus is raging like a forest fire, in the words of several public health officials. And some of them are raising the possibility that the outbreak-turned-full-fledged-epidemic could become fundamentally different from any other Ebola outbreak on record, in that it might stick around.

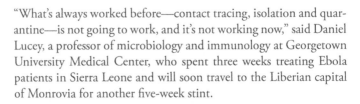

"What's always worked before—contact tracing, isolation and quarantine—is not going to work, and it's not working now," said Daniel Lucey, a professor of microbiology and immunology at Georgetown University Medical Center, who spent three weeks treating Ebola patients in Sierra Leone and will soon travel to the Liberian capital of Monrovia for another five-week stint.

"In my opinion," Lucey added, "a year from now, we won't have one or two cases; we'll have many cases of Ebola."

Unlike past outbreaks, in which Ebola emerged in the sparsely populated countryside of central Africa, this outbreak has become an exponentially spreading urban menace.

—Abby Phillip, "This Ebola Outbreak Could Be Here to Stay"

Unfortunately, the prediction proved to be more accurate than Phillip might have preferred.

You'll encounter additional kinds of logical structures as you create your own arguments. You'll find some of them in Chapter 12, "Fallacies of Argument," and still more in Chapter 14 on Toulmin argument.

12

Fallacies of Argument

Reading and Understanding Arguments

Left to right: Roy Delgado/www.Cartoonstock.com; © Bish/Cagle Cartoons, Inc.;
© Eric Allie/Cagle Cartoons, Inc.

Do these editorial cartoons strike a chord with you? All three are complicated. The first panel pokes fun at slippery slope arguments, which aim to thwart action by predicting dire consequences: chase that Frisbee and you'll soon be pulling milk carts. The second item uses a scare tactic (a potential fallacy of argument) to raise opposition to the educational reform called "Common Core," suggesting ominously that the program's cookie-cutter approach will produce children who all think alike. And the third cartoon points to a fallacy of argument that a prominent politician has perhaps slipped into—the sentimental appeal; it alludes to Hillary Clinton's comment in a 2014 interview with Diane Sawyer that she and husband Bill "came out of the White House not only dead broke but in debt."

Fallacies are argumentative moves flawed by their very nature or structure. Because such tactics can make productive principled argument more difficult, they potentially hurt everyone involved, including the people responsible for them. The worst sorts of fallacies muck up the frank but civil conversations that people should be able to have, regardless of their differences.

Yet it's hard to deny the power in offering audiences a compelling either/or choice or a vulnerable straw man in an argument. For exactly that reason, it's important that you can recognize and point out fallacies in the work of others—and avoid them in your own writing. This chapter aims to help you meet these goals: here we'll introduce you to fallacies of argument classified according to the emotional, ethical, and logical appeals we've discussed earlier (see Chapters 9, 10, and 11).

Fallacies of Emotional Argument

Emotional arguments can be powerful and suitable in many circumstances, and most writers use them frequently. However, writers who pull on their readers' heartstrings or raise their blood pressure too often can violate the good faith on which legitimate argument depends.

Scare Tactics

Politicians, advertisers, and public figures sometimes peddle their ideas by frightening people and exaggerating possible dangers well beyond their statistical likelihood. Such ploys work because it's easier to imagine something terrible happening than to appreciate its rarity.

Scare tactics can also be used to stampede legitimate fears into panic or prejudice. Laborers who genuinely worry about losing their jobs can be persuaded to fear immigrants who might work for less money. Seniors living on fixed incomes can be convinced that minor changes to entitlement programs represent dire threats to their well-being. Such tactics have the effect of closing off thinking because people who are scared often act irrationally. Even well-intended fear campaigns—like those directed against smoking, unprotected sex, or the use of illegal drugs—can misfire if their warnings prove too shrill. People just stop listening.

Either/Or Choices

Either/or choices can be well-intentioned strategies to get something accomplished. Parents use them all the time ("Eat your broccoli, or you won't get dessert"). But they become fallacious arguments when they reduce a complicated issue to excessively simple terms or when they're designed to obscure legitimate alternatives. Here, for example, is Riyad Mansour, the Palestinian representative to the United Nations, offering the nation of Israel just such a choice in an interview with Charlie Rose in January 2014:

> It is up to them [the Israelis] to decide what kind of a state they want to be. Do they want to be a democratic state where Israel will be the state for all of its citizens? Or do they want to be a state for the Jewish people, therefore excluding 1.6 million Palestinian Arabs who are Israelis from their society? That debate is not our debate. That debate is their debate.

But Joel B. Pollak, writing for Breitbart News Network, describes Mansour's claim as a "false choice" since Israel already is a Jewish state that nonetheless allows Muslims to be full citizens. The either/or argument Mansour presents, according to Pollack, does not describe the realities of this complex political situation.

A false choice?

© Adam Zyglis/Cagle Cartoons, Inc.

Slippery Slope

The **slippery slope** fallacy portrays today's tiny misstep as tomorrow's slide into disaster. Some arguments that aim at preventing dire consequences do not take the slippery slope approach (for example, the parent who corrects a child for misbehavior now is acting sensibly to prevent more serious problems as the child grows older). A slippery slope argument becomes wrong-headed when a writer exaggerates the likely consequences of an action, usually to frighten readers. As such, slippery slope arguments are also scare tactics. In recent years, the issue of gun ownership in America has evoked many slippery slope arguments. Here's one perspective on the tactic:

> The leadership of the NRA is exceptionally fond of the Slippery Slope argument. "Universal background checks will inevitably be followed by a national registry of gun-owners which will inevitably be followed by confiscation of all their guns." Or, "A ban on assault-style weapons and thirty+ round magazines will inevitably

be followed by a ban on hand guns with ten-round magazines, that will inevitably be followed by bans on all guns, including antique dueling pistols inherited from our Founding Fathers."

Problem number one with this slide down the fearsome slope is how much weaponry has changed since the days of militias with muskets. Even the NRA agrees that lines have to be drawn somewhere. They do not favor legalization of civilian use of rocket-propelled grenades, bazookas or stinger missiles. If there is a slippery slope we are starting approximately half-way down.

—Michael Wolkowitz, "Slippery Slopes, Imagined and Real"

Social and political ideas and proposals do have consequences, but they aren't always as dire as writers fond of slippery slope tactics would have you believe.

Overly Sentimental Appeals

Overly **sentimental appeals** use tender emotions excessively to distract readers from facts. Often, such appeals are highly personal and individual and focus attention on heartwarming or heartrending situations that make readers feel guilty if they challenge an idea, a policy, or a proposal. Emotions become an impediment to civil discourse when they keep people from thinking clearly.

This image, taken from a gun control protest, is designed to elicit sympathy by causing the viewer to think about the dangers guns pose to innocent children and, thus, support the cause.

Tim Boyle/Getty Images

Such sentimental appeals are a major vehicle of television news, where tugging at viewers' heartstrings can mean high ratings. For example, when a camera documents the day-to-day sacrifices of a single parent trying to meet mortgage payments and keep her kids in college, the woman's on-screen struggles can seem to represent the plight of an entire class of people threatened by callous bankers and college administrators. But while such human interest stories stir genuine emotions, they seldom give a complete picture of complex social or economic issues.

Bandwagon Appeals

Bandwagon appeals urge people to follow the same path everyone else is taking. Such arguments can be relatively benign and seem harmless. But they do push people to take the easier path rather than think independently about what choices to make or where to go.

Many American parents seem to have an innate ability to refute bandwagon appeals. When their kids whine, *Everyone else is going camping without chaperones,* the parents reply, *And if everyone else jumps off a cliff (or a railroad bridge or the Empire State Building), you will too?* The children groan—and then try a different line of argument.

Some bandwagon appeals work better than others.

Unfortunately, not all bandwagon approaches are so transparent. In recent decades, bandwagon issues have included a war on drugs, the nuclear freeze movement, campaigns against drunk driving, campaigns for immigration reform, bailouts for banks and businesses, and *many* fads in education from high-stakes testing to MOOCs. All these issues are too complex to permit the suspension of judgment that bandwagon tactics require.

Fallacies of Ethical Argument

Because readers give their closest attention to authors they respect or trust, writers usually want to present themselves as honest, well-informed, likable, or sympathetic. But not all the devices that writers use to gain the attention and confidence of readers are admirable. (For more on appeals based on character, see Chapter 10.)

Appeals to False Authority

Many academic research papers find and reflect on the work of reputable authorities and introduce these authorities through direct quotations or citations as credible evidence. (For more on assessing the reliability of sources, see Chapter 22.) **False authority**, however, occurs when writers offer themselves or other authorities as sufficient warrant for believing a claim:

Claim	X is true because I say so.
Warrant	What I say must be true.
Claim	X is true because Y says so.
Warrant	What Y says must be true.

Though they are seldom stated so baldly, claims of authority drive many political campaigns. American pundits and politicians are fond of citing the U.S. Constitution and its Bill of Rights (Canadians have their Charter of Rights and Freedoms) as ultimate authorities, a reasonable practice when the documents are interpreted respectfully. However, the rights claimed sometimes aren't in the texts themselves or don't mean what the speakers think they do. And most constitutional matters are debatable—as volumes of court records prove. Likewise, religious believers often base arguments on books or traditions that wield great authority in a particular religious community. But the power of such texts is usually limited to that group and less capable of persuading others solely on the grounds of authority.

In short, you should pay serious attention to claims supported by respected authorities, such as the Centers for Disease Control, the National Science Foundation, or the *Globe and Mail*. But don't accept information simply because it is put forth by such offices and agencies. To quote a Russian proverb made famous by Ronald Reagan, "Trust, but verify."

Dogmatism

A writer who asserts or assumes that a particular position is the *only one* that is conceivably acceptable is expressing **dogmatism**, a fallacy of character that undermines the trust that must exist between those who make and listen to arguments. When people or organizations write dogmatically, they imply that no arguments are necessary: the truth is self-evident and needs no support. Here is an extreme example of such an appeal, quoted in an *Atlantic* story by Tracy Brown Hamilton and describing an anti-smoking appeal made by the Third Reich:

> "Brother national socialist, do you know that your Fuhrer is against smoking and thinks that every German is responsible to the whole people for all his deeds and omissions, and does not have the right to damage his body with drugs?"
>
> —From Tracy Brown Hamilton, "The Nazis' Forgotten Anti-Smoking Campaign"

Subjects or ideas that can be defended with facts, testimony, and good reasons ought not to be off the table in a free society. In general, whenever someone suggests that even raising an issue for debate is totally unacceptable—whether on the grounds that it's racist, sexist, unpatriotic, blasphemous, insensitive, or offensive in some other way—you should be suspicious.

Ad Hominem *Arguments*

Ad hominem (Latin for "to the man") **arguments** attack the character of a person rather than the claims he or she makes: when you destroy the credibility of your opponents, you either destroy their ability to present reasonable appeals or distract from the successful arguments they may be offering. Such attacks, of course, aren't aimed at men only, as columnist Jamie Stiehm proved when she criticized Supreme Court Justice Sonia Sotomayor for delaying an Obamacare mandate objected to by the Little Sisters of the Poor, a Catholic religious order. Stiehm directly targets Sotomayor's religious beliefs:

> Et tu, Justice Sonia Sotomayor? Really, we can't trust you on women's health and human rights? The lady from the Bronx just dropped the ball on American women and girls as surely as she did the sparkling

ball at midnight on New Year's Eve in Times Square. Or maybe she's just a good Catholic girl.

—Jamie Stiehm, "The Catholic Supreme Court's War on Women"

Stiehm then widens her *ad hominem* assault to include Catholics in general:

> Sotomayor's blow brings us to confront an uncomfortable reality. More than WASPs, Methodists, Jews, Quakers or Baptists, Catholics often try to impose their beliefs on you, me, public discourse and institutions. Especially if "you" are female.

Arguably, *ad hominem* tactics like this turn arguments into two-sided affairs with good guys and bad guys (or gals), and that's unfortunate, since character often really *does* matter in argument. People expect the proponent of peace to be civil, a secretary of the treasury to pay his or her taxes, and the champion of family values to be a faithful spouse. But it's fallacious to attack an idea by uncovering the foibles of its advocates or by attacking their motives, backgrounds, or unchangeable traits.

Stacking the Deck

Just as gamblers try to stack the deck by arranging cards so they are sure to win, writers **stack the deck** when they show only one side of the story— the one in their favor. In a Facebook forum on the documentary film *Super Size Me* (which followed a 32-year-old man who ate three meals a day at McDonald's for thirty days with drastic health consequences), one student points out an example of stacking the deck:

> One of the fallacies was stacking the deck. Spurlock stated many facts and gave plenty of evidence of what can happen if you eat fast food in abundance. Weight gain, decline in health, habit forming, and a toll on your daily life. But he failed to show what could happen if you ate the fast food and participated in daily exercise and took vitamins. The fallacy is that he does not show us both sides of what can happen. Possibly you could eat McDonald's for three meals a day for thirty days and if you engaged in daily exercise and took vitamins maybe your health would be just fine. But we were not ever shown that side of the experiment.

> —Heather Tew Alleman, on a Facebook forum

In the same way, reviewers have been critical of documentaries by Michael Moore and Dinesh D'Souza that resolutely show only one side of a story or prove highly selective in their coverage. When you stack the deck, you take a big chance that your readers will react like Alleman and decide not to trust you: that's one reason it's so important to show that you have considered alternatives in making any argument.

Fallacies of Logical Argument

You'll encounter a problem in any argument when the claims, warrants, or proofs in it are invalid, insufficient, or disconnected. In theory, such problems seem easy enough to spot, but in practice, they can be camouflaged by a skillful use of words or images. Indeed, logical fallacies pose a challenge to civil argument because they often seem reasonable and natural, especially when they appeal to people's self-interests.

Hasty Generalization

A **hasty generalization** is an inference drawn from insufficient evidence: because *my* Fiat broke down, then *all* Fiats must be junk. It also forms the basis for most stereotypes about people or institutions: because *a few* people in a large group are observed to act in a certain way, *all* members of that group are inferred to behave similarly. The resulting conclusions are usually sweeping claims of little merit: *women are bad drivers*; *men are slobs*; *English teachers are nitpicky*; *computer jocks are . . .* , and on and on.

To draw valid inferences, you must always have sufficient evidence (see Chapter 21) and you must qualify your claims appropriately. After all, people do need generalizations to make reasonable decisions in life. Such claims can be offered legitimately if placed in context and tagged with sensible qualifiers—*some, a few, many, most, occasionally, rarely, possibly, in some cases, under certain circumstances, in my limited experience*.

Faulty Causality

In Latin, **faulty causality** is known as *post hoc, ergo propter hoc*, which translates as "after this, therefore because of this"—the faulty assumption that because one event or action follows another, the first causes the second. Consider a lawsuit commented on in the *Wall Street Journal* in which a writer sued Coors (unsuccessfully), claiming that drinking copious amounts of the company's beer had kept him from writing a novel.

Some actions do produce reactions. Step on the brake pedal in your car, and you move hydraulic fluid that pushes calipers against disks to create friction that stops the vehicle. In other cases, however, a supposed connection between cause and effect turns out to be completely wrong. For example, doctors now believe that when an elderly person falls and breaks a hip or leg, the injury usually caused the fall rather than the other way around.

That's why overly simple causal claims should always be subject to scrutiny. In summer 2008, writer Nicholas Carr posed a simple causal question in a cover story for the *Atlantic*: "Is Google Making Us Stupid?" Carr essentially answered yes, arguing that "as we come to rely on computers to mediate our understanding of the world, it is our own intelligence that flattens" and that the more one is online the less he or she is able to concentrate or read deeply.

But others, like Jamais Cascio (senior fellow at the Institute for Ethics and Emerging Technologies), soon challenged that causal connection: rather than making us stupid, Cascio argues, Internet tools like Google will lead to the development of "'fluid intelligence'—the ability to find meaning in confusion and to solve new problems, independent of acquired knowledge." The final word on this contentious causal relationship—the effects on the human brain caused by new technology—has yet to be written, and will probably be available only after decades of complicated research.

Begging the Question

Most teachers have heard some version of the following argument: *You can't give me a C in this course; I'm an A student.* A member of Congress accused of taking kickbacks can make much the same argument: *I can't be guilty of accepting such bribes; I'm an honest person.* In both cases, the claim is made on grounds that can't be accepted as true because those grounds themselves are in question. How can the accused bribe-taker defend herself on grounds of honesty when that honesty is in doubt? Looking at the arguments in Toulmin terms helps to see the fallacy:

Claim	You can't give me a C in this course . . .
Reason	. . . because I'm an A student.
Warrant	An A student is someone who can't receive Cs.

Claim	Representative X can't be guilty of accepting bribes . . .
Reason	. . . because she's an honest person.
Warrant	An honest person cannot be guilty of accepting bribes.

With the warrants stated, you can see why **begging the question**—assuming as true the very claim that's disputed—is a form of circular argument that goes nowhere. (For more on Toulmin argument, see Chapter 14.)

Equivocation

Equivocations—half truths or arguments that give lies an honest appearance—are usually based on tricks of language. Consider the plagiarist who copies a paper word for word from a source and then declares that "I wrote the entire paper myself"—meaning that she physically copied the piece on her own. But the plagiarist is using *wrote* equivocally and knows that most people understand the word to mean composing and not merely copying words.

Parsing words carefully can sometimes look like equivocation or be the thing itself. For example, early in 2014 Internal Revenue Service Commissioner John Koskinen promised to turn over to a committee of the House of Representatives all the relevant emails in a scandal involving the agency. Subsequently, the agency revealed that some of those requested emails had been destroyed by the failure of a computer's hard drive. But Koskinen defended his earlier promise by telling the chair of the committee, "I never said I would provide you emails we didn't have." A simple statement of fact or a slick equivocation?

Non Sequitur

A **non sequitur** is an argument whose claims, reasons, or warrants don't connect logically. You've probably detected a non sequitur when you react to an argument with a puzzled, "Wait, that doesn't follow." Children are adept at framing non sequiturs like this one: *You don't love me or you'd buy*

me a new bicycle! It doesn't take a parental genius to realize that love has little connection with buying children toys.

Non sequiturs often occur when writers omit steps in an otherwise logical chain of reasoning. For example, it might be a non sequitur to argue that since postsecondary education now costs so much, it's time to move colleges and university instruction online. Such a suggestion *may* have merit, but a leap from brick-and-mortar schools to virtual ones is extreme. Numerous issues and questions must be addressed step-by-step before the proposal can be taken seriously.

Politicians sometimes resort to non sequiturs to evade thorny issues or questions. Here for example is presidential candidate Mitt Romney in a 2011 CNBC Republican primary debate turning moderator John Harwood's question about changing political positions into one about demonstrating personal integrity:

> *Harwood*: . . . Your opponents have said you switched positions on many issues. . . . What can you say to Republicans to persuade them that the things you say in the campaign are rooted in something deeper than the fact that you are running for office?

> *Romney*: John, I think people know me pretty well. . . . I think people understand that I'm a man of steadiness and constancy. I don't think you are going to find somebody who has more of those attributes than I do. I have been married to the same woman for . . . 42 years. . . . I have been in the same church my entire life.

Conservative writer Matt K. Lewis took Romney to task for this move, pointing out that a steady personal life is no guarantor of a consistent political philosophy:

> This, of course, is not to say that values and character do not matter—they *do*—but it is to say that Romney's answer was a non sequitur. Everyone knows Mitt Romney is a decent, respectable person. The question is whether or not he can be trusted to advance conservatism as president.

Straw Man

Those who resort to the **straw man** fallacy attack arguments that no one is really making or portray opponents' positions as more extreme or far less coherent than they actually are. The speaker or writer thus sets up an argument that is conveniently easy to knock down (like a man of straw), proceeds to do so, and then claims victory over an opponent who may not even exist.

Straw men are especially convenient devices for politicians who want to characterize the positions of their opponents as more extreme than they actually are: consider obvious memes such as "war on women" and "war on Christmas." But straw man arguments are often more subtle. For instance, Steven Novella of Yale University argues that political commentator Charles Krauthammer slips into the fallacy when he misconstrues the meaning of "settled science" in a column on climate change. Novella rebuts Krauthammer's assertion that "There is nothing more anti-scientific than the very idea that science is settled, static, impervious to challenge" by explaining why such a claim is deceptive:

> Calling something an established scientific fact means that it is reasonable to proceed with that fact as a premise, for further research or for policy. It does not mean "static, impervious to challenge." That is the straw man. Both evolution deniers and climate change deniers use this tactic to misinterpret scientific confidence as an anti-scientific resistance to new evidence or arguments. It isn't. It does mean that the burden of proof has shifted to those opposing the theory that is now well-established (because it has already met a significant burden of proof).
>
> —Steven Novella, *NeuroLogica Blog*, February 25, 2014

In other words, Krauthammer's definition of *science* is not one that most scientists use.

Red Herring

This fallacy gets its name from the old British hunting practice of dragging a dried herring across the path of the fox in order to throw the hounds off the trail. A **red herring** fallacy does just that: it changes the subject abruptly or introduces an irrelevant claim or fact to throw readers or listeners off the trail. For example, people skeptical about climate change will routinely note that weather is always changing and point to the fact that Vikings settled in Greenland one thousand years ago before harsher conditions drove them away. True, scientists will say, but the point is irrelevant to arguments about worldwide global warming caused by human activity.

The red herring is not only a device writers and speakers use in the arguments they create, but it's also a charge used frequently to undermine someone else's arguments. Couple the term "red herring" in a Web search to just about any political or social cause and you'll come up with numerous articles complaining of someone's use of the device.

> climate change + red herring

> common core + red herring

> immigration reform + red herring

"Red herring" has become a convenient way of saying "I disagree with your argument" or "your point is irrelevant." And perhaps making a too-easy rebuttal like that can itself be a fallacy?

Faulty Analogy

Comparisons can help to clarify one concept by measuring it against another that is more familiar. Consider the power and humor of this comparison attributed to Mark Twain, an implicit argument for term limits in politics:

> Politicians and diapers must be changed often, and for the same reason.

When comparisons such as this one are extended, they become *analogies*—ways of understanding unfamiliar ideas by comparing them with something that's better known (see p. 200). But useful as such comparisons are, they may prove false if either taken on their own and pushed too far, or taken too seriously. At this point, they turn into **faulty analogies**—inaccurate or inconsequential comparisons between objects or concepts. Economist Paul Krugman provides an eye-opening analysis of a familiar but, as he sees it, false analogy between personal and government debt:

> Deficit-worriers portray a future in which we're impoverished by the need to pay back money we've been borrowing. They see America as being like a family that took out too large a mortgage, and will have a hard time making the monthly payments.

> This is, however, a really bad analogy in at least two ways.

First, families have to pay back their debt. Governments don't—all they need to do is ensure that debt grows more slowly than their tax base. The debt from World War II was never repaid; it just became increasingly irrelevant as the U.S. economy grew, and with it the income subject to taxation.

Second—and this is the point almost nobody seems to get—an overborrowed family owes money to someone else; U.S. debt is, to a large extent, money we owe to ourselves.

Whether you agree with the Nobel laureate or not, his explanation offers insight into how analogies work (or fail) and how to think about them critically.

RESPOND

1. Examine each of the following political slogans or phrases for logical fallacies.

    "Resistance is futile." (Borg message on *Star Trek: The Next Generation*)

    "It's the economy, stupid." (sign on the wall at Bill Clinton's campaign headquarters)

    "Make love, not war." (antiwar slogan popularized during the Vietnam War)

    "A chicken in every pot." (campaign slogan)

    "Guns don't kill, people do." (NRA slogan)

    "Dog Fighters Are Cowardly Scum." (PETA T-shirt)

    "If you can't stand the heat, get out of the kitchen." (attributed to Harry S Truman)

2. Choose a paper you've written for a college class and analyze it for signs of fallacious reasoning. Then find an editorial, a syndicated column, and a news report on the same topic and look for fallacies in them. Which has the most fallacies—and what kind? What may be the role of the audience in determining when a statement is fallacious?

3. Find a Web site that is sponsored by an organization (the Future of Music Coalition, perhaps), a business (Coca-Cola, Pepsi), or another group (the Democratic or Republican National Committee), and analyze the site for fallacious reasoning. Among other considerations,

look at the relationship between text and graphics and between individual pages and the pages that surround or are linked to them.

4. Political blogs such as *Mother Jones* and *InstaPundit* typically provide quick responses to daily events and detailed critiques of material in other media sites, including national newspapers. Study one such blog for a few days to see whether and how the site critiques the articles, political commentary, or writers it links to. Does the blog ever point out fallacies of argument? If so, does it explain the problems with such reasoning or just assume readers will understand the fallacies? Summarize your findings in a brief oral report to your class.

13

Rhetorical Analysis

Reading and Understanding Arguments

All images © Andy Anderson, Lone River Productions

If you watched the 2013 Super Bowl between the Baltimore Ravens and the San Francisco 49ers, you may remember the commercial. For two solemn minutes, still photographs of rural America and the people who work there moved across the screen accompanied by the unmistakable voice of the late Paul Harvey reading words he had first delivered in 1978. Maria Godoy of NPR described it this way: "It may not have been as dramatic as the stadium blackout that halted play for more than a half-hour, or as extravagant as Beyonce's halftime show. But for many viewers of Super Bowl XLVII, one of the standout moments was a deceptively simple ad for the Dodge Ram called 'God Made a Farmer.'" It was a fourth quarter interrupted by cattle, churches, snowy farmyards, bales of hay, plowed fields, hardworking men, and a few sturdy women. Occasionally, a slide discreetly showed a Ram truck, sponsor of the video, but there were no overt sales pitches—only a product logo in the final frame. Yet visits to the Ram Web site spiked immediately, and sales of Ram pickups did too. (The official video has been viewed on YouTube more than 17 million times.)

So how to account for the appeal of such an unconventional and unexpected commercial? That would be the work of a **rhetorical analysis**, the close reading of a text or, in this case, a video commercial, to figure out exactly how it functions. Certainly, the creators of "God Made a Farmer" counted on the strong emotional appeal of the photographs they'd commissioned, guessing perhaps that the expert images and Harvey's spellbinding words would contrast powerfully with the frivolity and emptiness of much Super Bowl ad fare:

> God said, "I need somebody willing to sit up all night with a newborn colt. And watch it die. Then dry his eyes and say, 'Maybe next year.'"

They pushed convention, too, by the length of the spot and the muted product connection, doubtless hoping to win the goodwill of a huge

audience suddenly all teary-eyed in the midst of a football game. And they surely gained the respect of a great many truck-buying farmers.

Rhetorical analyses can also probe the contexts that surround any argument or text—its impact on a society, its deeper implications, or even what it lacks or whom it excludes. Predictably, the widely admired Ram commercial (selected #1 Super Bowl XLVII spot by *Adweek*) acquired its share of critics, some attacking it for romanticizing farm life, others for ignoring the realities of industrial agriculture. And not a few writers noted what they regarded as glaring absences in its representation of farmers. Here, for instance, is copywriter and blogger Edye Deloch-Hughes, offering a highly personal and conflicted view of the spot in what amounts to an informal rhetorical analysis:

> . . . I was riveted by the still photography and stirring thirty-five-year-old delivery of legendary radio broadcaster Paul Harvey. But as I sat mesmerized, I waited to see an image that spoke to my heritage. What flashed before me were close-ups of stoic white men whose faces drowned out the obligatory medium shots of a minority token or two; their images minimized against the amber waves of grain.
>
> God made a Black farmer too. Where was my Grandpa, Grandma and Great Granny? My Auntie and Uncle Bolden? And didn't God make Hispanic and Native American farmers? They too were underrepresented.
>
> I am the offspring of a century and a half of African-American caretakers of the land, from Arkansas, Mississippi and Louisiana, who experienced their toils and troubles, their sun ups and sun downs. Their injustices and beat-downs. I wrestled with my mixed emotions; loving the commercial and feeling dejected at the same time.
>
> . . . Minimizing positive Black imagery and accomplishments is as American as wrestling cattle. We're often footnotes or accessories in history books, TV shows, movies and magazines as well as TV commercials. When content is exceptional, the omission is harder to recognize or criticize. Some friends of mine saw—or rather *felt*—the omission as I did. Others did not. I say be aware and vocal about how you are represented—if represented at all, otherwise your importance and relevance will be lost.
>
> —Edye Deloch-Hughes, "So God Made a Black Farmer Too"

As this example suggests, whenever you undertake a rhetorical analysis, follow your instincts and look closely. Why does an ad for a cell phone or breakfast sandwich make people want one immediately? How does an op-ed piece in the *Washington Post* suddenly change your long-held position on immigration? A rhetorical analysis might help you understand. Dig as deep as you can into the context of the item you are analyzing, especially when you encounter puzzling, troubling, or unusually successful appeals—ethical, emotional, or logical. Ask yourself what strategies a speech, editorial, opinion column, film, or ad spot employs to move your heart, win your trust, and change your mind—or why, maybe, it fails to do so.

Composing a Rhetorical Analysis

You perform a rhetorical analysis by analyzing how well the components of an argument work together to persuade or move an audience. You can study arguments of any kind—advertisements (as we've seen), editorials, political cartoons, and even songs, movies, or photographs. In every case, you'll need to focus your rhetorical analysis on elements that stand out or make the piece intriguing or problematic. You could begin by exploring *some* of the following issues:

- What is the purpose of this argument? What does it hope to achieve?

- Who is the audience for this argument? Who is ignored or excluded?

- What appeals or techniques does the argument use—emotional, logical, ethical?

- What type of argument is it, and how does the genre affect the argument? (You might challenge the lack of evidence in editorials, but you wouldn't make the same complaint about bumper stickers.)

- Who is making the argument? What ethos does it create, and how does it do so? What values does the ethos evoke? How does it make the writer or creator seem trustworthy?

- What authorities does the argument rely on or appeal to?

- What facts, reasoning, and evidence are used in the argument? How are they presented?

- What claims does the argument make? What issues are raised—or ignored or evaded?

- What are the contexts—social, political, historical, cultural—for this argument? Whose interests does it serve? Who gains or loses by it?

- How is the argument organized or arranged? What media does the argument use and how effectively?

- How does the language or style of the argument persuade an audience?

In answering questions like these, try to show *how* the key devices in an argument actually make it succeed or fail. Quote freely from a written piece, or describe the elements in a visual argument. (Annotating a visual text is one option.) Let readers know where and why an argument makes sense and where it falls apart. If you believe that an argument startles, challenges, insults, or lulls audiences, explain why that is the case and provide evidence. Don't be surprised when your rhetorical analysis itself becomes an argument. That's what it should be.

Understanding the Purpose of Arguments You Are Analyzing

To understand how well any argument works, begin with its purpose: Is it to sell running shoes? To advocate for limits to college tuition? To push a political agenda? In many cases, that purpose may be obvious. A conservative blog will likely advance right-wing causes; ads from a baby food company will likely show happy infants delighted with stewed prunes.

Funny, offensive, or both?

© Chris Maddaloni/CQ Roll Call

But some projects may hide their persuasive intentions. Perhaps you've responded to a mail survey or telephone poll only to discover that the questions are leading you to switch your cable service or buy apartment insurance. Do such stealthy arguments succeed? Do consumers resent the intrusion? Answering questions like these provides material for useful rhetorical analyses that assess the strengths, risks, and ethics of such strategies.

Understanding Who Makes an Argument

Knowing *who* is claiming *what* is key to any rhetorical analysis. That's why persuasive appeals usually have a name attached to them. Remember the statements included in TV ads during the last federal election: "Hello, I'm X—and I approve this ad"? Federal law requires such statements so we can tell the difference between ads a candidate endorses and ones sponsored by groups not even affiliated with the campaigns. Their interests and motives might be very different.

But knowing a name is just a starting place for analysis. You need to dig deeper, and you could do worse than to Google such people or groups to discover more about them. What else have they produced? Who publishes them: the *Wall Street Journal*, the blog *The Daily Kos*, or even a LiveJournal celebrity gossip site such as *Oh No They Didn't*? Check out related Web sites for information about goals, policies, contributors, and funding.

RESPOND

Describe a persuasive moment that you can recall from a speech, an editorial, an advertisement, a YouTube clip, or a blog posting. Or research one of the following famous persuasive moments and describe the circumstances—the historical situation, the issues at stake, the purpose of the argument—that make it so memorable.

Abraham Lincoln's Gettysburg Address (1863)

Elizabeth Cady Stanton's Declaration of Sentiments at the Seneca Falls Convention (1848)

Chief Tecumseh's address to General William Henry Harrison (1810)

Winston Churchill's radio addresses to the British people during World War II (1940)

Martin Luther King Jr.'s "Letter from Birmingham Jail" (1963)

Ronald Reagan's tribute to the *Challenger* astronauts (1986)

Toni Morrison's speech accepting the Nobel Prize (1993)

Will.i.am's "Yes We Can" song/collage on YouTube (2008)

Identifying and Appealing to Audiences

Most arguments are composed with specific audiences in mind, and their success depends, in part, on how well their strategies, content, tone, and language meet the expectations of that audience. So your rhetorical analysis of an argumentative piece should identify its target readers or viewers (see "Appealing to Audiences," p. 145) if possible, or make an educated guess about the audience, since most arguments suggest whom they intend to reach and in what ways.

Both a flyer stapled to a bulletin board in a college dorm ("Why you shouldn't drink and drive") and a forty-foot billboard for Bud Light might be aimed at the same general population—college students. But each will adjust its appeals for the different moods of that group in different moments. For starters, the flyer will appeal to students in a serious vein, while the beer ad will probably be visually stunning and virtually text-free.

You might also examine how a writer or an argument establishes credibility with an audience. One effective means of building credibility is to show respect for your readers or viewers, especially if they may not agree with you. In introducing an article on problems facing African American women in the workplace, editor in chief of *Essence* Diane Weathers considers the problems that she faced with respecting all her potential readers:

> We spent more than a minute agonizing over the provocative cover line for our feature "White Women at Work." The countless stories we had heard from women across the country told us that this was a workplace issue we had to address. From my own experience at several major magazines, it was painfully obvious to me that Black and White women are not on the same track. Sure, we might all start out in the same place. But early in the game, most sisters I know become stuck—and the reasons have little to do with intelligence or drive. At some point we bump our heads against that ceiling. And while White women may complain of a glass ceiling, for us, the ceiling is concrete.
>
> So how do we tell this story without sounding whiny and paranoid, or turning off our White-female readers, staff members, advertisers

and girlfriends? Our solution: Bring together real women (several of them highly successful senior corporate executives), put them in a room, promise them anonymity and let them speak their truth.

—Diane Weathers, "Speaking Our Truth"

Retailers like Walmart build their credibility by simple "straight talk" to shoppers: our low prices make your life better.

Beth Hall/Bloomberg News/Getty Images

Both paragraphs affirm Weathers's determination to treat audiences fairly *and* to deal honestly with a difficult subject. The strategy would merit attention in any rhetorical analysis.

Look, too, for signals that writers share values with readers or at least understand an audience. In the following passage, writer Jack Solomon is clear about one value that he hopes readers have in common—a preference for "straight talk":

There are some signs in the advertising world that Americans are getting fed up with fantasy advertisements and want to hear some straight talk. Weary of extravagant product claims . . . , consumers trained by years of advertising to distrust what they hear seem to be developing an immunity to commercials.

—Jack Solomon, "Masters of Desire:
The Culture of American Advertising"

But straight talk still requires common sense. If ever a major television ad seriously misread its audience, it may have been a spot that ran during the 2014 Winter Olympics for Cadillac's pricey new plug-in hybrid, the ELR. The company seemed to go out of its way to offend a great many people, foreign and domestic. As is typical strategy in rhetorical analyses, *Huffington Post*'s Carolyn Gregoire takes care to describe in detail the item she finds offensive:

> The opening shot shows a middle-aged man, played by the actor Neal McDonough, looking out over his backyard pool, asking the question: "Why do we work so hard? For this? For stuff?"
>
> As the ad continues, it becomes clear that the answer to this rhetorical question is actually a big fat YES. And it gets worse. "Other countries, they work," he says. "They stroll home. They stop by the cafe. They take August off. Off."
>
> Then he reveals just what it is that makes Americans better than all those lazy, espresso-sipping foreigners.
>
> "Why aren't you like that?" he says. "Why aren't we like that? Because we're crazy, driven, hard-working believers, that's why."
>
> — Carolyn Gregoire, "Cadillac Made a Commercial about the American Dream, and It's a Nightmare"

Her conclusion then is blistering, showing how readily a rhetorical analysis becomes an argument—and subject to criticism itself:

> Cadillacs have long been a quintessentially American symbol of wealth and status. But as this commercial proves, no amount of wealth or status is a guarantee of good taste. Now, the luxury car company is selling a vision of the American Dream at its worst: Work yourself into the ground, take as little time off as possible, and buy expensive sh*t (specifically, a 2014 Cadillac ELR).

Examining Arguments Based on Emotion: Pathos

Some emotional appeals are just ploys to win over readers with a pretty face, figurative or real. You've seen ads promising an exciting life and attractive friends if only you drink the right soda or wear a particular brand of clothes. Are you fooled by such claims? Probably not, if you pause to think about them. But that's the strategy—to distract you from thought just long enough to make a bad choice. It's a move worth commenting on in a rhetorical analysis.

How well does the emotional appeal here work?

Yet emotions can add real muscle to arguments, too, and that's worth noting. For example, persuading people not to drink and drive by making them fear death, injury, or arrest seems like a fair use of an emotional appeal. The public service announcement on this page uses an emotion-laden image to remind drivers to think of the consequences.

In a rhetorical analysis, you might note the juxtaposition of image with text, leading readers to connect casual notes left on windshields with the very serious consequences of drunk driving.

In analyzing emotional appeals, judge whether the emotions raised—anger, sympathy, fear, envy, joy, love, lust—advance the claims offered. Consider how columnist Ron Rosenbaum (whom we met in Chapter 9) makes the reasonable argument he offers for fatty foods all the more attractive by larding it with voluptuous language:

> The foods that best hit that sweet spot and "overwhelm the brain" with pleasure are high-quality fatty foods. They discourage us from overeating. A modest serving of short ribs or Peking duck will be both deeply pleasurable and self-limiting. As the brain swoons into

insensate delight, you won't have to gorge a still-craving cortex with mediocre sensations. "Sensory-specific satiety" makes a slam-dunk case (it's science!) for eating reasonable servings of superbly satisfying fatty foods.

—Ron Rosenbaum, "Let Them Eat Fat"

Does the use of evocative language ("swoons," "insensate delight," "superbly satisfying," "slam-dunk") convince you, or does it distract from considering the scientific case for "sensory-specific satiety"? Your task in a rhetorical analysis is to study an author's words, the emotions they evoke, and the claims they support and then to make this kind of judgment.

Healthy Food?

Kittipojn Pravalpatkul/Shutterstock

RESPOND

Browse YouTube or another Web site to find an example of a powerful emotional argument that's made visually, either alone or using words as well. In a paragraph, defend a claim about how the argument works. For example, does an image itself make a claim, or does it draw you in to consider a verbal claim? What emotion does the argument generate? How does that emotion work to persuade you?

Examining Arguments Based on Character: Ethos

It should come as no surprise: readers believe writers who seem honest, wise, and trustworthy. So in analyzing the effectiveness of an argument, look for evidence of these traits. Does the writer have the experience or authority to write on this subject? Are all claims qualified reasonably? Is evidence presented in full, not tailored to the writer's agenda? Are important objections to the author's position acknowledged and addressed? Are sources documented? Above all, does the writer sound trustworthy?

When a Norwegian anti-immigration extremist killed seventy-six innocent people in July 2011, Prime Minister Jens Stoltenberg addressed the citizens of Norway (and the world), and in doing so evoked the character or ethos of the entire nation:

> We will not let fear break us! The warmth of response from people in Norway and from the whole world makes me sure of this one thing: evil can kill a single person, but never defeat a whole people. The strongest weapon in the world—that is freedom of expression and democracy.

In analyzing this speech, you would do well to look at the way this passage deploys the deepest values of Norway—freedom of expression and democracy—to serve as a response to fear of terrorism. In doing so, Stoltenberg evokes ethical ideals to hold onto in a time of tragedy.

Or take a look at the following paragraph from a blog posting by Timothy Burke, a teacher at Swarthmore College and parent of a preschool child who is trying to think through the issue of homework for elementary school kids:

> So I've been reading a bit about homework and comparing notes with parents. There is a lot of variation across districts, not just in the amount of homework that kids are being asked to do, but in the kind of homework. Some districts give kids a lot of time-consuming busywork; other districts try to concentrate on having homework assignments be substantive work that is best accomplished independently. Some give a lot from a very early point in K–12 education; some give relatively little. As both a professional educator and an individual with personal convictions, I'd tend to argue against excessive amounts of

Burke establishes his ethos by citing his reading and his talks with other parents.

He underscores his right to address the matter.

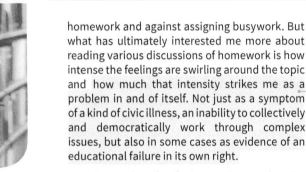

homework and against assigning busywork. But what has ultimately interested me more about reading various discussions of homework is how intense the feelings are swirling around the topic and how much that intensity strikes me as a problem in and of itself. Not just as a symptom of a kind of civic illness, an inability to collectively and democratically work through complex issues, but also in some cases as evidence of an educational failure in its own right.

He expresses concern about immoderate arguments and implies that he will demonstrate an opposite approach.

In considering the role of ethos in rhetorical analyses, pay attention to the details right down to the choice of words or, in an image, the shapes and colors. The modest, tentative tone that Burke uses in his blog is an example of the kind of choice that can shape an audience's perception of ethos. But these details need your interpretation. Language that's hot and extreme can mark a writer as either passionate or loony. Work that's sober and carefully organized can paint an institution as competent or overly cautious. Technical terms and abstract phrases can make a writer seem either knowledgeable or pompous.

Examining Arguments Based on Facts and Reason: Logos

In analyzing most arguments, you'll have to decide whether an argument makes a plausible claim and offers good reasons for you to believe it. Not all arguments will package such claims in a single neat sentence, or **thesis**—nor should they. A writer may tell a story from which you have to infer the claim. Visual arguments may work the same way: viewers have to assemble the parts and draw inferences in order to get the point.

Some conventional arguments (like those on an editorial page) may be perfectly obvious: writers stake out a claim and then present reasons that you should consider, or they may first present reasons and lay out a case that leads you to accept a claim in the conclusion. Consider the following example. In a tough opinion piece in *Time*, political commentator John McWhorter argues that filmmaker Spike Lee is being racist when he rails against hipsters moving into Fort Greene, a formerly all-black neighborhood in Brooklyn, New York. Lee fears that the whites are raising housing prices, pushing out old-time residents and diminishing the African American character of Fort Greene. McWhorter, an African American like Lee, sees matters differently:

Basically, black people are getting paid more money than they've ever seen in their lives for their houses, and a once sketchy neighborhood is now quiet and pleasant. And this is a bad thing . . . why?

Lee seems to think it's somehow an injustice whenever black people pick up stakes. But I doubt many of the blacks now set to pass fat inheritances on to their kids feel that way. This is not the old story of poor blacks being pushed out of neighborhoods razed down for highway construction. Lee isn't making sense.

— John McWhorter, "Spike Lee's Racism Isn't Cute"

When you encounter explicit charges like these, you analyze whether and how the claims are supported by good reasons and reliable evidence. A lengthy essay may, in fact, contain a series of claims, each developed to support an even larger point. Here's McWhorter, for instance, expanding his argument by suggesting that Lee's attitudes toward whites are irreconcilable.

"Respect the culture" when you move in, Lee growls. But again, he isn't making sense. We can be quite sure that if whites "respected" the culture by trying to participate in it, Lee would be one of the first in line to call it "appropriation." So, no whites better open up barbecue joints or spoken word cafes or try to be rappers. Yet if whites walk on by the culture in "respectful" silence, then the word on the street becomes that they want to keep blacks at a distance.

An anti-fur protestor in London makes a rather specific claim.

© Charles Platiau/Reuters/Corbis

Indeed, every paragraph in an argument may develop a specific and related idea. In a rhetorical analysis, you need to identify all these separate propositions and examine the relationships among them: Are they solidly linked? Are there inconsistencies that the writer should acknowledge? Does the end of the piece support what the writer said (and promised) at the beginning?

You'll also need to examine the quality of the information presented in an argument, assessing how accurately such information is reported, how conveniently it's displayed (in charts or graphs, for example), and how well the sources cited represent a range of *respected* opinions on a topic. (For more information on the use of evidence, see Chapter 11.)

Knowing how to judge the quality of sources is more important now than ever before because the digital universe is full of junk. In some ways, the computer terminal has become the equivalent of a library reference room, but the sources available online vary widely in quality and have not been evaluated by a library professional. As a consequence, you must know the difference between reliable, firsthand, or fully documented sources and those that don't meet such standards. (For using and documenting sources, see Chapters 22, 23, and 25.)

Examining the Arrangement and Media of Arguments

Aristotle carved the structure of logical argument to its bare bones when he observed that it had only two parts:

- statement

- proof

You could do worse, in examining an argument, than to make sure that every claim a writer makes is backed by sufficient evidence. Some arguments are written on the fly in the heat of the moment. Most arguments that you read and write, however, will be more than mere statements followed by proofs. Some writers will lay their cards on the table immediately; others may lead you carefully through a chain of claims toward a conclusion. Writers may even interrupt their arguments to offer background information or cultural contexts for readers. Sometimes they'll tell stories or provide anecdotes that make an argumentative point. They'll qualify the arguments they make, too, and often pause to admit that other points of view are plausible.

In other words, there are no formulas or acceptable patterns that fit all successful arguments. In writing a rhetorical analysis, you'll have to assess the organization of a persuasive text on its own merits.

It's fair, however, to complain about what may be *absent* from an argument. Most arguments of proposal (see Chapter 19), for example, include a section that defends the feasibility of a new idea, explaining how it might be funded or managed. In a rhetorical analysis, you might fault an editorial that supports a new stadium for a city without addressing feasibility issues. Similarly, analyzing a movie review that reads like an off-the-top-of-the-head opinion, you might legitimately ask what criteria of evaluation are in play (see Chapter 17).

Rhetorical analysis also calls for you to look carefully at an argument's transitions, headings and subheadings, documentation of sources, and overall tone or voice. Don't take such details for granted, since all of them contribute to the strength—or weakness—of an argument.

Nor should you ignore the way a writer or an institution uses media. Would an argument originally made in a print editorial, for instance, work better as a digital presentation (or vice versa)? Would a lengthy paper have more power if it included more images? Or do these images distract from a written argument's substance?

Finally, be open to the possibility of new or nontraditional structures of arguments. The visual arguments that you analyze may defy conventional principles of logic or arrangement—for example, making juxtapositions rather than logical transitions between elements or using quick cuts, fades, or other devices to link ideas. Quite often, these nontraditional structures will also resist the neatness of a thesis, leaving readers to construct at least a part of the argument in their heads. As we saw with the "God Made a Farmer" spot at the beginning of this chapter, advertisers are growing fond of soft-sell multimedia productions that can seem like something other than what they really are—product pitches. We may be asked not just to buy a product but also to live its lifestyle or embrace its ethos. Is that a reasonable or workable strategy for an argument? Your analysis might entertain such possibilities.

Looking at Style

Even a coherent argument full of sound evidence may not connect with readers if it's dull, off-key, or offensive. Readers naturally judge the credibility of arguments in part by how stylishly the case is made—even when they don't know exactly what style is. Consider how these simple, blunt sentences from the opening of an argument shape your image of the author and probably determine whether you're willing to continue to read the whole piece:

> We are young, urban, and professional. We are literate, respectable, intelligent, and charming. But foremost and above all, we are unemployed.
>
> —Julia Carlisle, "Young, Privileged, and Unemployed"

The strong, straightforward tone and the stark juxtaposition of being "intelligent" with "unemployed" set the style for this letter to the editor.

Now consider the brutally sarcastic tone of Nathaniel Stein's hilarious parody of the Harvard grading policy, a piece he wrote following up on a professor's complaint of out-of-control grade inflation at the school. Stein borrows the formal language of a typical "grading standards" sheet to mock the decline in rigor that the professor has lamented:

> The A+ grade is used only in very rare instances for the recognition of truly exceptional achievement.
>
> For example: A term paper receiving the A+ is virtually indistinguishable from the work of a professional, both in its choice of paper stock and its font. The student's command of the topic is expert, or at the very least intermediate, or beginner. Nearly every single word in the paper is spelled correctly; those that are not can be reasoned out phonetically within minutes. Content from Wikipedia is integrated with precision. The paper contains few, if any, death threats. . . .
>
> An overall course grade of A+ is reserved for those students who have not only demonstrated outstanding achievement in coursework but have also asked very nicely.
>
> Finally, the A+ grade is awarded to all collages, dioramas and other art projects.
>
> —Nathaniel Stein, "Leaked! Harvard's Grading Rubric"

Both styles probably work, but they signal that the writers are about to make very different kinds of cases. Here, style alone tells readers what to expect.

Manipulating style also enables writers to shape readers' responses to their ideas. Devices as simple as repetition, parallelism, or even paragraph length can give sentences remarkable power. Consider this passage from an essay by Sherman Alexie in which he explores the complex reaction of straight men to the announcement of NBA star Jason Collins that he is gay:

> Homophobic basketball fans will disparage his skills, somehow equating his NBA benchwarmer status with his sexuality. But let's not forget that Collins is still one of the best 1,000 basketball players in the world. He has always been better than his modest statistics would indicate, and his teams have been dramatically more efficient with him on the court. He is better at hoops than 99.9 percent of you are at anything you do. He might not be a demigod, but he's certainly a semi-demigod. Moreover, his basketball colleagues universally praise him as a physically and mentally tough player. In his prime, he ably battled that behemoth known as Shaquille O'Neal. Most of all, Collins is widely regarded as one of the finest gentlemen to ever play the game. Generous, wise, and supportive, he's a natural leader. And he has a degree from Stanford University.
>
> In other words, he's a highly attractive dude.
>
> —Sherman Alexie, "Jason Collins Is the Envy of Straight Men Everywhere"

In this passage, Alexie uses a sequence of short, direct, and roughly parallel sentences ("He is . . . He might . . . He ably battled . . . He has") to present evidence justifying the playful point he makes in a pointedly emphatic, one-sentence paragraph. The remainder of his short essay then amplifies that point.

Jason Collins

© Gary A. Vasquez/USA Today Sports Images

In a rhetorical analysis, you can explore such stylistic choices. Why does a formal style work for discussing one type of subject matter but not another? How does a writer use humor or irony to underscore an important point or to manage a difficult concession? Do stylistic choices, even something as simple as the use of contractions or personal pronouns, bring readers close to a writer, or do technical words and an impersonal voice signal that an argument is for experts only?

To describe the stylistic effects of visual arguments, you may use a different vocabulary and talk about colors, camera angles, editing, balance, proportion, fonts, perspective, and so on. But the basic principle is this: the look of an item—whether a poster, an editorial cartoon, or a film documentary—can support the message that it carries, undermine it, or muddle it. In some cases, the look will *be* the message. In a rhetorical analysis, you can't ignore style.

This poster, promoting travel to the bicycle-friendly city of Münster, Germany, demonstrates visually the amount of space needed to transport the same number of people by car, bicycle, and bus.

Foto Presseamt Münster, City of Münster, Press Office

RESPOND

Find a recent example of a visual argument, either in print or on the Internet. Even though you may have a copy of the image, describe it carefully in your paper on the assumption that your description is all readers may have to go on. Then make a judgment about its effectiveness, supporting your claim with clear evidence from the "text."

Examining a Rhetorical Analysis

On the following pages, well-known political commentator and columnist for the *New York Times* David Brooks argues that today's college graduates have been poorly prepared for life after school because of what he sees as a radical excess of supervision. Responding to his argument with a detailed analysis is Rachel Kolb, a student at Stanford University.

It's Not about You

DAVID BROOKS

Over the past few weeks, America's colleges have sent another class of graduates off into the world. These graduates possess something of inestimable value. Nearly every sensible middle-aged person would give away all their money to be able to go back to age 22 and begin adulthood anew.

© David Levene/
eyevine/
Redux Pictures

But, especially this year, one is conscious of the many ways in which this year's graduating class has been ill served by their elders. They enter a bad job market, the hangover from decades of excessive borrowing. They inherit a ruinous federal debt.

More important, their lives have been perversely structured. This year's graduates are members of the most supervised generation in American history. Through their childhoods and teenage years, they have been monitored, tutored, coached and honed to an unprecedented degree.

Yet upon graduation they will enter a world that is unprecedentedly wide open and unstructured. Most of them will not quickly get married, buy a home and have kids, as previous generations did. Instead, they will confront amazingly diverse job markets, social landscapes and lifestyle niches. Most will spend a decade wandering from job to job and clique to clique, searching for a role.

No one would design a system of extreme supervision to prepare people for a decade of extreme openness. But this is exactly what has emerged in modern America. College students are raised in an environment that demands one set of navigational skills, and they are then cast out into a different environment requiring a different set of skills, which they have to figure out on their own.

Worst of all, they are sent off into this world with the whole baby-boomer theology ringing in their ears. If you sample some of the commencement addresses being broadcast on C-Span these days, you see that many graduates are told to: Follow *your* passion, chart *your* own course, march to the beat of *your* own drummer, follow *your* dreams and find *your*self. This is the litany of expressive individualism, which is still the dominant note in American culture.

But, of course, this mantra misleads on nearly every front.

College grads are often sent out into the world amid rapturous talk of limitless possibilities. But this talk is of no help to the central business of adulthood, finding serious things to tie yourself down to. The successful young adult is beginning to make sacred commitments—to a spouse, a community and calling—yet mostly hears about freedom and autonomy.

Today's graduates are also told to find their passion and then pursue their dreams. The implication is that they should find themselves first and then go off and live their quest. But, of course, very few people at age 22 or 24 can take an inward journey and come out having discovered a developed self.

Most successful young people don't look inside and then plan a life. They look outside and find a problem, which summons their life. A relative suffers from Alzheimer's and a young woman feels called to help cure that disease. A young man works under a miserable boss and must develop management skills so his department can function. Another young woman finds herself confronted by an opportunity she never thought of in a job category she never imagined. This wasn't in her plans, but this is where she can make her contribution.

Most people don't form a self and then lead a life. They are called by a problem, and the self is constructed gradually by their calling.

The graduates are also told to pursue happiness and joy. But, of course, when you read a biography of someone you admire, it's rarely the things that made them happy that compel your admiration. It's the things they did to court unhappiness—the things they did that were arduous and miserable, which sometimes cost them friends and aroused hatred. It's excellence, not happiness, that we admire most.

Finally, graduates are told to be independent-minded and to express their inner spirit. But, of course, doing your job well often means suppressing yourself. As Atul Gawande mentioned during his countercultural address . . . at Harvard Medical School, being a good doctor often means being part of a team, following the rules of an institution, going down a regimented checklist.

Today's grads enter a cultural climate that preaches the self as the center of a life. But, of course, as they age, they'll discover that the tasks of a life are at the center. Fulfillment is a byproduct of how people engage their tasks, and can't be pursued directly. Most of us are egotistical and most are self-concerned most of the time, but it's nonetheless true that life comes to a point only in those moments when the self dissolves into some task. The purpose in life is not to find yourself. It's to lose yourself.

Understanding Brooks's Binaries

RACHEL KOLB

Courtesy of
Rachel Kolb

As a high school and college student, I was given an incredible range of educational and extracurricular options, from interdisciplinary studies to summer institutes to student-organized clubs. Although today's students have more opportunities to adapt their educations to their specific personal goals, as I did, David Brooks argues that the structure of the modern educational system nevertheless leaves young people ill-prepared to meet the challenges of the real world. In his *New York Times* editorial "It's Not about You," Brooks illustrates excessive supervision and uncontrolled individualistic rhetoric as opposing problems that complicate young people's entry into adult life, which then becomes less of a natural progression than an outright paradigm shift. Brooks's argument itself mimics the pattern of moving from "perversely structured" youth to "unprecedentedly wide open" adulthood: it operates on the basis of binary oppositions, raising familiar notions about how to live one's life and then dismantling them. Throughout, the piece relies less on factual evidence than on Brooks's own authoritative tone and skill in using rhetorical devices.

In his editorial, Brooks objects to mainstream cultural messages that sell students on individuality, but bases his conclusions more on general observations than on specific facts. His argument is, in itself, a loose form of rhetorical

Connects article to personal experience to create an ethical appeal.

Provides brief overview of Brooks's argument.

States Brooks's central claim.

Transition sentence.

analysis. It opens by telling us to "sample some of the commencement addresses being broadcast on C-Span these days," where we will find messages such as: "Follow *your* passion, chart *your* own course, march to the beat of *your* own drummer, follow *your* dreams and find *your*self." As though moving down a checklist, it then scrutinizes the problems with this rhetoric of "expressive individualism." Finally, it turns to Atul Gawande's "countercultural address" about working collectively, en route to confronting the individualism of modern America. C-Span and Harvard Medical School aside, however, Brooks's argument is astonishingly short on external sources. He cites no basis for claims such as "this year's graduates are members of the most supervised generation in American history" or "most successful young people don't look inside and then plan a life," despite the fact that these claims are fundamental to his observations. Instead, his argument persuades through painting a picture—first of "limitless possibilities," then of young men and women called into action by problems that "summon their life"—and hoping that we will find the illustration familiar.

Comments critically on author's use of evidence.

Instead of relying on the logos of his argument, Brooks assumes that his position as a baby boomer and *New York Times* columnist will provide a sufficient enough ethos to validate his claims. If this impression of age and social status did not enter our minds along with his bespectacled portrait, Brooks reminds us of it. Although he refers to the theology of the baby boomer generation as the "worst of all," from the beginning of his editorial he allots himself as another "sensible middle-aged person" and

Analyzes author's intended audience.

distances himself from college graduates by referring to them as "they" or as "today's grads," contrasting with his more inclusive reader-directed "you." Combined with his repeated use of passive sentence constructions that create a confusing sense of responsibility ("The graduates are sent off into the world"; "graduates are told"), this sense of distance could be alienating to the younger audiences for which this editorial seems intended. Granted, Brooks compensates for it by embracing themes of "excellence" and "fulfillment" and by opening up his message to "most of us" in his final paragraph, but nevertheless his self-defined persona has its limitations. Besides dividing his audience, Brooks risks reminding us that, just as his observations belong only to this persona, his arguments apply only to a subset of American society. More specifically, they apply only to the well-educated middle to upper class who might be more likely to fret after the implications of "supervision" and "possibilities," or the readers who would be most likely to flip through the *New York Times*.

Brooks overcomes his limitations in logos and ethos through his piece's greatest strength: its style. He effectively frames cultural messages in binaries in order to reinforce the disconnect that exists between what students are told and what they will face as full members of society. Throughout his piece, he states one assumption after another, then prompts us to consider its opposite. "Serious things" immediately take the place of "rapturous talk"; "look[ing] inside" replaces "look[ing] outside"; "suppressing yourself" becomes an alternative to being "independent-minded." Brooks's argument

Closely analyzes Brooks's style.

is consumed with dichotomies, culminating with his statement "It's excellence, not happiness, that we admire most." He frames his ideas within a tight framework of repetition and parallel structure, creating muscular prose intended to engage his readers. His repeated use of the phrase "but, of course" serves as a metronomic reminder, at once echoing his earlier assertions and referring back to his air of authority.

Analyzes author's conclusion.

Brooks illustrates the power of words in swaying an audience, and in his final paragraph his argument shifts beyond commentary. Having tested our way of thinking, he now challenges us to change. His editorial closes with one final binary, the claim that "The purpose in life is not to find yourself" but "to lose yourself." And, although some of Brooks's previous binaries have clanged with oversimplification, this one rings truer. In accordance with his adoption of the general "you," his concluding message need not apply only to college graduates. By unfettering its restrictions at its climax, Brooks liberates his argument. After all, only we readers bear the responsibility of reflecting, of justifying, and ultimately of determining how to live our lives.

WORK CITED

Brooks, David. "It's Not about You." *Everything's an Argument*, 7th ed., by Andrea A. Lunsford and John J. Ruszkiewicz, Bedford/St. Martin's, 2016, pp. 106-8. Reprint of "It's Not about You," *The New York Times*, 30 May 2011.

GUIDE TO WRITING A RHETORICAL ANALYSIS

Finding a Topic

A rhetorical analysis is usually assigned: you're asked to show how an argument works and to assess its effectiveness. When you can choose your own subject for analysis, look for one or more of the following qualities:

- a complex verbal or visual argument that challenges you—or disturbs or pleases you

- a text that raises current or enduring issues of substance

- a text that you believe should be taken more seriously

Look for arguments to analyze in the editorial and op-ed pages of any newspaper, political magazines such as the *Nation* or *National Review*, Web sites of organizations and interest groups, political blogs such as *Huffington Post* or *Power Line*, corporate Web sites that post their TV ad spots, videos and statements posted to YouTube, and so on.

Researching Your Topic

Once you've got a text to analyze, find out all you can about it. Use library or Web resources to explore:

- who the author is and what his or her credentials are

- if the author is an institution, what it does, what its sources of funding are, who its members are, and so on

- who is publishing or sponsoring the piece, and what the organization typically publishes

- what the leanings or biases of the author and publisher might be

- what the context of the argument is—what preceded or provoked it and how others have responded to it

GUIDE **TO WRITING A RHETORICAL ANALYSIS**

Formulating a Claim

Begin with a hypothesis. A full thesis might not become evident until you're well into your analysis, but your final thesis should reflect the complexity of the piece that you're studying. In developing a thesis, consider questions such as the following:

- How can I describe what this argument achieves?

- What is the purpose, and is it accomplished?

- What audiences does the argument address and what audiences does it ignore, and why?

- Which of its rhetorical features will likely influence readers most: ethos of the author? emotional appeals? logical progression? style?

- What aspects of the argument work better than others?

- How do the rhetorical elements interact?

Here's the hardest part for most writers of rhetorical analyses: whether you agree or disagree with an argument usually doesn't matter in a rhetorical analysis. You've got to stay out of the fray and pay attention only to how—and to how well—the argument works.

Examples of Possible Claims for a Rhetorical Analysis

- Some people admire the directness and confidence of Hillary Clinton; others are put off by her bland and sometimes tone-deaf rhetoric. A close look at several of her speeches and public appearances will illuminate both sides of this debate.

- Today's editorial in the *Daily Collegian* about campus crimes may scare first-year students, but its anecdotal reporting doesn't get down to hard numbers—and for a good reason. Those statistics don't back the position taken by the editors.

GUIDE TO WRITING A RHETORICAL ANALYSIS

- The imageboard 4chan has been called an "Internet hate machine," yet others claim it as a great boon to creativity. A close analysis of its homepage can help to settle this debate.

- The original design of New York's Freedom Tower, with its torqued surfaces and evocative spire, made a stronger argument about American values than its replacement, a fortress-like skyscraper stripped of imagination and unable to make any statement except "I'm 1,776 feet tall."

Preparing a Proposal

If your instructor asks you to prepare a proposal for your rhetorical analysis, here's a format you might use:

- Provide a copy of the work you're analyzing, whether it's a print text, a photograph, a digital image, or a URL, for instance.

- Offer a working hypothesis or tentative thesis.

- Indicate which rhetorical components seem especially compelling and worthy of detailed study and any connections between elements. For example, does the piece seem to emphasize facts and logic so much that it becomes disconnected from potential audiences? If so, hint at that possibility in your proposal.

- Indicate background information you intend to research about the author, institution, and contexts (political, economic, social, and religious) of the argument.

- Define the audience you'd like to reach. If you're responding to an assignment, you may be writing primarily for a teacher and classmates. But they make up a complex audience in themselves. If you can do so within the spirit of the assignment, imagine that your analysis will be published in a local newspaper, Web site, or blog.

GUIDE TO WRITING A RHETORICAL ANALYSIS

- Conclude by briefly discussing the key challenges you anticipate in preparing a rhetorical analysis.

Considering Format and Media

Your instructor may specify that you use a particular format and/
or medium. If not, ask yourself these questions to help you make
a good choice:

- What format is most appropriate for your rhetorical analysis?
  Does it call for an academic essay, a report, an infographic, a
  brochure, or something else?

- What medium is most appropriate for your analysis? Would
  it be best delivered orally to a live audience? Presented as an
  audio essay or podcast? Presented in print only or in print
  with illustrations?

- Will you need visuals, such as moving or still images, maps,
  graphs, charts—and what function will they play in your
  analysis? Make sure they are not just "added on" but are necessary components of the analysis.

Thinking about Organization

Your rhetorical analysis is likely to include the following:

- Facts about the text you're analyzing: Provide the author's
  name; the title or name of the work; its place of publication
  or its location; the date it was published or viewed.

- Contexts for the argument: Readers need to know where the
  text is coming from, to what it may be responding, in what
  controversies it might be embroiled, and so on. Don't assume
  that they can infer the important contextual elements.

- A synopsis of the text that you're analyzing: If you can't attach the original argument, you must summarize it in enough

detail so that a reader can imagine it. Even if you attach a copy of the piece, the analysis should include a summary.

- Some claim about the work's rhetorical effectiveness: It might be a simple evaluative claim or something more complex. The claim can come early in the paper, or you might build up to it, providing the evidence that leads toward the conclusion you've reached.

- A detailed analysis of how the argument works: Although you'll probably analyze rhetorical components separately, don't let your analysis become a dull roster of emotional, ethical, and logical appeals. Your rhetorical analysis should be an argument itself that supports a claim; a simple list of rhetorical appeals won't make much of a point.

- Evidence for every part of the analysis.

- An assessment of alternative views and counterarguments to your own analysis.

Getting and Giving Response: Questions for Peer Response

If you have access to a writing center, discuss the text that you intend to analyze with a writing consultant before you write the paper. Try to find people who agree with the argument and others who disagree, and take notes on their observations. Your instructor may assign you to a peer group for the purpose of reading and responding to one another's drafts; if not, share your draft with someone on your own. You can use the following questions to evaluate a draft. If you're evaluating someone else's draft, be sure to illustrate your points with examples. Specific comments are always more helpful than general observations.

GUIDE TO WRITING A RHETORICAL ANALYSIS

The Claim

- Does the claim address the rhetorical effectiveness of the argument itself rather than the opinion or position that it takes?

- Is the claim significant enough to interest readers?

- Does the claim indicate important relationships between various rhetorical components?

- Would the claim be one that the creator of the piece would regard as serious criticism?

Evidence for the Claim

- Is enough evidence given to support all your claims? What evidence do you still need?

- Is the evidence in support of the claim simply announced, or are its significance and appropriateness analyzed? Is a more detailed discussion needed?

- Do you use appropriate evidence, drawn from the argument itself or from other materials?

- Do you address objections readers might have to the claim, criteria, or evidence?

- What kinds of sources might you use to explain the context of the argument? Do you need to use sources to check factual claims made in the argument?

- Are all quotations introduced with appropriate signal phrases (for instance, "As Áida Álvarez points out"), and do they merge smoothly into your sentences?

GUIDE TO WRITING A RHETORICAL ANALYSIS

Organization and Style

- How are the parts of the argument organized? How effective is this organization? Would some other structure work better?

- Will readers understand the relationships among the original text, your claims, your supporting reasons, and the evidence you've gathered (from the original text and any other sources you've used)? If not, what could be done to make those connections clearer? Are more transitional words and phrases needed? Would headings or graphic devices help?

- Are the transitions or links from point to point, sentence to sentence, and paragraph to paragraph clear and effective? If not, how could they be improved?

- Is the style suited to the subject and appropriate to your audience? Is it too formal? Too casual? Too technical? Too bland or boring?

- Which sentences seem particularly effective? Which ones seem weakest, and how could they be improved? Should some short sentences be combined, or should any long ones be separated into two or more sentences?

- How effective are the paragraphs? Do any seem too skimpy or too long? Do they break the analysis at strategic points?

- Which words or phrases seem particularly effective, accurate, and powerful? Do any seem dull, vague, unclear, or inappropriate for the audience or your purpose? Are definitions provided for technical or other terms that readers might not know?

GUIDE TO WRITING A RHETORICAL ANALYSIS

Spelling, Punctuation, Mechanics, Documentation, and Format

- Check the spelling of the author's name, and make sure that the name of any institution involved with the work is correct. Note that the names of many corporations and institutions use distinctive spelling and punctuation.

- Get the title of the text you're analyzing right.

- Are there any errors in spelling, punctuation, capitalization, and the like?

- Does the assignment require a specific format? Check the original assignment sheet to be sure.

RESPOND

Find an argument on the editorial page or op-ed page in a recent newspaper. Then analyze it rhetorically, using principles discussed in this chapter. Show how it succeeds, fails, or does something else entirely. Perhaps you can show that the author is unusually successful in connecting with readers but then has nothing to say. Or perhaps you discover that the strong logical appeal is undercut by a contradictory emotional argument. Be sure that the analysis includes a summary of the original essay and basic publication information about it (its author, place of publication, and publisher).

PART 2

WRITING ARGUMENTS

14

Structuring Arguments

Writing Arguments

I get hives after eating ice cream.
My mouth swells up when
I eat cheese.
Yogurt triggers my asthma.
↓
Dairy products make me sick.

Dairy products make me sick.
Ice cream is a dairy product.
↓
Ice cream makes me sick.

These two sets of statements illustrate the most basic ways in which Western culture structures logical arguments. The first piles up specific examples and draws a conclusion from them: that's **inductive reasoning** and structure. The second sets out a general principle (the major premise of a syllogism) and applies it to a specific case (the minor premise) in order to reach a conclusion: that's **deductive reasoning** and structure. In everyday reasoning, we often omit the middle statement, resulting in what Aristotle called an *enthymeme*: "Since dairy products make me sick, I better leave that ice cream alone." (See p. 197 for more on enthymemes.)

But the arguments you will write in college call for more than just the careful critical thinking offered within inductive and deductive reasoning. You will also need to define claims, explain the contexts in which you are offering them, consider counterarguments fairly and carefully, defend your assumptions, offer convincing evidence, appeal to particular audiences, and more. And you will have to do so using a clear structure that moves your argument forward. This chapter introduces you to three helpful ways to structure arguments. Feel free to borrow from all of them!

The Classical Oration

The authors of this book once examined a series of engineering reports and found that—to their great surprise—these reports were generally structured in ways similar to those used by Greek and Roman rhetors two thousand years ago. Thus, this ancient structuring system is alive and well in twenty-first-century culture. The classical oration has six parts, most of which will be familiar to you, despite their Latin names:

>   ***Exordium:*** You try to win the attention and goodwill of an audience while introducing a topic or problem.

Narratio: You present the facts of the case, explaining what happened when, who is involved, and so on. The narratio puts an argument in context.

Partitio: You divide up the topic, explaining what the claim is, what the key issues are, and in what order they will be treated.

Confirmatio: You offer detailed support for the claim, using both logical reasoning and factual evidence.

Refutatio: You carefully consider and respond to opposing claims or evidence.

Peroratio: You summarize the case and move the audience to action.

This structure is powerful because it covers all the bases: readers or listeners want to know what your topic is, how you intend to cover it, and what evidence you have to offer. And you probably need a reminder to present a pleasing *ethos* when beginning a presentation and to conclude with enough *pathos* to win an audience over completely. Here, in outline form, is a five-part updated version of the classical pattern, which you may find useful on many occasions:

Introduction

- gains readers' interest and willingness to listen
- establishes your qualifications to write about your topic
- establishes some common ground with your audience
- demonstrates that you're fair and even-handed
- states your claim

Background

- presents information, including personal stories or anecdotes that are important to your argument

Lines of Argument

- presents good reasons, including logical and emotional appeals, in support of your claim

Alternative Arguments

- carefully considers alternative points of view and opposing arguments
- notes the advantages and disadvantages of these views
- explains why your view is preferable to others

Conclusion

- summarizes the argument
- elaborates on the implications of your claim
- makes clear what you want the audience to think or do
- reinforces your credibility and perhaps offers an emotional appeal

Not every piece of rhetoric, past or present, follows the structure of the oration or includes all its components. But you can identify some of its elements in successful arguments if you pay attention to their design. Here are the words of the 1776 Declaration of Independence:

When in the Course of human events, it becomes necessary for one people to dissolve the political bands which have connected them with another, and to assume among the powers of the earth, the separate and equal station to which the Laws of Nature and of Nature's God entitle them, a decent respect to the opinions of mankind requires that they should declare the causes which impel them to the separation.

Opens with a brief *exordium* explaining why the document is necessary, invoking a broad audience in acknowledging a need to show "a decent respect to the opinions of mankind." Important in this case, the lines that follow explain the assumptions on which the document rests.

We hold these truths to be self-evident, that all men are created equal, that they are endowed by their Creator with certain unalienable Rights, that among these are Life, Liberty, and the pursuit of Happiness—that to secure these rights, Governments are instituted among Men, deriving their just powers from the consent of the governed—That whenever any Form of Government becomes destructive to these ends, it is the Right of the People to alter or to abolish it and to institute new Government, laying its Foundation on such principles and organizing its powers in such form, as to them shall seem most likely to effect their Safety and Happiness. Prudence, indeed, will dictate that Governments long established should not be changed for light and transient causes; and accordingly all experience hath shewn that mankind are more disposed to suffer, while evils are sufferable, than to right themselves by abolishing the forms to which they are accustomed. But when a long train of abuses and usurpations, pursuing invariably the same Object evinces a design to reduce them under absolute Despotism, it is their right, it is their duty, to throw off such Government and to provide new Guards for their future security. Such has been the patient sufferance of these Colonies; and such is now the necessity which constrains them to alter their former Systems of Government. The history of the present King of Great Britain is a history of repeated injuries and usurpations, all having in direct object the establishment of an absolute Tyranny over these States. To prove this, let Facts be submitted to a candid world.

A *narratio* follows, offering background on the situation: because the government of George III has become destructive, the framers of the Declaration are obligated to abolish their allegiance to him.

Arguably, the *partitio* begins here, followed by the longest part of the document (not reprinted here), a *confirmatio* that lists the "long train of abuses and usurpations" by George III.

—Declaration of Independence, July 4, 1776

The authors might have structured this argument by beginning with the last two sentences of the excerpt and then listing the facts intended to prove the king's abuse and tyranny. But by choosing first to explain the purpose and "self-evident" assumptions behind their argument and only then moving on to demonstrate how these "truths" have been denied by the British, the authors forge an immediate connection with readers and build up to the memorable conclusion. The structure is both familiar and inventive—as your own use of key elements of the oration should be in the arguments you compose.

The Declaration of Independence

National Archives

Rogerian and Invitational Arguments

In trying to find an alternative to confrontational and angry arguments like those that so often erupt in legislative bodies around the world, scholars and teachers of rhetoric have adapted the nonconfrontational principles employed by psychologist Carl Rogers in personal therapy sessions. In simple terms, Rogers argued that people involved in disputes should not respond to each other until they could fully, fairly, and even sympathetically state the other person's position. Scholars of rhetoric Richard E. Young,

Alton L. Becker, and Kenneth L. Pike developed a four-part structure that is now known as Rogerian argument:

1. **Introduction:** You describe an issue, a problem, or a conflict in terms rich enough to show that you fully understand and respect any alternative position or positions.

2. **Contexts:** You describe the contexts in which alternative positions may be valid.

3. **Writer's position:** You state your position on the issue and present the circumstances in which that opinion would be valid.

4. **Benefits to opponent:** You explain to opponents how they would benefit from adopting your position.

The key to Rogerian argumentation is a willingness to think about opposing positions and to describe them fairly. In a Rogerian structure, you have to acknowledge that alternatives to your claims exist and that they might be reasonable under certain circumstances. In tone, Rogerian arguments steer clear of heated and stereotypical language, emphasizing instead how all parties in a dispute might gain from working together.

In the same vein, feminist scholars Sonja Foss and Cindy Griffin have outlined a form of argument they label "invitational," one that begins with careful attention to and respect for the person or the audience you are in conversation with. Foss and Griffin show that such listening—in effect, walking in the other person's shoes—helps you see that person's points of view more clearly and thoroughly and thus offers a basis for moving together toward new understandings. The kind of argument they describe is what another rhetorician, Krista Ratcliffe, calls "rhetorical listening," which helps to establish productive connections between people and thus helps enable effective cross-cultural communications.

Invitational rhetoric has as its goal not winning over opponents but getting people and groups to work together and identify with each other; it strives for connection, collaboration, and the mutually informed creation of knowledge. As feminist scholar Sally Miller Gearhart puts it, invitational argument offers a way to disagree without hurting one another, to disagree with respect. This kind of argument is especially important in a society that increasingly depends on successful collaboration to get things done. In college, you may have opportunities to practice invitational rhetoric in peer-review sessions, when each member of a group listens carefully in order to work through problems and issues. You may also practice invitational rhetoric looking at any contested issue from other people's points of view, taking them into account, and engaging them fairly and respectfully in your own argument. Students we know who are working in high-tech industries also tell us how much such arguments are valued, since they fuel innovation and "out of the box" thinking.

Invitational arguments, then, call up structures that more resemble good two-way conversations or free-ranging dialogues than straight-line marches from thesis to conclusion. Even conventional arguments benefit from invitational strategies by giving space early on to a full range of perspectives, making sure to present them thoroughly and clearly. Remember that in such arguments your goal is enhanced understanding so that you can open up a space for new perceptions and fresh ideas.

Consider how Frederick Douglass tried to broaden the outlook of his audiences when he delivered a Fourth of July oration in 1852. Most nineteenth-century Fourth of July speeches followed a pattern of praising the Revolutionary War heroes and emphasizing freedom, democracy, and justice. Douglass, a former slave, had that tradition in mind as he delivered his address, acknowledging the "great principles" that the "glorious anniversary" celebrates. But he also asked his (white) listeners to see the occasion from another point of view:

> Fellow-citizens, pardon me, allow me to ask, why am I called upon to speak here today? What have I, or those I represent, to do with your national independence? Are the great principles of political freedom and natural justice, embodied in the Declaration of Independence, extended to us? And am I, therefore, called upon to bring our humble offering to the national altar, and to confess the benefits and express devout gratitude for the blessings resulting from your independence to us? . . . I say it with a sad sense of the disparity between us. I am not included within the pale of this glorious anniversary! Your high independence only reveals the immeasurable distance between us. The blessings in which you, this day, rejoice, are not enjoyed in common. The rich inheritance of justice, liberty, prosperity and independence, bequeathed by your fathers, is shared by you, not by me. The sunlight that brought life and healing to you, has brought stripes and death to me. This Fourth of July is yours, not mine. You may rejoice, I must mourn.
>
> —Frederick Douglass,
> "What to the Slave Is the Fourth of July?"

Frederick Douglass

© World History Archive/Alamy

Although his speech is in some ways confrontational, Douglass is also inviting his audience to see a version of reality that they could have discovered on their own had they dared to imagine the lives of African Americans living in the shadows of American liberty. Issuing that invitation, and highlighting its consequences, points a way forward in the conflict between slavery and freedom, black and white, oppression and justice, although response to Douglass's invitation was a long time in coming.

In May 2014, First Lady Michelle Obama used elements of invitational argument in delivering a speech to high school graduates from several high schools in Topeka, Kansas. Since the speech occurred on the sixtieth anniversary of the Supreme Court's decision to disallow "separate but equal" schools in the landmark *Brown v. Board of Education* case, which was initiated in Topeka, Mrs. Obama invited the audience to experience the ups and downs of students before and after the decision, putting themselves in the places of the young African Americans who, in 1954, desperately wanted the freedom to attend well-funded schools open to white students. So she tells the stories of some of these young people, inviting those there to walk a while in their shoes. And she concludes her speech with a call for understanding and cooperation:

> Every day, you have the same power to choose our better history—
> by opening your hearts and minds, by speaking up for what you

know is right, by sharing the lessons of Brown v. Board of Education, the lessons you learned right here in Topeka, wherever you go for the rest of our lives. I know you all can do it. I am so proud of all of you, and I cannot wait to see everything you achieve in the years ahead.

Michelle Obama speaking in Topeka, Kansas

AP Photo/Orlin Wagner

In this speech, Mrs. Obama did not castigate audience members for failing to live up to the ideals of *Brown v. Board of Education* (though she could have done so), nor does she dwell on current ills in Topeka. Rather, she invokes "our better history" and focuses on the ways those in Topeka have helped to write that history. She identifies with her audience and asks them to identify with her—and she aims to inspire the young graduates to follow her example.

The use of invitational argument and careful listening in contemporary political life are rare, but in spite of much evidence to the contrary (think of the repeatedly demonstrated effectiveness of political attack ads), the public claims to prefer nonpartisan and invitational rhetoric to one-on-one, winner-take-all battles, suggesting that such an approach strikes a chord in many people, especially in a world that is increasingly open to issues of diversity. The lesson to take from Rogerian or invitational argument is that it makes good sense in structuring your own arguments to learn opposing positions well enough to state them accurately and honestly, to strive to understand the points of view of your opponents, to acknowledge those views fairly in your own work, and to look for solutions that benefit as many people as possible.

Choose a controversial topic that is frequently in the news, and decide how you might structure an argument on the subject, using the general principles of the classical oration. Then look at the same subject from a Rogerian or invitational perspective. How might your argument differ? Which approach would work better for your topic? For the audiences you might want to address?

Toulmin Argument

In *The Uses of Argument* (1958), British philosopher Stephen Toulmin presented structures to describe the way that ordinary people make reasonable arguments. Because Toulmin's system acknowledges the complications of life—situations when we qualify our thoughts with words such as *sometimes*, *often*, *presumably*, *unless*, and *almost*—his method isn't as airtight as formal logic that uses syllogisms (see p. 261 in this chapter and p. 195 in Chapter 11). But for that reason, Toulmin logic has become a powerful and, for the most part, practical tool for understanding and shaping arguments in the real world.

Toulmin argument will help you come up with and test ideas and also figure out what goes where in many kinds of arguments. Let's take a look at the basic elements of Toulmin's structure:

Claim	the argument you wish to prove
Qualifiers	any limits you place on your claim
Reason(s)/ Evidence	support for your claim
Warrants	underlying assumptions that support your claim
Backing	evidence for warrant

If you wanted to state the relationship between them in a sentence, you might say:

> My claim is true, to a qualified degree, because of the following reasons, which make sense if you consider the warrant, backed by these additional reasons.

These terms—claim, evidence, warrants, backing, and qualifiers—are the building blocks of the Toulmin argument structure. Let's take them one at a time.

Making Claims

Toulmin arguments begin with **claims**, debatable and controversial statements or assertions you hope to prove.

A claim answers the question *So what's your point?* or *Where do you stand on that?* Some writers might like to ignore these questions and avoid stating a position. But when you make a claim worth writing about, then it's worth standing up and owning it.

Is there a danger that you might oversimplify an issue by making too bold a claim? Of course. But making that sweeping claim is a logical first step toward eventually saying something more reasonable and subtle. Here are some fairly simple, undeveloped claims:

Congress should enact legislation that establishes a path to citizenship for illegal immigrants.

It's time for the World Health Organization (WHO) to exert leadership in coordinating efforts to stem the Ebola epidemic in West Africa.

NASA should launch a human expedition to Mars.

Veganism is the most responsible choice of diet.

Military insurance should not cover the cost of sex change surgery for service men and women.

Good claims often spring from personal experiences. You may have relevant work or military or athletic experience—or you may know a lot about music, film, sustainable agriculture, social networking, inequities in government services—all fertile ground for authoritative, debatable, and personally relevant claims.

RESPOND

Claims aren't always easy to find. Sometimes they're buried deep within an argument, and sometimes they're not present at all. An important skill in reading and writing arguments is the ability to identify claims, even when they aren't obvious.

Collect a sample of six to eight letters to the editor of a daily newspaper (or a similar number of argumentative postings from a political blog). Read each item, and then identify every claim that the writer makes.

When you've compiled your list of claims, look carefully at the words that the writer or writers use when stating their positions. Is there a common vocabulary? Can you find words or phrases that signal an impending claim? Which of these seem most effective? Which ones seem least effective? Why?

Offering Evidence and Good Reasons

You can begin developing a claim by drawing up a list of reasons to support it or finding **evidence** that backs up the point.

Evidence and Reason(s) ⟶ **So** Claim

One student writer wanted to gather good reasons in support of an assertion that his college campus needed more official spaces for parking bicycles. He did some research, gathering statistics about parking-space allocation, numbers of people using particular designated slots, and numbers of bicycles registered on campus. Before he went any further, however, he listed his primary reasons for wanting to increase bicycle parking:

- **Personal experience:** At least twice a week for two terms, he was unable to find a designated parking space for his bike.

- **Anecdotes:** Several of his friends told similar stories. One even sold her bike as a result.

- **Facts:** He found out that the ratio of car to bike parking spaces was 100 to 1, whereas the ratio of cars to bikes registered on campus was 25 to 1.

- **Authorities:** The campus police chief told the college newspaper that she believed a problem existed for students who tried to park bicycles legally.

On the basis of his preliminary listing of possible reasons in support of the claim, this student decided that his subject was worth more research. He was on the way to amassing a set of good reasons and evidence that were sufficient to support his claim.

In shaping your own arguments, try putting claims and reasons together early in the writing process to create enthymemes. Think of these enthymemes as test cases or even as topic sentences:

Bicycle parking spaces should be expanded because the number of bikes on campus far exceeds the available spots.

It's time to lower the driving age because I've been driving since I was fourteen and it hasn't hurt me.

National legalization of marijuana is long overdue since it is already legal in over twenty states, has shown to be less harmful than alcohol, and provides effective relief from pain associated with cancer.

Violent video games should be carefully evaluated and their use monitored by the industry, the government, and parents because these games cause addiction and psychological harm to players.

As you can see, attaching a reason to a claim often spells out the major terms of an argument.

"I know your type, you're the type who'll make me prove every claim I make."

Anticipate challenges to your claims.

© 2009 Charles Barsotti/The New Yorker Collection/The Cartoon Bank

But your work is just beginning when you've put a claim together with its supporting reasons and evidence—because readers are certain to begin questioning your statement. They might ask whether the reasons and evidence that you're offering really do support the claim: should the driving age really be changed just because you've managed to drive since you were fourteen? They might ask pointed questions about your evidence: exactly how do you know that the number of bikes on campus far exceeds the number of spaces available? Eventually, you've got to address potential questions about the quality of your assumptions and the quality of your

evidence. The connection between claim and reason(s) is a concern at the next level in Toulmin argument.

Determining Warrants

Crucial to Toulmin argument is appreciating that there must be a logical and persuasive connection between a claim and the reasons and data supporting it. Toulmin calls this connection the **warrant**. It answers the question *How exactly do I get from the data to the claim?* Like the warrant in legal situations (a search warrant, for example), a sound warrant in an argument gives you authority to proceed with your case.

The warrant tells readers what your (often unstated) assumptions are—for example, that any practice that causes serious disease should be banned by the government. If readers accept your warrant, you can then present specific evidence to develop your claim. But if readers dispute your warrant, you'll have to defend it before you can move on to the claim itself.

Stating warrants can be tricky because they can be phrased in various ways. What you're looking for is the general principle that enables you to justify the move from a reason to a specific claim—the bridge connecting them. The warrant is the assumption that makes the claim seem believable. It's often a value or principle that you share with your readers. Here's an easy example:

> Don't eat that mushroom: it's poisonous.

The warrant supporting this enthymeme can be stated in several ways, always moving from the reason (*it's poisonous*) to the claim (*Don't eat that mushroom*):

> Anything that is poisonous shouldn't be eaten.

> If something is poisonous, it's dangerous to eat.

Here's the relationship, diagrammed:

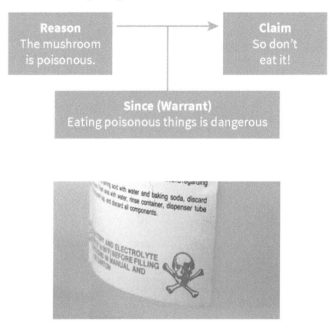

A simple icon—a skull and crossbones—can make a visual argument that implies a claim, a reason, and a warrant.

PhotoLink/Getty Images

Perfectly obvious, you say? Exactly—and that's why the statement is so convincing. If the mushroom in question is a death cap or destroying angel (and you might still need expert testimony to prove that it is), the warrant does the rest of the work, making the claim that it supports seem logical and persuasive.

Let's look at a similar example, beginning with the argument in its basic form:

> We'd better stop for gas because the gauge has been reading empty for more than thirty miles.

In this case, you have evidence that is so clear (a gas gauge reading empty) that the reason for getting gas doesn't even have to be stated: the tank is almost empty. The warrant connecting the evidence to the claim is also pretty obvious:

> If the fuel gauge of a car has been reading empty for more than
> thirty miles, then that car is about to run out of gas.

Since most readers would accept this warrant as reasonable, they would
also likely accept the statement the warrant supports.

Naturally, factual information might undermine the whole argument: the
fuel gauge might be broken, or the driver might know that the car will go
another fifty miles even though the fuel gauge reads empty. But in most
cases, readers would accept the warrant.

Now let's consider how stating and then examining a warrant can help you
determine the grounds on which you want to make a case. Here's a political enthymeme of a familiar sort:

> Flat taxes are fairer than progressive taxes because they treat all
> taxpayers in the same way.

Warrants that follow from this enthymeme have power because they appeal to a core American value—equal treatment under the law:

> Treating people equitably is the American way.

> All people should be treated in the same way.

You certainly could make an argument on these grounds. But stating the
warrant should also raise a flag if you know anything about tax policy.
If the principle is obvious and universal, then why do federal and many
progressive state income taxes require people at higher levels of income to
pay at higher tax rates than people at lower income levels? Could the warrant not be as universally popular as it seems at first glance? To explore the
argument further, try stating the contrary claim and warrants:

> Progressive taxes are fairer than flat taxes because people with more
> income can afford to pay more, benefit more from government,
> and shelter more of their income from taxes.

> People should be taxed according to their ability to pay.

> People who benefit more from government and can shelter more of
> their income from taxes should be taxed at higher rates.

Now you see how different the assumptions behind opposing positions really are. If you decided to argue in favor of flat taxes, you'd be smart to recognize that some members of your audience might have fundamental reservations about your position. Or you might even decide to shift your entire argument to an alternative rationale for flat taxes:

> Flat taxes are preferable to progressive taxes because they simplify the tax code and reduce the likelihood of fraud.

Here, you have two stated reasons that are supported by two new warrants:

> Taxes that simplify the tax code are desirable.

> Taxes that reduce the likelihood of fraud are preferable.

Whenever possible, you'll choose your warrant knowing your audience, the context of your argument, and your own feelings.

Be careful, though, not to suggest that you'll appeal to any old warrant that works to your advantage. If readers suspect that your argument for progressive taxes really amounts to *I want to stick it to people who work harder than I,* your credibility may suffer a fatal blow.

Examples of Claims, Reasons, and Warrants

E-cigarettes legitimize smoking among youth and entice children by using flavors like bubblegum.

→ **So** the federal government should ban e-cigarettes from all public places.

Since
The Constitution was established to "promote the general welfare," and citizens are thus entitled to protection from harmful actions by others.

The Electoral College gives small states undue influence.

→ **So** it should be abolished.

Since
No states should have undue influence on presidential elections.

I've been drinking since age fourteen without problems.

→ **So** the legal age for drinking should be lowered.

Since
What works for me should work for everyone else.

At their simplest, warrants can be stated as "X is good" or "X is bad." Return to the letters to the editor or blog postings that you analyzed in the exercise on p. 271, this time looking for the warrant that is behind each claim. As a way to start, ask yourself these questions:

> If I find myself agreeing with the letter writer, what assumptions about the subject matter do I share with him/her?
>
> If I disagree, what assumptions are at the heart of that disagreement?

The list of warrants you generate will likely come from these assumptions.

Offering Evidence: Backing

The richest, most interesting part of a writer's work—backing—remains to be done after the argument has been outlined. Clearly stated claims and warrants show you how much evidence you will need. Take a look at this brief argument, which is both debatable and controversial, especially in tough economic times:

> NASA should launch a human expedition to Mars because Americans need a unifying national goal.

Here's one version of the warrant that supports the enthymeme:

> What unifies the nation ought to be a national priority.

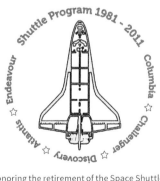

Sticker honoring the retirement of the Space Shuttle program

© Steven Barrymore

To run with this claim and warrant, you'd first need to place both in context. Human space exploration has been debated with varying intensity following the 1957 launch of the Soviet Union's Sputnik satellite, after the losses of the U.S. space shuttles Challenger (1986) and Columbia (2003), and after the retirement of the Space Shuttle program in 2011. Acquiring such background knowledge through reading, conversation, and inquiry of all kinds will be necessary for making your case. (See Chapter 10 for more on gaining authority.)

There's no point in defending any claim until you've satisfied readers that questionable warrants on which the claim is based are defensible. In Toulmin argument, evidence you offer to support a warrant is called **backing**.

Warrant

What unifies the nation ought to be a national priority.

Backing

Americans want to be part of something bigger than themselves. (Emotional appeal as evidence)

In a country as diverse as the United States, common purposes and values help make the nation stronger. (Ethical appeal as evidence)

In the past, government investments such as the Hoover Dam and the *Apollo* moon program enabled many—though not all—Americans to work toward common goals. (Logical appeal as evidence)

In addition to evidence to support your warrant (backing), you'll need evidence to support your claim:

Argument in Brief (Enthymeme/Claim)

NASA should launch a human expedition to Mars because Americans now need a unifying national goal.

Evidence

The American people are politically divided along lines of race, ethnicity, religion, gender, and class. (Fact as evidence)

A common challenge or problem often unites people to accomplish great things. (Emotional appeal as evidence)

A successful Mars mission would require the cooperation of the entire nation—and generate tens of thousands of jobs. (Logical appeal as evidence)

A human expedition to Mars would be a valuable scientific project for the nation to pursue. (Appeal to values as evidence)

As these examples show, appeals to values and emotions can be just as appropriate as appeals to logic and facts, and all such claims will be stronger if a writer presents a convincing ethos. In most arguments, appeals work together rather than separately, reinforcing each other. (See Chapter 10 for more on ethos.)

Using Qualifiers

Experienced writers know that qualifying expressions make writing more precise and honest. Toulmin logic encourages you to acknowledge limitations to your argument through the effective use of **qualifiers**. You can save time if you qualify a claim early in the writing process. But you might not figure out how to limit a claim effectively until after you've explored your subject or discussed it with others.

Qualifiers		
few	more or less	often
it is possible	in some cases	perhaps
rarely	many	under these conditions
it seems	typically	possibly
some	routinely	for the most part
it may be	most	if it were so
sometimes	one might argue	in general

Never assume that readers understand the limits you have in mind. Rather, spell them out as precisely as possible, as in the following examples:

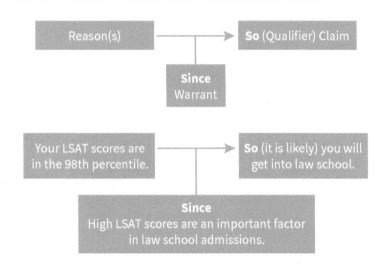

The new NEA logo

Unqualified Claim	People who don't go to college earn less than those who do.
Qualified Claim	*In most cases,* people who don't go to college earn less than those who do.

Understanding Conditions of Rebuttal

In the Toulmin system, potential objections to an argument are called **conditions of rebuttal**. Understanding and reacting to these conditions are essential to support your own claims where they're weak and also to recognize and understand the reasonable objections of people who see the world differently. For example, you may be a big fan of the Public Broadcasting Service (PBS) and the National Endowment for the Arts (NEA) and prefer that federal tax dollars be spent on these programs. So you offer the following claim:

Claim	The federal government should support the arts.

You need reasons to support this thesis, so you decide to present the issue as a matter of values:

Argument in Brief	The federal government should support the arts because it also supports the military.

Now you've got an enthymeme and can test the warrant, or the premises of your claim:

Warrant	If the federal government can support the military, then it can also support other programs.

But the warrant seems frail: you can hear a voice over your shoulder saying, "In essence, you're saying that *Because we pay for a military, we should pay for everything!*" So you decide to revise your claim:

Revised Argument	If the federal government can spend huge amounts of money on the military, then it can afford to spend moderate amounts on arts programs.

Now you've got a new warrant, too:

Revised Warrant	A country that can fund expensive programs can also afford less expensive programs.

This is a premise that you can defend, since you believe strongly that the arts are just as essential as a strong military is to the well-being of the country. Although the warrant now seems solid, you still have to offer strong grounds to support your specific and controversial claim. So you cite statistics from reputable sources, this time comparing the federal budgets for the military and the arts. You break them down in ways that readers can visualize, demonstrating that much less than a penny of every tax dollar goes to support the arts.

But then you hear those voices again, saying that the "common defense" is a federal mandate; the government is constitutionally obligated to support a military, and support for the arts is hardly in the same league! Looks like you need to add a paragraph explaining all the benefits the arts provide for very few dollars spent, and maybe you should suggest that such funding

falls under the constitutional mandate to "promote the general welfare." Though not all readers will accept these grounds, they'll appreciate that you haven't ignored their point of view: you've gained credibility by anticipating a reasonable objection.

Dealing with conditions of rebuttal is an essential part of argument. But it's important to understand rebuttal as more than mere opposition. Anticipating objections broadens your horizons, makes you more open to alternative viewpoints, and helps you understand what you need to do to support your claim.

Within Toulmin argument, conditions of rebuttal remind us that we're part of global conversations: Internet newsgroups and blogs provide potent responses to positions offered by participants in discussions; instant messaging and social networking let you respond to and challenge others; links on Web sites form networks that are infinitely variable and open. In cyberspace, conditions of rebuttal are as close as your screen.

RESPOND

Using an essay or a project you are composing, do a Toulmin analysis of the argument. When you're done, see which elements of the Toulmin scheme are represented. Are you short of evidence to support the warrant? Have you considered the conditions of rebuttal? Have you qualified your claim adequately? Next, write a brief revision plan: How will you buttress the argument in the places where it is weakest? What additional evidence will you offer for the warrant? How can you qualify your claim to meet the conditions of rebuttal? Then show your paper to a classmate and have him/her do a Toulmin analysis: a new reader will probably see your argument in different ways and suggest revisions that may not have occurred to you.

Outline of a Toulmin Argument

Consider the claim that was mentioned on p. 278:

Claim	The federal government should ban e-cigarettes.
Qualifier	The ban would be limited to public spaces.
Good Reasons	E-cigarettes have not been proven to be harmless. E-cigarettes legitimize smoking and also are aimed at recruiting teens and children with flavors like bubble-gum and cotton candy.
Warrants	The Constitution promises to "promote the general welfare." Citizens are entitled to protection from harmful actions by others.
Backing	The United States is based on a political system that is supposed to serve the basic needs of its people, including their health.
Evidence	Analysis of advertising campaigns that reveal direct appeals to children Lawsuits recently won against e-cigarette companies, citing the link between e-cigarettes and a return to regular smoking Examples of bans on e-cigarettes already imposed in many public places
Authority	Cite the FDA and medical groups on effect of e-cigarette smoking.
Conditions of Rebuttal	E-cigarette smokers have rights, too. Smoking laws should be left to the states. Such a ban could not be enforced.
Responses	The ban applies to public places; smokers can smoke in private.

A Toulmin Analysis

You might wonder how Toulmin's method holds up when applied to an argument that is longer than a few sentences. Do such arguments really work the way that Toulmin predicts? In the following short argument, well-known linguist and author Deborah Tannen explores the consequences of a shift in the meaning of one crucial word: *compromise.* Tannen's essay, which originally appeared as a posting on Politico.com on June 15, 2011, offers a series of interrelated claims based on reasons, evidence, and warrants that culminate in the last sentence of the essay. She begins by showing that the word *compromise* is now rejected by both the political right and the political left and offers good reasons and evidence to support that claim. She then moves back to a time when "a compromise really was considered great," and offers three powerful pieces of evidence in support of that claim. The argument then comes back to the present, with a claim that the compromise and politeness of the nineteenth century have been replaced by "growing enmity." That claim is supported with reasoning and evidence that rest on an underlying warrant that "vituperation and seeing opponents as enemies is corrosive to the human spirit." The claims in the argument—that *compromise* has become a dirty word and that enmity and an adversarial spirit are on the rise—lead to Tannen's conclusion: rejecting compromise breaks the trust necessary for a democracy and thus undermines the very foundation of our society. While she does not use traditional qualifying words, she does say that the situation she describes is a "threat" to our nation, which qualifies the claim to some extent: the situation is not the "death" of our nation but rather a "threat." Tannen's annotated essay follows.

Why Is "Compromise" Now a Dirty Word?

DEBORAH TANNEN

Photo: Stephen Voss, courtesy of Deborah Tannen

When did the word "compromise" get compromised?

When did the negative connotations of "He was caught in a compromising position" or "She compromised her ethics" replace the positive connotations of "They reached a compromise"?

House Speaker John Boehner said it outright on *60 Minutes* last year. When talking about "compromise," Boehner said, "I reject the word."

Contextual information leading up to initial claim

"When you say the word 'compromise,'" he explained, ". . . a lot of Americans look up and go, 'Uh-oh, they're gonna sell me out.'" His position is common right now.

In the same spirit, Tony Perkins wrote in a recent CNN.com op-ed piece, "When it comes to conservative principles, compromise is the companion of losers."

The political right is particularly vehement when it comes to compromise. Conservatives are now strongly swayed by the tea party movement, whose clarion call is a refusal to compromise, regardless of the practical consequences.

But the rejection of compromise is more widespread than that. The left regularly savages President Barack Obama for compromising too soon, too much or on the wrong issues. Many

who fervently sought universal health coverage, for example, could not celebrate its near accomplishment because the president gave up the public option.

Initial claim

The death of compromise has become a threat to our nation as we confront crucial issues such as the debt ceiling and that most basic of legislative responsibilities: a federal budget.

Reason

At stake is the very meaning of what had once seemed unshakable: "the full faith and credit" of the U.S. government.

Evidence

Back when the powerful nineteenth-century senator Henry Clay was called "the great compromiser," achieving a compromise really was considered great. On three occasions, the Kentucky statesman helped the Senate preserve the Union by crafting compromises between the deadlocked slave-holding South and the Northern free states. In 1820, his Missouri Compromise stemmed the spread of slavery. In 1833, when the South was poised to defy federal tariff laws favored by the North and the federal government was about to authorize military action, Clay found a last-minute compromise. And his Compromise of 1850 averted civil war for at least a decade.

It was during an 1850 Senate debate that Clay stated his conviction: "I go for honorable compromise whenever it can be made." Something else he said then holds a key to how the dwindling respect for compromise is related to larger and more dangerous developments in our nation today.

Warrant

"All legislation, all government, all society," Clay said, "is formed upon the principle of mutual concession, politeness, comity, courtesy; upon these, everything is based."

Concession, politeness, comity, courtesy—none of these words could be uttered now with the assurance of listeners' approval. The word "comity" is rarely heard; "concession" sounds weak; "politeness" and "courtesy" sound quaint—much like the contemporary equivalent, "civility."

That Clay lauded both compromise and civil discourse in the same speech reveals the link between, on the one hand, the word "compromise" falling into disrepute, and, on the other, the glorification of aggression that I wrote about in my book, *The Argument Culture: Stopping America's War of Words.*

Today we have an increasing tendency to approach every task—and each other—in an ever more adversarial spirit. Nowhere is this more evident, or more destructive, than in the Senate.

Though the two-party system is oppositional by nature, there is plenty of evidence that a certain (yes) comity has been replaced by growing enmity. We don't have to look as far back as Clay for evidence. In 1996, for example, an unprecedented fourteen incumbent senators announced that they would not seek reelection. And many, in farewell essays, described an increase in vituperation and partisanship that made it impossible to do the work of the Senate.

"The bipartisanship that is so crucial to the operation of Congress," Howell Heflin of Alabama wrote, "especially the Senate, has

Margin labels: Claim · Reason (paragraph 2); Evidence (paragraph 3); Claim (paragraph 4); Rebuttal · Evidence (paragraph 5); Evidence (paragraph 6)

been abandoned." J. James Exon of Nebraska described an "ever-increasing vicious polarization of the electorate" that had "all but swept aside the former preponderance of reasonable discussion."

Claim

But this is not happening only in the Senate. There is a rising adversarial spirit among the people and the press. It isn't only the obvious invective on TV and radio. A newspaper story that criticizes its subject is praised as "tough"; one that refrains from criticism is scorned as a "puff piece."

Reason

Evidence

The notion of "balance" today often leads to a search for the most extreme opposing views— so they can be presented as "both sides," leaving no forum for subtlety, multiple perspectives or the middle ground, where most people stand. Framing issues in this polarizing way reinforces the impression that Boehner voiced: that compromising is selling out.

Warrant

Claim

Being surrounded by vituperation and seeing opponents as enemies is corrosive to the human spirit. It's also dangerous to our democracy. The great anthropologist Margaret Mead explained this in a 1962 speech.

Reason

"We are essentially a society which must be more committed to a two-party system than to either party," Mead said. "The only way you can have a two-party system is to belong to a party formally and to fight to the death . . ." not for your party to win but "for the right of the other party to be there too."

Today, this sounds almost as quaint as "comity" in political discourse.

Mead traced our two-party system to our unique revolution: "We didn't kill a king and we didn't execute a large number of our people, and we came into our own without the stained hands that have been associated with most revolutions."

Reason

With this noble heritage, Mead said, comes "the obligation to keep the kind of government we set up"—where members of each party may "disagree mightily" but still "trust in each other and trust in our political opponents."

Losing that trust, Mead concluded, undermines the foundation of our democracy. That trust is exactly what is threatened when the very notion of compromise is rejected.

Conclusion

What Toulmin Teaches

As Tannen's essay demonstrates, few arguments you read have perfectly sequenced claims or clear warrants, so you might not think of Toulmin's terms in building your own arguments. Once you're into your subject, it's easy to forget about qualifying a claim or finessing a warrant. But remembering what Toulmin teaches will always help you strengthen your arguments:

- Claims should be clear, reasonable, and carefully qualified.

- Claims should be supported with good reasons and evidence. Remember that a Toulmin structure provides the framework of an argument, which you fill out with all kinds of data, including facts, statistics, precedents, photographs, and even stories.

- Claims and reasons should be based on assumptions your audience will likely accept. Toulmin's focus on warrants can be confusing because it asks us to look at the assumptions that underlie our arguments—something many would rather not do. Toulmin pushes us to probe the values that support any argument and to think of how those values relate to particular audiences.

- Effective arguments respectfully anticipate objections readers might offer. Toulmin argument acknowledges that any claim can crumble under certain conditions, so it encourages a complex view that doesn't demand absolute or unqualified positions.

It takes considerable experience to write arguments that meet all these conditions. Using Toulmin's framework brings them into play automatically. If you learn it well enough, constructing good arguments can become a habit.

CULTURAL CONTEXTS FOR ARGUMENT

Organization

As you think about organizing your argument, remember that cultural factors are at work: patterns that you find persuasive are probably ones that are deeply embedded in your culture. In the United States, many people expect a writer to "get to the point" as directly as possible and to articulate that point efficiently and unambiguously. The organizational patterns favored by many in business hold similarities to the classical oration — a highly explicit pattern that leaves little or nothing unexplained — introduction and thesis, background, overview of the parts that follow, evidence, other viewpoints, and conclusion. If a piece of writing follows this pattern, American readers ordinarily find it "well organized."

So it's no surprise that student writers in the United States are expected to make their structures direct and their claims explicit, leaving little unspoken. Their claims usually appear early in an argument, often in the first paragraph.

But not all cultures take such an approach. Some expect any claim or thesis to be introduced subtly, indirectly, and perhaps at the end of a work, assuming that audiences will "read between the lines" to understand what's being said. Consequently, the preferred structure of arguments (and face-to-face negotiations, as well) may be elaborate, repetitive, and full of digressions. Those accustomed to such writing may find more direct Western styles overly simple, childish, or even rude.

When arguing across cultures, look for cues to determine how to structure your presentations effectively. Here are several points to consider:

- Do members of your audience tend to be very direct, saying explicitly what they mean? Or are they restrained, less likely to call a spade a spade? Consider adjusting your work to the expectations of the audience.

- Do members of your audience tend to respect authority and the opinions of groups? They may find blunt approaches disrespectful or contrary to their expectations.

- Consider when to state your thesis: At the beginning? At the end? Somewhere else? Not at all?

- Consider whether digressions are a good idea, a requirement, or an element to avoid.

15

Arguments
of Fact

Writing Arguments

Chapter 15, "Arguments of Fact," from *Everything's an Argument*, Seventh Edition, by Andrea A. Lunsford and John J. Ruszkiewicz, pp. 151–184 (Chapter 8). Copyright © 2016 by Bedford/St. Martin's.

Left to right: Zoonar/N.Sorokin/age fototstock; Alfred Eisenstaedt/Getty Images;
© David R. Frazier, Photolibrary, Inc./Alamy

Many people believe that extensive use of the Internet, and especially social media, is harmful to memory and to learning, but recent research by scholars of literacy provides evidence suggesting that they are probably wrong.

In the past, female screen stars like Marilyn Monroe could be buxom and curvy, less concerned about their weight than actresses today. Or so the legend goes. But measuring the costumes worn by Monroe and other actresses reveals a different story.

When an instructor announces a tough new attendance policy for her course, a student objects that there is no evidence that students who regularly attend classes perform any better than those who do not. The instructor begs to differ.

Understanding Arguments of Fact

Factual arguments come in many varieties, but they all try to establish whether something is or is not so, answering questions such as *Is a historical legend true? Has a crime occurred?* or *Are the claims of a scientist accurate?* At first glance, you might object that these aren't arguments at all but just a matter of looking things up and then writing reports. And you'd be correct to an extent: people don't usually argue factual matters that are settled or undisputed (*The earth revolves around the sun*), that might be decided with simple research (*The Mendenhall Glacier has receded 1.75 miles since 1958*), or that are the equivalent of a rule (*One mile measures 5,280 feet*). Reporting facts, you might think, should be free of the friction of argument.

Yet facts become arguments whenever they're controversial on their own or challenge people's beliefs and lifestyles. Disagreements about childhood obesity, endangered species, or energy production ought to have a kind of clean, scientific logic to them. But that's rarely the case because the facts surrounding them must be interpreted. Those interpretations then determine what we feed children, where we can build a dam, or how we heat our homes. In other words, serious factual arguments almost always have consequences. *Can we rely on wind and solar power to solve our energy needs? Will the Social Security trust fund really go broke? Is it healthy to eat fatty foods?* People need well-reasoned factual arguments on subjects of this kind to make informed decisions. Such arguments educate the public.

For the same reason, we need arguments to challenge beliefs that are common in a society but held on the basis of inadequate or faulty information. Corrective arguments appear daily in the media, often based on studies written by scientists or researchers that the public would not encounter on their own. Many people, for example, believe that talking on a cell phone while driving is just like listening to the radio. But their intuition is not based on hard data: scientific studies show that using a cell phone in a car is comparable to driving under the influence of alcohol. That's a fact. As a result, fourteen states (and counting) have banned the use of handheld phones in cars.

Factual arguments also routinely address broad questions about how we understand the past. For example, are the accounts that we have of the American founding—or the Civil War, Reconstruction, or the heroics of the "Greatest Generation" in World War II—accurate? Or do the "facts" that we teach today sometimes reflect the perspectives and prejudices of earlier times or ideologies? The telling of history is almost always controversial and rarely settled: the British and Americans will always tell different versions of what happened in North America in 1776.

© Bagley/Cagle Cartoons, Inc.

The Internet puts mountains of information at our fingertips, but we need to be sure to confirm whether or not that information is fact, using what Howard Rheingold calls "crap detection," the ability to distinguish between accurate information and inaccurate information, misinformation, or disinformation. (For more on "crap detection," see Chapter 22, "Evaluating Sources.")

As you can see, arguments of fact do much of the heavy lifting in our world. They report on what has been recently discovered or explore the implications of that new information. They also add interest and complexity to our lives, taking what might seem simple and adding new dimensions to it. In many situations, they're the precursors to other forms of analysis, especially causal and proposal arguments. Before we can explore why things happen as they do or solve problems, we need to do our best to determine the facts.

RESPOND

For each topic in the following list, decide whether the claim is worth arguing to a college audience, and explain why or why not.

Earthquakes are increasing in number and intensity.

Many people die annually of heart disease.

Fewer people would be obese if they followed the Paleo Diet.

Japan might have come to terms more readily in 1945 if the Allies in World War II hadn't demanded unconditional surrender.

Boys would do better in school if there were more men teaching in elementary and secondary classrooms.

The sharp drop in oil prices could lead drivers to go back to buying gas-guzzling trucks and SUVs.

There aren't enough high-paying jobs for college graduates these days.

Hydrogen may never be a viable alternative to fossil fuels because it takes too much energy to change hydrogen into a usable form.

Proponents of the Keystone Pipe Line have exaggerated the benefits it will bring to the American economy.

Characterizing Factual Arguments

Factual arguments are often motivated by simple human curiosity or suspicion: *Are people who earn college degrees happier than those who don't? If being fat is so unhealthy, why aren't mortality rates rising?* Researchers may notice a pattern that leads them to look more closely at some phenomenon or behavior, exploring questions such as *What if?* or *How come?* Or maybe a writer first notes something new or different or unexpected and wants to draw attention to that fact: *Contrary to expectations, suicide rates are much higher in rural areas than in urban ones.*

Such observations can lead quickly to **hypotheses**—that is, toward tentative and plausible statements of fact whose merits need to be examined more closely. *Maybe being a little overweight isn't as bad for people as we've been told? Maybe people in rural areas have less access to mental health services?* To support such hypotheses, writers then have to uncover evidence that reaches well beyond the casual observations that triggered an initial interest—like a news reporter motivated to see whether there's a verifiable story behind a source's tip.

For instance, the authors of *Freakonomics*, Stephen J. Dubner and Steven D. Levitt, were intrigued by the National Highway Traffic Safety Administration's claim that car seats for children were 54 percent effective in preventing deaths in auto crashes for children below the age of four. In a *New York Times* op-ed column entitled "The Seat-Belt Solution," they posed an important question about that factual claim:

> But 54 percent effective compared with what? The answer, it turns out, is this: Compared with a child's riding completely unrestrained.

Their initial question about that claim led them to a more focused inquiry, then to a database on auto crashes, and then to a surprising conclusion: for kids above age twenty-four months, those in car seats were statistically safer than those without any protection but weren't safer than those confined by seat belts (which are much simpler, cheaper, and more readily available devices). Looking at the statistics every which way, the authors wonder if children older than two years would be just as well off physically—and their parents less stressed and better off financially—if the government mandated seat belts rather than car seats for them.

What kinds of evidence typically appear in sound factual arguments? The simple answer might be "all sorts," but a case can be made that factual arguments try to rely more on "hard evidence" than do "constructed" arguments based on logic and reason (see Chapter 11). Even so, some pieces of evidence are harder than others!

Developing a Factual Argument

Entire Web sites are dedicated to finding and posting errors from news and political sources. Some, like Media Matters for America and Accuracy in Media, take overtly partisan stands. Here's a one-day sampling of headlines from Media Matters:

> Hillary Clinton Overcompensates on Foreign Policy Because She's a Woman

> Fox Host Defends Calling Michelle Obama Fat

> Fox News Decries Granting Undocumented Children Their Right to Public Education

And here's a listing from Accuracy in Media:

> An Inside Look at How Democrats Rig the Election Game

> Why Obamacare Is Unfixable

> The American Left: Friends to Our Country's Enemies

It would be hard to miss the blatant political agendas at work on these sites.

Other fact-checking organizations have better reputations when it comes to assessing the truths behind political claims and media presentations. Though both are also routinely charged with bias, Pulitzer Prize–winning PolitiFact.com and FactCheck.org at least make an effort to be fair-minded across a broader political spectrum. FactCheck, for example, provides a detailed analysis of the claims it investigates in relatively neutral and denotative language, and lists the sources its researchers used—just as if its writers were doing a research paper. At its best, FactCheck.org demonstrates what one valuable kind of factual argument can accomplish.

Any factual argument that you might compose—from how you state your claim to how you present evidence and the language you use—should be similarly shaped by the occasion for the argument and a desire to serve the audiences that you hope to reach. We can offer some general advice to help you get started.

PolitiFact uses a meter to rate political claims from "True" to "Pants on Fire."

RESPOND

The Annenberg Public Policy Center at the University of Pennsylvania hosts FactCheck.org, a Web site dedicated to separating facts from opinion or falsehood in the area of politics. It claims to be politically neutral. Find a case that interests you, either a recent controversial item listed on its homepage or another from its archives. Carefully study the item. Pay attention to the devices that FactCheck uses to suggest or ensure objectivity and the way that it handles facts and statistics. Then offer your own brief *factual* argument about the site's objectivity.

Identifying an Issue

To offer a factual argument of your own, you need to identify an issue or problem that will interest you and potential readers. Look for situations or phenomena—local or national—that seem out of the ordinary in the expected order of things. For instance, you might notice that many people you know are deciding not to attend college. How widespread is this change, and who are the people making this choice?

Or follow up claims that strike you as at odds with the facts as you know them or believe them. Maybe you doubt explanations being offered for your favorite sport team's current slump or for the declining number of minority men in your college courses. Or you might give a local spin to factual questions that other people have already formulated on a national level. Do people in your town seem to be flocking to high-MPG vehicles or resisting bans on texting while driving or smoking in public places outdoors? You will likely write a better paper if you take on a factual question that genuinely interests you.

In fact, whole books are written when authors decide to pursue factual questions that intrigue them. But you want to be careful not to argue matters that pose no challenge for you or your audiences. You're not offering anything new if you just try to persuade readers that smoking is harmful to their well-being. So how about something fresh in the area of health?

Quick preliminary research and reading might allow you to move from an intuition to a hypothesis, that is, a tentative statement of your claim: *Having a dog is good for your health.* As noted earlier, factual arguments often provoke other types of analysis. In developing this claim, you'd need to explain what "good for your health" means, potentially an argument of definition. You'd also likely find yourself researching causes of the phenomenon if you can demonstrate that it is factual. As it turns out, your canine hypothesis would have merit if you defined "good for health" as "encouraging exercise." Here's the lead to a *New York Times* story reporting recent research:

> If you're looking for the latest in home exercise equipment, you may want to consider something with four legs and a wagging tail.
>
> Several studies now show that dogs can be powerful motivators to get people moving. Not only are dog owners more likely to take regular walks, but new research shows that dog walkers are more active overall than people who don't have dogs.
>
> One study even found that older people are more likely to take regular walks if the walking companion is canine rather than human.
>
> —Tara Parker-Pope, "Forget the Treadmill. Get a Dog,"
> March 14, 2011

As always, there's another side to the story: what if people likely to get dogs are the very sort already inclined to be more physically active? You could explore that possibility as well (and researchers have) and then either modify your initial hypothesis or offer a new one. That's what hypotheses are for. They are works in progress.

Moving is the best medicine.
Keeping active and losing weight are just two of the ways that you can fight osteoarthritis pain. In fact, for every pound you lose, that's four pounds less pressure on each knee. For information on managing pain, go to fightarthritispain.org.

Here's an actual ad based on the claim that exercise (and dog ownership) is good for health.

RESPOND

Working with a group of colleagues, generate a list of twenty favorite "mysteries" explored on TV shows, in blogs, or in tabloid newspapers. Here are three to get you started—the alien crash landing at Roswell, the existence of Atlantis, and the uses of Area 51. Then decide which—if any— of these puzzlers might be resolved or explained in a reasonable factual argument and which ones remain eternally mysterious and improbable. Why are people attracted to such topics? Would any of these items provide material for a noteworthy factual argument?

Researching Your Hypothesis

How and where you research your subject will depend, naturally, on your subject. You'll certainly want to review Chapter 20, "Finding Evidence," Chapter 21, "Evaluating Sources," and Chapter 22, "Using Sources," be- fore constructing an argument of fact. Libraries and the Web will provide you with deep resources on almost every subject. Your task will typically be to separate the best sources from all the rest. The word *best* here has many connotations: some reputable sources may be too technical for your audiences; some accessible sources may be pitched too low or be too far removed from the actual facts.

You'll be making judgment calls like this routinely. But do use primary sources whenever you can. For example, when gathering a comment from a source on the Web, trace it whenever possible to its original site, and read the comment in its full context. When statistics are quoted, follow them back to the source that offered them first to be sure that they're recent and reputable. Instructors and librarians can help you appreciate the differences. Understand that even sources with pronounced biases can furnish useful information, provided that you know how to use them, take their limitations into account, and then share what you know about the sources with your readers.

Sometimes, you'll be able to do primary research on your own, especially when your subject is local and you have the resources to do it. Consider conducting a competent survey of campus opinions and attitudes, for example, or study budget documents (often public) to determine trends in faculty salaries, tuition, student fees, and so on. Primary research of this sort can be challenging because even the simplest surveys or polls have to be intelligently designed and executed in a way that samples a representative population (see Chapter 11). But the work could pay off in an argument that brings new information to readers.

Refining Your Claim

As you learn more about your subject, you might revise your hypothesis to reflect what you've discovered. In most cases, these revised hypotheses will grow increasingly complex and specific. Following are three versions of essentially the same claim, with each version offering more information to help readers judge its merit:

- Americans really did land on the moon, despite what some people think!

- Since 1969, when the *Eagle* supposedly landed on the moon, some people have been unjustifiably skeptical about the success of the United States' *Apollo* program.

- Despite plentiful hard evidence to the contrary—from *Saturn V* launches witnessed by thousands to actual moon rocks tested by independent labs worldwide—some people persist in believing falsely that NASA's moon landings were actually filmed on deserts in the American Southwest as part of a massive propaganda fraud.

The additional details about the subject might also suggest new ways to develop and support it. For example, conspiracy theorists claim that the absence of visible stars in photographs of the moon landing is evidence that it was staged, but photographers know that the camera exposure needed to capture the foreground—astronauts in their bright space suits—would

have made the stars in the background too dim to see. That's a key bit of evidence for this argument.

'...And, of course, there are the conspiracy theorists who say that it was all a big hoax and I didn't jump over it at all.'

© KES/CartoonStock.com

As you advance in your research, your thesis will likely pick up even more qualifying words and expressions, which help you to make reasonable claims. Qualifiers—words and phrases such as *some, most, few, for most people, for a few users, under specific conditions, usually, occasionally, seldom,* and so on—will be among your most valuable tools in a factual argument. (See p. 281 in Chapter 14 for more on qualifiers.)

Sometimes it is important to set your factual claim into a context that helps explain it to others who may find it hard to accept. You might have to concede some ground initially in order to see the broader picture. For instance, professor of English Vincent Carretta anticipated strong objections after he uncovered evidence that Olaudah Equiano—the author of *The Interesting Narrative* (1789), a much-cited autobiographical account of his Middle Passage voyage and subsequent life as a slave—may actually have been born in South Carolina and not in western Africa. Speaking to the *Chronicle of Higher Education* about why Equiano may have fabricated his African origins to serve a larger cause, Carretta explains:

"Whether [Equiano] invented his African birth or not, he knew that what that movement needed was a first-person account. And because they were going after the slave trade, it had to be an account of someone who had been born in Africa and was brought across the Middle Passage. An African American voice wouldn't have done it."

—Jennifer Howard, "Unraveling the Narrative"

Carretta asks readers to appreciate that the new facts that he has discovered about *The Interesting Narrative* do not undermine the work's historical significance. If anything, his research has added new dimensions to its meaning and interpretation.

Deciding Which Evidence to Use

In this chapter, we've blurred the distinction between factual arguments for scientific and technical audiences and those for the general public (in magazines, blogs, social media sites, television documentaries, and so on). In the former kind of arguments, readers will expect specific types of evidence arranged in a formulaic way. Such reports may include a hypothesis, a review of existing research on the subject, a description of methods, a presentation of results, and finally a formal discussion of the findings. If you are thinking "lab report," you are already familiar with an academic form of a factual argument with precise standards for evidence.

Less scientific factual arguments—claims about our society, institutions, behaviors, habits, and so on—are seldom so systematic, and they may draw on evidence from a great many different media. For instance, you might need to review old newspapers, scan videos, study statistics on government Web sites, read transcripts of congressional hearings, record the words of eyewitnesses to an event, glean information by following experts on Twitter, and so on. Very often, you will assemble your arguments from material found in credible, though not always concurring, authorities and resources—drawing upon the factual findings of scientists and scholars, but perhaps using their original insights in novel ways.

For example, you might be intrigued by a comprehensive report from the Kaiser Family Foundation (2010) providing the results of a study of more than 2,000 eight- to eighteen-year-old American children:

The study found that the average time spent reading books for pleasure in a typical day rose from 21 minutes in 1999 to 23 minutes in 2004, and finally to 25 minutes in 2010. The rise of screen-based media has not melted children's brains, despite ardent warnings otherwise: "It does not appear that time spent using screen media (TV, video games and computers) displaces time spent with print media," the report stated. Teens are not only reading more books, they're involved in communities of like-minded book lovers.

—Hannah Withers and Lauren Ross,
"Young People Are Reading More Than You"

Reading about these results, however, may raise some new questions for you: Is twenty-five minutes of reading a day really something to be happy about? What is the quality of what these young people are reading? Such questions might lead you to do a new study that could challenge the conclusion of the earlier research by bringing fresh facts to the table.

Often, you may have only a limited number of words or pages in which to make a factual argument. What do you do then? You present your best evidence as powerfully as possible. But that's not difficult. You can make a persuasive factual case with just a few examples: three or four often suffice to make a point. Indeed, going on too long or presenting even good data in ways that make it seem uninteresting or pointless can undermine a claim.

Presenting Your Evidence

In *Hard Times* (1854), British author Charles Dickens poked fun at a pedagogue he named Thomas Gradgrind, who preferred hard facts before all things human or humane. When poor Sissy Jupe (called "girl number twenty" in his awful classroom) is unable at his command to define *horse*, Gradgrind turns to his star pupil:

"Bitzer," said Thomas Gradgrind. "Your definition of a horse."

"Quadruped. Graminivorous. Forty teeth, namely twenty-four grinders, four eyeteeth, and twelve incisive. Sheds coat in the spring; in marshy countries, sheds hoofs, too. Hoofs hard, but requiring to be shod with iron. Age known by marks in mouth."
Thus (and much more) Bitzer.

"Now girl number twenty," said Mr. Gradgrind. "You know what a horse is."

—Charles Dickens, **Hard Times**

But does Bitzer? Rattling off facts about a subject isn't quite the same thing as knowing it, especially when your goal is, as it is in an argument of fact, to educate and persuade audiences. So you must take care how you present your evidence.

Factual arguments, like any others, take many forms. They can be as simple and pithy as a letter to the editor (or Bitzer's definition of a horse) or as comprehensive and formal as a senior thesis or even a dissertation. Such a thesis might have just two or three readers mainly interested in the facts you are presenting and the competence of your work. So your presentation can be lean and relatively simple.

But to earn the attention of readers in some more public forum, you may need to work harder to be persuasive. For instance, Pew Research Center's May 2014 formal report, *Young Adults, Student Debt, and Economic Well-Being*, which spends time introducing its authors and establishing their expertise, is twenty-three pages long, cites a dozen sources, and contains sixteen figures and tables. Like many such studies, it also includes a foreword, an overview, and a detailed table of contents. All these elements help readers find the facts they need while also establishing the ethos of the work, making it seem serious, credible, well conceived, and worth reading.

Considering Design and Visuals

When you prepare a factual argument, consider how you can present your evidence most effectively. Precisely because factual arguments often rely on evidence that can be measured, computed, or illustrated, they benefit from thoughtful, even artful presentation of data. If you have lots of examples, you might arrange them in a list (bulleted or otherwise) and keep the language in each item roughly parallel. If you have an argument that can be translated into a table, chart, or graph, try it. And if there's a more dramatic medium for your factual argument—a Prezi slide show, a multimedia mashup, a documentary video posted via a social network—experiment with it, checking to be sure it would satisfy the assignment.

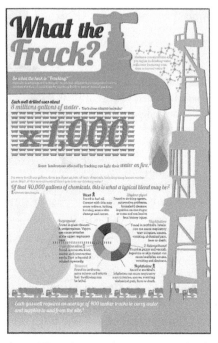

"What the Frack?" uses images to present its case against fracking.

© Jess Nelson Design

Images and photos—from technical illustrations to imaginative re-creations—have the power to document what readers might otherwise have to imagine, whether actual conditions of drought, poverty, or a disaster like devastating typhoon Haiyan that displaced over 4 million people in the Philippines in 2013, or the dimensions of the Roman forum as it existed in the time of Julius Caesar. Readers today expect the arguments they read to include visual elements, and there's little reason not to offer this assistance if you have the technical skills to create them.

Consider the rapid development of the genre known as infographics—basically data presented in bold visual form. These items can be humorous and creative, but many, such as "Learning Out of Poverty" on the preceding page, make powerful factual arguments even when they leave it to viewers to draw their own conclusions. Just search "infographics" on the Web to find many examples.

Infographics like this one turn facts and data into arguments.

USAID

GUIDE TO WRITING AN ARGUMENT OF FACT

Finding a Topic

You're entering an argument of fact when you:

- make a claim about fact or existence that's controversial or surprising: *Climate change is threatening species in all regions by extending the range of non-native plants and animals.*

- correct an error of fact: *The overall abortion rate is not increasing in the United States, though rates are increasing in some states.*

- challenge societal myths: *Many Mexicans fought alongside Anglos in battles that won Texas its independence from Mexico.*

- wish to discover the state of knowledge about a subject or examine a range of perspectives and points of view: *The rationales of parents who homeschool their children reveal some surprising differences.*

Researching Your Topic

Use both a library and the Web to locate the information you need. A research librarian is often a valuable resource, as are experts or eyewitnesses. Begin research by consulting the following types of sources:

- scholarly books on your subject

- newspapers, magazines, reviews, and journals (online and print)

- online databases

- government documents and reports

- Web sites, blogs, social networking sites, and listservs or newsgroups

- experts in the field, some of whom might be right on your campus

GUIDE TO WRITING AN ARGUMENT OF FACT

Do field research if appropriate—a survey, a poll, or systematic observation. Or invite people with a stake in the subject to present their interpretations of the facts. Evaluate all sources carefully, making sure that each is authoritative and credible.

Formulating a Hypothesis

Don't rush into a thesis. Instead, begin with a hypothesis that expresses your beliefs at the beginning of the project but that may change as you learn more. It's OK to start with a question to which you don't have an answer or with a broad, general interest in a subject:

- **Question:** Have higher admissions standards at BSU reduced the numbers of entering first-year students from small, rural high schools?

- **Hypothesis:** Higher admissions standards at BSU are reducing the number of students admitted from rural high schools, which tend to be smaller and less well-funded than those in suburban and urban areas.

- **Question:** Have music sites like Pandora and Spotify reduced the amount of illegal downloading of music?

- **Hypothesis:** Services like Pandora and Spotify may have done more than lawsuits by record companies to discourage illegal downloads of music.

- **Question:** How dangerous is nuclear energy, really?

- **Hypothesis:** The danger posed by nuclear power plants is far less than that attributable to other viable energy sources.

- **Question:** Why can't politicians and citizens agree about the threat posed by the huge federal deficit?

- **Hypothesis:** People with different points of view read different threats into the budget numbers and so react differently.

GUIDE **TO WRITING AN ARGUMENT OF FACT**

Examples of Arguable Factual Claims

* A campus survey that shows that far more students have read *Harry Potter and the Prisoner of Azkaban* than *Hamlet* indicates that our current core curriculum lacks depth.

* Evidence suggests that the European conquest of the Americas may have had more to do with infectious diseases than any superiority in technology or weaponry.

* In the long run, dieting may be more harmful than moderate overeating.

Preparing a Proposal

If your instructor asks you to prepare a proposal for your project, here's a format that may help:

State your thesis or hypothesis completely. If you are having trouble doing so, try outlining it in Toulmin terms:

Claim:

Reason(s):

Warrant(s):

Alternatively, you might describe the complications of a factual issue you hope to explore in your project, with the thesis perhaps coming later.

* Explain why the issue you're examining is important, and provide the context for raising the issue. Are you introducing new information, making available information better known, correcting what has been reported incorrectly, or complicating what has been understood more simply?

* Identify and describe those readers you most hope to reach with your argument. Why is this group of readers most

appropriate for your project? What are their interests in the subject? How might you involve them in the paper?

- Discuss the kinds of evidence you expect to use in the project and the research the paper will require.

- Briefly discuss the key challenges you anticipate in preparing your argument.

Considering Format and Media

Your instructor may specify that you use a particular format and/or medium. If not, ask yourself these questions to help you make a good choice:

- What format is most appropriate for your argument of fact? Does it call for an academic essay, a report, an infographic, a brochure, or something else?

- What medium is most appropriate for your argument? Would it be best delivered orally to a live audience? Presented as an audio essay or podcast? Presented in print only or in print with illustrations?

- Will you need visuals, such as moving or still images, maps, graphs, charts—and what function will they play in your argument? Make sure they are not just "added on" but are necessary components of the argument.

Thinking about Organization

The simplest structure for a factual argument is to make a claim and then prove it. But even a basic approach needs an introductory section that provides a context for the claim and a concluding section that assesses the implications of the argument. A factual argument that corrects an error or provides an alternative view of some familiar concept or historical event will also need a

GUIDE **TO WRITING AN ARGUMENT OF FACT**

section early on explaining what the error or the common belief is. Be sure your opening section answers the *who, what, where, when, how,* and (maybe) *why* questions that readers will bring to the case.

Factual arguments offered in some academic fields follow formulas and templates. A format favored in the hard sciences and also in the social and behavioral sciences is known by its acronym, IMRAD, which stands for Introduction, Methods, Research, and Discussion. Another typical format calls for an abstract, a review of literature, a discussion of method, an analysis, and a references list. When you have flexibility in the structure of your argument, it makes sense to lead with a striking example to interest readers in your subject and then to conclude with your strongest evidence. Pay particular attention to transitions between key points.

If you are defending a specific claim, anticipate the ways people with different points of view might respond to your argument. Consider how to address such differences respectfully in the body of your argument. But don't let a factual argument with a persuasive thesis end with concessions or refutations, especially in pieces for the general public. Such a strategy leaves readers thinking about problems with your claim at precisely the point when they should be impressed by its strengths. On the other hand, if your factual argument becomes exploratory, you may find yourself simply presenting a range of positions.

Getting and Giving Response: Questions for Peer Response

Your instructor may assign you to a group for the purpose of reading and responding to each other's drafts. If not, ask for responses from serious readers or consultants at a writing center. Use the following questions to evaluate a colleague's draft. Since specific comments help more than general observations, be sure

GUIDE TO WRITING AN ARGUMENT OF FACT

to illustrate your comments with examples. Some of the questions below assume a conventional, thesis-driven project, but more exploratory or invitational arguments of fact also need to be clearly phrased, organized, and supported with evidence.

The Claim

- Does the claim clearly raise a serious and arguable factual issue?

- Is the claim as clear and specific as possible?

- Is the claim qualified? If so, how?

Evidence for the Claim

- Is the evidence provided enough to persuade readers to believe your claim? If not, what additional evidence would help? Does any of the evidence seem inappropriate or ineffective? Why?

- Is the evidence in support of the claim simply announced, or do you explain its significance and appropriateness? Is more discussion needed?

- Are readers' potential objections to the claim or evidence addressed adequately? Are alternative positions understood thoroughly and presented fairly?

- What kinds of sources are cited? How credible and persuasive will they be to readers? What other kinds of sources might work better?

- Are all quotations introduced with appropriate signal phrases (such as "As Tyson argues, . . .") and blended smoothly into the writer's sentences?

- Are all visuals titled and labeled appropriately? Have you introduced them and commented on their significance?

GUIDE **TO WRITING AN ARGUMENT OF FACT**

Organization and Style

- How are the parts of the argument organized? Is this organization effective?

- Will readers understand the relationships among the claims, supporting reasons, warrants, and evidence? If not, how might those connections be clearer? Is the function of every visual clear? Are more transitions needed? Would headings or graphic devices help?

- Are the transitions or links from point to point, sentence to sentence, and paragraph to paragraph clear and effective? If not, how could they be improved?

- Are all visuals carefully integrated into the text? Is each visual introduced and commented on to point out its significance? Is each visual labeled as a figure or a table and given a caption as well as a citation?

- Is the style suited to the subject? Is it too formal, casual, or technical? Can it be improved?

- Which sentences seem effective? Which ones seem weaker, and how could they be improved? Should short sentences be combined, and any longer ones be broken up?

- How effective are the paragraphs? Too short or too long? How can they be improved?

- Which words or phrases seem effective? Do any seem vague or inappropriate for the audience or the writer's purpose? Are technical or unfamiliar terms defined?

GUIDE **TO WRITING AN ARGUMENT OF FACT**

Spelling, Punctuation, Mechanics, Documentation, and Format

- Are there any errors in spelling, punctuation, capitalization, and the like?

- Is an appropriate and consistent style of documentation used for parenthetical citations and the list of works cited or references? (See Chapter 24.)

- Does the paper or project follow an appropriate format? Is it appropriately designed and attractively presented? How could it be improved?

PROJECTS

1. Turn a database of information you find in the library or online into a traditional argument or, alternatively, into an infographic that offers a variety of potential claims. FedStats, a government Web site, provides endless data, but so can the sports or financial sections of a newspaper. Once you find a rich field of study, examine the data and draw your ideas from it, perhaps amplifying these ideas with material from other related sources of information. If you decide to create an infographic, you'll find good examples at VizWorld or Cool Infographics online. Software tools you can use to create infographics include Piktochart and Google Public Data. Have fun.

2. Write an argument about one factual matter you are confident—based on personal experience or your state of knowledge—that most people get wrong, time and again. Use your expertise to correct this false impression.

3. Tough economic and political times sometimes reinforce and sometimes undermine cultural myths. With your classmates, generate a list of common beliefs about education, employment, family life, marriage, social progress, technology, and so on that seem to be under unusual

scrutiny today. *Does it still pay to invest in higher education? Do two-parent households matter as much as they used to? Can children today expect to do better than their parents? Is a home still a good investment?* Pick one area to explore in depth, narrow the topic as much as you can, and then gather facts that inform it by doing research, perhaps working collaboratively to expand your findings. Turn your investigation into a factual argument.

4. Since critic and writer Nicholas Carr first asked "Is Google Making Us Stupid?" many have answered with a resounding "yes," arguing that extensive time online is reducing attention spans and leaving readers less critical than ever. Others have disagreed, saying that new technologies are doing just the opposite—expanding our brain power. Do some research on this controversy, on the Web or in the library, and consult with a wide range of people interested in the subject, perhaps gathering them together for a discussion or panel discussion. Then offer a factual argument based on what you uncover, reflecting the range of perspectives and opinions you have encountered.

Two Sample Factual Arguments

Why You Should Fear Your Toaster More Than Nuclear Power

TAYLOR PEARSON

> Readers will certainly notice the title.

For the past month or so, headlines everywhere have been warning us of the horrible crises caused by the damaged Japanese nuclear reactors. Titles like "Japan Nuclear Disaster Tops Scale" have fueled a new wave of protests against anything nuclear—namely, the construction of new nuclear plants or even the continued operation of existing plants. However, all this reignited fear of nuclear energy is nothing more than media sensationalism. We need nuclear energy. It's clean, it's efficient, it's economic, and it's probably the only thing that will enable us to quickly phase out fossil fuels.

> A recent nuclear disaster in Japan provides a challenge context for Pearson's claim: we need nuclear energy.

> The first-person plural point of view (*we*) helps Pearson to connect with his audience.

Death Toll

First, let's address what is probably everyone's main concern about nuclear energy: the threat it poses to us and the likelihood of a nuclear power plant killing large numbers of people. The actual number of deaths caused by nuclear power plant accidents, even in worst-case scenarios, have been few. Take the Chernobyl

---

Taylor Pearson wrote "Why You Should Fear Your Toaster More Than Nuclear Power" while he was a sophomore at the University of Texas at Austin. The assignment asked for a public argument—one good enough to attract readers who could put it down if they lost interest. In other words, a purely academic argument wouldn't work. So Pearson allows himself to exercise his sense of humor. Nor did the paper have to be formally documented. However, Pearson was expected to identify crucial sources the way writers do in magazines and newspapers. The paper provides an example of a factual argument with a clear thesis: "We need nuclear energy."

Pearson deflates fears by putting deaths caused by nuclear plants in perspective.

accident—the worst and most lethal nuclear incident to date. As tragic as it was, the incident has killed only eighty-two people. More specifically, according to a 2005 release by the World Health Organization, thirty-two were killed in the effort to put out the fires caused by the meltdown and thirty-eight died within months of the accident as a result of acute radiation poisoning. Since the accident occurred in 1986, an additional twelve people have died from the radiation they were exposed to during the accident. Almost all deaths were highly exposed rescue workers. Other nuclear power accidents have been few and never resulted in more than ten deaths per incident. Still think that's too dangerous? To provide some perspective, let's consider an innocuous household appliance, the toaster: over three thousand people died from toaster accidents the first year the appliances were produced and sold in the 1920s, and they still cause around fifty accident-related deaths every year in the United States. So your toaster is far more likely to kill you than any nuclear power plant and subsequently give you a painfully embarrassing epitaph.

In fact, in comparison to the other major means of energy production in the United States, nuclear power is remarkably safe. According to the U.S. Department of Labor, coal mining currently causes about sixty-five deaths and eleven thousand injuries per year, while oil drilling is responsible for approximately 125 deaths per year in the United States. Annual death tolls fluctuate depending upon the demand for these resources and the subsequent drilling or mining required, but the human cost is still exponentially more than that of nuclear energy. However, in the decades that nuclear power has been used in the United States, there have been zero deaths caused by nuclear power accidents—none at all. That's much better than the thousands of lives coal, oil, and toasters have cost us. If you care about saving human lives, then you should like nuclear energy.

Radiation

Despite nuclear energy causing remarkably few deaths, people are also terrified of another aspect of nuclear power—radiation. Everyone's scared of developing a boulder-size tumor or our apples growing to similar size as a result of the awful radiation given off by nuclear power plants or their potential meltdowns. However, it should comfort you to know (or perhaps not) that you receive more radiation from a brick wall than from a nuclear power plant.

We live in a radioactive world—nearly everything gives off at least a trace amount of radiation; that includes brick walls. Yes, while such a wall emits about 3.5 millirems of radiation per year, a nuclear power plant gives off about .3 millirems per year. (Millirem is just a unit of radiation dosage.) Of course, this low level of emission is a result of the numerous safeguards set up around the reactors to suppress radiation. So what happens if those safeguards fail? Will everyone surrounding the plant turn into a mutant?

The argument uses technical terms but makes sure they are accessible to readers.

To answer that question, let's examine the reactor failures in the recent Japanese nuclear crisis

following several devastating earthquakes. The damage from the quakes took out the power to several nuclear plants, which caused their core cooling systems to go offline. To prevent reactor meltdowns, workers had to douse the failing reactors in thousands of gallons of seawater to cool the fuel rods, which contain all the radioactive materials. Worries about the resulting radioactive seawater contaminating the ocean and sea life flared as a result. But just how radioactive is the water? Officials from Tokyo Electric Power Company said the water "would have to be drunk for a whole year in order to accumulate one millisievert." People are generally exposed to about 1 to 10 millisieverts each year from background radiation caused by substances in the air and soil. "You would have to eat or drink an awful lot to get any level of radiation that would be harmful," said British nuclear expert Laurence Williams. You get exposed to 5 millisieverts during a coast-to-coast flight across the United States. According to the U.S. Food and Drug Administration, you receive between 5 and 60 millisieverts in a CAT scan, depending on the type. So drinking water for a year that was in direct contact with containers of radioactive material used in those Japanese nuclear plants will expose you to a fifth of the radiation you would get from the weakest CAT scan. How dangerous!

The argument is full of data and statistics from what seem to be reputable authorities and sources.

As the argument explores various aspects of nuclear energy, headings keep the reader on track.

Waste

But even if we have little to fear from nuclear power plants themselves, what about the supposedly deadly by-products of these plants?

Pearson strategically concedes a downside of nuclear energy.

Opponents of nuclear energy cite the fact that while nuclear power plants don't emit greenhouse gases, they do leave behind waste that remains radioactive for thousands of years. However, this nuclear waste problem is exaggerated. According to Professor Emeritus of Computer Science at Stanford University, John McCarthy, a 1,000-megawatt reactor produces only 1.5 cubic meters of waste after a year of operation. The current solution is to put the waste in protective containers and store them in caverns cut in granite. At the very least, with such a small amount of waste per reactor, the caverns don't have to be dug very fast.

Nuclear power plants do produce waste that needs to be kept away from living things, but the actual amount of waste produced is small and therefore manageable. If the United States got all its power from nuclear plants, the amount of waste produced would be equivalent to one pill of aspirin per person, per year—tiny compared to the amount of waste produced by plants that use fossil fuels; the U.S. Energy Information Administration notes that coal alone produces about 1.8 billion metric tons of CO_2 emissions per year.

Quantity is not the only factor that has been exaggerated—the amount of time the waste remains dangerously radioactive has also been inflated. After about five hundred years, the fission products' radiation levels drop to below the level at which we typically find them in nature; the thousands of years opponents of nuclear energy refer to are the years the waste will be radioactive, not excessively so. You

don't want to stand right next to this material even after those first five hundred years, but if it can exist in nature without doing any noticeable damage, then it doesn't pose any serious threat. Essentially, everything is radioactive; to criticize something for being radioactive without specifying the level of radioactivity means nothing.

Meeting Our Energy Demands

Although I've done a lot here in an attempt to defend nuclear energy, I still acknowledge it's not perfect. While the nuclear waste problem isn't something to be too worried about, it would still be better if we could satisfy our demand for energy without producing waste, radioactive or otherwise. However, I believe nuclear energy is the only realistic option we have to one day achieve an entirely clean energy reality.

We live in an age dominated by energy—to power our cars, our homes, and our computers. Let's face it: we're not going to give up the lifestyle that energy gives us. But under the current means of energy production—primarily coal in the United States—we're pumping out billions of tons of greenhouse gases that will eventually destroy our planet. So we have a dilemma. While we want to do something about global warming, we don't want to change our high-energy-consumption way of life. What are our options?

The concluding paragraphs compare nuclear power to potential alternatives.

Currently, completely clean sources of energy haven't been developed enough to make them a realistic option to supply all our energy needs. For solar energy to match the energy production of nuclear power plants presently in use, we would have to cover an area the size of New Jersey with solar panels. That's not a realistic option; we're not going to build that many panels just to get ourselves off of our addiction to fossil fuels. The same is true of the other renewable energy sources: wind, geothermal, hydroelectric, etc. The technologies simply aren't mature enough.

However, nuclear power *is* realistic. We have the means and the technology to make enough nuclear power plants to satisfy our electricity demands. Nuclear plants produce a lot of power with relatively little waste. Moving from coal to nuclear plants could provide us with adequate power until we develop more efficient renewable sources of electricity.

So what's stopping us? Of course, those heavily invested in coal and other fossil fuels lobby the government to keep their industries profitable, but a large source of opposition is also the American public. Because of the atom bombs of World War II, the Cold War, and Chernobyl, we're scared of all things nuclear. Anytime we hear the word "radiation," images of mushroom clouds and fallout enter our minds. But nuclear power plants aren't bombs. No matter what happens to them, they will never explode. Strong as it might be, our fear of nuclear power is overblown and keeping us from using a source of energy that could literally save our planet. We need to stop the fearmongering before we burn our planet to a crisp.

> Pearson ends his argument by asking readers to acknowledge that their fears of nuclear power aren't based in fact.

Of course, that's if our toasters don't kill us first.

What the Numbers Show about N.F.L. Player Arrests

NEIL IRWIN

Off-the-field violence by professional football players is coming under new focus this week after the release of a video involving the star Baltimore Ravens running back Ray Rice, followed by a bungled response by the National Football League.

But what do the numbers show about N.F.L. players' tangles with the law more broadly? Are some teams' players more likely to get into legal trouble? Are arrests rising or falling? What are the most common offenses?

USA Today maintains a database of arrests, charges, and citations of N.F.L. players for anything more serious than a traffic citation. Maintained by Brent Schrotenboer, it goes back to 2000 and covers, to date, 713 instances in which pro football players have had a run-in with the law that was reported by the news media.

Ray Rice was arraigned on domestic violence charges in May 2014. He was fired by the Baltimore Ravens in September 2014.

AP Photo/The Philadelphia Inquirer, Tom Gralish, Pool

The data set is imperfect; after all, it depends on news media outlets finding out about every time a third-string offensive lineman is pulled over for driving drunk, and so some arrests may well fall through the cracks. Moreover, arrests are included even if charges are dropped or the player is found not guilty, so it presumably includes legal run-ins in which the player did nothing wrong.

Finally, for purposes of these tabulations, a simple drug possession charge in which no one was hurt counts the same as a case like that of Mr. Rice, who is on tape punching his fiancée out cold (she is now his wife), or even that of the former New England Patriot Aaron Hernandez, who is in jail awaiting trial on murder charges.

But with those caveats aside, here's what the data show about how pro football players are interacting with the law. The numbers show a league in which drunk-driving arrests are a continuing problem and domestic violence charges are surprisingly common; in which the teams that have the most players getting in legal trouble don't always fit the impressions fans might have; and in which teams with high arrest rates tend to stay that way over time.

One N.F.L. player in 40 is arrested in a given year. There are 32 teams, each with 53 players on its roster plus another eight on its practice squad (plus more players who show up for training camp but do not make the team, but we didn't attempt to account for them). Thus over the nearly 15 years that the *USA Today* data goes back, the 713 arrests mean that 2.53 percent of players have had a serious run-in with the law in an average year. That may sound bad, but the arrest rate is lower than the national average for men in that age range.

Arrests peaked in the mid-2000s, and are way down this year. The peak year for arrests of N.F.L. players was 2006, followed closely by 2007 and 2008. (These are calendar years, not N.F.L. seasons.) One important caveat: The apparent increase could be a result of increased coverage of professional athletes' legal troubles by Internet media. In other words, we don't know for sure whether more N.F.L. players were being arrested in those years, or whether TMZ and other outlets were better positioned to find out about it.

Despite the Ray Rice episode, 2014 is on track to be the year with the fewest arrests of N.F.L. players on record. Through Sept. 10, there had only been 21. If the final four months of the year proceed at the same pace of arrests as the first eight, that will come to 28, well below the previous low of 36 in 2004.

The most common accusation is driving while drunk, but domestic violence is a big problem. Some 28 percent of the arrests in the database were for driving under the influence, with 202 incidents. Other frequent categories of charges include assault and battery (88 cases) and drug-related offenses (82). This data is also a reminder that domestic violence has been a problem among N.F.L. players since long before Ray and Janay Rice got on that Atlantic City elevator: There have been 85 charges for domestic violence and related offenses since 2000.

The Minnesota Vikings have had the most players arrested since 2000. The number of arrests by team range from a low of 11 (tie between the Arizona Cardinals and St. Louis Rams) versus a high of 44 (the Vikings), with the Cincinnati Bengals and Denver Broncos close behind. (The Houston Texans also have 11 but started playing in 2002.)

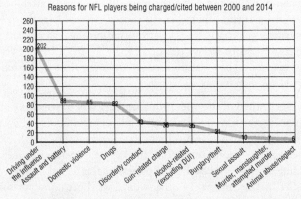

Although driving under the influence is the top reason NFL players ran into trouble with the law, the next three biggest reasons are very concerning.

Data from *USA Today*

To look at it a different way, across the league from 2000 through 2013, 2.53 percent of players were arrested per year, but for the Vikings, that number is 5 percent. For the teams tied for fewest arrests, it is 1.3 percent.

The Ravens have received negative publicity over Rice, whom they fired, and over other players' legal troubles this year, but their 22 player arrests since 2000 make them right at the leaguewide average. The Oakland Raiders have cultivated an image of being a franchise for tough, rowdy bad boys. The team's players, however, have had 19 scrapes with the law since 2000, below average.

The frequency of arrests in a franchise tends to be consistent over time. One might imagine that the number of players from a given franchise who are arrested is a random phenomenon. Maybe, in the rankings above, for example, the Vikings and the Bengals were just unlucky and the Cardinals and Rams were just lucky.

But there's a simple way to test that. If the results were random, you would expect there to be no correlation between the number of player arrests in one time period with a subsequent time period. You could even imagine a negative correlation, if teams that had a run of players getting in trouble took extra care not to sign players reputed to have character issues.

But that is not what happened over the last 14 years. If you chart the number of arrests of players from each franchise in the first seven years of the data, 2000 to 2006, versus the number of arrests that franchise experienced from 2007 to 2013, the correlation is a pretty solid 53 percent. [This] shows a clear pattern in which those franchises with high numbers of arrests in the early years also tended to have high numbers of arrests in later years and vice versa.

The data don't tell us anything about why these patterns are so persistent, but there are two possibilities that seem to stand out. First, there could be club culture. The top management of a franchise may send a message to personnel scouts and coaches that they are either more or less tolerant of signing players who have

had legal problems in the past. (One might imagine that the personal style of the coach could play a role as well, but coaches tend not to have long tenures in the modern N.F.L.; no coach has led his team continuously for the entirety of the time covered by this arrest data, though the Patriots' Bill Belichick misses that honor by only a few weeks, having been hired in late January 2000.)

Second, there is geography. Different cities have different patterns of living and different approaches to law enforcement. Perhaps players for the Jets and the Giants (both with persistently low arrest rates) are at less risk of arrest for D.U.I. because people are less likely to need to drive themselves to nightclubs in Manhattan. Or perhaps in some cities, young African-American men driving expensive cars attract more police attention than in others.

Regardless of the reasons, a handful of franchises have persistently higher numbers of players who end up being arrested, and may want to learn from their rivals in other cities as to why.

16

Arguments of Definition

Writing Arguments

Left to right: AP Photo/Seth Wenig; Bill Wight/Getty Images; Frederick M. Brown/Getty Images

A student writes a cookbook for her master's thesis, hoping to make it easier for people to eat good, healthy food for less money. Her work helps redefine current definitions of *thesis*.

A panel of judges must decide whether computer-enhanced images will be eligible in a contest for landscape photography. At what point is an electronically manipulated image no longer a *photograph*?

A conservative student group accuses the student government on campus of sponsoring a lecture series featuring a disproportionate number of "left-wing" writers and celebrities. A spokesperson for the student government defends its program by questioning the definition of *left-wing* used to classify some of the speakers.

Understanding Arguments of Definition

Definitions matter. Just ask a scientist, a mathematician, an engineer, a judge—or just an everyday person who wants to marry someone of the same sex. In 1996, the Congress passed, and President Clinton signed, the Defense of Marriage Act (DOMA), which defined marriage in federal law this way:

> In determining the meaning of any Act of Congress, or of any ruling, regulation, or interpretation of the various administrative bureaus and agencies of the United States, the word "marriage" means only a legal union between one man and one woman as husband and wife, and the word "spouse" refers only to a person of the opposite sex who is a husband or a wife. 1 U.S.C. 7.

This decision and its definitions of *marriage* and *spouse* have been challenged over and over again in the ensuing decades, leading eventually to another Supreme Court decision, in the summer of 2013, that declared

DOMA unconstitutional. The majority opinion, written by Justice Kennedy, found that the earlier law was discriminatory and that it labeled same-sex unions as "less worthy than the marriage of others." In so ruling, the court affirmed that the federal government cannot differentiate between a "marriage" of heterosexuals and one of homosexuals. Laws regarding marriage—and thus attempting to define or redefine the term—are still ongoing, and you might want to check the status of such controversies in your own state.

In any case, such decisions demonstrate that arguments of definition aren't abstract academic exercises: they are contentious and very often have important consequences for ordinary people. That's because they wield the power to say what someone or something is or can be. Such arguments can both include or exclude: A wolf in Montana either is an endangered species or it isn't. An unsolicited kiss is or is not sexual harassment. A person merits official political refugee status in the United States or doesn't. Another way of approaching definitional arguments, however, is to think of what falls between *is* and *is not* in a definitional claim. In fact, many definitional disputes occur in that murky realm.

Consider the controversy over how to define *human intelligence.* Some argue that human intelligence is a capacity that is measured by tests of verbal and mathematical reasoning. In other words, it's defined by IQ and SAT scores. Others define *intelligence* as the ability to perform specific practical tasks. Still others interpret *intelligence* in emotional terms as a competence in relating to other people. Any of these positions could be defended reasonably, but perhaps the wisest approach would be to construct a definition of *intelligence* that is rich enough to incorporate all these perspectives—and maybe more.

The fact is that crucial political, social, and scientific terms—such as *intelligence, social justice, war, or marriage*—are reargued, reshaped, and updated for the times.

The use of drones in air strikes—and the loss of civilian lives involved— has led to a heated national controversy. Commenting in *The Daily Kos*, MinistryOfTruth wrote:

> We all cringe when we hear of the innocent lives lost at war and
> civilians caught in the crossfire. These civilian deaths are always
> sad and tragic reminders of the cost of war. The Military/Industrial
> Complex doesn't like that. Reports of civilian deaths make the wars
> unpopular, and that's not the right way to continue to justify an

ever growing military budget full of expensive drone missiles and the longest war in American history, is it? Nope. So what do they do? Re-define the dead civilians.

—MinistryOfTruth, in *The Daily Kos*

Blogger MinistryOfTruth goes on to quote from a lengthy article in the *New York Times* concluding that the administration "embraced a disputed method for counting civilian casualties that . . . in effect counts all military-age males in a strike zone as combatants, . . . unless there is explicit intelligence posthumously proving them innocent." As this example illustrates, during war times it is especially important to watch how definitions get shifted and changed to shape or change reality.

Red DaxLuma Gallery/Shutterstock

The argument over how to define *militants* and *combatants* will not be settled simply by consulting a dictionary, no matter how up to date it is. In fact, dictionaries inevitably reflect the way that particular groups of people use words at a specified time and place. And like any form of writing, these reference books mirror the prejudices of their makers—as shown, perhaps most famously, in the entries of lexicographer Samuel Johnson (1709–1784), who gave the English language its first great dictionary. Johnson, no friend of the Scots, defined *oats* as "a grain which in England is generally given to horses, but in Scotland supports the people." (To be fair, he also defined *lexicographer* as "a writer of dictionaries, a harmless drudge.") Thus, it's possible to disagree with dictionary definitions or to regard them merely as starting points for arguments.

The *Dictionary for Landlubbers* defines words according to their point of view!

Excerpted from SAILING: *A Dictionary for Landlubbers, Old Salts, & Armchair Drifters.*
Copyright © 1981 by Henry Beard and Roy McKie. Used by permission of
Workman Publishing Co., Inc., New York. All rights reserved.

RESPOND

Briefly discuss how you might define the italicized terms in the following controversial claims of definition. Compare your definitions of the terms with those of your classmates.

Graphic novels are *serious literature*.

Burning a nation's flag is a *hate crime*.

Matt Drudge and Arianna Huffington aren't *journalists*.

College sports programs have become *big businesses*.

Plagiarism can be an act of *civil disobedience*.

Satanism is a *religion* properly protected by the First Amendment.

Campaign contributions are acts of *free speech* that should never be regulated.

The District of Columbia should not have all the privileges of an American *state*.

Polygamous couples should have the legal privileges of *marriage*.

Kinds of Definition

Because there are different kinds of definitions, there are also different ways to make a definition argument. Fortunately, identifying a particular type of definition is less important than appreciating when an issue of definition is at stake. Let's explore some common definitional issues.

Formal Definitions

Formal definitions are what you find in dictionaries. Such definitions place a term in its proper **genus** and **species**—first determining its class and then identifying the features or criteria that distinguish it from other members of that class. That sounds complicated, but a definition will help you see the principle. To define *hybrid car*, you might first place it in a general class—*passenger vehicles*. Then the formal definition would distinguish hybrid cars from other passenger vehicles: *they can move using two or more sources of power, either separately or in combination.* So the full definition might look like this: *a hybrid car is a passenger vehicle* (genus) *that can operate using two or more sources of power, separately or in combination* (species).

2014 Honda Insight: fully hybrid or something else?

PHOTOEDIT/PhotoEdit, Inc.

Many arguments involve deciding whether an object meets the criteria set by a formal definition. For instance, suppose that you are considering whether a Toyota Prius and a Honda Insight are comparable hybrid

vehicles. Both are clearly passenger cars, so the genus raises no questions. But not all vehicles that claim to be hybrids are powered by two sources: some of them are just electrically *assisted* versions of a regular gasoline car. That's the species question. Looking closely, you discover that a Prius can run on either gas or electric power alone. But does the Insight have that flexibility? Not quite. It has an electric motor that assists its small gas engine, but the vehicle never runs on electricity alone. So technically the Insight is labeled a *mild hybr*id whereas the Prius is called a *full hybrid*. This definitional distinction obviously has consequences for consumers concerned about CO_2 emissions.

Operational Definitions

Operational definitions identify an object or idea by what it does or by what conditions create it. For example, someone's offensive sexual imposition on another person may not meet the technical definition of *harassment* unless it is considered *unwanted*, *unsolicited*, and *repeated*. These three conditions then define what makes an act that might be acceptable in some situations turn into harassment. But they might also then become part of a highly contentious debate: were the conditions actually present in a given case? For example, could an offensive act really be harassment if the accused believed sexual interest was mutual and therefore solicited?

As you might imagine, arguments arise from operational definitions whenever people disagree about what the conditions define or whether these conditions have been fulfilled. Here are some examples of those types of questions:

Questions Related to Conditions

- Can institutional racism occur in the absence of specific and individual acts of racism?

- Can someone who is paid for their community service still be called a volunteer?

- Can an offensive act be termed harassment if the accused believed sexual interest was mutual and therefore solicited?

Questions Related to Fulfillment of Conditions

- Has an institution supported traditions or policies that have led to widespread racial inequities?

- Was the compensation given to a volunteer really "pay" or simply "reimbursement" for expenses?

- Should a person be punished for harassment if he or she believed the offensive action to be solicited?

THE PRINCE RECONSIDERS:

IS WAKING SLEEPING BEAUTY WITH A KISS SEXUAL HARASSMENT?

Prince Charming considers whether an action would fulfill the conditions for an operational definition.

Cartoonstock Ltd./www.CartoonStock.com

RESPOND

This chapter opens with several rhetorical situations that center on definitional issues. Select one of these situations, and then, using the strategy of formal definition, set down some criteria of definition. For example, identify the features of a photograph that make it part of a larger class (*art, communication method, journalistic technique*). Next, identify the features that make it distinct from other members of that larger class. Then use the strategy of operational definition to establish criteria for the same object: what does it do? Remember to ask questions related to conditions (*Is a computer-scanned photograph still a photograph?*) and questions related to fulfillment of conditions (*Does a good photocopy of a photograph achieve the same effect as the photograph itself?*).

Definitions by Example

Resembling operational definitions are **definitions by example**, which define a class by listing its individual members. Such definitions can be helpful when it is easier to illustrate or show what related people or things have in common than to explain each one in precise detail. For example, one might define the broad category of *tablets* by listing the major examples of these products or define *heirloom tomatoes* by recalling all those available at the local farmers' market.

An app like Discovr Music defines musical styles by example when it connects specific artists or groups to others who make similar sounds.

Discovr Music 2012

Arguments of this sort may focus on who or what may be included in a list that defines a category—*classic movies, worst natural disasters, groundbreaking painters*. Such arguments often involve comparisons and contrasts with the items that most readers would agree belong in this list. One could ask why Washington, D.C., is denied the status of a state: how does it differ from the fifty recognized American states? Or one might wonder why the status of planet is denied to asteroids, when both planets and asteroids are bodies that orbit the sun. A comparison between planets and asteroids might suggest that size is one essential feature of the eight recognized planets that asteroids don't meet. (In 2006, in a famous exercise in definitional argument, astronomers decided to deny poor Pluto its planetary classification.)

Developing a Definitional Argument

Definitional arguments don't just appear out of the blue; they often evolve out of daily life. You might get into an argument over the definition of *ordinary wear and tear* when you return a rental car with some soiled upholstery. Or you might be asked to write a job description for a new position to be created in your office: you have to define the job position in a way that doesn't step on anyone else's turf. Or maybe employees on your campus object to being defined as *temporary workers* when they've held their same jobs for years. Or someone derides one of your best friends as *just a nerd*. In a dozen ways every day, you encounter situations that are questions of definition. They're so frequent and indispensable that you barely notice them for what they are.

Formulating Claims

In addressing a question of definition, you'll likely formulate a *tentative claim*—a declarative statement that represents your first response to such situations. Note that such initial claims usually don't follow a single definitional formula.

CLAIMS OF DEFINITION

A person paid to do public service is not a **volunteer**.

Institutional racism can exist—maybe even thrive—in the absence of overt civil rights violations.

Political bias has been consistently practiced by the mainstream media.

Theatergoers shouldn't confuse **musicals** with **operas**.

White lies are hard to define but easy to recognize.

None of the statements listed here could stand on its own because it likely reflects a first impression and gut reaction. But that's fine because making a claim of definition is typically a starting point, a cocky moment that

doesn't last much beyond the first serious rebuttal or challenge. Statements like these aren't arguments until they're attached to reasons, data, warrants, and evidence (see Chapter 14).

Finding good reasons to support a claim of definition usually requires formulating a general definition by which to explore the subject. To be persuasive, the definition must be broad and not tailored to the specific controversy:

> A volunteer is . . .
>
> Institutional racism is . . .
>
> Political bias is . . .
>
> A musical is . . . but an opera is . . .
>
> A white lie is . . .

Now consider how the following claims might be expanded with a general definition to become full-fledged definitional arguments:

ARGUMENTS OF DEFINITION

> Someone paid to do public service is not a volunteer because volunteers are people who . . .
>
> Institutional racism can exist even in the absence of overt violations of civil rights because, by definition, institutional racism is . . .
>
> Political bias in the media is evident when . . .
>
> Musicals focus on words first while operas . . .
>
> The most important element of a white lie is its destructive nature; the act of telling one hurts both the receiver and the sender.

Notice, too, that some of the issues can involve comparisons between things—such as operas and musicals.

Crafting Definitions

Imagine that you decide to tackle the concept of *paid volunteer* in the following way:

Participants in the federal AmeriCorps program are not really volunteers because they receive "education awards" for their public service. Volunteers are people who work for a cause without receiving compensation.

In Toulmin terms, as explained in Chapter 14, the argument looks like this:

Claim	Participants in AmeriCorps aren't volunteers . . .
Reason	. . . because they are paid for their service.
Warrant	People who are compensated for their services are, ordinarily, employees.

As you can see, the definition of *volunteers* will be crucial to the shape of the argument. In fact, you might think you've settled the matter with this tight little formulation. But now it's time to listen to the readers over your shoulder (again, see Chapter 14), who are pushing you further. Do the terms of your definition account for all pertinent cases of volunteerism—in particular, any related to the types of public service AmeriCorps members might be involved in? What do you do with unpaid interns: how do they affect your definition of *volunteers*? Consider, too, the word *cause* in your original claim of the definition:

Volunteers are people who work for a cause without receiving compensation.

Cause has political connotations that you may or may not intend. You'd better clarify what you mean by *cause* when you discuss its definition in your paper. Might a phrase such as *the public good* be a more comprehensive or appropriate substitute for *a cause*? And then there's the matter of *compensation* in the second half of your definition:

Volunteers are people who work for a cause without receiving compensation.

Aren't people who volunteer to serve on boards, committees, and commissions sometimes paid, especially for their expenses? What about members of the so-called all-volunteer military? They're financially compensated during their years of service, and they enjoy benefits after they complete their tours of duty.

As you can see, you can't just offer up a definition as part of an argument and expect that readers will accept it. Every part of a definition has to be interrogated, critiqued, and defended. So investigate your subject in the

library, on the Internet, and in conversation with others, including experts if you can. You might then be able to present your definition in a single paragraph, or you may have to spend several pages coming to terms with the complexity of the core issue.

After conducting research of this kind, you'll be in a better position to write an extended definition that explains to your readers what you believe makes a volunteer a volunteer, how to identify institutional racism, or how to distinguish between a musical and an opera.

Matching Claims to Definitions

Once you've formulated a definition that readers will accept—a demanding task in itself—you might need to look at your particular subject to see if it fits your general definition. It should provide evidence of one of the following:

- It is a clear example of the class defined.

- It clearly falls outside the defined class.

- It falls between two closely related classes or fulfills some conditions of the defined class but not others.

- It defies existing classes and categories and requires an entirely new definition.

How do you make this key move in an argument? Here's an example from an article by Anthony Tommasini entitled "Opera? Musical? Please Respect the Difference." Early in the piece, Tommasini argues that a key element separates the two musical forms:

> Both genres seek to combine words and music in dynamic, fe-
> licitous and, to invoke that all-purpose term, artistic ways. But in
> opera, music is the driving force; in musical theater, words come
> first.

His claim of definition (or of difference) makes sense because it clarifies aspects of the two genres.

> This explains why for centuries opera-goers have revered works
> written in languages they do not speak. . . . As long as you basically
> know what is going on and what is more or less being said, you can
> be swept away by a great opera, not just by music, but by visceral
> drama. .

In contrast, imagine if the exhilarating production of Cole Porter's *Anything Goes* now on Broadway . . . were to play in Japan without any kind of titling technology. The wit of the musical is embedded in its lyrics. . . .

But even after having found a distinction so perceptive, Tommasini (like most writers making arguments of definition) still has to acknowledge exceptions.

Theatergoing audiences may not care much whether a show is a musical or an opera. But the best achievements in each genre . . . have been from composers and writers who grounded themselves in a tradition, *even while reaching across the divide*. [emphasis added]

If evidence you've gathered while developing an argument of definition suggests that similar limitations may be necessary, don't hesitate to modify your claim. It's amazing how often seemingly cut-and-dried matters of definition become blurry—and open to compromise and accommodation—as you learn more about them. That has proved to be the case as various campuses across the country have tried to define *hate speech* or *internship*—tricky matters. And even the Supreme Court has never said exactly what *pornography* is. Just when matters seem to be settled, new legal twists develop. Should virtual child pornography created with software be illegal, as is the real thing? Or is a virtual image—even a lewd one—an artistic expression that is protected (as other works of art are) by the First Amendment?

Considering Design and Visuals

In thinking about how to present your argument of definition, you may find a simple visual helpful, such as the Venn diagram on page 198 from Wikimedia Commons that defines *sustainability* as the place where our society and its economy intersect with the environment. Such a visual might even suggest a structure for an oral presentation.

Remember too that visuals like photographs, charts, and graphs can also help you make your case. Such items might demonstrate that the conditions for a definition have been met—as the widely circulated and horrific photographs from Abu Ghraib prison in Iraq helped to define *torture*. Or you might create a graphic yourself to illustrate a concept you are defining, perhaps through comparison and contrast.

Finally, don't forget that basic design elements—such as boldface and italics, headings, or links in online text—can contribute to (or detract from) the credibility and persuasiveness of your argument of definition.

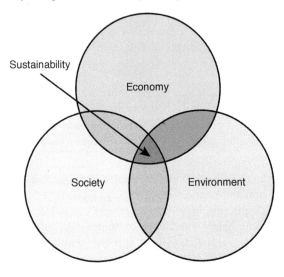

GUIDE **TO WRITING AN ARGUMENT OF DEFINITION**

Finding a Topic

You're entering an argument of definition when you:

- formulate a controversial or provocative definition: *The American Dream, which once meant a McMansion in a gated community, now has taken on a new definition.*

- challenge a definition: *For most Americans today, the American Dream involves not luxury but the secure pensions, cheap energy costs, and health insurance that workers in the 1950s and 1960s supposedly enjoyed.*

- try to determine whether something fits an existing definition: *Expanding opportunity is (or is not) central to the American Dream.*

- seek to broaden an existing definition or create a new definition to accommodate wider or differing perspectives: *In a world where information is easily and freely shared, it may be time to explore alternative understandings of the American Dream.*

Look for issues of definition in your everyday affairs—for instance, in the way that jobs are classified at work, that key terms are used in your academic major, that politicians characterize social issues that concern you, and so on. Be especially alert to definitional arguments that may arise when you or others deploy adjectives such as *true, real, actual,* or *genuine*: *a true patriot, real reform, authentic Mexican food.*

Researching Your Topic

You can research issues of definition by using the following sources:

- college dictionaries and encyclopedias

- unabridged dictionaries

GUIDE **TO WRITING AN ARGUMENT OF DEFINITION**

- specialized reference works and handbooks, such as legal and medical dictionaries

- your textbooks (check their glossaries)

- newsgroups and blogs that focus on particular topics, especially political ones

- community or advocacy groups that are engaged in legal or social issues

- social media postings by experts you respect

Browse in your library reference room and use the electronic indexes and databases to determine how often disputed or contentious terms or phrases occur in influential online newspapers, journals, and Web sites.

When dealing with definitions, ask librarians about the most appropriate and reliable sources. For instance, to find the definition of a legal term, *Black's Law Dictionary* or a database such as FindLaw may help. Check USA.gov for how the government defines terms.

Formulating a Claim

After exploring your subject, try to formulate a thesis that lets readers know where you stand or what issues are at stake. Begin with the following types of questions:

- questions related to genus: *Is assisting in suicide a crime?*

- questions related to species: *Is marijuana a harmful addictive drug or a useful medical treatment?*

- questions related to conditions: *Must the imposition of sexual attention be both unwanted and unsolicited to be considered sexual harassment?*

- questions related to fulfillment of conditions: *Has our college kept in place traditions or policies that might constitute racial discrimination?*

- questions related to membership in a named class: *Can a story put together out of thirty-one retweets be called a novel, or even a short story?*

If you start with a thesis, it should be a complete statement that makes a claim of definition and states the reasons supporting it. You may later decide to separate the claim from its supporting reasons. But a working thesis should be a fully articulated thought that spells out all the details and qualifications: *Who? What? Where? When? How many? How regularly? How completely?*

However, since arguments of definition are often exploratory and tentative, an initial thesis (if you have one) may simply describe problems in formulating a particular definition: *What we mean by X is likely to remain unsettled until we can agree more fully about Y and Z; The key to understanding what constitutes X may lie in appreciating how different groups approach Y and Z.*

Examples of Definitional Claims

- Assisting a gravely ill person in committing suicide should not be considered *murder* when the motive for the act is to ease a person's suffering and not to benefit from the death.

- Although somewhat addictive, marijuana should not be classified as a *dangerous drug* because it damages individuals and society less than heroin or cocaine and because it helps people with life-threatening diseases live more comfortably.

- Giving college admission preference to all racial minorities can be an example of *class discrimination* because such policies may favor middle- and upper-class students who are already advantaged.

- Attempts to define the concept of *freedom* need to take into account the way the term is historically understood in cultures worldwide, not just in the countries of Western Europe and North America.

Preparing a Proposal

If your instructor asks you to prepare a proposal for your project, here's a format that may help:

State your thesis or hypothesis completely. If you're having trouble doing so, try outlining it in Toulmin terms:

Claim:

Reason(s):

Warrant(s):

Alternatively, you might describe the complications of a definitional issue you hope to explore in your project, with the thesis perhaps coming later.

- Explain why this argument of definition deserves attention. What's at stake? Why is it important for your readers to consider?

- Identify whom you hope to reach through your argument and why these readers would be interested in it. How might you involve them in the paper?

- Briefly discuss the key challenges that you anticipate in preparing your argument.

- Determine what sources you expect to consult: Web? Databases? Dictionaries? Encyclopedias? Periodicals?

- Determine what visuals to include in your definitional argument.

GUIDE TO WRITING AN ARGUMENT OF DEFINITION

Considering Format and Media

Your instructor may specify that you use a particular format and/ or medium. If not, ask yourself these questions to help you make a good choice:

- What format is most appropriate for your argument of definition? Does it call for an academic essay, a report, an infographic, a brochure, or something else?

- What medium is most appropriate for your argument? Would it be best delivered orally to a live audience? Presented as an audio essay or podcast? Presented in print only or in print with illustrations?

- Will you need visuals, such as moving or still images, maps, graphs, charts—and what function will they play in your argument? Make sure they are not just "added on" but are necessary components of the argument.

Thinking about Organization

Your argument of definition is likely to include some of the following parts:

- a claim involving a question of definition

- a general definition of some key concept

- a careful look at your subject in terms of that general definition

- evidence for every part of the argument, including visual evidence if appropriate

- a careful consideration of alternative views and counterarguments

- a conclusion drawing out the implications of the argument

GUIDE TO WRITING AN ARGUMENT OF DEFINITION

It's impossible, however, to predict what emphasis each of those parts might receive or what the ultimate shape of an argument of definition will be. Try to account for the ways people with different points of view will likely respond to your argument. Then, consider how to address such differences civilly in the body of your argument.

Getting and Giving Response: Questions for Peer Response

Your instructor may assign you to a group for the purpose of reading and responding to each other's drafts. If not, ask for responses from serious readers or consultants at a writing center. Use the following questions to evaluate a colleague's draft. Be sure to illustrate your comments with examples; specific comments help more than general observations.

The Claim

- Is the claim clearly an issue of definition?

- Is the claim significant enough to interest readers?

- Are clear and specific criteria established for the concept being defined? Do the criteria define the term adequately? Using this definition, could most readers identify what's being defined and distinguish it from other related concepts?

Evidence for the Claim

- Is enough evidence furnished to explain or support the definition? If not, what kind of additional evidence is needed?

- Is the evidence in support of the claim simply announced, or are its significance and appropriateness analyzed? Is a more detailed discussion needed?

GUIDE TO WRITING AN ARGUMENT OF DEFINITION

- Are all the conditions of the definition met in the concept being examined?

- Are any objections readers might have to the claim, criteria, evidence, or way the definition is formulated adequately addressed? Have you represented other points of view completely and fairly?

- What kinds of sources are cited? How credible and persuasive will they be to readers? What other kinds of sources might work better?

- Are all quotations introduced with appropriate signal phrases (such as "As Tyson argues, . . .") and blended smoothly into the writer's sentences?

- Are all visual sources labeled, introduced, and commented upon?

Organization and Style

- How are the parts of the argument organized? Is this organization effective?

- Will readers understand the relationships among the claims, supporting reasons, warrants, and evidence? If not, how might those connections be clearer? Is the function of every visual clear? Are more transitions needed? Would headings or graphic devices help?

- Are the transitions or links from point to point, sentence to sentence, and paragraph to paragraph clear and effective? If not, how could they be improved?

- Are all visuals (or other elements such as audio or video clips) carefully integrated into the text? Is each visual introduced and commented on to point out its significance? Is each visual labeled as a figure or a table and given a caption as well as a citation?

- Is the style suited to the subject? Is it too formal, casual, or technical? Can it be improved?

- Which sentences seem effective? Which ones seem weaker, and how could they be improved? Should short sentences be combined, and any longer ones be broken up?

- How effective are the paragraphs? Too short or too long? How can they be improved?

- Which words or phrases seem effective? Do any seem vague or inappropriate for the audience or the writer's purpose? Are technical or unfamiliar terms defined?

Spelling, Punctuation, Mechanics, Documentation, and Format

- Are there any errors in spelling, punctuation, capitalization, and the like?

- Is the documentation appropriate and consistent? (See Chapter 25.)

- Does the paper or project follow an appropriate format? Is it appropriately designed and attractively presented?

PROJECTS

1. Write an argument of definition about a term such as *military combatants* or *illegal alien* that has suddenly become culturally significant or recently changed in some important way. Either defend the way the term has come to be defined or raise questions about its appropriateness, offensiveness, inaccuracy, and so on. Consider words or expressions such as *terrorism, marriage equality, racist, assisted suicide, enhanced interrogation, tea partier, collateral damage, forcible rape, net neutrality,* etc.

2. Write an essay in which you compare or contrast the meaning of two related terms, explaining the differences between them by using one or more methods of definition: formal definition, operational definition, definition by example. Be clever in your choice of the initial terms: look for a pairing in which the differences might not be immediately apparent to people unfamiliar with how the terms are used in specific communities. Consider terms such as *liberal/ progressive*, *classy/cool*, *lead soprano/prima donna*, *student athlete/ jock*, *highbrow /intellectual*, and so on.

3. In an essay at the end of this chapter, Natasha Rodriguez explores the adjective *underprivileged*, trying to understand why this label bothers her so much. She concludes that needing financial aid should not be conflated with being disadvantaged. After reading this selection carefully, respond to Rodriguez's argument in an argument of definition of your own. Or, alternatively, explore a concept similar to "underprivileged" with the same intensity that Rodriguez brings to her project. Look for a term to define and analyze either from your major or from an area of interest to you.

4. Because arguments of definition can have such important consequences, it helps to develop one by first getting input from lots of "stakeholders," that is, from people or groups likely to be affected by any change in the way a term is defined. Working with a small group, identify a term in your school or wider community that might need a fresh formulation or a close review. It could be a familiar campus word or phrase such as *nontraditional student*, *diversity*, *scholastic dishonesty*, or *social justice*; or it may be a term that has newly entered the local environment, perhaps reflecting an issue of law enforcement, safety, transportation, health, or even entertainment. Once you have settled on a significant term, identify a full range of stakeholders. Then, through some systematic field research (interviews, questionnaires) or by examining existing documents and materials (such as library sources, Web sites, pamphlets, publications), try to understand how the term currently functions in your community. Your definitional argument will, in effect, be what you can learn about the meanings that word or phrase has today for a wide variety of people.

Two Sample Definitional Agruments

Who Are You Calling Underprivileged?

NATASHA RODRIGUEZ

Courtesy of
Natasha Rodríguez

I have come to loathe the word "underprivi-leged." When I filled out my college applica-tions, I checked off the Latino/Hispanic box whenever I was asked to give my ethnicity. My parents in turn indicated their income, hoping that we would qualify for financial aid. But while I waited for acceptances and rejections, several colleges I was considering sent me ma-terial that made me feel worthless rather than excited about attending those institutions.

The author questions the connotations of *underprivi-leged*.

The first mailing I received was a brochure that featured a photograph of African-American, Asian, and Latino teens standing around in a cluster, their faces full of laughter and joy. The title of the brochure was "Help for Underprivileged Students." At first I was confused: "Underprivileged" was not a word that I associated with myself. But there was the handout, with my name printed boldly on the surface.

The text went on to inform me that, since I was a student who had experienced an under-privileged life, I could qualify for several kinds of financial aid and scholarships. While I ap-preciated the intent, I was turned off by that one word—"underprivileged."

Natasha Rodriguez is a student at Sarah Lawrence College, where she edits the features section of her school newspaper, the *Phoenix*.

I had never been called that before. The word made me question how I saw myself in the world. Yes, I needed financial aid, and I had received generous scholarships to help me attend a private high school on the Upper East Side of New York. Surely that didn't mean that I had lived a less-privileged life than others. My upbringing had been very happy.

What does "underprivileged" actually mean? According to most dictionaries, the word refers to a person who does not enjoy the same standard of living or rights as a majority of people in a society. I don't fit that definition. Even though my family does not have a lot of money, we have always had enough to get by, and I have received an excellent education.

> The author then gives a standard definition for *underprivileged* and explains why she refuses the label.

What angered me most about the label was why colleges would ever use such a term. Who wants to be called underprivileged? I'm sure that even those who have had no opportunities would not want their social status rubbed in their faces so blatantly. People should be referred to as underprivileged only if they're the ones who are calling themselves that.

Misfortune, like beauty, is in the eye of the beholder. It's not appropriate to slap labels on people that they might not like or even agree with. Social research has found that those who are negatively labeled usually have lower self-esteem than others who are not labeled in that way. So why does the label of "underprivileged" persist?

Most colleges brag about the diversity of their students. But I don't want to be bragged about if my ethnicity is automatically associated with "underprivileged." Several colleges

> The author examines the assumptions colleges make based on ethnicity and income.

that had not even received information on my parents' finances just assumed that I was underprivileged because I had checked "Latino/Hispanic" on their applications.

That kind of labeling has to stop. Brochures and handouts could be titled "Help for Students in Need" rather than "Help for Underprivileged Students." I am sure that many people, myself included, are more than willing to admit that they require financial aid, and would feel fine about a college that referred to them as a student in need.

The essay concludes with the author's own self-definition.

That's a definition I can agree with. I am a student in need; I'm just not an underprivileged one.

Friending: The Changing Definition of Friendship in the Social Media Era

JOYCE XINRAN LIU

March 6, 2014

In just two months, I boosted my LinkedIn connections from 300 to almost 500. I was proud of winning the numbers game. However, recently when I was trying to request an informational interview via LinkedIn, I was depressed that less than 5% actually responded to me. I think I know most of them, but I actually don't. Or they don't think so. Maybe this is social media's fault. It creates the illusion of intimacy and closeness that doesn't actually exist. Maybe I should blame myself. I rushed to think of my social media connections as true friends that I could rely on.

I forgot the rules of friendship. Social media is a new platform for communication that expands and accelerates the way we connect and engage people, but the old rules of thumb for building relationships are still there. To understand what makes a friend a "friend" in social media, we'd better step back and think about the chemistry needed in true friendship (sans social media).

To make a true friend, we first need to get to know the person well, such that we understand what she likes and dislikes, what experiences have made her who she is today, and what her values are in life. Yet knowing someone does not guarantee a lasting friendship. For example, some people know their boss pretty well, yet they may not define their boss as a friend. In addition to knowing each other well, building friendships takes time; it's necessary for both sides to have some investment in the relationship.

Joyce Xinran Liu is a graduate in Integrated Marketing Communications at Northwestern University's Medill School. She posted this piece on a blog called Vitamin IMC, a site developed by the graduate students in the program to "educate marketers, potential students and companies about integrated marketing communications—what it is, how it's applied and how it builds profit within organizations."

Now let's get back to the world of social media and reconsider the process of making friends. Facebook, Twitter, LinkedIn, and many other social media platforms have provided tons of personal information—both ongoing and historical—about people we want to know. For example, we can gain insights into someone's social life and interests through Facebook, get up-to-the-minute status updates from Twitter, and read someone's full professional experience on LinkedIn. A five-minute search on a social media platform can make us feel that we are old friends of the person we want to make friends with. But this is only one side of the story since the person we are searching into may not feel the same way as we do. This is often the case. A one-way connection without reciprocal engagement can never be thought of as a friendship, even on social media.

When acquaintances share their joys, complaints or even private information on social media, does it mean that they deem all of these online connections as real friends? Probably not. But why share their private information then? My argument is that they sacrifice their privacy in exchange for intimacy. Some people may want to make more friends, attract more attention, or even enhance self-esteem with the inflated intimacy they receive from friends, acquaintances and mere strangers on social media. These shared social media updates make people feel close, but it doesn't always mean they are close.

It's not social media's fault that it helps us develop a wide net of connections, yet still leaves us wanting more. We've created the myth of building strong relationships via social media. It's possible to build friendship online, but more often we need to integrate online engagement with offline interaction. Overall, social media has changed ways people interact with each other, but it has not affected the rooted norms and socialization process of making friends either online or offline. And it's time to adjust our expectations for building relationships in this new media space.

17

Evaluations

Writing Arguments

Chapter 17, "Evaluations," from *Everything's an Argument*, Seventh Edition, by Andrea A. Lunsford and John J. Ruszkiewicz, pp. 210–239 (Chapter 10). Copyright © 2016 by Bedford/St. Martin's.

Left to right: Mario Tama/Getty Images; Jonah Willihnganz, The Stanford Storytelling Project; Hulton Archive/Getty Images

"We don't want to go there for coffee. Their beans aren't fair trade, the drinks are high in calories, and the stuff is *way* overpriced."

The campus storytelling project has just won a competition sponsored by NPR, and everyone involved is thrilled. Then they realize that this year all but one of the leaders of this project will graduate and that they have very few new recruits. So they put their heads together to figure out what qualities they need in new recruits that will help maintain the excellence of their project.

Orson Welles's masterpiece *Citizen Kane* is playing at the Student Union for only one more night, but the new *Captain America* is featured across the street in 3-D. Guess which movie your roomie wants to see? You intend to set her straight.

Understanding Evaluations

Evaluations are everyday arguments. By the time you leave home in the morning, you've likely made a dozen informal evaluations: You've selected dressy clothes because you have a job interview with a law firm. You've chosen low-fat yogurt and fruit over the pancakes you really love. You've queued up the perfect playlist on your iPhone for your hike to campus. In each case, you've applied criteria to a particular problem and then made a decision. That's evaluating on the fly.

Some professional evaluations require more elaborate standards, evidence, and paperwork (imagine an aircraft manufacturer certifying a new jet for passenger service), but they don't differ structurally from the simpler choices that people make all the time. People love to voice their opinions, and they always have. In fact, a mode of ancient rhetoric—called the *ceremonial* or *epideictic* (see Chapter 8)—was devoted entirely to speeches of praise and blame.

Today, rituals of praise and blame are a significant part of American life. Adults who would choke at the notion of debating causal or definitional claims will happily spend hours appraising the Oakland Raiders, Boston Red Sox, or Tampa Bay Rays. Other evaluative spectacles in our culture include awards shows, beauty pageants, most-valuable-player presentations, lists of best-dressed or worst-dressed celebrities, "sexiest people" magazine covers, literary prizes, political opinion polls, consumer product magazines, and—the ultimate formal public gesture of evaluation—elections. Indeed, making evaluations is a form of entertainment in America and generates big audiences (think of *The Voice*) and revenues.

Arguments about sports are usually evaluations of some kind.

Cal Sport Media via AP Images

RESPOND

The last ten years have seen a proliferation of "reality" talent shows—*Dancing with the Stars*, *So You Think You Can Dance*, *American* (or *Canadian* or *Australian* or many other) *Idol*, *America's Got Talent*, *The Voice*, and so on. Write a short opinion piece assessing the merits of a particular "talent" show. What should a proper event of this kind accomplish? Does the event you're reviewing do so?

Criteria of Evaluation

Arguments of evaluation can produce simple rankings and winners or can lead to profound decisions about our lives, but they always involve standards. The particular standards we establish for judging anything—whether an idea, a work of art, a person, or a product—are called **criteria of evaluation**. Sometimes criteria are self-evident: a car that gets fifteen miles per gallon is a gas hog, and a piece of fish that smells even a little off shouldn't be eaten. But criteria get complicated when a subject is abstract: *What features make a song a classic? What constitutes a fair wage? How do we measure a successful foreign policy or college career?* Struggling to identify such difficult criteria of evaluation can lead to important insights into your values, motives, and preferences.

Why make such a big deal about criteria when many acts of evaluation seem effortless? We should be suspicious of our judgments especially when we make them casually. It's irresponsible simply to think that spontaneous and uninformed quips should carry the same weight as well-informed and well-reasoned opinions. Serious evaluations always require reflection, and when we look deeply into our judgments, we sometimes discover important questions that typically go unasked, many prefaced by *why*:

- You challenge the grade you received in a course, but you don't question the practice of grading.

- You argue passionately that a Republican Congress is better for America than a Democratic alternative, but you fail to ask why voters get only two choices.

- You argue that buying a hybrid car makes more sense than keeping an SUV, but you don't ask whether taking alternative forms of transportation (like the bus or a bike) makes the most sense of all.

Push an argument of evaluation hard enough and even simple judgments become challenging and intriguing.

In fact, for many writers, grappling with criteria is the toughest step in producing an evaluation. When you offer an opinion about a topic you know reasonably well, you want readers to learn something from your judgment. So you need time to think about and then justify the criteria for your opinion, whatever the subject.

Do you think, for instance, that you could explain what (if anything) makes a veggie burger good? Though many people have eaten veggie burgers, they probably haven't spent much time thinking about them. But it wouldn't be enough to claim merely that a proper one should be juicy or tasty—such trite claims are not even interesting. The following criteria offered on the *Cook's Illustrated* Web site show what happens when experts give the issue a closer look:

> We wanted to create veggie burgers that even meat eaters would love. We didn't want them to taste like hamburgers, but we did

want them to act like hamburgers, *having a modicum of chew, a harmonious blend of savory ingredients, and the ability to go from grill to bun without falling apart.* [emphasis added]

—*Cook's Illustrated*

After a lot of experimenting, *Cook's Illustrated* came up with a recipe that met these criteria.

What criteria of evaluation are embedded in this visual argument?

© Ildi Papp/age fotostock

Criteria of evaluation aren't static, either. They differ according to time and audience. Much market research, for example, is designed to find out what particular consumers want now and may want in the future—what their criteria are for buying a product. In good times, people may demand homes with soaring entryways, lots of space, and premium appliances. In tougher times, they may care more about efficient use of space, quality insulation, and energy-efficient stoves and dishwashers. Shifts in values, attitudes, and criteria happen all the time.

RESPOND

Choose one item from the following list that you understand well enough to evaluate. Develop several criteria of evaluation that you could defend to distinguish excellence from mediocrity in the area. Then choose an item that you don't know much about and explain the research you might do to discover reasonable criteria of evaluation for it.

smartwatches	U.S. vice presidents
NFL quarterbacks	organic vegetables
social networking sites	all-electric cars
TV journalists	spoken word poetry
video games	athletic shoes
graphic narratives	country music bands
Navajo rugs	sci-fi films

Characterizing Evaluation

One way of understanding evaluative arguments is to consider the types of evidence they use. A distinction explored in Chapter 11 between hard evidence and constructed arguments based on reason is helpful here: we defined **hard evidence** as facts, statistics, testimony, and other kinds of arguments that can be measured, recorded, or even found—the so-called smoking gun in a criminal investigation. We defined constructed arguments based on reason as those that are shaped by language and various kinds of logic.

We can talk about arguments of evaluation the same way, looking at some as quantitative and others as qualitative. **Quantitative arguments** of evaluation rely on criteria that can be measured, counted, or demonstrated in some mechanical fashion (something is taller, faster, smoother, quieter, or more powerful than something else). In contrast, **qualitative arguments** rely on criteria that must be explained through language and media, relying on such matters as values, traditions, and emotions (something is more ethical, more beneficial, more handsome, or more noble than something else). A claim of evaluation might be supported by arguments of both sorts.

Quantitative Evaluations

At first glance, quantitative evaluations seem to hold all the cards, especially in a society as enamored of science and technology as our own is. Making judgments should be easy if all it involves is measuring and counting—and in some cases, that's the way things work out. *Who's the tallest or heaviest or loudest person in your class?* If your classmates allow themselves to be measured, you could find out easily enough, using the right equipment

and internationally sanctioned standards of measurement—the meter, the kilo, or the decibel.

But what if you were to ask, *Who's the smartest person in class?* You could answer this more complex question quantitatively, using IQ tests or college entrance examinations that report results numerically. In fact, almost all college-bound students in the United States submit to this kind of evaluation, taking either the SAT or the ACT to demonstrate their verbal and mathematical prowess. Such measures are widely accepted by educators and institutions, but they are also vigorously challenged. What do they actually measure? They predict likely academic success only in college, which is one kind of intelligence.

Quantitative measures of evaluation can be enormously useful, but even the most objective measures have limits. They've been devised by fallible people who look at the world from their own inevitably limited perspectives.

Qualitative Evaluations

Many issues of evaluation that are closest to people's hearts aren't subject to quantification. *What makes a movie great?* If you suggested a quantitative measure like length, your friends would probably hoot, "Get serious!" But what about box-office receipts, adjusted for inflation? Would films that made the most money—an easily quantifiable measure—be the "best pictures"? That select group would include movies such as *Star Wars, The Sound of Music, Gone with the Wind, Titanic, Avatar, and E.T.* An interesting group of films—but the best?

To define the criteria for "great movie," you'd more likely look for the standards and evidence that serious critics explore in their arguments, abstract or complicated issues such as their societal impact, cinematic technique, dramatic structures, intelligent casting, and so on. Most of these markers of quality could be defined and identified with some precision but not measured or counted. You'd also have to make your case rhetorically, convincing the audience to accept the markers of quality you are offering and yet appreciating that they might not. A movie reviewer making qualitative judgments might spend as much time defending criteria of evaluation as providing evidence that these standards are present in a particular film. But putting those standards into action can be what makes a review something worth reading. Consider how Roger Ebert, in writing about *Toy Story, the first all-computer-made feature film,* teaches his readers how to find evidence of quality in a great movie:

Toy Story creates a universe out of a couple of kids' bedrooms, a gas station, and a stretch of suburban highway. Its heroes are toys, which come to life when nobody is watching. Its conflict is between an old-fashioned cowboy who has always been a little boy's favorite toy, and the new space ranger who may replace him. The villain is the mean kid next door who takes toys apart and puts them back together again in macabre combinations. And the result is a visionary roller-coaster ride of a movie.

Web sites such as Netflix and Rotten Tomatoes offer recommendations for films based on users' past selections and the ratings of other users and critics. Sometimes those judgments are at odds. Then whom do you trust?

© Denis ALLARD/REA/Redux

For the kids in the audience, a movie like this will work because it tells a fun story, contains a lot of humor, and is exciting to watch. Older viewers may be even more absorbed, because *Toy Story*, the first feature made entirely by computer, achieves a three-dimensional reality and freedom of movement that is liberating and new. The more you know about how the movie was made, the more you respect it.

RESPOND

For examples of powerful evaluation arguments, search the Web or your library for eulogies or obituaries of famous, recently deceased individuals. Try to locate at least one such item, and then analyze the types of claims it makes about the accomplishments of the deceased. What types of criteria of evaluation hold the obituary or eulogy together? Why should we respect or admire the person?

Developing an Evaluative Argument

Developing an argument of evaluation can seem like a simple process, especially if you already know what your claim is likely to be. To continue the movie theme for one more example:

> *Citizen Kane* is the finest film ever made by an American director.

Having established a claim, you would then explore the implications of your belief, drawing out the reasons, warrants, and evidence that might support it:

Claim	*Citizen Kane* is the finest film ever made by an American director . . .
Reason	. . . because it revolutionizes the way we see the world.
Warrant	Great films change viewers in fundamental ways.
Evidence	Shot after shot, *Citizen Kane* presents the life of its protagonist through cinematic images that viewers can never forget.

The warrant here is, in effect, an implied statement of criteria—in this case, the quality that defines "great film" for the writer. It may be important for the writer to share that assumption with readers and perhaps to identify other great films that similarly make viewers appreciate new perspectives.

As you can see, in developing an evaluative argument, you'll want to pay special attention to criteria, claims, and evidence.

Formulating Criteria

Although even casual evaluations (*The band sucks!*) might be traced to reasonable criteria, most people don't defend their positions until they are challenged (*Oh yeah?*). Similarly, writers who address readers with whom they share core values rarely discuss their criteria in great detail. A film critic like the late Roger Ebert (see p. 370) isn't expected to restate all his principles every time he writes a movie review. Ebert assumes that his readers will—over time—come to appreciate his standards. Still, criteria can make or break a piece.

So spend time developing your criteria of evaluation. What exactly makes a shortstop an all-star? Why is a standardized test an unreliable measure of intelligence? Fundamentally, what distinguishes an inspired rapper from a run-of-the-mill one? List the possibilities and then pare them down to the essentials. If you offer vague, dull, or unsupportable principles, expect to be challenged.

You're most likely to be vague about your beliefs when you haven't thought (or read) enough about your subject. Push yourself at least as far as you imagine readers will. Anticipate readers looking over your shoulder, asking difficult questions. Say, for example, that you intend to argue that anyone who wants to stay on the cutting edge of personal technology will obviously want Apple's latest iPad because it does so many amazing things. But what does that mean exactly? What makes the device "amazing"? Is it that it gives access to email and the Web, has a high-resolution screen, offers an astonishing number of apps, and makes a good e-reader? These are particular features of the device. But can you identify a more fundamental quality to explain the product's appeal, such as an iPad user's experience, enjoyment, or feeling of productivity? You'll often want to raise your evaluation to a higher level of generality like this so that your appraisal of a product, book, performance, or political figure works as a coherent argument, and not just as a list of random observations.

Be certain, too, that your criteria of evaluation apply to more than just your topic of the moment. Your standards should make sense on their own merits and apply across the board. If you tailor your criteria to get the outcome you want, you are doing what is called "special pleading." You might be pleased when you prove that the home team is awesome, but it won't take skeptics long to figure out how you've cooked the books.

RESPOND

Local news and entertainment magazines often publish "best of" issues or articles that catalog their readers' and editors' favorites in such categories as "best place to go on a first date," "best ice cream sundae," and "best dentist." Sometimes the categories are specific: "best places to say 'I was retro before retro was cool'" or "best movie theater seats." Imagine that you're the editor of your own local magazine and that you want to put out a "best of" issue tailored to your hometown. Develop ten categories for evaluation. For each category, list the evaluative criteria that you would use to make your judgment. Next, consider that because your criteria are warrants, they're especially tied to audience. (The criteria for "best dentist," for example, might be tailored to people whose major concern is avoiding pain, to those whose children will be regular patients, or to those who want the cheapest possible dental care.) For

several of the evaluative categories, imagine that you have to justify your judgments to a completely different audience. Write a new set of criteria for that audience.

Making Claims

In evaluations, claims can be stated directly or, more rarely, strongly implied. For most writers, strong statements followed by reasonable qualifications work best. Consider the differences between the following three claims and how much greater the burden of proof is for the first claim:

> Jessica Williams is the funniest "correspondent" ever on *The Daily Show*.

> Jessica Williams has emerged as one of the funniest of *The Daily Show's* "correspondents."

> Jessica Williams may come to be regarded as one of the funniest and most successful of the "correspondents" on *The Daily Show*.

The funniest of all? Jessica Williams reporting on The Daily Show.

Here's a second set of examples demonstrating the same principle, that qualifications generally make a claim of evaluation easier to deal with and smarter:

> The Common Core Standards movement sure is a dumb idea.

> The Common Core Standards movement in educational reform is likely to do more harm than good.

> While laudable in their intentions to raise standards and improve student learning, the Common Core Standards adopted throughout the United States continue to put so high a premium on testing that they may well undermine the goals they seek to achieve.

The point of qualifying a statement isn't to make evaluative claims bland but to make them responsible and reasonable. Consider how Reagan Tankersley uses the criticisms of a musical genre he enjoys to frame a claim he makes in its defense:

> Structurally, dubstep is a simple musical form, with formulaic progressions and beats, something that gives a musically tuned ear little to grasp or analyze. For this reason, a majority of traditionally trained musicians find the genre to be a waste of time. These people have a legitimate position. . . . However, I hold that it is the simplicity of dubstep that makes it special: the primal nature of the song is what digs so deeply into fans. It accesses the most primitive area in our brains that connects to the uniquely human love of music.
>
> —Reagan Tankersley, "Dubstep: Why People Dance"

Tankersley doesn't pretend that dubstep is something it's not, nor does he expect his argument to win over traditionally minded critics. Yet he still makes a claim worth considering.

Dubstep DJs Benga, Artwork, and Skream of Magnetic Man perform.
Chiaki Nozu/Wire Image/Getty Images

One tip: Nothing adds more depth to an opinion than letting others challenge it. When you can, use the resources of the Internet or local discussion

boards to get responses to your opinions or topic proposals. It can be eye-opening to realize how strongly people react to ideas or points of view that you regard as perfectly normal. Share your claim and then, when you're ready, your first draft with friends and classmates, asking them to identify places where your ideas need additional support, either in the discussion of criteria or in the presentation of evidence.

Presenting Evidence

Generally, the more evidence in an evaluation the better, provided that the evidence is relevant. For example, in evaluating the performance of two laptops, the speed of their processors would be essential; the quality of their keyboards or the availability of service might be less crucial yet still worth mentioning. But you have to decide how much detail your readers want in your argument. For technical subjects, you might make your basic case briefly and then attach additional supporting documents at the end—tables, graphs, charts—for those who want more data.

Just as important as relevance in selecting evidence is presentation. Not all pieces of evidence are equally convincing, nor should they be treated as such. Select evidence that is most likely to influence your readers, and then arrange the argument to build toward your best material. In most cases, that best material will be evidence that's specific, detailed, memorable, and derived from credible sources. The details in these paragraphs from Sean Wilsey's review of *Fun Home: A Family Tragicomic*, a graphic novel by Alison Bechdel, tell you precisely what makes the work "lush," "absorbing," and well worth reading:

> It is a pioneering work, pushing two genres (comics and memoir) in multiple new directions, with panels that combine the detail and technical proficiency of R. Crumb with a seriousness, emotional complexity, and innovation completely its own. Then there are the actual words. Generally this is where graphic narratives stumble. Very few cartoonists can also write—or, if they can, they manage only to hit a few familiar notes. But *Fun Home* quietly succeeds in telling a story, not only through well-crafted images but through words that are equally revealing and well chosen. Big words, too! In 232 pages this memoir sent me to the dictionary five separate times (to look up "bargeboard," "buss," "scutwork," "humectant," and "perseverated").

A comic book for lovers of words! Bechdel's rich language and precise images combine to create a lush piece of work—a memoir where concision and detail are melded for maximum, obsessive density. She has obviously spent years getting this memoir right, and it shows. You can read *Fun Home* in a sitting, or get lost in the pictures within the pictures on its pages. The artist's work is so absorbing you feel you are living in her world.

—Sean Wilsey, "The Things They Buried"

The details in this passage make the case that Alison Bechdel's novel is one that pushes both comics and memoirs in new directions.

In evaluation arguments, don't be afraid to concede a point when evidence goes contrary to the overall claim you wish to make. If you're really skillful, you can even turn a problem into an argumentative asset, as Bob Costas does in acknowledging the flaws of baseball great Mickey Mantle in the process of praising him:

None of us, Mickey included, would want to be held to account for every moment of our lives. But how many of us could say that our best moments were as magnificent as his?

—Bob Costas, "Eulogy for Mickey Mantle"

RESPOND

Take a close look at the cover of Alison Bechdel's graphic novel *Fun Home: A Family Tragicomic*. In what various ways does it make an argument of evaluation designed to make you want to read the work? Examine other books, magazines, or media packages (such as video game or software boxes) and describe any strategies they use to argue for their merit.

Fun Home: A Family Tragicomic by Alison Bechdel. Cover illustration © 2007 by Alison Bechdel. Reprinted by permission of Houghton Mifflin Harcourt Publishing Company. All rights reserved.

Considering Design and Visuals

Visual components play a significant role in many arguments of evaluation, especially those based on quantitative information. As soon as numbers are involved in supporting a claim, think about ways to arrange them in tables, charts, graphs, or infographics to make the information more accessible to readers. Visual elements are especially helpful when comparing items. Indeed, a visual spread like the one in the federal government's comparison of electric and hybrid cars (see p. 379) becomes an argument in itself about the vehicles the government has analyzed for fuel economy. The facts seem to speak for themselves because they are presented with care and deliberation. In the same way, you will want to make sure that you use similar care when using visuals to inform and persuade readers.

But don't ignore other basic design features of a text—such as headings for the different criteria you're using or, in online evaluations, links to material related to your subject.

Compare Side-by-Side

| Fuel Economy | Energy and Environment | Safety | Specs |

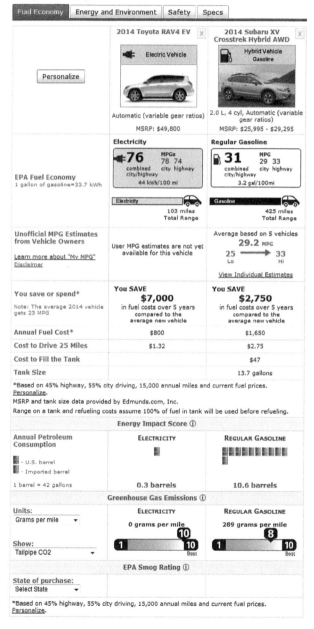

	2014 Toyota RAV4 EV ⊗	2014 Subaru XV Crosstrek Hybrid AWD ⊗
Personalize	Electric Vehicle	Hybrid Vehicle Gasoline
	Automatic (variable gear ratios)	2.0 L, 4 cyl, Automatic (variable gear ratios)
	MSRP: $49,800	MSRP: $25,995 - $29,295

	Electricity	**Regular Gasoline**
EPA Fuel Economy 1 gallon of gasoline=33.7 kWh	**76** MPGe / 78 74 combined city highway city/highway / 44 kWh/100 mi	**31** MPG / 29 33 combined city highway city/highway / 3.2 gal/100mi
	Electricity / 103 miles Total Range	Gasoline / 425 miles Total Range
Unofficial MPG Estimates from Vehicle Owners Learn more about "My MPG" Disclaimer	User MPG estimates are not yet available for this vehicle	Average based on 5 vehicles **29.2** MPG / 25 → 33 Lo Hi / View Individual Estimates
You save or spend* Note: The average 2014 vehicle gets 23 MPG	You SAVE **$7,000** in fuel costs over 5 years compared to the average new vehicle	You SAVE **$2,750** in fuel costs over 5 years compared to the average new vehicle
Annual Fuel Cost*	$800	$1,650
Cost to Drive 25 Miles	$1.32	$2.75
Cost to Fill the Tank		$47
Tank Size		13.7 gallons

*Based on 45% highway, 55% city driving, 15,000 annual miles and current fuel prices. Personalize.
MSRP and tank size data provided by Edmunds.com, Inc.
Range on a tank and refueling costs assume 100% of fuel in tank will be used before refueling.

Energy Impact Score ⓘ

Annual Petroleum Consumption	ELECTRICITY	REGULAR GASOLINE
▪ - U.S. barrel ▪ - Imported barrel 1 barrel = 42 gallons	0.3 barrels	10.6 barrels

Greenhouse Gas Emissions ⓘ

Units: Grams per mile ▾	ELECTRICITY	REGULAR GASOLINE
	0 grams per mile **10**	289 grams per mile **8**
Show: Tailpipe CO2 ▾	1 ━━ 10 Best	1 ━━ 10 Best

EPA Smog Rating ⓘ

| State of purchase: Select State ▾ | | |

*Based on 45% highway, 55% city driving, 15,000 annual miles and current fuel prices. Personalize.

GUIDE TO WRITING AN EVALUATION

Finding a Topic

You're entering an argument of evaluation when you:

- make a judgment about quality: Citizen Kane *is probably the finest film ever made by an American director.*

- challenge such a judgment: Citizen Kane *is vastly overrated by most film critics.*

- construct a ranking or comparison: Citizen Kane *is a more intellectually challenging movie than* Casablanca.

- explore criteria that might be used in making evaluative judgments: *Criteria for judging films are evolving as the production and audiences of films become ever more international.*

Issues of evaluation crop up everywhere—in the judgments you make about public figures or policies; in the choices you make about instructors and courses; in the recommendations you offer about books, films, or television programs; in the preferences you exercise in choosing products, activities, or charities. Evaluations typically use terms that indicate value or rank—*good/bad, effective/ineffective, best/worst, competent/incompetent, successful/unsuccessful.* When you can choose a topic for an evaluation, consider writing about something on which others regularly ask your opinion or advice.

Researching Your Topic

You can research issues of evaluation by using the following sources:

- journals, reviews, and magazines (for current political and social issues)

- books (for assessing judgments about history, policy, etc.)

- biographies (for assessing people)

GUIDE TO WRITING AN EVALUATION

- research reports and scientific studies

- books, magazines, and Web sites for consumers

- periodicals and Web sites that cover entertainment and sports

- blogs and social media sites that explore current topics

Surveys and polls can be useful in uncovering public attitudes: *What kinds of movies are young people seeing today? Who are the most admired people in the country? What activities or businesses are thriving or waning?* You'll discover that Web sites, newsgroups, and blogs thrive on evaluation. (Ever receive an invitation to "like" something on social media?) Browse these public forums for ideas, and, when possible, explore your own topic ideas there. But remember that all sources need to be evaluated themselves; examine each source carefully, making sure that it is legitimate and credible.

Formulating a Claim

After exploring your subject, try to draw up a full and specific claim that lets readers know where you stand and on what criteria you'll base your judgments. Come up with a thesis that's challenging enough to attract readers' attention. In developing a thesis, you might begin with questions like these:

- What exactly is my opinion? Where do I stand?

- Can I make my judgment more clear-cut?

- Do I need to narrow or qualify my claim?

- By what standards will I make my judgment?

- Will readers accept my criteria, or will I have to defend them, too? What criteria might others offer?

- What evidence or major reasons can I offer in support of my evaluation?

GUIDE TO WRITING AN EVALUATION

For a conventional evaluation, your thesis should be a complete statement. In one sentence, make a claim of evaluation and state the reasons that support it. Be sure your claim is specific. Anticipate the questions readers might have: *Who? What? Where? Under what conditions? With what exceptions? In all cases?* Don't expect readers to guess where you stand.

For a more exploratory argument, you might begin (and even end) with questions about the process of evaluation itself. *What are the qualities we seek—or ought to—in our political leaders? What does it say about our cultural values when we find so many viewers entertained by so-called reality shows on television? What might be the criteria for collegiate athletic programs consistent with the values of higher education?* Projects that explore topics like these might not begin with straightforward theses or have the intention to persuade readers.

Examples of Evaluative Claims

- Though they may never receive Oscars for their work, Tom Cruise and Keanu Reeves deserve credit as actors who have succeeded in a wider range of film roles than most of their contemporaries.

- People are returning to cities because they find life there more civilized than in the suburbs.

- Lena Dunham's writing and acting on *Girls* is the most honest presentation of the lives of twentysomething women today.

- Jimmy Carter has been highly praised for his work as a former president of the United States, but history may show that even his much-derided term in office laid the groundwork for the foreign policy and economic successes now attributed to later administrations.

GUIDE **TO WRITING AN EVALUATION**

- Young adults today are shying away from diving into the housing market because they no longer believe that home-ownership is a key element in economic success.

Preparing a Proposal

If your instructor asks you to prepare a proposal for your project, here's a format that may help:

State your thesis completely. If you're having trouble doing so, try outlining it in Toulmin terms:

Claim:

Reason(s):

Warrant(s):

Alternatively, you might describe your intention to explore a particular question of evaluation in your project, with the thesis perhaps coming later.

- Explain why this issue deserves attention. What's at stake?

- Identify whom you hope to reach through your argument and why these readers would be interested in it.

- Briefly discuss the key challenges you anticipate in preparing your argument.

- Determine what research strategies you'll use. What sources do you expect to consult?

Considering Format and Media

Your instructor may specify that you use a particular format and/or medium. If not, ask yourself these questions to help you make a good choice:

GUIDE TO WRITING AN EVALUATION

- What format is most appropriate for your argument of evaluation? Does it call for an academic essay, a report, an infographic, a brochure, or something else?

- What medium is most appropriate for your argument? Would it be best delivered orally to a live audience? Presented as an audio essay or podcast? Presented in print only or in print with illustrations?

- Will you need visuals, such as moving or still images, maps, graphs, charts—and what function will they play in your argument? Make sure they are not just "added on" but are necessary components of the argument.

Thinking about Organization

Your evaluation will likely include elements such as the following:

- an evaluative claim that makes a judgment about a person, idea, or object

- the criterion or criteria by which you'll measure your subject

- an explanation or justification of the criteria (if necessary)

- evidence that the particular subject meets or falls short of the stated criteria

- consideration of alternative views and counterarguments

All these elements may be present in arguments of evaluation, but they won't follow a specific order. In addition, you'll often need an opening paragraph to explain what you're evaluating and why. Tell readers why they should care about your subject and take your opinion seriously.

GUIDE TO WRITING AN EVALUATION

Getting and Giving Response: Questions for Peer Response

Your instructor may assign you to a group for the purpose of reading and responding to each other's drafts. If not, ask for responses from serious readers or consultants at a writing center. Use the following questions to evaluate a colleague's draft. Be sure to illustrate your comments with examples; specific comments help more than general observations.

The Claim

- Is the claim an argument of evaluation? Does it make a judgment about something?

- Does the claim establish clearly what's being evaluated?

- Is the claim too sweeping? Does it need to be qualified?

- Will the criteria used in the evaluation be clear to readers? Do the criteria need to be defined more precisely?

- Are the criteria appropriate ones to use for this evaluation? Are they controversial? Should they be defended?

Evidence for the Claim

- Is enough evidence provided to show that what's being evaluated meets the established criteria? If not, what additional evidence is needed?

- Is the evidence in support of the claim simply announced, or are its significance and appropriateness analyzed? Is more detailed discussion needed?

- Are any objections readers might have to the claim, criteria, or evidence adequately addressed?

- What kinds of sources are cited? How credible and persuasive will they be to readers? What other kinds of sources might work better?

- Are all quotations introduced with appropriate signal phrases (such as "As Tyson argues, . . .") and blended smoothly into the writer's sentences?

- Are all visual sources labeled, introduced, and commented upon?

Organization and Style

- How are the parts of the argument organized? Is this organization effective?

- Will readers understand the relationships among the claims, supporting reasons, warrants, and evidence? If not, how might those connections be clearer? Is the function of every visual clear? Are more transitions needed? Would headings or graphic devices help?

- Are the transitions or links from point to point, sentence to sentence, and paragraph to paragraph clear and effective? If not, how could they be improved?

- Are all visuals carefully integrated into the text? Is each visual introduced and commented on to point out its significance? Is each visual labeled as a figure or a table and given a caption as well as a citation?

- Is the style suited to the subject? Is it too formal, casual, or technical? Can it be improved?

- Which sentences seem effective? Which ones seem weaker, and how could they be improved? Should short sentences be combined, and any longer ones be broken up?

GUIDE TO WRITING AN EVALUATION

- How effective are the paragraphs? Too short or too long? How can they be improved?

- Which words or phrases seem effective? Do any seem vague or inappropriate for the audience or the writer's purpose? Are technical or unfamiliar terms defined?

Spelling, Punctuation, Mechanics, Documentation, and Format

- Are there any errors in spelling, punctuation, capitalization, and the like?

- Is the documentation appropriate and consistent? (See Chapter 25.)

- Does the paper or project follow an appropriate format? Is it appropriately designed and attractively presented?

PROJECTS

1. What kinds of reviews or evaluations do you consult most often or read regularly—those of TV shows, sports teams, video games, fashions, fishing gear, political figures? Try composing an argument of evaluation in your favorite genre: make and defend a claim about the quality of some object, item, work, or person within your area of interest or special knowledge. Let the paper demonstrate an expertise you have gained by your reading. If it helps, model your evaluation upon the work of a reviewer or expert you particularly respect.

2. Prepare a project in which you challenge what you regard as a wrong-headed evaluation, providing sound reasons and solid evidence for challenging this existing and perhaps commonly held view. Maybe you believe that a classic novel you had to read in high school is overrated or that people who criticize video games really don't understand them. Explain why the topic of your evaluation needs to be reconsidered and provide reasons, evidence, and, if necessary, different criteria of evaluation for doing so. For an example of this type of evaluation, see Sean Kamperman's "The Wikipedia Game" on pp. 389–95.

3. Write an evaluation in which you compare or assess the contributions or achievements of two or three notable people working within the same field or occupation. They may be educators, entrepreneurs, artists, legislators, editorial cartoonists, fashion designers, programmers, athletes—you name it. While your first instinct might be to rank these individuals and pick a "winner," this evaluation will work just as well if you can help readers appreciate the different paths by which your subjects have achieved distinction.

4. Within this chapter, the authors claim that criteria of evaluation can change depending on times and circumstances: "In good times, people may demand homes with soaring entryways, lots of space, and premium appliances. In tougher times, they may care more about efficient use of space, quality insulation, and energy-efficient stoves and dishwashers." Working in a group, discuss several scenarios of change and then explore how those circumstances could alter the way we evaluate particular objects, activities, or productions. For example, what impact might global warming have upon the way we determine desirable places to live or vacation? How might a continued economic downturn change the criteria by which we judge successful careers or good educational paths for our children? If people across the globe continue to put on weight, how might standards of personal beauty or fashion alter? If government institutions continue to fall in public esteem, how might we modify our expectations for elected officials? Following the discussion, write a paper or prepare a project in which you explore how one scenario for change might revise customary values and standards of evaluation.

Two Sample Evaluations

The Wikipedia Game: Boring, Pointless, or Neither?

SEAN KAMPERMAN

When most people think about Wikipedia—the self-styled "free, Web-based, collaborative, multilingual encyclopedia project"—they are likely reminded of the preliminary research they did for that term paper on post-structuralism, or of the idle minutes they may've spent exploring an interesting topic just for the heck of it—the neuroanatomy of purple-striped jellyfish, for example, or *Jersey Shore*. First and foremost a layman's tool, Wikipedia has struggled to find legitimacy alongside more reputable reference sources such as *Encyclopaedia Britannica*, even in spite of the outstanding quality of many of its entries. But fortunately for the makers of the Free Encyclopedia—and for the rest of us—Wikipedia's usefulness goes far beyond its intended "encyclopedic" purpose. Under the right circumstances, it can be as much a source of entertainment as one of knowledge and self-improvement.

> Opening paragraph provides a context and a subtle evaluative thesis: "Wikipedia's usefulness goes far beyond its intended 'encyclopedic' purpose."

Sean Kamperman wrote "The Wikipedia Game: Boring, Pointless, or Neither?" in spring 2010 for a lower-division course on rhetoric and media at the University of Texas at Austin. In his topic proposal he briefly described Wikipedia games familiar to many students and then indicated what he intended to explore: "A lot of scholars have been very critical of Wikipedia—some going so far as to discourage its use altogether, even for the purpose of gathering background info. Does the fact that games like these use Wikipedia detract from their educational value? Or do the games in some way rebut these criticisms, demonstrating that the practical uses of user-generated online encyclopedias go beyond traditional research and, by extension, considerations of factual correctness?" His paper is the answer to those questions.

WikiHunt is introduced as a cultural phenomenon.

A prime example of this fact is a phenomenon identified as the Wikipedia game—or, as it's now known to users of Apple and Android smart phones, "WikiHunt." WikiHunt is a simple game whose rules draw upon the unique architectural features of wikis, in that players perform "moves" by following the links that connect one Wikipedia entry to another. Driven by cultural conditions of dilettantism and the spurts of creativity that tend to come on in times of extreme boredom, dozens if not hundreds of Wikipedia users in high school computer labs, college dormitories, and professional workspaces around the globe have "discovered" the game on their own. Some have even gone so far as to claim sole proprietorship—as in the case of two of my friends, who swear they invented the game while sitting through a lecture on academic dishonesty. Questions of original authorship aside, the Wikipedia game would appear to be a bona fide grassroots phenomenon—and one well worth examining if we consider its possible implications for learning and education.

Understanding that not every reader will know WikiHunt, Kamperman offers a detailed explanation.

If you've never played the Wikipedia game, it's fun—educational—and, for the most part, free; indeed, all you'll need is one or more friends, two computers, and an Internet connection. To begin, navigate to the Wikipedia homepage and click the "Random article" link on the left-hand side of the screen. As advertised, this link will lead you and your friend to two randomly generated Wikipedia articles. The objective from here is to get from your article to your opponent's using nothing but links to other articles. These links, which appear within the text of the articles themselves, are bits of hypertext denoted in blue; click on any of them, and you'll be instantly transported to another article and another set of links. Depending on which version of the rules you're going by, either the player who finishes first or the one who gets to his or her opponent's page using the fewest number of links is the winner. Easy, right?

Not exactly. What makes the Wikipedia game hard—and coincidentally, what makes it so much fun—is the vastness of the Web site's encyclopedic content. Click the "Random article" button enough times, and you'll see a pattern emerge: the majority of articles that pop up are short ones covering extremely obscure topics, usually having to do with something related to European club soccer. Entries such as these, labeled "orphans" for their relative paucity of length and links, in fact comprise the majority of Wikipedia articles. So the chances of you or your opponent hitting the randomly-generated-article jackpot and getting a "Jesus" or an "Adolf Hitler"—two pages with tons of links—are pretty slim. Rather, the task at hand usually requires that players navigate from orphan to orphan, as was the case in a game I played just last night with my friends David and Paige. They were unlucky enough to pull up an article on the summer village of Whispering Hills, Alberta, and I was no less unfortunate to get one on "blocking," an old 3D computer animation technique that makes characters and objects look like they're moving. Between these two pages, we were supplied with a total of nineteen links—they had nine doors to choose from, whereas I had ten. That's not a lot to work with. As you can

The paper returns to its thesis when it notes how unexpectedly hard WikiHunt is.

probably surmise, games like this one take more than a few idle minutes—not to mention a heck of a lot of brainpower and spontaneous strategizing.

Kamperman uses his own experience to show precisely how WikiHunt tracks users' processes of thought and "knowledge sets."

Indeed, what makes the Wikipedia game interesting is that it welcomes comparison between the players' respective strategies and methods for getting from point A to point B, highlighting differences between their thought processes and respective knowledge sets. To elaborate using the aforementioned example, I initially knew nothing about either Whispering Hills, Alberta, or "Blocking (animation)." What I did know, however, was that in order to get to Canada, I'd have to go through the good old U.S. of A. So I clicked a link at the bottom of the page entitled "Categories: animation techniques," and from there looked for a well-known technique that I knew to be associated with an American software company. Selecting "PowerPoint animation," I was led from there to the article on Microsoft—which, thanks to the company's late '90s monopolistic indiscretions, furnished me with a link to the U.S. Department of Justice. Five clicks later and I was in Alberta, looking for a passageway to Whispering Hills, one of the province's smallest, obscurest villages. I finally found it in a series of lists on communities in Alberta—but not before my opponents beat me to the punch and got to my page on "blocking" first. David, a computer science major, had taken a different approach to clinch the win; rather than drawing upon his knowledge of a macroscopic, big-picture subject like geography, he skipped from the article on Canada to a page entitled "Canadian industrial research and development organizations," from which he quickly bored through twelve articles on various topics in the computer sciences before falling on "Blocking (animation)." In his case, specialized knowledge was the key to winning.

But did David and Paige really win? Perhaps—but in the wide world of the Wikipedia game, there are few hard-and-fast rules to go by. Whereas my opponents got to their destination quicker than I, my carefully planned journey down the funnel from big ("United States") to small ("List of summer villages in Alberta") got me to Whispering Hills using two fewer links than they. So in this example, one sees not a clear-cut lesson on how to win the game, but rather a study in contrasting styles. A player can rely on specialized knowledge, linking quickly to familiar domains and narrowing the possibilities from there; or, she/he may choose to take a slower, more methodical approach, employing abstract, top-down reasoning skills to systematically sift through broader categories of information. Ultimately, victory is possible in either case.

Its more casual, entertaining uses aside, Wikipedia gets a bad rap, especially in the classroom. Too many college professors and high school English teachers have simply written it off, some even going so far as to expressly forbid their students from using it while at school. These stances and attitudes are understandable. Teaching students how to find good sources and properly credit them is hard enough without the competing influence of the Wikipedia community, whose definition of an acceptably accurate source seems to

extend not only to professionally or academically vetted articles, but to blogs as well, some obviously plagiarized. But to deny Wikipedia a place in the classroom is to deny both students and teachers alike the valuable experience of playing a game that shows us not only what we know, but how we know—how our brains work when posed with the everyday challenge of having to connect ostensibly unrelated pieces of information, and furthermore, how they work differently in that respect.

Acknowledging reservations about Wikipedia, the paper asserts that WikiHunt shows players "how we know."

Knowledge building is a connective or associative process, as the minds behind Wikipedia well know. A casual perusal of any Wikipedia article reveals reams and reams of blue hypertext—bits of text that, when set in isolation, roughly correspond to discrete categories of information about the world. In a sense, the visual rhetoric of Wikipedia invokes the verbal rhetoric of exploration, prompting intrepid Web-using truth seekers to go sailing through a bright blue sea of information that is exciting by virtue of its seeming limitlessness. It should comfort teachers to know that, in quickly navigating through linked knowledge categories to reach their respective destinations, Wikipedia gamers aren't relying too much on their understanding of the articles themselves; rather, what they're relying on is their ability to understand relationships.

Argues that WikiHunt is about learning relationships between ideas.

The fact that so many people have independently found the fun at the heart of Wikipedia should be a heads-up. The Wikipedia game is a grassroots technological innovation that sheds new light on what it means to know—and, perhaps more importantly, one that reminds us that, yes, learning can be fun. It isn't too hard to imagine versions of the game that could be played by kids in school, and how teachers could then use the game to learn more about the stuff of their trade—namely, learning and how it works. So the next time you hear a friend, teacher, or coworker dismiss the Free Encyclopedia as "unreliable" or "unacademic," do knowledge a favor and challenge them to the following:

> "Villa of Livia" to "List of Montreal Expos broadcasters" . . .
>
> . . . no click-backs . . .
>
> . . . twenty links or less.
>
> Go.

Defends Wikipedia as supporting a game that proves to be about "learning and how it works."

My Awkward Week with Google Glass

HAYLEY TSUKAYAMA

The Washington
Post/Getty Images

April 29, 2014

It's a Wednesday night, and I'm turning heads on the sidewalk.
People are slowing halfway down the block as I approach. They're
whispering about me as I walk through the room. Strangers are
watching me, sometimes even stopping me on the street.

Why? Because I'm wearing Google Glass. And I hate it.

I shouldn't feel this way. I like new technology—I've been a tech
reporter at the *Washington Post* for more than three years. And I
admire the vision of technology that Google promises Glass can
offer: a device that lets you keep track of e-mails, texts and other
messages in a seamless way—all through a screen that's perched
just over your right eye.

Headed into a week with Glass, on loan from a co-worker, I was
prepared to review a buggy product. Glass, after all, is still in
testing, and has only been released to developers, media and just
a handful of "normal" people who were willing to spend $1,500
on an untested product. I expected tension headaches from constantly trying to focus on a floating screen above my line of vision. (I got only one headache, for what it's worth.) I even prepared myself to be comfortable talking aloud to the product in
public because you can control Glass through voice commands.

What I wasn't prepared for was the attention I got. Sporting Glass
put me among only a handful of people in Washington, and that
meant getting a lot of looks. Most of it was good attention from

---

Hayley Tsukayama covers consumer technology for the *Washington Post*.

curious people, but it still made me miserable. For wallflowers like me, wearing something that draws constant attention is more or less my personal idea of hell.

I've heard just about every privacy concern raised about Glass, but, as the one wearing the device, I wasn't expecting that the privacy most invaded would be my own. That type of anxiety should lessen over time, particularly as Google works with designer labels such as Luxottica's Oakley and Ray-Ban to make prettier models. But anyone who opts to buy Glass should be ready and willing to become a constant topic of conversation and to answer questions from strangers. Wearing Google Glass in public is like wearing a sandwich-board that says "Talk to me!" And, given the rare but highly publicized fights, robberies and other major incidents some Glass users have experienced, I was a little wary about wearing the device in public.

In the name of fairness, though, I did wear them—nearly everywhere: to work, to the grocery store, out with friends, even to choir rehearsal. Here's a sample of what I heard (or overheard) from friends and strangers in the week I spent with Glass:

"Is she wearing Google Glass?" "Is that what I think that is?" "Are you recording, like, right now?" "You look ridiculous."

Or, my personal favorite, delivered deadpan, from a friend: "Oh, *Hayley*."

But beyond the personal privacy issues, I found that Google Glass is an intriguing device that has a lot of flaws. After more than two years in development, the number of remaining technical bugs is surprising.

On the hardware side, the problems ranged from the device becoming too warm—sometimes after just 10 minutes of use—to needing to be charged multiple times a day. The sensors on the device were far from perfect, and there were many times when I had to re-tap, re-swipe or (and maybe this was the worst part) jerk my head up repeatedly to wake up the device when it went dormant. I probably reset the device at least half a dozen times in the course of normal use because it wouldn't respond to my frantic taps, or refused to connect to my smartphone even when there were no other network problems.

Glass works better with Google's Android phones (in my case, an HTC One M8 on loan from HTC) than with the iPhone, if only because the integration between the Google systems is much smoother. As for software, developers have been smart about designing Glass apps to minimize the amount of data bombarding users. Big names such as Facebook, Twitter and CNN provide a strong app core for Glass. The CNN app, for example, will let you see headlines for top stories, or by subject, and serves headlines, photos and short video.

There are other apps that would be nice to have, however, particularly more photo apps to take advantage of the point-of-view vantage you get with the device.

The iPhone experience with Glass is improving. In fact, Google added a feature allowing Glass users to see iPhone text notifications during the week I wore the device. And some functions of Glass, such as the ability to project what a Glass user sees to a paired phone, were fantastic and useful in ways I didn't anticipate.

But though I tried, very hard, to make Glass a part of my life, I simply didn't feel comfortable with the screen hovering just out of my line of sight. I didn't get any direct challenges about filming others without their permission—not that I ever did film people without permission—but nearly every person who questioned me about Glass asked if I was filming.

What struck me most, however, was what happened when I let others try on the device, giving me a glimpse of how I appeared when I was wearing Glass: a conversation partner who was like a dinner guest who keeps looking at the door, as if to check if there's another person in the room they'd rather be talking to. Think of every person wearing earbuds or a Bluetooth headset who has annoyed you for the same reason. Now multiply it by a factor of 10.

All of which goes against what Glass is supposedly all about: the idea that you can avoid those awkward moments when you try to sneak a peek at your smartphone, which is always much more obvious than you think.

After a few earnest days of trying to make the thing work, I stopped trying to force the issue and used it as I would in real life—in situations when I needed to watch something hands-free, or when I wasn't required to actively engage with other people. In those cases, Glass worked as promised. It delivered updates to keep me informed without overwhelming me and acted as a useful second screen to my smartphone.

But that also meant that, more often than not, Glass ended up perched on the top of my head—the way you wear your sunglasses indoors—or discreetly tucked into my bag, in order to keep it from being the only subject of conversation.

Would I buy Google Glass? Not now, especially with that $1,500 price tag. The device has a lot of evolving to do before it's ready for the world. The world has some evolving to do before it's ready for Glass, too.

18

Causal
Arguments

Writing Arguments

Chapter 18, "Causal Arguments," from *Everything's an Argument*, Seventh Edition, by Andrea A. Lunsford and John J. Ruszkiewicz, pp. 240–271 (Chapter 11). Copyright © 2016 by Bedford/St. Martin's.

Left to right: c. byatt-norman/Shutterstock; Robyn Beck/AFP/Getty Images; AP Photo/Jeff Roberson

In spite of the fact that they have thrived for over fifty million years, around nine years ago colonies of bees started dying . . . and dying. Are pesticides the cause? Or perhaps it's the move agriculture has made from planting cover crops like alfalfa and clover that create natural fertilizers to using synthetic fertilizers that cater to crop monocultures but leave no food support for bees? Scientists believe a combination of these factors account for the current loss of bees.

Small business owners and big companies alike still seem reluctant to hire new employees. Is it because of complex government regulations, continuing uncertainties about health care costs, worries about debt, improvements in productivity—or all of the above? People needing jobs want to know.

Most state governments use high taxes to discourage the use of tobacco products. But when anti-smoking campaigns and graphic warning labels convince people to quit smoking, tax revenues decline, reducing support for health and education programs. Will raising taxes even higher restore that lost revenue?

Understanding Causal Arguments

Americans seem to be getting fatter, so fat in fact that we hear often about the "obesity crisis" in the United States. But what is behind this rise in weight? Rachel Berl, writing for *U.S. News and World Report*, points to unhealthy foods and a sedentary lifestyle:

> "There is no single, simple answer to explain the obesity patterns" in America, says Walter Willett, who chairs the department of nutrition at the Harvard School of Public Health. "Part of this is due to lower incomes and education, which result in purchases of cheap foods that are high in refined starch and sugar. More deeply,

this also reflects lower public investment in education, public transportation, and recreational facilities," he says. The bottom line: cheap, unhealthy foods mixed with a sedentary lifestyle have made obesity the new normal in America. And that makes it even harder to change, Willett says.

—Rachel Pomerance Berl

Many others agree that as processed fast food and other things such as colas have gotten more and more affordable, consumption of them has gone up, along with weight. But others offer different theories for the rise in obesity.

Whatever the reasons for our increased weight, the consequences can be measured by everything from the width of airliner seats to the rise of diabetes in the general population. Many explanations are offered by scientists, social critics, and health gurus, and some are refuted. Figuring out what's going on is a national concern—and an important exercise in cause-and-effect argument.

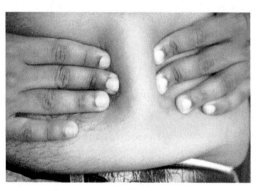

© Bartomeu Amengual/age fotostock

Causal arguments—from the causes of poverty in rural communities to the consequences of ocean pollution around the globe—are at the heart of many major policy decisions, both national and international. But arguments about causes and effects also inform many choices that people make every day. Suppose that you need to petition for a grade change because you were unable to turn in a final project on time. You'd probably enumerate the reasons for your failure—the death of your cat, followed by an attack of the hives, followed by a crash of your computer—hoping that an associate dean reading the petition might see these explanations as tragic enough to change your grade. In identifying the causes of the situation, you're implicitly arguing that the effect (your failure to submit the project on time) should be considered in a new light. Unfortunately, the administrator might accuse you of faulty causality (see p. 213) and judge that failure to complete the project is due more to your procrastination than to the reasons you offer.

Causal arguments exist in many forms and frequently appear as part of other arguments (such as evaluations or proposals). It may help focus your work on causal arguments to separate them into three major categories:

Arguments that state a cause and then examine its effects

Arguments that state an effect and then trace the effect back to its causes

Arguments that move through a series of links: A causes B, which leads to C and perhaps to D

Cause A → leads to Cause B → leads to Cause C → leads to Effect D

Arguments That State a Cause and Then Examine Its Effects

What would happen if Congress suddenly came together and passed immigration reform that gave millions of people in the United States a legal pathway to citizenship? Before such legislation could be enacted, the possible effects of this "cause" would have to be examined in detail and argued intensely. Groups on various sides of this hot-button issue are actually doing so now, and the sides present very different scenarios. In this debate, you'd be successful if you could convincingly describe the consequences of

such a change. Alternatively, you could challenge the causal explanations made by people you don't agree with. But speculation about causes and effects is always risky because life is complicated.

Consider the following passage from researcher Gail Tverberg's blog Our Finite World, from 2011, describing possible consequences of the commitment to increase the production of ethanol from corn:

> At the time the decision was made to expand corn ethanol production, we seemed to have an excess of arable land, and corn prices were low. Using some corn for ethanol looked like it would help farmers, and also help increase fuel for our vehicles. There was also a belief that cellulosic ethanol production might be right around the corner, and could substitute, so there would not be as much pressure on food supplies.

Paresh Nath, cartoonist for India's *National Herald*, personifies the causes for a world food crisis in this item from March 2011.

© Paresh Nath, Cagle Cartoons, Inc.

> Now the situation has changed. Food prices are much higher, and the number of people around the world with inadequate food supply is increasing. The ethanol we are using for our cars is much more in direct competition with the food people around the world are using, and the situation may very well get worse, if there are crop failures.

—Gail Tverberg, *Our Finite World*

Note that the researcher here begins by pointing out the cause-effect relationship that the government was hoping for and then points to the potential effects of that policy when circumstances change. As it turns out, using corn for fuel did have many unintended consequences, for example, inflating the price not only of corn but of wheat and soybeans as well, leading to food shortages and even food riots around the globe.

Arguments That State an Effect and Then Trace the Effect Back to Its Causes

This type of argument might begin with a specific effect (a catastrophic drop in sales of music CDs) and then trace it to its most likely causes (the introduction of MP3 technology, new modes of music distribution, a preference for single song purchases). Or you might examine the reasons that music executives offer for their industry's dip and decide whether their causal analyses pass muster.

Like other kinds of causal arguments, those tracing effects to a cause can have far-reaching significance. In 1962, for example, the scientist Rachel Carson seized the attention of millions with a famous causal argument about the effects that the overuse of chemical pesticides might have on the environment. Here's an excerpt from the beginning of her book-length study of this subject. Note how she begins with the effects before saying she'll go on to explore the causes:

> [A] strange blight crept over the area and everything began to change. Some evil spell had settled on the community: mysterious maladies swept the flocks of chickens; the cattle and sheep sickened and died. Everywhere was a shadow of death. The farmers spoke of much illness among their families. . . . There had been several sudden and unexplained deaths, not only among adults but even among children, who would be stricken suddenly while at play and die within a few hours. The roadsides, once so attractive, were now lined with browned and withered vegetation as though swept by fire. These, too, were silent, deserted by all living things. Even the streams were now lifeless. Anglers no longer visited them, for all the fish had died.
>
> In the gutters under the eaves and between the shingles of the roofs, a white granular powder still showed a few patches; some weeks before it had fallen like snow upon the roofs and lawns, the

fields and streams. No witchcraft, no enemy action had silenced the rebirth of new life in this stricken world. The people had done it themselves. . . . What has silenced the voices of spring in countless towns in America? This book is an attempt to explain.

—Rachel Carson, *Silent Spring*

Today, one could easily write a causal argument of the first type about *Silent Spring* and the environmental movement that it spawned.

Arguments That Move through a Series of Links: A Causes B, Which Leads to C and Perhaps to D

In an environmental science class, for example, you might decide to argue that, despite reductions in acid rain, tightened national regulations regarding smokestack emissions from utility plants are still needed for the following reasons:

1.   Emissions from utility plants in the Midwest still cause significant levels of acid rain in the eastern United States.

2.   Acid rain threatens trees and other vegetation in eastern forests.

3.   Powerful lobbyists have prevented midwestern states from passing strict laws to control emissions from these plants.

4.   As a result, acid rain will destroy most eastern forests by 2030.

In this case, the first link is that emissions cause acid rain; the second, that acid rain causes destruction in eastern forests; and the third, that states have not acted to break the cause-and-effect relationship that is established by the first two points. These links set the scene for the fourth link, which ties the previous points together to argue from effect: unless X, then Y.

RESPOND

The causes of some of the following events and phenomena are well known and frequently discussed. But do you understand these causes well enough to spell them out to someone else? Working in a group, see how well (and in how much detail) you can explain each of the following events or phenomena. Which explanations are relatively clear, and which seem more open to debate?

earthquakes/tsunamis

popularity of Lady Gaga or Taylor Swift or the band Wolf Alice

Cold War

Edward Snowden's leak of CIA documents

Ebola crisis in western Africa

popularity of the *Transformers* films

swelling caused by a bee sting

sharp rise in cases of autism or asthma

climate change

Characterizing Causal Arguments

Causal arguments tend to share several characteristics.

They Are Often Part of Other Arguments.

Many stand-alone causal arguments address questions that are fundamental to our well-being: *Why are juvenile asthma and diabetes increasing so dramatically in the United States? What are the causes of the rise in cases of malaria in Africa, and what can we do to counter this rise? What will happen to Europe if its birthrate continues to decline?*

But causal analyses often work to support other arguments—especially proposals. For example, a proposal to limit the time that children spend playing video games might first draw on a causal analysis to establish that playing video games can have bad results—such as violent behavior, short attention spans, and decreased social skills. The causal analysis provides a rationale that motivates the proposal. In this way, causal analyses can be useful in establishing good reasons for arguments in general.

They Are Almost Always Complex.

The complexity of most causal relationships makes it difficult to establish causes and effects. For example, in 2011 researchers at Northwestern University reported a startling correlation: youths who participated in church activities were far more likely to grow into obese adults than their counterparts who were not engaged in religious activities. How does one even begin to explain such a peculiar and unexpected finding? Too many church socials? Unhealthy food at potluck meals? More regular social engagement? Perhaps.

Or consider the complexity of analyzing the causes of food poisoning when they strike large populations: in 2008, investigators spent months trying to discover whether tomatoes, cilantro, or jalapeño peppers were the cause of a nationwide outbreak of salmonella. More than seventeen states were affected. But despite such challenges, whenever it is possible to demonstrate convincing causal connections between X and Y, we gain important knowledge and powerful arguments. That's why, for example, great effort went into establishing an indisputable link between smoking and lung cancer. Once proven, decisive legal action could finally be taken to warn smokers.

They Are Often Definition Based.

One reason that causal arguments are complex is that they often depend on careful definitions. Recent figures from the U.S. Department of Education, for example, show that the number of high school dropouts is rising and that this rise has caused an increase in youth unemployment. But exactly how does the study define *dropout*? A closer look may suggest that some students (perhaps a lot) who drop out later "drop back in" and complete high school or that some who drop out become successful entrepreneurs or business owners. Further, how does the study define *employment*? Until you can provide definitions for all key terms in a causal claim, you should proceed cautiously with your argument.

"The rise in unemployment, however, which was somewhat offset by an expanding job market, was countered by an upturn in part-time dropouts, which, in turn, was diminished by seasonal factors, the anticipated summer slump, and, over-all, a small but perceptible rise in actual employment."

Causal arguments can also be confusing.

© Ed Arno/The New Yorker Collection/The Cartoon Bank

They Usually Yield Probable Rather Than Absolute Conclusions.

Because causal relationships are almost always complex or subtle, they seldom can yield more than a high degree of probability. Consequently, they are almost always subject to criticism or open to charges of false causality. (We all know smokers who defy the odds to live long, cancer-free lives.) Scientists in particular are wary when making causal claims.

Even after an event, proving precisely what caused it can be hard. During the student riots of the late 1960s, for example, a commission was charged with determining the causes of riots on a particular campus. After two years of work and almost a thousand pages of evidence and reports, the commission was unable to pinpoint anything but a broad network of contributing causes and related conditions. And how many years is it likely to take to unravel all the factors responsible for the extended recession and economic decline in the United States that began in 2008? After all, serious scholars are still arguing about the forces responsible for the Great Depression of 1929.

To demonstrate that X caused Y, you must find the strongest possible evidence and subject it to the toughest scrutiny. But a causal argument doesn't fail just because you can't find a single compelling cause. In fact, causal arguments are often most effective when they help readers appreciate how tangled our lives and landscapes really are.

Developing Causal Arguments

Exploring Possible Claims

To begin creating a strong causal claim, try listing some of the effects— events or phenomena—that you'd like to know the causes of:

- Why do college tuition costs routinely outstrip the rate of inflation?

- What's really behind the slow pace of development of alternative energy sources?

- Why are almost all the mothers in animated movies either dead to begin with or quickly killed off?

- Why is same-sex marriage more acceptable to American society than it was a decade ago?

- Why do so few younger Americans vote, even in major elections?

Or try moving in the opposite direction, listing some phenomena or causes you're interested in and then hypothesizing what kinds of effects they may produce:

- How will the growing popularity of e-readers change our relationships to books?

- What will happen as the result of efforts to repeal the Affordable Health Care Act?

- What will be the consequences if more liberal (or conservative) judges are appointed to the U.S. Supreme Court?

- What will happen as China and India become dominant industrialized nations?

Read a little about the causal issues that interest you most, and then try them out on friends and colleagues. They might suggest ways to refocus or clarify what you want to do or offer leads to finding information about your subject. After some initial research, map out the causal relationship you want to explore in simple form:

X might cause (or might be caused by) **Y** for the following reasons:

    1.

    2.

    3. (add more as needed)

Such a statement should be tentative because writing a causal argument should be an exercise in which you uncover facts, not assume them to be true. Often, your early assumptions (*Tuition was raised to renovate the stadium*) might be undermined by the facts you later discover (*Tuition doesn't fund the construction or maintenance of campus buildings*).

You might even decide to write a wildly exaggerated or parodic causal argument for humorous purposes. Humorist Dave Barry does this when he explains the causes of El Niño and other weather phenomena: "So we see that the true cause of bad weather, contrary to what they have been claiming all these years, is TV weather forecasters, who have also single-handedly destroyed the ozone layer via overuse of hair spray." Most of the causal reasoning you do, however, will take a serious approach to subjects that you, your family, and your friends care about.

Working with a group, write a big *Why?* on a sheet of paper or computer screen, and then generate a list of *why* questions. Don't be too critical of the initial list:

Why

—*do people laugh?*

—*do swans mate for life?*

—*do college students binge drink?*

—*do teenagers drive fast?*

—*do babies cry?*

—*do politicians take risks on social media?*

Generate as lengthy a list as you can in fifteen minutes. Then decide which of the questions might make plausible starting points for intriguing causal arguments.

© Bill Coster/age fotostock

Defining the Causal Relationships

In developing a causal claim, you can examine the various types of causes and effects in play in a given argument and define their relationship. Begin by listing all the plausible causes or effects you need to consider. Then decide which are the most important for you to analyze or the easiest to defend or critique. The following chart on "Causes" may help you to appreciate some important terms and relationships.

Type of Causes	What It Is or Does	What It Looks Like
Sufficient cause	Enough for something to occur on its own	Lack of oxygen is sufficient to cause death Cheating on an exam is sufficient to fail a course
Necessary cause	Required for something to occur (but in combination with other factors)	Fuel is necessary for fire Capital is necessary for economic growth
Precipitating cause	Brings on a change	Protest march ignites a strike by workers Plane flies into strong thunderstorms
Proximate cause	Immediately present or visible cause of action	Strike causes company to declare bankruptcy Powerful wind shear causes plane to crash
Remote cause	Indirect or underlying explanation for action	Company was losing money on bad designs and inept manufacturing Wind shear warning failed to sound in cockpit
Reciprocal causes	One factor leads to a second, which reinforces the first, creating a cycle	Lack of good schools leads to poverty, which further weakens education, which leads to even fewer opportunities . . .

Even the most everyday causal analysis can draw on such distinctions among reasons and causes. What persuaded you, for instance, to choose the college you decided to attend? *Proximate* reasons might be the location of the school or the college's curriculum in your areas of interest. But what are the *necessary* reasons—the ones without which your choice of that college could not occur? Adequate financial support? Good test scores and academic record? The expectations of a parent?

Once you've identified a causal claim, you can draw out the reasons, warrants, and evidence that can support it most effectively:

Claim	Certain career patterns cause women to be paid less than men.
Reason	Women's career patterns differ from men's.
Warrant	Successful careers are made during the period between ages twenty-five and thirty-five.
Evidence	Women often drop out of or reduce work during the decade between ages twenty-five and thirty-five to raise families.

Claim	Lack of community and alumni support caused the football coach to lose his job.
Reason	Ticket sales and alumni support have declined for three seasons in a row despite a respectable team record.
Warrant	Winning over fans is as important as winning games for college coaches in smaller athletic programs.
Evidence	Over the last ten years, coaches at several programs have been sacked because of declining support and revenues.

RESPOND

Here's a schematic causal analysis of one event, exploring the difference among precipitating, necessary, and sufficient causes. Critique and revise the analysis as you see fit. Then create another of your own, beginning with a different event, phenomenon, incident, fad, or effect.

Event: Traffic fatality at an intersection

Precipitating cause: A pickup truck that runs a red light, totals a Prius, and injures its driver

Necessary cause: Two drivers who are navigating Friday rush-hour traffic (if no driving, then no accident)

Sufficient cause: A truck driver who is distracted by a cell-phone conversation

Supporting Your Point

In drafting your causal argument, you'll want to do the following:

- Show that the causes and effects you've suggested are highly probable and backed by evidence, or show what's wrong with the faulty causal reasoning you may be critiquing.

- Assess any links between causal relationships (what leads to or follows from what).

- Show that your explanations of any causal chains are accurate, or identify where links in a causal chain break down.

- Show that plausible cause-and-effect explanations haven't been ignored or that the possibility of multiple causes or effects has been considered.

In other words, you will need to examine your subject carefully and find appropriate ways to support your claims. There are different ways to accomplish that goal.

For example, in studying effects that are physical (as they would be with diseases or climate conditions), you can offer and test *hypotheses*, or theories about possible causes. That means researching such topics thoroughly because you'll need to draw upon authorities and research articles for your explanations and evidence. (See Chapter 20, "Academic Arguments," and Chapter 21, "Finding Evidence.") Don't be surprised if you find yourself debating which among conflicting authorities make the most plausible causal or explanatory arguments. Your achievement as a writer may be simply that you present these differences in an essay, leaving it to readers to make judgments of their own—as John Tierney does in "Can a Playground Be Too Safe?" at the end of this chapter (see p. 434).

But not all the evidence in compelling causal arguments needs to be strictly scientific or scholarly. Many causal arguments rely on **ethnographic observations**—the systematic study of ordinary people in their daily routines. How would you explain, for example, why some people step aside when they encounter someone head-on and others do not? In an argument that attempts to account for such behavior, investigators Frank Willis, Joseph Gier, and David Smith observed "1,038 displacements involving 3,141 persons" at a Kansas City shopping mall. In results that surprised the investigators, "gallantry" seemed to play a significant role in causing people to step aside for one another—more so than other causes that the investigators had anticipated (such as deferring to someone who's physically stronger or higher in status). Doubtless you've read of other such studies, perhaps in psychology courses. You may even decide to do a little fieldwork on your own—which raises the possibility of using personal experiences in support of a causal argument.

Indeed, people's experiences generally lead them to draw causal conclusions about things they know well. Personal experience can also help build your credibility as a writer, gain the empathy of listeners, and thus support a causal claim. Although one person's experiences cannot ordinarily be universalized, they can still argue eloquently for causal relationships. Listen to Sara Barbour, a recent graduate of Columbia University, as she draws upon her own carefully described experiences to bemoan what may happen when e-readers finally displace printed books:

> In eliminating a book's physical existence, something crucial is lost forever. Trapped in a Kindle, the story remains but the book can no longer be scribbled in, hoarded, burned, given, or received. We may be able to read it, but we can't share it with others in the same way, and its ability to connect us to people, places, and ideas is that much less powerful.
>
> I know the Kindle will eventually carry the day—an electronic reader means no more embarrassing coffee stains, no more library holds and renewals, no more frantic flipping through pages for a lost quote, or going to three bookstores in one afternoon to track down an evasive title. Who am I to advocate the doom of millions of trees when the swipe of a finger can deliver all 838 pages of *Middlemarch* into my waiting hands?
>
> But once we all power up our Kindles something will be gone, a kind of language. Books communicate with us as readers—but as important, we communicate with each other through books themselves. When that connection is lost, the experience of reading—and our lives—will be forever altered.
>
> —Sara Barbour, "Kindle vs. Books: The Dead Trees Society,"
> *Los Angeles Times*, June 17, 2011

All these strategies—testing hypotheses, presenting experimental evidence, and offering personal experience—can help you support a causal argument or undermine a causal claim you regard as faulty.

RESPOND

One of the fallacies of argument discussed in Chapter 12 is the *post hoc, ergo propter hoc* ("after this, therefore because of this") fallacy. Causal arguments are particularly prone to this kind of fallacious reasoning, in which a writer asserts a causal relationship between two entirely unconnected events. When Angelina Jolie gave birth to twins in 2008, for instance, the stock market rallied by nearly six hundred points, but it would be difficult to argue that either event is related to the other.

Because causal arguments can easily fall prey to this fallacy, you might find it instructive to create and defend an absurd connection of this kind. Begin by asserting a causal link between two events or phenomena that likely have no relationship: *The enormous popularity of* Doctor Who *is partially due to global warming.* Then spend a page or so spinning out an imaginative argument to defend the claim. It's OK to have fun with this exercise, but see how convincing you can be at generating plausibly implausible arguments.

The comparative size of successive generations across time when fertility is constant at 1.3 births per woman

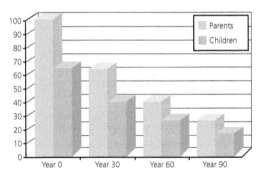

A simple graph can provide dramatic evidence for a causal claim—in this case, the effect of reduced fertility rates on a population.

Data from Statistics Bureau, MIC; Ministry of Health, Labour and Welfare

Considering Design and Visuals

You may find that the best way to illustrate a causal relationship is to present it visually. Even a simple bar graph or chart can demonstrate a relationship between two variables that might be related to a specific cause, like the one above showing the dramatic effects of lowered birthrates. The report that uses this figure explores the effects that such a change would have on the economies of the world.

Or you may decide that the most dramatic way to present important causal information about a single issue or problem is via an infographic, cartoon, or public service announcement. Our arresting example on the next page is part of a campaign by People for the Ethical Treatment of Animals (PETA). An organization that advocates for animal rights, PETA promotes campaigns that typically try to sway people to adopt vegetarian diets by depicting the practices of the agriculture industry as cruel.

PETA's ad campaign expands its focus to environmentalists by explaining through causal links why they should consider vegetarian diets.

Courtesy of People for the Ethical Treatment of Animals; peta.org

(Many of us have also seen their celebrity anti-fur campaigns; see p. 235 for one example.) Their "Meat's Not Green!" campaign, however, attempts to reach an audience that might not buy into the animal rights argument. Instead, it appeals to people who have environmentalist beliefs by presenting data that claims a causal link between animal farming and environmental destruction. How much of this data surprises you?

GUIDE TO WRITING A CAUSAL ARGUMENT

Finding a Topic

You're entering a causal argument when you:

- state a cause and then examine its effects: *The ongoing economic downturn has led more people to return to college to enhance their job market credentials.*

- describe an effect and trace it back to its causes: *There has been a recent surge in the hiring of part-time contract workers, likely due to the reluctance of businesses to hire permanent employees who would be subject to new health care regulations.*

- trace a string of causes to figure out why something happened: *The housing and financial markets collapsed in 2008 after government mandates to encourage homeownership led banks to invent questionable financial schemes in order to offer subprime mortgages to borrowers who bought homes they could not afford with loans they could not pay back.*

- explore plausible consequences (intended or not) of a particular action, policy, or change: *The ban on incandescent lightbulbs may draw more attention to climate change than any previous government action.*

Spend time brainstorming possibilities for causal arguments. Many public issues lend themselves to causal analysis and argument: browse the homepage of a newspaper or news source on any given day to discover plausible topics. Consider topics that grow from your own experiences.

It's fair game, too, to question the accuracy or adequacy of existing arguments about causality. You can write a strong paper by raising doubts about the facts or assumptions that others have made and perhaps offering a better causal explanation on your own.

GUIDE TO WRITING A CAUSAL ARGUMENT

Researching Your Topic

Causal arguments will lead you to many different resources:

- current news media—especially magazines and newspapers (online or in print)

- online databases

- scholarly journals

- books written on your subject (here you can do a keyword search, either in your library or online)

- blogs, Web sites, or social networking sites

In addition, why not carry out some field research? Conduct interviews with appropriate authorities on your subject, create a questionnaire aimed at establishing a range of opinions on your subject, or arrange a discussion forum among people with a stake in the issue. The information you get from interviews, questionnaires, or open-ended dialogue might provide ideas to enrich your argument or evidence to back up your claims.

Formulating a Claim

For a conventional causal analysis, try to formulate a claim that lets readers know where you stand on some issue involving causes and effects. First, identify the kind of causal argument that you expect to make (see pp. 403–08 for a review of these kinds of arguments) or decide whether you intend, instead, to debunk an existing cause-and-effect claim. Then explore your relationship to the claim. What do you know about the subject and its causes and effects? Why do you favor (or disagree with) the claim? What significant reasons can you offer in support of your position?

End this process by formulating a thesis—a complete sentence that says, in effect, *A causes (or does not cause or is caused by) B*, followed by a summary of the reasons supporting this causal

GUIDE TO WRITING A CAUSAL ARGUMENT

relationship. Make your thesis as specific as possible and be sure that it's sufficiently controversial or intriguing to hold a reader's interest. Of course, feel free to revise any such claim as you learn more about a subject.

For causal topics that are more open-ended and exploratory, you may not want to take a strong position, particularly at the outset. Instead, your argument might simply present a variety of reasonable (and possibly competing) explanations and scenarios.

Examples of Causal Claims

- Right-to-carry gun laws have led to increased rates of crime in states that have approved such legislation.

- Sophisticated use of social media is now a must for any political candidate who hopes to win.

- Grade inflation is lowering the value of a college education.

- The proliferation of images in film, television, and computer-generated texts is changing the way we read and use information.

- Experts don't yet agree on the long-term impact that sophisticated use of social media will have on American political campaigns, though some effects are already evident.

Preparing a Proposal

If your instructor asks you to prepare a proposal for your project, here's a format that may help:

State your thesis completely. If you're having trouble doing so, try outlining it in Toulmin terms:

GUIDE TO WRITING A CAUSAL ARGUMENT

Claim:

Reason(s):

Warrant(s):

Alternatively, you might indicate an intention to explore a particular causal question in your project, with the thesis perhaps coming later.

- Explain why this issue deserves attention. What's at stake?

- Identify whom you hope to reach through your argument and why this group of readers would be interested in it.

- Briefly discuss the key challenges you anticipate in preparing your argument.

- Determine what research strategies you'll use. What sources do you expect to consult?

- Briefly identify and explore the major stakeholders in your argument and what alternative perspectives you may need to consider as you formulate your argument.

Considering Format and Media

Your instructor may specify that you use a particular format and/or medium. If not, ask yourself these questions to help you make a good choice:

- What format is most appropriate for your causal argument? Does it call for an academic essay, a report, an infographic, a brochure, or something else?

- What medium is most appropriate for your argument? Would it be best delivered orally to a live audience? Presented as an audio essay or podcast? Presented in print only or in print with illustrations?

- Will you need visuals, such as moving or still images, maps, graphs, charts—and what function will they play in your argument? Make sure they are not just "added on" but are necessary components of the argument.

Thinking about Organization

Your causal argument will likely include elements such as the following:

- a specific causal claim somewhere in the paper—or the identification of a significant causal issue

- an explanation of the claim's significance or importance

- evidence sufficient to support each cause or effect—or, in an argument based on a series of causal links, evidence to support the relationships among the links

- a consideration of other plausible causes and effects, and evidence that you have thought carefully about these alternatives before offering your own ideas

Getting and Giving Response: Questions for Peer Response

Your instructor may assign you to a group for the purpose of reading and responding to each other's drafts. If not, ask for responses from serious readers or consultants at a writing center. Use the following questions to evaluate a colleague's draft. Be sure to illustrate your comments with examples; specific comments help more than general observations.

GUIDE **TO WRITING A CAUSAL ARGUMENT**

The Claim

- Does the claim state a causal argument?

- Does the claim identify clearly what causes and effects are being examined?

- What about the claim will make it appeal to readers?

- Is the claim too sweeping? Does it need to be qualified? How might it be narrowed and focused?

- How strong is the relationship between the claim and the reasons given to support it? How could that relationship be made more explicit?

Evidence for the Claim

- What's the strongest evidence offered for the claim? What, if any, evidence needs to be strengthened?

- Is enough evidence offered to show that these causes are responsible for the identified effect, that these effects result from the identified cause, or that a series of causes and effects are linked? If not, what additional evidence is needed? What kinds of sources might provide this evidence?

- How credible will the sources be to potential readers? What other sources might be more persuasive?

- Is evidence in support of the claim analyzed logically? Is more discussion needed?

- Have alternative causes and effects been considered? Have objections to the claim been carefully considered and presented fairly? Have these objections been discussed?

GUIDE **TO WRITING A CAUSAL ARGUMENT**

Organization and Style

- How are the parts of the argument organized? Is this organization effective?

- Will readers understand the relationships among the claims, supporting reasons, warrants, and evidence? If not, how might those connections be clearer? Is the function of every visual clear? Are more transitions needed? Would headings or graphic devices help?

- Are the transitions or links from point to point, sentence to sentence, and paragraph to paragraph clear and effective? If not, how could they be improved?

- Are all visuals (or other elements such as audio or video clips) carefully integrated into the text? Is each visual introduced and commented on to point out its significance? Is each visual labeled as a figure or a table and given a caption as well as a citation?

- Is the style suited to the subject? Is it too formal, casual, or technical? Can it be improved?

- Which sentences seem effective? Which ones seem weaker, and how could they be improved? Should short sentences be combined, and any longer ones be broken up?

- How effective are the paragraphs? Too short or too long? How can they be improved?

- Which words or phrases seem effective? Do any seem vague or inappropriate for the audience or the writer's purpose? Are technical or unfamiliar terms defined?

GUIDE **TO WRITING A CAUSAL ARGUMENT**

Spelling, Punctuation, Mechanics, Documentation, and Format

● Are there any errors in spelling, punctuation, capitalization, and the like?

● Is the documentation appropriate and consistent? (See Chapter 25.)

● Does the paper or project follow an appropriate format? Is it appropriately designed and attractively presented?

PROJECTS

1. Develop an argument exploring one of the cause-and-effect topics mentioned in this chapter. Just a few of those topics are listed below:

   Disappearance of honeybees in the United States

   Causes of long-term unemployment or declining job markets

   Using the tax code to discourage/encourage specific behaviors (i.e., smoking, eating unhealthy foods, hiring more workers)

   Increasing numbers of obese children and/or adults

   Ramifications of increasing amounts of time spent on social media sites

   Results of failing to pass immigration reform legislation

   Repercussions of U.S. ethanol policy

   What is lost/gained as paper books disappear

2. Write a causal argument about a subject you know well, even if the topic does not strike you as particularly "academic": *What accounts for the popularity of* The Hunger Games *trilogy? What are the likely consequences of students*

living more of their lives via social media? How are video games chang-ing the way students you know learn? Why do women love shoes? In this argument, be sure to separate precipitating or proximate causes from sufficient or necessary ones. In other words, do a deep and revealing causal analysis about your subject, giving readers new insights.

3. John Tierney's essay "Can a Playground Be Too Safe?" (see p. 434) explores some unintended consequences of noble-minded efforts in recent decades to make children's playgrounds safer. After read-ing the Tierney piece, list any comparable situations you know of where unintended consequences may have undermined the good (or maybe even bad?) intentions of those who took action or imple-mented some change. Choose the most intriguing situation, do the necessary research, and write a causal argument about it.

4. Raven Jiang's "Dota 2: The Face of Professional Gaming" (see p. 429) argues that crowdfunding and netstreaming are two major causes in the rise of big-money professional gaming, which he sees as a phenomenon that is here to stay ("Watch out NFL, America's sport is about to change"). In a project of your own, describe the causes that have led to a particular effect on your campus or in your commu-nity or place of work. You may point out, as Jiang does, both advan-tages and disadvantages of the change brought about by the causes you analyze.

Two Sample Causal Arguments

Dota 2: The Face of Professional Gaming

RAVEN JIANG

August 5, 2014

Just over a week ago, history was made when a team of five young Chinese men left Seattle with $5 million in winnings. The game they were playing was not poker but "Dota 2," a multiplayer online game made by the Bellevue-based gaming company Valve. This year's annual "Dota 2" Internationals tournament, the fourth one since its creation, presented the largest prize pool ever seen in professional gaming—a total of $10.9 million. ESPN covered the matches and it seemed like every media outlet was trying to get in on the story, if only as a human interest piece. There is a sense that we are entering new uncharted territories.

> The introductory paragraph presents the "effect": a huge rise in professional online gaming.

Since the early 2000s, much has been written and said about the slow but steady rise of professional video gaming. What happened this month at Seattle is a coming-of-age story that we are all familiar with, but it is also so much more. A confluence of factors had brought the 2014 "Dota 2" Internationals into the mainstream consciousness and they represent an interesting microcosm of the technological forces that are shaping our future, gaming and otherwise.

> A causal claim is stated.

Raven Jiang is an undergraduate at Stanford University, studying computer science. His piece was first published in the *Stanford Daily*, a student-produced newspaper founded in 1892.

The first cause is introduced: crowdfunding.

Kickstarter brought the idea of crowdfunding into our daily lives, but Valve made it addictive with "Dota 2." Unlike past video gaming tournaments that relied solely on sponsorships for prize money, which were often the first thing on the chopping boards when it came to corporate budget cuts, the Internationals were almost entirely crowdfunded via in-game item purchases by online players. In the weeks leading up to the event, fans could purchase tournament-related in-game items to contribute to the prize pool and to eventually earn vanity visual effects that they could show off in-game on their characters. And just like a Kickstarter campaign, there was a counter tracking the amount raised, with final rewards that fans earn determined by the final total—think Kickstarter fundraising goals. For example, the reward for hitting $3.5 million this time was access to special chat emoticons. In this way, much like purchasing swag at an indie concert, fans not only contribute to the prize pool but feel like they get something back in return.

The benefits of crowdfunding are stated.

So, fans pay both to support the goal of having a more exciting tournament with bigger stakes and to gain personal items; Valve takes a cut as profits and professional Dota players get to make a career out of their passion. As Michael Scott once said, this is a win-win-win outcome. The final prize pool of $10.9 million was more than three times that of last year. To put that into perspective, the second placing team this year won more money than last year's winning team. That's a growth rate that would make Bernie Madoff jealous.

The author points out benefits to the winners as well as the viewers.

The successful use of crowdfunding by Valve is a great example of the value of crowdfunding as a whole. The reason why corporate sponsorships have historically been unreliable is because they are a poor indirect proxy for consumer demand. Much like the homemade gadgets that find their audience on Kickstarter, Valve is tapping into an underserved demand by getting the consumers to directly pay for the cost of production.

The other major force behind the modern "Dota 2" juggernaut is live game streaming. YouTube brought us video sharing and Netflix brought us the Internet's take on cable TV, but online gaming is helping to turn a very different form of visual entertainment into its own industry. Just like the Super Bowl, we now have the huge events that draw millions of viewers in the likes of the Internationals. But beyond that familiar format, there is also a burgeoning cottage industry of individual gamers who stream their gaming sessions live online and make money off of advertising and product placements. A popular full-time game streamer can take home a six-digit income doing what his parents say will never amount to much, probably right in their basement.

The second major cause is presented to support the claim.

The prevalence of game streaming has created the interesting situation in which many fans of popular online games seldom ever actually feel the need to play them, because watching is so much less stressful, less time-consuming, and more readily accessible. In some sense, "Dota 2," a game notorious for its complex game mechanics, can probably thank the rise of stream watching for the success of its annual

championship events, because let's face it: If every sports fan had to be able to play the game in order to understand and enjoy watching it, then college football would be bankrupt. With the professionalization of online gaming that parallels the paths taken by its traditional counterparts, it is no wonder Google recently decided to fork out a cool billion dollars to acquire the major game streaming site Twitch.tv.

The point is that online gaming is going to be a big deal. And it is a big deal not just because video gaming is becoming big money, but because its rise is symbolic of the same technological shifts that are changing all other aspects of our lives.

The author gives proof that online video gaming is already big time in South Korea and the United States.

The future is already here in South Korea, where professional "Starcraft" gamers are literally national celebrities. Significant milestones like the recent "Dota 2" Internationals suggest that the U.S. is on its way there. Watching the live stream of the Internationals with its extremely professional production value, the seasoned commentators throwing team and player stats at each other and the incredible amount of skill and concentration exhibited by the competitors, an alien visitor from Alpha Centauri would be hard-pressed to say what exactly differentiates "Dota 2" from sports. (I suppose there has not been any accusation of steroid abuse. Yet.)

The downsides of the dramatic rise in online gaming are presented.

That said, it is not all rainbows and unicorns. There is a general feeling that this year's matches at the Internationals have not been as exciting and eventful as last year's. Perhaps the unprecedented prize pool this year was causing players to be more risk-averse, leading to fewer clutch plays and comebacks from behind. Both of the teams in the final were also Chinese, who are known for being more methodological both in play style and training processes. The old fan favorite Na'Vi, the Eastern European past championship winners known for their dramatic comebacks and eccentric play styles, did not manage to get into the final four this year. Still, even if "Dota 2" does falter, it has already pushed the boundaries for professional gaming and paved the way for the future.

The concluding sentence assures readers that even if Dota 2 itself fails, what it represents has already had a major impact on the future of gaming.

Watch out NFL, America's sport is about to change.

Can a Playground Be Too Safe?

JOHN TIERNEY

A childhood relic: jungle gyms, like this one in Riverside Park in Manhattan, have disappeared from most American playgrounds in recent decades.

© Dith Pran/The New York Times/Redux

When seesaws and tall slides and other perils were disappearing from New York's playgrounds, Henry Stern drew a line in the sandbox. As the city's parks commissioner in the 1990s, he issued an edict concerning the ten-foot-high jungle gym near his childhood home in northern Manhattan.

"I grew up on the monkey bars in Fort Tryon Park, and I never forgot how good it felt to get to the top of them," Mr. Stern said. "I didn't want to see that playground bowdlerized. I said that as long as I was parks commissioner, those monkey bars were going to stay."

His philosophy seemed reactionary at the time, but today it's shared by some researchers who question the value of safety-first

---

John Tierney is a journalist and coauthor of the book *Willpower: Rediscovering the Greatest Human Strength* (2011). He writes the science column "Findings" for the *New York Times*, where this piece was originally published on July 18, 2011. You will note that, as a journalist, Tierney cites sources without documenting them formally. An academic version of this argument might offer both in-text citations and a list of sources at the end.

playgrounds. Even if children do suffer fewer physical injuries—and the evidence for that is debatable—the critics say that these playgrounds may stunt emotional development, leaving children with anxieties and fears that are ultimately worse than a broken bone.

"Children need to encounter risks and overcome fears on the playground," said Ellen Sandseter, a professor of psychology at Queen Maud University in Norway. "I think monkey bars and tall slides are great. As playgrounds become more and more boring, these are some of the few features that still can give children thrilling experiences with heights and high speed."

After observing children on playgrounds in Norway, England, and Australia, Dr. Sandseter identified six categories of risky play: exploring heights, experiencing high speed, handling dangerous tools, being near dangerous elements (like water or fire), rough-and-tumble play (like wrestling), and wandering alone away from adult supervision. The most common is climbing heights.

"Climbing equipment needs to be high enough, or else it will be too boring in the long run," Dr. Sandseter said. "Children approach thrills and risks in a progressive manner, and very few children would try to climb to the highest point for the first time they climb. The best thing is to let children encounter these challenges from an early age, and they will then progressively learn to master them through their play over the years."

Sometimes, of course, their mastery fails, and falls are the common form of playground injury. But these rarely cause permanent damage, either physically or emotionally. While some psychologists—and many parents—have worried that a child who suffered a bad fall would develop a fear of heights, studies have shown the opposite pattern: A child who's hurt in a fall before the age of nine is less likely as a teenager to have a fear of heights.

By gradually exposing themselves to more and more dangers on the playground, children are using the same habituation techniques developed by therapists to help adults conquer phobias, according to Dr. Sandseter and a fellow psychologist, Leif Kennair, of the Norwegian University for Science and Technology.

"Risky play mirrors effective cognitive behavioral therapy of anxiety," they write in the journal *Evolutionary Psychology*, concluding that this "anti-phobic effect" helps explain the evolution of children's fondness for thrill-seeking. While a youthful zest for exploring heights might not seem adaptive—why would natural selection favor children who risk death before they have a chance to reproduce?—the dangers seemed to be outweighed by the benefits of conquering fear and developing a sense of mastery.

"Paradoxically," the psychologists write, "we posit that our fear of children being harmed by mostly harmless injuries may result in more fearful children and increased levels of psychopathology."

The old tall jungle gyms and slides disappeared from most American playgrounds across the country in recent decades because of parental concerns, federal guidelines, new safety standards set by manufacturers and—the most frequently cited factor—fear of lawsuits.

Shorter equipment with enclosed platforms was introduced, and the old pavement was replaced with rubber, wood chips, or other materials designed for softer landings. These innovations undoubtedly prevented some injuries, but some experts question their overall value.

"There is no clear evidence that playground safety measures have lowered the average risk on playgrounds," said David Ball, a professor of risk management at Middlesex University in London. He noted that the risk of some injuries, like long fractures of the arm, actually increased after the introduction of softer surfaces on playgrounds in Britain and Australia.

"This sounds counterintuitive, but it shouldn't, because it is a common phenomenon," Dr. Ball said. "If children and parents believe they are in an environment which is safer than it actually is, they will take more risks. An argument against softer surfacing is that children think it is safe, but because they don't understand its properties, they overrate its performance."

Reducing the height of playground equipment may help toddlers, but it can produce unintended consequences among bigger children. "Older children are discouraged from taking healthy exercise on playgrounds because they have been designed with the safety of the very young in mind," Dr. Ball said. "Therefore, they may play in more dangerous places, or not at all."

Fear of litigation led New York City officials to remove seesaws, merry-go-rounds, and the ropes that young Tarzans used to swing from one platform to another. Letting children swing on tires became taboo because of fears that the heavy swings could bang into a child.

"What happens in America is defined by tort lawyers, and unfortunately that limits some of the adventure playgrounds," said Adrian Benepe, the current parks commissioner. But while he misses the Tarzan ropes, he's glad that the litigation rate has declined, and he's not nostalgic for asphalt pavement.

"I think safety surfaces are a godsend," he said. "I suspect that parents who have to deal with concussions and broken arms wouldn't agree that playgrounds have become too safe." The ultra-safe enclosed platforms of the 1980s and 1990s may have been an overreaction, Mr. Benepe said, but lately there have been more creative alternatives.

"The good news is that manufacturers have brought out new versions of the old toys," he said. "Because of height limitations, no one's building the old monkey bars anymore, but kids can go up smaller climbing walls and rope nets and artificial rocks."

Still, sometimes there's nothing quite like being ten feet off the ground, as a new generation was discovering the other afternoon at Fort Tryon Park. A soft rubber surface carpeted the pavement, but the jungle gym of Mr. Stern's youth was still there. It was the prime destination for many children, including those who'd never seen one before, like Nayelis Serrano, a ten-year-old from the South Bronx who was visiting her cousin.

When she got halfway up, at the third level of bars, she paused, as if that was high enough. Then, after a consultation with her mother, she continued to the top, the fifth level, and descended to recount her triumph.

"I was scared at first," she explained. "But my mother said if you don't try, you'll never know if you could do it. So I took a chance and kept going. At the top I felt very proud." As she headed back for another climb, her mother, Orkidia Rojas, looked on from a bench and considered the pros and cons of this unfamiliar equipment.

"It's fun," she said. "I'd like to see it in our playground. Why not? It's kind of dangerous, I know, but if you just think about danger you're never going to get ahead in life."

19

Proposals

Writing Arguments

Chapter 19, "Proposals," from *Everything's an Argument*, Seventh Edition,
by Andrea A. Lunsford and John J. Ruszkiewicz, pp. 272–304 (Chapter 12).
Copyright © 2016 by Bedford/St. Martin's.

A student looking forward to spring break proposes to two friends that they join a group that will spend the vacation helping to build a school in a Haitian village.

The members of a club for undergrad business majors talk about their common need to create informative, appealing, interactive résumés. After much talk, three members suggest that the club develop a résumé app especially for business majors looking for a first job.

A project team at a large architectural firm works for three months developing a response to an RFP (request for proposal) to convert a university library into a digital learning center.

Understanding and Categorizing Proposals

We live in an era of big proposals—complex programs for health care reform, bold dreams to privatize space exploration, multibillion-dollar designs for high-speed rail systems, ceaseless calls to improve education, and so many other such ideas brought down to earth by sobering proposals for budget reform and deficit reduction. As a result, there's often more talk than action because persuading people (or legislatures) to do something— or *anything*!—is always hard. But that's what *proposal arguments* do: they provide thoughtful reasons for supporting or sometimes resisting change.

Such arguments, whether national or local, formal or casual, are important not only on the national scene but also in all of our lives. How many proposals do you make or respond to in one day? A neighbor might suggest that you volunteer to help clean up an urban creek bed; a campus group might demand that students get better seats at football games; a supervisor might ask for ideas to improve customer satisfaction at a restaurant; you might offer an ad agency reasons to hire you as a summer intern—or propose to a friend that you take in the latest zombie film. In each case, the proposal implies that some action should take place and suggests that there are sound reasons why it should.

This cartoon, by Steve Breen, suggests that high-speed rail proposals are going to run into a major obstacle in California.

By permission of Steve Breen and Creators Syndicate, Inc.

In their simplest form, proposal arguments look something like this:

A should do B because of C.

┌─────────A─────────┐ ┌──────────────B──────────────┐
Our student government should endorse the Academic Bill of Rights

┌──────────────C──────────────┐
because students should not be punished in
their courses for their personal political views.

Proposals come at us so routinely that it's not surprising that they cover a dizzyingly wide range of possibilities. So it may help to think of proposal arguments as divided roughly into two kinds—those that focus on specific practices and those that focus on broad matters of policy. Here are several examples of each kind:

Proposals about Practices

- The college should allow students to pay tuition on a month-by-month basis.

- Commercial hotels should stop opposing competitors like Airbnb.

- College athletes should be paid for the services they provide.

Proposals about Policies

- The college should adopt a policy guaranteeing that students in all majors can graduate in four years.

- The United Nations should make saving the oceans from pollution a global priority.

- Major Silicon Valley firms should routinely reveal the demographic makeup of their workforces.

RESPOND

People write proposal arguments to solve problems and to change the way things are. But problems aren't always obvious: what troubles some people might be no big deal to others. To get an idea of the range of problems people face on your campus (some of which you may not even have thought of as problems), divide into groups, and brainstorm about things that annoy you on and around campus, including wastefulness in the cafeterias, 8:00 a.m. classes, and long lines for football or concert tickets. Ask each group to aim for at least a dozen gripes. Then choose three problems, and as a group, discuss how you'd prepare a proposal to deal with them.

Characterizing Proposals

Proposals have three main characteristics:

1. They call for change, often in response to a problem.

2. They focus on the future.

3. They center on the audience.

Proposals always call for some kind of action. They aim at getting something done—or sometimes at *preventing* something from being done. Proposals marshal evidence and arguments to persuade people to choose a course of action: *Let's build a completely green house. Let's oppose the latest*

Supreme Court ruling on Internet privacy. Let's create a campus organization for first-generation college students. Let's ban drones from campus airspace, especially at sporting events. But you know the old saying, "You can lead a horse to water, but you can't make it drink." It's usually easier to *convince* audiences what a good course of action is than to *persuade* them to take it (or pay for it). Even if you present a cogent proposal, you may still have work to do.

Proposal arguments must appeal to more than good sense. Ethos matters, too. It helps if a writer suggesting a change carries a certain gravitas earned by experience or supported by knowledge and research. If your word and credentials carry weight, then an audience is more likely to listen to your proposal. So when the commanders of three *Apollo* moon missions, Neil Armstrong, James Lovell, and Eugene Cernan, wrote an open letter to President Obama expressing their dismay at his administration's decision to cancel NASA's plans for advanced spacecraft and new lunar missions, they won a wide audience:

> For The United States, the leading space faring nation for nearly half a century, to be without carriage to low Earth orbit and with no human exploration capability to go beyond Earth orbit for an indeterminate time into the future, destines our nation to become one of second or even third rate stature. While the President's plan envisages humans traveling away from Earth and perhaps toward Mars at some time in the future, the lack of developed rockets and spacecraft will assure that ability will not be available for many years.

> Without the skill and experience that actual spacecraft operation provides, the USA is far too likely to be on a long downhill slide to mediocrity. America must decide if it wishes to remain a leader in space. If it does, we should institute a program which will give us the very best chance of achieving that goal.

But even their considerable ethos was not enough to carry the day with the space agency and the man who made the decision.

Yet, as the space program example obviously demonstrates, proposal arguments focus on the future—what people, institutions, or governments should do over the upcoming weeks, months, or, in the NASA moon-mission example, decades. This orientation toward the future presents special challenges, since few of us have crystal balls. Proposal arguments must therefore offer the best evidence available to suggest that actions we recommend will achieve what they promise.

All that remains of the American space program?

Michael Williamson/The Washington Post/Getty Images

In May 2014, Senator Elizabeth Warren introduced legislation aimed at reducing student loan debt, in part by allowing for refinancing. In an interview in *Rolling Stone,* Senator Warren explained:

> Homeowners refinance their loans when interest rates go down. Businesses refinance their loans. But right now, there's no way for students to be able to do that. I've proposed that we reduce the interest rate on the outstanding loan debt to the same rate Republicans and Democrats came together last year to set on new loans [3.86 percent]. For millions of borrowers, that would cut interest rates in half or more.

Yet Warren's proposal soon came under fire, particularly from senators who argued that the proposed bill did little to reduce borrowing or lower the cost of higher education. So despite the concerns of bankers and economists that the $1.1 trillion student loan debt is dampening the national economy, the bill was turned aside on June 11, 2014.

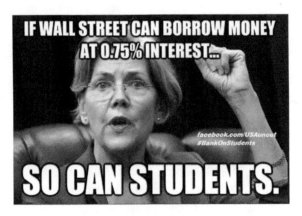

IF WALL STREET CAN BORROW MONEY AT 0.75% INTEREST...

SO CAN STUDENTS.

facebook.com/USAunout
#BankOnStudents

http://www.ClassWarfareExists.com

Which raises the matter of audiences, and we are left asking whether Senator Warren's bill spoke equally well to students, parents, bankers, and members of Congress. Some of those audiences failed to be convinced.

Some proposals are tailored to general audiences; consequently, they avoid technical language, make straightforward and relatively simple points, and sometimes use charts, graphs, and tables to make data comprehensible. You can find such arguments, for example, in newspaper editorials, letters to the editor, and political documents like Senator Warren's proposed legislation. And such appeals to a broad group make sense when a proposal—say, to finance new toll roads or build an art museum—must surf on waves of community support and financing.

But often proposals need to win the approval of specific groups or individuals (such as financiers, developers, public officials, and legislators) who have the power to make change actually happen. Such arguments will usually be more technical, detailed, and comprehensive than those aimed at the general public because people directly involved with an issue have a stake in it. They may be affected by it themselves and thus have in-depth knowledge of the subject. Or they may be responsible for implementing the proposal. You can expect them to have specific questions about it and, possibly, formidable objections. So identifying your potential audiences is critical to the success of any proposal. On your own campus, for example, a plan to alter admissions policies might be directed both to students in general and (perhaps in a different form) to the university president, members of the faculty council, and admissions officers.

Proposals have to take audience values into account. Shooting deer, even when they're munching on garden flowers, is unacceptable to most suburbanites.

Ron Sanford/Science Source*/Photo Researchers

An effective proposal also has to be compatible with the values of the audience. Some ideas may make good sense but cannot be enacted. For example, many American towns and cities have a problem with expanding deer populations. Without natural predators, the deer are moving closer to homes, dining on gardens and shrubbery, and endangering traffic. Yet one obvious and feasible solution—culling the herds through hunting—is usually not saleable to communities (perhaps too many people remember *Bambi*).

RESPOND

Work in a group to identify about half a dozen problems on your campus or in the local community, looking for a wide range of issues. (Don't focus on problems in individual classes.) Once you have settled on these issues, then use various resources—the Web, the phone book (if you can find one), a campus directory—to locate specific people, groups, or offices whom you might address or influence to deal with the issues you have identified.

Developing Proposals

In developing a proposal, you will have to do some or all of the following:

- Define a problem that needs a solution or describe a need that is not currently addressed.

- Make a strong claim that addresses the problem or need. Your solution should be an action directed at the future.

- Show why your proposal will fix the problem or address the need.

- Demonstrate that your proposal is feasible.

This might sound easy, but writing a proposal argument can be a process of discovery. At the outset, you think you know exactly what ought to be done, but by the end, you may see (and even recommend) other options.

Defining a Need or Problem

To make a proposal, first establish that a need or problem exists. You'll typically dramatize the problem that you intend to fix at the beginning of your project and then lead up to a specific claim. But in some cases, you could put the need or problem right after your claim as the major reason for adopting the proposal:

> Let's ban cell phones on campus now. Why? Because we've become a school of walking zombies. No one speaks to or even acknowledges the people they meet or pass on campus. Half of our students are so busy chattering to people that they don't participate in the community around them.

How can you make readers care about the problem you hope to address? Following are some strategies:

- Paint a vivid picture of the need or problem.

- Show how the need or problem affects people, both those in the immediate audience and the general public as well.

- Underscore why the need or problem is significant and pressing.

- Explain why previous attempts to address the issue may have failed.

For example, in proposing that the military draft be restored in the United States or that all young men and women give two years to national service (a tough sell!), you might begin by drawing a picture of a younger generation that is self-absorbed, demands instant gratification, and doesn't understand what it means to participate as a full member of society. Or you might note how many young people today fail to develop the life skills they need to strike out on their own. Or like congressional representative Charles Rangel (D-New York), who regularly proposes a Universal

National Service Act, you could define the issue as a matter of fairness, arguing that the current all-volunteer army shifts the burden of national service to a small and unrepresentative sample of the American population. Speaking on CNN on January 26, 2013, Rangel said:

> Since we replaced the compulsory military draft with an all-volunteer force in 1973, our nation has been making decisions about wars without worry over who fights them. I sincerely believe that reinstating the draft would compel the American public to have a stake in the wars we fight as a nation. That is why I wrote the Universal National Service Act, known as the "draft" bill, which requires all men and women between ages 18 and 25 to give two years of service in any capacity that promotes our national defense.

Of course, you would want to cite authorities and statistics to prove that any problem you're diagnosing is real and that it touches your likely audience. Then readers *may* be ready to hear your proposal.

File this cartoon under "anticipate objections to your proposal."

© Mike Keefe/Cagle Cartoons, Inc.

In describing a problem that your proposal argument intends to solve, be sure to review earlier attempts to fix it. Many issues have a long history that you can't afford to ignore (or be ignorant of). Understand too that some problems seem to grow worse every time someone tinkers with them. You might pause before proposing any new attempt to reform the current system of financing federal election campaigns when you discover that previous reforms have resulted in more bureaucracy, more restrictions on political expression, and more unregulated money flowing into the system. *"Enough is enough"* can be a potent argument when faced with such a mess.

If you review "Let's Charge Politicians for Wasting Our Time" at the end of this chapter, a brief proposal by political and culture writer/blogger Virginia Postrel, you'll see that she spends quite a bit of time pointing out the irritation caused by unwanted political robocalls to her landline, even though she recognizes that such calls are illegal on cell phones. Does this focus on the landline take away from her proposal that the politicians should have to pay a fee for such calls as well as for unsolicited email messages they send, a proposal also put forward by technology guru Esther Dyson? Would you advise her to revise her argument—and if so, how?

Making a Strong and Clear Claim

After you've described and analyzed a problem, you're prepared to offer a fix. Begin with your claim (a proposal of what X or Y should do), followed by the reason(s) that X or Y should act and the effects of adopting the proposal:

Claim	Communities should encourage the development of charter schools.
Reason	Charter schools are not burdened by the bureaucracy that is associated with most public schooling.
Effects	Instituting such schools will bring more effective education to communities and offer an incentive to the public schools to improve their programs.

Having established a claim, you can explore its implications by drawing out the reasons, warrants, and evidence that can support it most effectively:

Claim	In light of a recent U.S. Supreme Court decision that ruled that federal drug laws cannot be used to prosecute doctors who prescribe drugs for use in suicide, our state should immediately pass a bill legalizing physician-assisted suicide for patients who are terminally ill.
Reason	Physician-assisted suicide can relieve the suffering of those who are terminally ill and will die soon.
Warrant	The relief of suffering is desirable.

Evidence	Oregon voters have twice approved the state's Death with Dignity Act, which has been in effect since 1997, and to date the suicide rate has not risen sharply, nor have doctors given out a large number of prescriptions for death-inducing drugs. Several other states are considering ballot initiatives in favor of doctor-assisted suicide.

The *reason* sets up the need for the proposal, whereas the *warrant* and *evidence* demonstrate that the proposal is just and could meet its objective. Your actual argument would develop each point in detail.

RESPOND

For each problem and solution below, make a list of readers' likely objections to the solution offered. Then propose a solution of your own, and explain why you think it's more workable than the original.

Problem	Future deficits in the Social Security system
Solution	Raise the age of retirement to seventy-two.

Problem	Severe grade inflation in college courses
Solution	Require a prescribed distribution of grades in every class: 10% A; 20% B; 40% C; 20% D; 10% F.

Problem	Increasing rates of obesity in the general population
Solution	Ban the sale of high-fat sandwiches and entrees in fast-food restaurants.

Problem	Inattentive driving because drivers are texting
Solution	Institute a one-year mandatory prison sentence for the first offense.

Problem	Increase in sexual assaults on and around campus
Solution	Establish a 10:00 p.m. curfew on weekends.

A proposal argument in four panels. You might compare this argument with Taylor Pearson's "Why You Should Fear Your Toaster More Than Nuclear Power" in Chapter 15.

© Andy Singer/Cagle Cartoons, Inc.

Showing That the Proposal Addresses the Need or Problem

An important but tricky part of making a successful proposal lies in relating the claim to the need or problem that it addresses. Facts and probability are your best allies. Take the time to show precisely how your solution will fix a problem or at least improve upon the current situation. Sometimes an emotional appeal is fair play, too. Here's former NBA player John Amaechi using that approach when he asks superstar Kobe Bryant of the L.A. Lakers not to appeal a $100,000 penalty he received for hurling an antigay slur at a referee:

> Kobe, stop fighting the fine. You spoke ill-advised words that shot out like bullets, and if the emails I received from straight and gay young people and sports fans in Los Angeles alone are anything to go by, you did serious damage with your outburst.
>
> A young man from a Los Angeles public school emailed me. You are his idol. He is playing up, on the varsity team, he has your posters all over his room, and he hopes one day to play in college

and then in the NBA with you. He used to fall asleep with images of passing you the ball to sink a game-winning shot. He watched every game you played this season on television, but this week he feels less safe and less positive about himself because he stared adoringly into your face as you said the word that haunts him in school every single day.

Kobe, stop fighting the fine. Use that money and your influence to set a new tone that tells sports fans, boys, men, and the society that looks up to you that the word you said in anger is not OK, not ever. Too many athletes take the trappings of their hard-earned success and leave no tangible legacy apart from "that shot" or "that special game."

—John Amaechi, "A Gay Former NBA Player
Responds to Kobe Bryant"

Left: John Amaechi; right: Kobe Bryant.

Left: Chris Goodney/Bloomberg News/Getty Images; right: © Lucy Nicholson/Reuters/LANDOV

The paragraph describing the reaction of the schoolboy provides just the tie that Amaechi needs between his proposal and the problem it would address. The story also gives his argument more power.

Alternatively, if you oppose an idea, these strategies work just as well in reverse: if a proposal doesn't fix a problem, you have to show exactly why. Here are a few paragraphs from an editorial posting by Doug Bandow for *Forbes* in which he refutes a proposal for reinstating military conscription:

All told, shifting to conscription would significantly weaken the military. New "accessions," as the military calls them, would be less bright, less well educated, and less positively motivated. They would be less likely to stay in uniform, resulting in a less experienced force. The armed forces would be less effective in combat, thereby costing America more lives while achieving fewer foreign policy objectives.

Why take such a step?

One argument, most recently articulated by Thomas Ricks of the Center for a New American Security, is that a draft would save "the government money." That's a poor reason to impress people into service.

First, conscription doesn't save much cash. It costs money to manage and enforce a draft—history demonstrates that not every inductee would go quietly. Conscripts serve shorter terms and re-enlist less frequently, increasing turnover, which is expensive. And unless the government instituted a Czarist lifetime draft, everyone beyond the first ranks would continue to expect to be paid.

Second, conscription shifts rather than reduces costs. Ricks suggested that draftees should "perform tasks currently outsourced at great cost to the Pentagon: paperwork, painting barracks, mowing lawns, driving generals around." Better to make people do grunt work than to pay them to do it? Force poorer young people into uniform in order to save richer old people tax dollars. Ricks believes that is a good reason to jail people for refusing to do as the government demands?

The government could save money in the same way by drafting FBI agents, postal workers, Medicare doctors, and congressmen. Nothing warrants letting old politicians force young adults to pay for Washington's profligacy. Moreover, by keeping some people who want to serve out while forcing others who don't want to serve in—creating a veritable evasion industry along the way—conscription would raise total social costs. It would be a bad bargain by any measure.

—Doug Bandow, "A New Military Draft Would Revive
a Very Bad Old Idea"

Finally, if your own experience backs up your claim or demonstrates the need or problem that your proposal aims to address, then consider using it to develop your proposal (as John Amaechi does in addressing his proposal to Kobe Bryant). Consider the following questions in deciding when to include your own experiences in showing that a proposal is needed or will in fact do what it claims:

- Is your experience directly related to the need or problem that you seek to address or to your proposal about it?

- Will your experience be appropriate and speak convincingly to the audience? Will the audience immediately understand its significance, or will it require explanation?

- Does your personal experience fit logically with the other reasons that you're using to support your claim?

Be careful. If a proposal seems crafted to serve mainly your own interests, you won't get far.

Showing That the Proposal Is Feasible

To be effective, proposals must be *feasible*—that is, the action proposed can be carried out in a reasonable way. Demonstrating feasibility calls on you to present evidence—from similar cases, from personal experience, from observational data, from interview or survey data, from Internet research, or from any other sources—showing that what you propose can indeed be done with the resources available. "Resources available" is key: if the proposal calls for funds, personnel, or skills beyond reach or reason, your audience is unlikely to accept it. When that's the case, it's time to reassess your proposal, modify it, and test any new ideas against these revised criteria. This is also when you can reconsider proposals that others might suggest are better, more effective, or more workable than yours. There's no shame in admitting that you may have been wrong. When drafting a proposal, ask friends to think of counterproposals. If your own proposal can stand up to such challenges, it's likely a strong one.

Considering Design and Visuals

Because proposals often address specific audiences, they can take a number of forms—a letter, a memo, a Web page, a feasibility report, an infographic, a brochure, a prospectus, or even an editorial cartoon (see Andy

Singer's "No Exit" item on p. 452). Each form has different design requirements. Indeed, the design may add powerfully to—or detract significantly from—the effectiveness of the proposal. Typically, though, proposals are heavy in photographs, tables, graphs, comparison charts, and maps, all designed to help readers understand the nature of a problem and how to solve it. Needless to say, any visual items should be handsomely presented: they contribute to your ethos.

Lengthy reports also usually need headings—or, in an oral report, slides—that clearly identify the various stages of the presentation. Those headings, which will vary, would include items such as Introduction, Nature of the Problem, Current Approaches or Previous Solutions, Proposal/Recommendations, Advantages, Counterarguments, Feasibility, Implementation, and so on. So before you produce a final copy of any proposal, be sure its design enhances its persuasiveness.

A related issue to consider is whether a graphic image might help readers understand key elements of the proposal—what the challenge is, why it demands action, and what exactly you're suggesting—and help make the idea more attractive. That strategy is routinely used in professional proposals by architects, engineers, and government agencies.

The Bionic Arch proposes to do more than add retail and office space.

AP/Wide World Photos

For example, the artist rendering above shows the Bionic Arch, a proposed skyscraper in Taiwan designed by architect Vincent Callebaut. As a proposal, this one stands out because it not only suggests an addition to the city skyline, but it also offers architectural innovations to make the structure more environmentally friendly. If you look closely, you'll notice that each floor of the building includes suspended "sky gardens" that, according to the proposal, will help solve the problem of city smog by siphoning away toxic fumes. According to Callebaut, "The skyscraper reduces our ecological footprint in the urban area. It respects the environment and gives a new symbiotic ecosystem for the biodiversity of Taiwan. The Bionic Arch is the new icon of sustainable development." Who wouldn't support a building that looked great *and* helped clean the air?

GUIDE **TO WRITING A PROPOSAL**

Finding a Topic or Identifying a Problem

You're entering a proposal argument when you:

- make a claim that supports a change in practice: *Bottled water should carry a warning label describing the environmental impact of plastic.*

- make a claim that supports a change in policy: *Government workers, especially legislators and administrative officials, should never be exempt from laws or programs imposed on other citizens.*

- make a claim that resists suggested changes in practice or policy: *The surest way to guarantee that HOV lanes on freeways improve traffic flow is not to build any.*

- explore options for addressing existing issues or investigate opportunities for change: *Urban planners need to examine the long-term impact digital technologies may have on transportation, work habits, housing patterns, power usage, and entertainment opportunities in cities of the future.*

Since your everyday experience often calls on you to consider problems and to make proposals, begin your brainstorming for topics with practical topics related to your life, education, major, or job. Or make an informal list of proposals that you would like to explore in broader academic or cultural areas—problems you see in your field or in the society around you. Or do some freewriting on a subject of political concern, and see if it leads to a call for action.

Researching Your Topic

For many proposals, you can begin your research by consulting the following types of sources:

- newspapers, magazines, reviews, and journals (online and print)

- television or radio news reports

- online databases

- government documents and reports

- Web sites, blogs, social networking sites, listservs, or newsgroups

- books

- experts in the field, some of whom might be right on your campus

Consider doing some field research, if appropriate—a survey of student opinions on Internet accessibility, for example, or interviews with people who have experienced the problem you are trying to fix.

Finally, remember that your proposal's success can depend on the credibility of the sources you use to support it, so evaluate each source carefully (see Chapter 22).

Formulating a Claim

As you think about and explore your topic, begin formulating a claim about it. To do so, come up with a clear thesis that makes a proposal and states the reasons that this proposal should be adopted. To start formulating a claim, explore and respond to the following questions:

- What do I know about the proposal that I'm making?

- What reasons can I offer to support my proposal?

- What evidence do I have that implementing my proposal will lead to the results I want?

Rather than make a specific proposal, you may sometimes want to explore the range of possibilities for addressing a particular situation or circumstance. In that case, a set of open-ended questions

might be a more productive starting point than a focused thesis, suggesting, for instance, what goals any plausible proposal might have to meet.

Examples of Proposal Claims

- Because lowering the amount of fuel required to be blended with ethanol would lower greenhouse gas emissions by millions of tons and decrease land use that is releasing unhealthy amounts of carbon into the atmosphere, the EPA proposal to reduce ethanol produced from corn should be adopted.

- Every home should be equipped with a well-stocked emergency kit that can sustain inhabitants for at least three days in a natural disaster.

- Congress should repeal the Copyright Extension Act, since it disrupts the balance between incentives for creators and the right of the public to information as set forth in the U.S. Constitution.

- To simplify the lives of consumers and eliminate redundant products, industries that manufacture rechargeable batteries should agree on a design for a universal power adapter.

- People from different economic classes, age groups, political philosophies, and power groups (government, Main Street, Wall Street) all have a stake in reforming current budget and tax policies. But how do we get them to speak and to listen to each other? That is the challenge we face if we hope to solve our national economic problems.

Preparing a Proposal

If your instructor asks you to prepare a proposal for your project, here's a format that may help:

GUIDE TO WRITING A PROPOSAL

State the thesis of your proposal completely. If you're having trouble doing so, try outlining it in Toulmin terms:

Claim:

Reason(s):

Warrant(s):

Alternatively, you might describe your intention to explore a particular problem in your project, with the actual proposal (and thesis) coming later.

- Explain why this issue deserves attention. What's at stake?

- Identify and describe those readers whom you hope to reach with your proposal. Why is this group of readers appropriate? Can you identify individuals who can actually fix a problem?

- Briefly discuss the major difficulties that you foresee for your proposal. How will you demonstrate that the action you propose is necessary and workable? Persuade the audience to act? Pay for the proposal?

- Determine what research strategies you'll use. What sources do you expect to consult?

Considering Format and Media

Your instructor may specify that you use a particular format and/or medium. If not, ask yourself these questions to help you make a good choice:

- What format is most appropriate for your proposal? Does it call for an academic essay, a report, an infographic, a brochure, or something else?

- What medium is most appropriate for your argument? Would it be best delivered orally to a live audience? Presented as an audio essay or podcast? Presented in print only or in print with illustrations?

- Will you need visuals, such as moving or still images, maps, graphs, charts—and what function will they play in your argument? Make sure they are not just "added on" but are necessary components of the argument.

Thinking about Organization

Proposals can take many different forms but generally include the following elements:

- a description of the problem you intend to address or the state of affairs that leads you to propose the action

- a strong and specific proposal, identifying the key reasons for taking the proposed action and the effects that taking this action will have

- a clear connection between the proposal and a significant need or problem

- a demonstration of ways in which the proposal addresses the need

- evidence that the proposal will achieve the desired outcome

- a consideration of alternative ways to achieve the desired outcome and a discussion of why these may not be feasible

- a demonstration that the proposal is feasible and an explanation of how it may be implemented

GUIDE **TO WRITING A PROPOSAL**

Getting and Giving Response: Questions for Peer Response

Your instructor may assign you to a group for the purpose of reading and responding to each other's drafts. If not, ask for responses from serious readers or consultants at a writing center. Use the following questions to evaluate a colleague's draft. Since specific comments help more than general observations, be sure to illustrate your comments with examples. Some of the questions below assume a conventional, thesis-driven project, but more exploratory, open-ended proposal arguments also need to be clearly phrased, organized, and supported with evidence.

The Claim

- Does the claim clearly call for action? Is the proposal as clear and specific as possible? Is it realistic or possible to accomplish?

- Is the proposal too sweeping? Does it need to be qualified? If so, how?

- Does the proposal clearly address the problem that it intends to solve? If not, how could the connection be strengthened?

- Is the claim likely to get the audience to act rather than just to agree? If not, how could it be revised to do so?

Evidence for the Claim

- Is enough evidence furnished to get the audience to support the proposal? If not, what kind of additional evidence is needed? Does any of the evidence provided seem inappropriate or otherwise ineffective? Why?

- Is the evidence in support of the claim simply announced, or are its significance and appropriateness analyzed? Is a more detailed discussion needed?

- Are objections that readers might have to the claim or evidence adequately and fairly addressed?

GUIDE TO WRITING A PROPOSAL

- What kinds of sources are cited? How credible and persuasive will they be to readers? What other kinds of sources might work better?

- Are all quotations introduced with appropriate signal phrases (such as "As Tyson argues, . . .") and blended smoothly into the writer's sentences?

- Are all visual sources labeled, introduced, and commented upon?

Organization and Style

- How are the parts of the argument organized? Is this organization effective?

- Will readers understand the relationships among the claims, supporting reasons, warrants, and evidence? If not, how might those connections be clearer? Is the function of every visual clear? Are more transitions needed? Would headings or graphic devices help?

- Are the transitions or links from point to point, sentence to sentence, and paragraph to paragraph clear and effective? If not, how could they be improved?

- Are all visuals carefully integrated into the text? Is each visual introduced and commented on to point out its significance? Is each visual labeled as a figure or a table and given a caption as well as a citation?

- Is the style suited to the subject? Is it too formal, casual, or technical? Can it be improved?

- Which sentences seem effective? Which ones seem weaker, and how could they be improved? Should short sentences be combined, and any longer ones be broken up?

- How effective are the paragraphs? Too short or too long? How can they be improved?

GUIDE **TO WRITING A PROPOSAL**

- Which words or phrases seem effective? Do any seem vague or inappropriate for the audience or the writer's purpose? Are technical or unfamiliar terms defined?

Spelling, Punctuation, Mechanics, Documentation, and Format

- Are there any errors in spelling, punctuation, capitalization, and the like?

- Is the documentation appropriate and consistent? (See Chapter 25.)

- Does the paper or project follow an appropriate format? Is it appropriately designed and attractively presented?

PROJECTS

1. Identify a proposal currently in the news or one advocated unrelentingly by the media that you *really* don't like. It may be a political initiative, a cultural innovation, a transportation alternative, or a lifestyle change. Spend time studying the idea more carefully than you have before. And then compose a proposal argument based on your deeper understanding of the proposal. You may still explain why you think it's a bad idea. Or you may endorse it, using your new information and your interesting perspective as a former dissenter.

2. The uses and abuses of technology and media—from smartphones and smartwatches to social networks— seem to be on everyone's mind. Write a proposal argument about some pressing dilemma caused by the digital screens that are changing (ruining?) our lives. You might want to explain how to bring traditional instructors into the digital age or establish etiquette for people who walk in traffic using handheld electronic devices. Or maybe you

want to keep parents off of social networks. Or maybe you have a great idea for separating professional and private lives online. Make your proposal in some pertinent medium: print op-ed, cartoon, photo essay, infographic, set of PowerPoint or Prezi slides, podcast.

3. Write a proposal to yourself diagnosing some minor issue you would like to address, odd behavior you'd like to change, or obsession you'd like to curb. Explore the reasons behind your mania and the problems it causes you and others. Then come up with a plausible proposal to resolve the issue and prove that you can do it. Make the paper hilarious.

4. Working in a group initially, come up with a list of problems—local, national, or international—that seem just about insoluble, from persuading nations to cut down on their CO_2 emissions to figuring out how to keep tuition costs in check. After some discussion, focus on just one or two of these matters and then discuss not the issues themselves but the general reasons that the problems have proven intractable. What exactly keeps people from agreeing on solutions? Are some people content with the status quo? Do some groups profit from the current arrangements? Are alternatives to the status quo just too costly or not feasible for other reasons? Do people find change uncomfortable? Following the discussion, work alone or collaboratively on an argument that examines the general issue of *change*: What makes it possible in any given case? What makes it difficult? Use the problems you have discussed as examples to illustrate your argument. Your challenge as a writer may be to make such an open-ended discussion interesting to general readers.

Two Sample Proposals

A Call to Improve Campus Accessibility

MANASI DESHPANDE

Introduction

Courtesy of
Manasi Deshpande

Wes Holloway, a sophomore at the University of Texas at Austin (UT), never considered the issue of campus accessibility during his first year on campus. But when an injury his freshman year left him wheelchair-bound, he was astonished to realize that he faced an unexpected challenge: maneuvering around the UT campus. Hills that he had effortlessly traversed became mountains; doors that he had easily opened became anvils; and streets that he had mindlessly crossed became treacherous terrain. Says Wes: "I didn't think about accessibility until I had to deal with it, and I think most people are the same way."

For the ambulatory individual, access for the mobility impaired on the UT campus is easy to overlook. Automatic door entrances and bathrooms with the universal handicapped symbol make the campus seem sufficiently accessible. But for many students and faculty at UT, including me, maneuvering the UT campus in a wheelchair is a daily experience of stress and frustration. Although the University

The paper opens with a personal example and dramatizes the issue of campus accessibility.

Both problem and solution are previewed here, with more details provided in subsequent sections of the paper.

Manasi Deshpande wrote a longer version of this essay for a course preparing her to work as a consultant in the writing center at the University of Texas at Austin. We have edited it to emphasize the structure of her complex proposal. Note, too, how she reaches out to a general audience to make an argument that might seem to have a narrow constituency. This essay is documented using MLA style.

has made a concerted and continuing effort to improve access, students and faculty with physical disabilities still suffer from discriminatory hardship, unequal opportunity to succeed, and lack of independence.

The University must make campus accessibility a higher priority and take more seriously the hardship that the campus at present imposes on people with mobility impairments. Better accessibility would also benefit the numerous students and faculty with temporary disabilities and help the University recruit a more diverse body of students and faculty.

The introduction's final paragraph summarizes the argument.

Assessment of Current Efforts

The author's fieldwork (mainly interviews) enhances her authority and credibility.

The current state of campus accessibility leaves substantial room for improvement. There are approximately 150 academic and administrative buildings on campus (Grant). Eduardo Gardea, intern architect at the Physical Plant, estimates that only about nineteen buildings comply fully with the Americans with Disabilities Act (ADA). According to Penny Seay, PhD, director of the Center for Disability Studies at UT Austin, the ADA in theory "requires every building on campus to be accessible." However, as Bill Throop, associate director of the Physical Plant, explains, there is "no legal deadline to make the entire campus accessible"; neither the ADA nor any other law mandates that certain buildings be made compliant by a certain time. Though not bound by specific legal obligation, the University should strive to fulfill the spirit of the law and recognize campus accessibility as a pressing moral obligation.

The Benefits of Change

Benefits for People with Permanent Mobility Impairments

Improving campus accessibility would significantly enhance the quality of life of students and faculty with mobility impairments. The campus at present poses discriminatory hardship on these individuals by making daily activities such as getting to class and using the bathroom unreasonably difficult. Before Wes Holloway leaves home, he must plan his route carefully to avoid hills, use ramps that are easy to maneuver, and enter the side of the building with the accessible entrance. As he goes to class, Wes must go out of his way to avoid poorly paved sidewalks and roads. Sometimes he cannot avoid them and must take an uncomfortable and bumpy ride across potholes and uneven pavement. If his destination does not have an automatic door, he must wait for someone to open the door for him because it is too heavy for him to open himself. To get into Burdine Hall, he has to ask a stranger to push him through the heavy narrow doors because his fingers would get crushed if he pushed himself. Once in the classroom, Wes must find a suitable place to sit, often far away from his classmates because stairs block him from the center of the room.

Other members of the UT community with mobility impairments suffer the same daily hardships as Wes. According to Mike Gerhardt, student affairs administrator of Services for Students with Disabilities (SSD), approximately eighty students with physical disabilities, including twenty to twenty-five

The paper uses several layers of headings to organize its diverse materials.

The author outlines the challenges faced by a student with mobility impairment.

Accessibility issues are given a human face with examples of the problems that mobility-impaired people face on campus.

students using wheelchairs, are registered with SSD. However, the actual number of students with mobility impairments is probably higher because some students choose not to seek services from SSD. The current state of campus accessibility discriminates against all individuals with physical disabilities in the unnecessary hardship it imposes and in the ways it denies them independence.

Benefits for People with Temporary Mobility Impairments

The author broadens the appeal of her proposal by showing how improved accessibility will benefit everyone on campus.

In addition to helping the few members of the UT campus with permanent mobility impairments, a faster rate of accessibility improvement would also benefit the much larger population of people with temporary physical disabilities. Many students and faculty will become temporarily disabled from injury at some point during their time at the University. They will encounter difficulties similar to those facing people with permanent disabilities, including finding accessible entrances, opening doors without automatic entrances, and finding convenient classroom seating. And, according to Dr. Jennifer Maedgen, assistant dean of students and director of SSD, about 5 to 10 percent of the approximately one thousand students registered with SSD at any given time have temporary disabilities. By improving campus accessibility, the University would in fact reach out to all of its members, even those who have never considered the possibility of mobility impairment or the state of campus accessibility.

Numbers provide hard evidence for an important claim.

Benefits for the University

Better accessibility would also benefit the University as a whole by increasing recruitment of handicapped individuals and thus promoting a more diverse campus. When prospective students and faculty with disabilities visit the University, they might decide not to join the UT community because of poor access. On average, about one thousand students, or 2 percent of the student population, are registered with SSD. Mike Gerhardt reports that SSD would have about 1,500 to 3,000 registered students if the University reflected the community at large with respect to disability. These numbers suggest that the University can recruit more students with disabilities by taking steps to ensure that they have an equal opportunity to succeed.

The author offers a new but related argument: enhanced accessibility could bolster recruitment efforts.

Counterarguments

Arguments against devoting more effort and resources to campus accessibility have some validity but ultimately prove inadequate. Some argue that accelerating the rate of accessibility improvements and creating more efficient services require too much spending on too few people. However, this spending actually enhances the expected quality of life of all UT community members rather than just the few with permanent physical disabilities. Unforeseen injury can leave anyone with a permanent or temporary disability at any time. In making decisions about campus accessibility, administrators must realize that having a disability is not a choice and that bad luck does

The paper briefly notes possible objections to the proposal.

not discriminate. They should consider how their decisions would affect their campus experience if they became disabled. Despite the additional cost, the University should make accessibility a priority and accommodate more accessibility projects in its budget.

Recommendations

Foster Empathy and Understanding for Long-Term Planning

After establishing a case for enhanced campus accessibility, the author offers specific suggestions for action.

The University should make campus accessibility a higher priority and work toward a campus that not only fulfills legal requirements but also provides a user-friendly environment for the mobility impaired. It is difficult for the ambulatory person to empathize with the difficulties faced by these individuals. Recognizing this problem, the University should require the administrators who allocate money to ADA projects to use wheelchairs around the campus once a year. Administrators must realize that people with physical disabilities are not a small, distant, irrelevant group; anyone can join their ranks at any time. Administrators should ask themselves if they would find the current state of campus accessibility acceptable if an injury forced them to use a wheelchair on a permanent basis.

In addition, the University should actively seek student input for long-term improvements to accessibility. The University is in the process of creating the ADA Accessibility Committee, which, according to the office of the Dean of Students' Web site, will "address institution-wide, systemic issues that fall under the scope of the Americans with Disabilities Act." Students should play a prominent and powerful role in this new ADA Accessibility Committee. The Committee should select its student representatives carefully to make sure that they are driven individuals committed to working for progress and representing the interests of students with disabilities. The University should consider making Committee positions paid so that student representatives can devote sufficient time to their responsibilities.

Improve Services for the Mobility Impaired

The University should also work toward creating more useful, transparent, and approachable services for its members with physical disabilities by making better use of online technology and helping students take control of their own experiences.

First, SSD can make its Web site more useful by updating it frequently with detailed information on construction sites that will affect accessible routes. The site should delineate alternative accessible routes and approximate the extra time required to use the detour. This information would help people with mobility impairments to plan ahead and avoid delays, mitigating the stress of maneuvering around construction sites.

The University should also develop software for an interactive campus map. The software would work like MapQuest or Google Maps but would provide detailed descriptions of accessible routes on campus from one building

to another. It would be updated frequently with new ADA improvements and information on construction sites that impede accessible routes.

Since usefulness of services is most important for students during their first encounters with the campus, SSD should hold one-on-one orientations for new students with mobility impairments. SSD should inform students in both oral and written format of their rights and responsibilities and make them aware of problems that they will encounter on the campus. Beyond making services more useful, these orientations would give students the impression of University services as open and responsive, encouraging students to report problems that they encounter and assume the responsibility of self-advocacy.

As a continuing resource for people with physical disabilities, the SSD Web site should include an anonymous forum for both general questions and specific complaints and needs. Many times, students notice problems but do not report them because they find visiting or calling SSD time-consuming or because they do not wish to be a burden. The anonymity and immediate feedback provided by the forum would allow for more freedom of expression and provide students an easier way to solve the problems they face.

Services for the mobility impaired should also increase their transparency by advertising current accessibility projects on their Web sites. The University should give its members with mobility impairments a clearer idea of its efforts to improve campus accessibility. Detailed online descriptions of ADA projects, including the cost of each project, would affirm its resolve to create a better environment for its members with physical disabilities.

Conclusion

Although the University has made progress in accessibility improvements on an old campus, it must take bolder steps to improve the experience of its members with mobility impairments. At present, people with permanent mobility impairments face unreasonable hardship, unequal opportunity to succeed, and lack of independence. To enhance the quality of life of all of its members and increase recruitment of disabled individuals, the University should focus its resources on increasing the rate of accessibility improvements and improving the quality of its services for the mobility impaired.

The writer reiterates her full proposal.

As a public institution, the University has an obligation to make the campus more inclusive and serve as an example for disability rights. With careful planning and a genuine desire to respond to special needs, practical and cost-effective changes to the University campus can significantly improve the quality of life of many of its members and prove beneficial to the future of the University as a whole.

WORKS CITED

Gardea, Eduardo. Personal interview, 24 Mar. 2005.

Gerhardt, Michael. Personal interview, 8 Apr. 2005.

Grant, Angela. "Making Campus More Accessible." *Daily Texan Online,* 14 Oct. 2003, www.dailytexanonline.com/2003/11/14/making-campus-more-accessible.

Holloway, Wesley Reed. Personal interview, 5 Mar. 2005.

Maedgen, Jennifer. Personal interview, 25 Mar. 2005.

Office of the Dean of Students. ADA Student Forum. *University of Texas at Austin,* 6 Apr. 2005, ddce.utexas.edu/disability/2005/04/april-6th-ada-student-forums/.

Seay, Penny. Personal interview, 11 Mar. 2005.

Throop, William. Personal interview, 6 Apr. 2005.

Let's Charge Politicians for Wasting Our Time

VIRGINIA POSTREL

There's an election today here in California, and that means my landline at home is ringing constantly with robocalls from assorted public figures whose recorded voices urge me to get out and vote for their favorite candidates. One called the other day while I was conducting an interview on the mobile phone I use for most purposes. I didn't answer, but it interrupted the flow of the conversation. Yesterday I picked up the receiver to find five voice mails, all from recorded political voices (including two identical messages from the same sheriff candidate).

Our phone number is on the National Do Not Call Registry, but those rules for telemarketers don't apply to political campaigns. The folks who make the laws aren't about to do away with a technique that works.

Political robocalls are illegal to mobile phones but OK to most landlines, as long as they meet disclosure requirements. Everyone I know hates such calls, and even political consultants know they're a problem. "Some voters get turned off by too many robocalls," cautions a political-strategy website. The cumulative annoyance, it warns, means that voters may resent yours even if they're rare. Yep.

Recorded, automatically dialed messages arguably constitute a legitimate and potentially important form of political speech. If I weren't so annoyed, I might actually like to know who's endorsing whom for sheriff. But it's ridiculous that the only way to limit the onslaught is to pay someone $24.99 to tell organizations, who may or may not listen, that I don't want them bothering me.

Here's a better idea: You should be able to set a charge for calling you. Every number that isn't on your "free" list would

Virginia Postrel posted this column on the Bloomberg View on June 3, 2014. She has also written for *Forbes*, the *Wall Street Journal*, the *New York Times*, and the *Atlantic*.

automatically be assessed a fee. The phone company would get a percentage of the revenue, and you'd be able to adjust the fee to different levels at different times of the day or for different seasons. (The nearer the election, the higher I'd make my charge.) If candidates really think it's valuable to call me, they should be willing to pay. Otherwise, they're just forcing me to subsidize their political efforts with my time and attention.

Technology investor Esther Dyson has for years been pushing a similar idea for e-mail. Unsolicited phone calls are much more annoying, and the technological challenges of "reversing the charges" should be much easier. Although you can't track down the true scamsters who break the do-not-call law and peddle fraudulent schemes from phony numbers, the politicians and charities that pester us for support aren't trying to hide. They're just trying to get something scarce and precious—our time and attention—for free.

PART 3

RESEARCH AND ARGUMENTS

20

Academic Arguments

Research and Arguments

Left to right: Imaginechina via AP Images; AP/Invision/Charles Sykes; © Javier Larrea/age fotostock

Much of the writing you will do in college (and some of what you will no doubt do later in your professional work) is generally referred to as *academic discourse* or *academic argument*. Although this kind of writing has many distinctive features, in general it shares these characteristics:

• It is based on research and uses evidence that can be documented.

• It is written for a professional, academic, or school audience likely to know something about its topic.

• It makes a clear and compelling point in a fairly formal, clear, and sometimes technical style.

• It follows agreed-upon conventions of format, usage, and punctuation.

• It is documented, using some professional citation style.

Academic writing is serious work, the kind you are expected to do whenever you are assigned a term essay, research paper, or capstone project. Manasi Deshpande's proposal "A Call to Improve Campus Accessibility" in Chapter 19 is an example of an academic argument of the kind you may write in college. You will find other examples of such work throughout this book.

Understanding What Academic Argument Is

Academic argument covers a wide range of writing, but its hallmarks are an appeal to reason and a faith in research. As a consequence, such arguments cannot be composed quickly, casually, or off the top of one's head. They require careful reading, accurate reporting, and a conscientious commitment to truth. But academic pieces do not tune out all appeals to ethos or emotion: today, we know that these arguments often convey power and authority through their impressive lists of sources and their immediacy.

But an academic argument crumbles if its facts are skewed or its content proves to be unreliable.

Look, for example, how systematically Susannah Fox and Lee Rainie, director and codirector of the Pew Internet Project, present facts and evidence in arguing that the Internet has been, overall, a big plus for society and individuals alike.

> [Today,] 87% of American adults now use the Internet, with near-saturation usage among those living in households earning $75,000 or more (99%), young adults ages 18–29 (97%), and those with college degrees (97%). Fully 68% of adults connect to the Internet with mobile devices like smartphones or tablet computers.

> The adoption of related technologies has also been extraordinary: Over the course of Pew Research Center polling, adult ownership of cell phones has risen from 53% in our first survey in 2000 to 90% now. Ownership of smartphones has grown from 35% when we first asked in 2011 to 58% now.

> Impact: Asked for their overall judgment about the impact of the Internet, toting up all the pluses and minuses of connected life, the public's verdict is overwhelmingly positive: 90% of Internet users say the Internet has been a good thing for them personally and only 6% say it has been a bad thing, while 3% volunteer that it has been some of both. 76% of Internet users say the Internet has been a good thing for society, while 15% say it has been a bad thing and 8% say it has been equally good and bad.

> —Susannah Fox and Lee Rainie, "The Web at 25 in the U.S."

Note, too, that these writers draw their material from research and polls conducted by the Pew Research Center, a well-known and respected organization. Chances are you immediately recognize that this paragraph is an example of a researched academic argument.

You can also identify academic argument by the way it addresses its audiences. Some academic writing is clearly aimed at specialists in a field who are familiar with both the subject and the terminology that surrounds it. As a result, the researchers make few concessions to general readers unlikely to encounter or appreciate their work. You see that single-mindedness in this abstract of an article about migraine headaches in a scientific journal: it quickly becomes unreadable to nonspecialists.

ABSTRACT

Migraine is a complex, disabling disorder of the brain that manifests itself as attacks of often severe, throbbing head pain with sensory sensitivity to light, sound and head movement. There is a clear familial tendency to migraine, which has been well defined in a rare autosomal dominant form of familial hemiplegic migraine (FHM). FHM mutations so far identified include those in CACNA1A (P/Q voltage-gated Ca(2+) channel), ATP1A2 (N(+)-K(+)-ATPase) and SCN1A (Na(+) channel) genes. Physiological studies in humans and studies of the experimental correlate—cortical spreading depression (CSD)—provide understanding of aura, and have explored in recent years the effect of migraine preventives in CSD. . . .

—Peter J. Goadsby, "Recent Advances in Understanding Migraine Mechanisms, Molecules, and Therapeutics," ***Trends in Molecular Medicine*** (January 2007)

Yet this very article might later provide data for a more accessible argument in a magazine such as *Scientific American*, which addresses a broader (though no less serious) readership. Here's a selection from an article on migraine headaches from that more widely read journal (see also the infographic on p. 486):

> At the moment, only a few drugs can prevent migraine. All of them were developed for other diseases, including hypertension, depression and epilepsy. Because they are not specific to migraine, it will come as no surprise that they work in only 50 percent of patients—and, in them, only 50 percent of the time—and induce a range of side effects, some potentially serious.
>
> Recent research on the mechanism of these antihypertensive, antiepileptic and antidepressant drugs has demonstrated that one of their effects is to inhibit cortical spreading depression. The drugs' ability to prevent migraine with and without aura therefore supports the school of thought that cortical spreading depression contributes to both kinds of attacks. Using this observation as a starting point, investigators have come up with novel drugs that specifically inhibit cortical spreading depression. Those drugs are now being tested in migraine sufferers with and without aura. They

work by preventing gap junctions, a form of ion channel, from opening, thereby halting the flow of calcium between brain cells.

—David W. Dodick and J. Jay Gargus, "Why Migraines Strike," *Scientific American* (August 2008)

Such writing still requires attention, but it delivers important and comprehensible information to any reader seriously interested in the subject and the latest research on it.

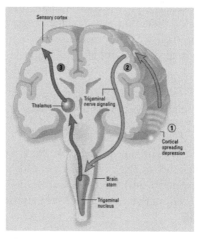

Infographic: The Root of Migraine Pain

© Tolpa Studios, Inc.

Even when academic writing is less technical and demanding, its style will retain a degree of formality. In academic arguments, the focus is on the subject or topic rather than the authors, the tone is straightforward, the language is largely unadorned, and all the *i*'s are dotted and *t*'s crossed. Here's an abstract for an academic paper written by a scholar of communications on the Burning Man phenomenon, demonstrating those qualities:

Every August for more than a decade, thousands of information technologists and other knowledge workers have trekked out into a barren stretch of alkali desert and built a temporary city devoted to art, technology, and communal living: Burning Man. Drawing on extensive archival research, participant observation, and interviews, this paper explores the ways that Burning Man's bohemian ethos supports new forms of production emerging in Silicon Valley and especially at Google. It shows how elements of the Burning Man world—including the building of a socio-technical commons, participation in project-based artistic labor, and the fusion of social and professional interaction—help shape and legitimate the collaborative manufacturing processes driving the growth of Google and other firms. The paper thus develops the notion that Burning Man serves as a key cultural infrastructure for the Bay Area's new media industries.

—Fred Turner, "Burning Man at Google:
A Cultural Infrastructure for New Media Production"

You might imagine a different and far livelier way to tell a story about the annual Burning Man gathering in Nevada, but this piece respects the conventions of its academic field.

A scene from Burning Man
Mike Nelson/AFP/Getty Images

Another way you likely identify academic writing—especially in term papers or research projects—is by the way it draws upon sources and builds arguments from research done by experts and reported in journal articles and books. Using an evenhanded tone and dealing with all points of view fairly, such writing brings together multiple voices and intriguing ideas. You can see these moves in just one paragraph from a heavily documented student essay examining the comedy of Chris Rock:

The breadth of passionate debate that [Chris] Rock's comedy elicits from intellectuals is evidence enough that he is advancing discussion of the foibles of black America, but Rock continually insists that he has no political aims: "Really, really at the end of the day, the only important thing is being funny. I don't go out of my way to be political" (qtd. in Bogosian 58). His unwillingness to view himself as a black leader triggers Justin Driver to say, "[Rock] wants to be caustic and he wants to be loved" (32). Even supporters wistfully sigh, "One wishes Rock would own up to the fact that he's a damned astute social critic" (Kamp 7).

> —Jack Chung, "The Burden of Laughter:
> Chris Rock Fights Ignorance His Way"

Readers can quickly tell that author Jack Chung has read widely and thought carefully about how to support his argument.

As you can see even from these brief examples, academic arguments cover a broad range of topics and appear in a variety of media—as a brief note in a journal like *Nature*, for example, a poster session at a conference on linguistics, a short paper in *Physical Review Letters*, a full research report in microbiology, or an undergraduate honors thesis in history. What do all these projects have in common? One professor we know defines academic argument as "carefully structured research," and that seems to us to be a pretty good definition.

Conventions in Academic Argument Are Not Static.

Far from it. In fact, the rise of new technologies and the role that blogs, wikis, social media sites, and other digital discourses play in all our lives are affecting academic writing as well. Thus, scholars today are pushing the envelope of traditional academic writing in some fields. Physicians, for example, are using narrative (rather than charts) more often in medicine to communicate effectively with other medical personnel. Professional journals now sometimes feature serious scholarly work in new formats—such as comics (as in legal scholar Jamie Boyle's work on intellectual property, or Nick Sousanis's Columbia University PhD dissertation, which is entirely in comic form). And student writers are increasingly producing serious academic arguments using a wide variety of modalities, including sound, still and moving images, and more.

Developing an Academic Argument

In your first years of college, the academic arguments you make will probably include the features and qualities we've discussed above—and which you see demonstrated in the sample academic arguments at the end of this chapter. In addition, you can make a strong academic argument by following some time-tested techniques.

Choose a topic you want to explore in depth. Unless you are assigned a topic (and remember that even assigned topics can be tweaked to match your interests), look for a subject that intrigues you—one you *want* to learn more about. One of the hardest parts of producing an academic argument is finding a topic narrow enough to be manageable in the time you have to work on it but also rich enough to sustain your interest over the same period. Talk with friends about possible topics and explain to them why you'd like to pursue research on this issue. Look through your Twitter feeds and social network postings to identify themes or topics that leap out as compelling. Browse through books and articles that interest you, make a list of potential subjects, and then zero in on one or two top choices.

Get to know the conversation surrounding your topic. Once you've chosen a topic, expect to do even more reading and browsing—a lot more. Familiarize yourself with what's been said about your subject and especially with the controversies that currently surround it. Where do scholars agree, and where do they disagree? What key issues seem to be at stake? You can start by exploring the Internet, using key terms that are associated with your topic. But you may be better off searching the more specialized databases at your library with the assistance of a librarian who can help you narrow your search and make it more efficient. Library databases will also give you access to materials not available via Google or other online search engines—including, for example, full-text versions of journal articles. For much more on identifying appropriate sources, see Chapter 21, "Finding Evidence."

Assess what you know and what you need to know. As you read about your topic and discuss it with others, keep notes on what you have learned, including what you already know about it. Such notes should soon reveal where the gaps are in your knowledge. For instance, you may discover a need to learn about legal issues and thus end up doing research in a law school library. Or perhaps talking with experts about your topic might be helpful. Instructors on your campus may have the knowledge you need, so explore your school's Web site to find faculty or staff to talk with. Make

an appointment to visit them during office hours and bring the sorts of questions to your meeting that show you've done basic work on the subject. And remember that experts are now only a click away: a student we know, working on Internet privacy concerns, wrote a brief message to one of the top scholars in the field asking for help with two particular questions—and got a response within two days!

Come up with a claim about your topic. The chapters in Part 2, "Writing Arguments," offer instruction in formulating thesis statements, which most academic arguments must have. Chapters 15–19, in particular, explain how to craft claims tailored to individual projects ranging from arguments of fact to proposals. Remember here, though, that good claims are controversial. After all, you don't want to debate something that everyone already agrees upon or accepts.

In addition, your claim needs to say something consequential about that important or controversial topic and be supported with strong evidence and good reasons (see Chapter 21). Here, for example, is the claim that student Charlotte Geaghan-Breiner makes after observing the alienation of today's children from the natural world and arguing for the redesign of schoolyards that invite children to interact with nature: "As a formative geography of childhood, the schoolyard serves as the perfect place to address nature deficit disorder." Charlotte develops her claim and supports it with evidence about the physical, psychological, academic, and social benefits of interacting with the natural world. She includes images illustrating the contrast between traditional schoolyards and "biophilic," or nature-oriented, schoolyards and establishes guidelines for creating natural play landscapes. (See Charlotte's complete essay, reprinted at the end of this chapter.)

Consider your rhetorical stance and purpose. Once you have a claim, ask yourself where you stand with respect to your topic and how you want to represent yourself to those reading your argument:

- You may take the stance of a reporter: you review what has been said about the topic; analyze and evaluate contributions to the conversation surrounding it; synthesize the most important strands of that conversation; and finally draw conclusions based on them.

- You may see yourself primarily as a critic: you intend to point out the problems and mistakes associated with some view of your topic.

- You may prefer the role of an advocate: you present research that strongly supports a particular view on your topic.

Whatever your perspective, remember that in academic arguments you want to come across as fair and evenhanded, especially when you play the advocate. Your stance will always be closely tied to your purpose, which in most of your college writing will be at least twofold: to do the best job in fulfilling an assignment for a course and to support the claim you are making to the fullest extent possible. Luckily, these two purposes work well together.

Think about your audience(s). Here again, you will often find that you have at least two audiences—and maybe more. First, you will be writing to your instructor, so take careful notes when the assignment is given and, if possible, set up a conference to nail down your teacher's expectations: what will it take to convince this audience that you have done a terrific job of writing an academic argument? Beyond your instructor, you should also think of your classmates as an audience—informed, intelligent peers who will be interested in what you have to say. Again, what do you know about these readers, and what will they expect from your project?

Finally, consider yet another important audience—people who are already discussing your topic. These will include the authors whose work you have read and the larger academic community of which they are now a part. If your work appears online or in some other medium, you will reach more people than you initially expect, and most if not all of them will be unknown to you. As a result, you need to think carefully about the various ways your argument could be read—or misread—and plan accordingly.

Concentrate on the material you are gathering. Any academic argument is only as good as the evidence it presents to support its claims. Give each major piece of evidence (say, a lengthy article that addresses your subject directly) careful scrutiny:

- Summarize its main points.
- Analyze how those points are pertinent.
- Evaluate the quality of the supporting evidence.
- Synthesize the results of your analysis and evaluation.
- Summarize what you think about the article.

In other words, test each piece of evidence and then decide which to keep—and which to throw out. But do not gather only materials that favor your take on the topic. You want, instead, to look at all legitimate perspectives on your claim, and in doing so, you may even change your mind.

That's what good research for an academic argument can do: remember the "conscientious commitment to truth" we mentioned earlier? Keep yourself open to discovery and change. (See Chapter 22, "Evaluating Sources," and Chapter 23, "Using Sources.")

Give visual and nonprint materials the same scrutiny you would to print sources, since these days you will likely be gathering or creating such materials in many fields. Remember that the graphic representation of data always involves an interpretation of that material: numbers can lie and pictures distort. In addition, infographics today often make complex academic arguments in a visual form. (See p. 309 for one such example.)

Take special care with documentation. As you gather materials for your academic argument, record where you found each source so that you can cite it accurately. For print sources, develop a working bibliography either on your computer or in a notebook you can carry with you. For each book, write the name of the author, the title of the book, the city of publication, the publisher, the date of publication, and the place that you found it (the section of the library, for example, and the call number for the book). For each print article, write the name of the author, the title of the article, the title of the periodical, and the volume, issue, publication date, and exact page numbers. Include any other information you may later need in preparing a works cited list or references list.

For electronic sources, keep a careful record of the information you'll need in a works cited list or references list. Write the author and title information, the name of the database or other online site where you found the source, the full URL, the date the document was first produced, the date it was published on the Web or most recently updated, and the date you accessed and examined it. The simplest way to ensure that you have this information is to print a copy of the source, highlight source information, and write down any other pertinent information.

Remember, too, that different academic fields use different systems of documentation, so if your instructor has not recommended a style of documentation to you, ask in class about it. Scholars have developed these systems over long periods of time to make research in an area reliable and routine. Using documentation responsibly shows that you understand the conventions of your field or major and that you have paid your dues, thereby establishing your position as a member of the academic community. (For more detailed information, see Chapter 25, "Documenting Sources.")

Think about organization. As you review the research materials you have gathered, you are actually beginning the work of drafting and designing your project. Study the way those materials are organized, especially any from professional journals, whether print or digital. You may need to include in your own argument some of the sections or features you find in professional research:

- Does the article open with an abstract, summarizing its content?

- Does the article give any information about the author or authors and their credentials?

- Is there a formal introduction to the subject or a clear statement of a thesis or hypothesis?

- Does the article begin with a "review of literature," summarizing recent research on its topic?

- Does the piece describe its methods of research?

- How does the article report its results and findings?

- Does the article use charts and graphs or other visuals to report data?

- Does the piece use headings and subheadings?

- How does the work summarize its findings or how does it make recommendations?

- Does the essay offer a list of works cited or references?

Anticipate some variance in the way materials are presented from one academic field to another.

As you organize your own project, check with your instructor to see if there is a recommended pattern for you to follow. If not, create a scratch outline or storyboard to describe how your essay will proceed. In reviewing your evidence, decide which pieces support specific points in the argument. Then try to position your strongest pieces of evidence in key places—near the beginning of paragraphs, at the end of the introduction, or toward a powerful conclusion. In addition, strive to achieve a balance between, on the one hand, your own words and argument and, on the other hand, the sources that you use or quote in support of the argument. The sources of evidence are important supports, but they shouldn't overpower the structure of your argument itself. Finally, remember that your organization needs to take into account the placement of visuals—charts, tables, photographs, and so on. (For specific advice on structuring arguments, review the "Thinking about Organization" sections in the "Guides to Writing" for Chapters 15–19.)

Consider style and tone. Most academic argument adopts the voice of a reasonable, fair-minded, and careful thinker who is interested in coming as close to the truth about a topic as possible. A style that achieves that tone may have some of the following features:

- It strives for clarity and directness, though it may use jargon appropriate to a particular field.

- It favors denotative rather than connotative language.

- It is usually impersonal, using first person (*I*) sparingly.

- In some fields, it may use the passive voice routinely.

- It uses technical language, symbols, and abbreviations for efficiency.

- It avoids colloquialisms, slang, and sometimes even contractions.

The examples at the end of this chapter demonstrate traditional academic style, though there is, as always, a range of possibilities in its manner of expression.

Consider genre, design, and visuals. Most college academic arguments look more like articles in professional journals than like those one might find in a glossier periodical like *Scientific American*—that is, they are still usually black on white, use a traditional font size and type (like 11-point Times New Roman), and lack any conscious design other than inserted tables or figures. But such conventions are changing.

Indeed, student writers today can go well beyond print, creating digital documents that integrate a variety of media and array data in strikingly original ways. But always consider what genres best suit your topic, purpose, and audience and then act accordingly. As you think about the design possibilities for your academic argument, you may want to consult your instructor—and to test your ideas and innovations on friends or classmates.

In choosing visuals to include in your argument, be sure each one makes a strong contribution to your message and is appropriate and fair to your topic and your audience. Treat visuals as you would any other sources and integrate them into your text. Like quotations, paraphrases, and summaries, visuals need to be introduced and commented on in some way. In addition, label and number ("Figure 1," "Table 2," and so on) each visual, provide a caption that includes source information and describes the visual, and cite the source in your references page or works cited list. Even if you create a visual (such as a bar graph) by using information from a source (the results, say, of a Gallup poll), you must cite the source. If you use a photograph you took yourself, cite it as a personal photograph.

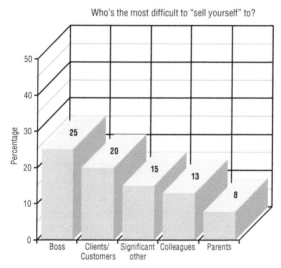

Who's the most difficult to "sell yourself" to?

This bar chart, based on data from a Sandler Training survey of 1,053 adults, would be listed in your works cited or references under the authors' names.

Data from Sandler Training survey of 1,053 adults.

Reflect on your draft and get responses. As with any important piece of writing, an academic argument calls for careful reflection on your draft. You may want to do a "reverse outline" to test whether a reader can pull a logical and consistent pattern out of the paragraphs or sections you have written. In addition, you can also judge the effectiveness of your overall argument, assessing what each paragraph contributes and what may be missing. Turning a critical eye to your own work at the draft stage can save much grief in the long run. Be sure to get some response from classmates and friends too: come up with a set of questions to ask them about your draft and push them for honest responses. Find out what in your draft is confusing or unclear to others, what needs further evidence, and so on.

Edit and proofread your text. Proofread an academic argument at least three times. First review it for ideas, making sure that all your main points and supporting evidence make sense and fit nicely together. Give special attention to transitions and paragraph structure and the way you have

arranged information, positioned headings, and captioned graphic items. Make sure the big picture is in focus.

Then read the text word by word to check spelling, punctuation, quotation marks, apostrophes, abbreviations—in short, all the details that can go wrong simply because of a slip in attention. To keep their focus at this level, some readers will even read an entire text backwards. Notice too where your computer's spelling and grammar checkers may be underlining particular words and phrases. Don't ignore these clear signals.

Finally, check that every source mentioned in the academic argument appears in the works cited or references list and that every citation is correct. This is also the time to make any final touchups to your overall design. Remember that how the document looks is part of what establishes its credibility.

RESPOND

1. Look closely at the following five passages, each of which is from an opening of a published work, and decide which ones provide examples of academic argument. How would you describe each one, and what are its key features? Which is the most formal and academic? Which is the least? How might you revise them to make them more—or less—academic?

    > During the Old Stone Age, between thirty-seven thousand and eleven thousand years ago, some of the most remarkable art ever conceived was etched or painted on the walls of caves in southern France and northern Spain. After a visit to Lascaux, in the Dordogne, which was discovered in 1940, Picasso reportedly said to his guide, "They've invented everything." What those first artists invented was a language of signs for which there will never be a Rosetta stone; perspective, a technique that was not redis-covered until the Athenian Golden Age; and a bestiary of such vitality and finesse that, by the flicker of torchlight, the animals seem to surge from the walls, and move across them like figures in a magic-lantern show (in that sense, the artists invented ani-mation). They also thought up the grease lamp—a lump of fat, with a plant wick, placed in a hollow stone—to light their work-place; scaffolds to reach high places; the principles of stenciling and Pointillism; powdered colors, brushes, and stumping cloths; and, more to the point of Picasso's insight, the very concept of an image. A true artist reimagines that concept with every blank canvas—but not from a void.
    >
    > —Judith Thurman, "First Impressions," *The New Yorker*

I stepped over the curb and into the street to hitchhike. At the age of ten I'd put some pretty serious mileage on my thumb. And I knew how it was done. Hold your thumb up, not down by your hip as though you didn't much give a damn whether you got a ride or not. Always hitch at a place where a driver could pull out of traffic and give you time to get in without risking somebody tailgating him.

—Harry Crews, "On Hitchhiking," *Harper's*

Coral reef ecosystems are essential marine environments around the world. Host to thousands (and perhaps millions) of diverse organisms, they are also vital to the economic well-being of an estimated 0.5 billion people, or 8% of the world's population who live on tropical coasts (Hoegh-Guldberg 1999). Income from tourism and fishing industries, for instance, is essential to the economic prosperity of many countries, and the various plant and animal species present in reef ecosystems are sources for different natural products and medicines. The degradation of coral reefs can therefore have a devastating impact on coastal populations, and it is estimated that between 50% and 70% of all reefs around the world are currently threatened (Hoegh-Guldberg). Anthropogenic influences are cited as the major cause of this degradation, including sewage, sedimentation, direct trampling of reefs, over-fishing of herbivorous fish, and even global warming (Umezawa et al. 2002; Jones et al. 2001; Smith et al. 2001).

—Elizabeth Derse, "Identifying the Sources of Nitrogen to Hanalei Bay, Kauai, Utilizing the Nitrogen Isotope Signature of Macroalgae," *Stanford Undergraduate Research Journal*

While there's a good deal known about invertebrate neurobiology, these facts alone haven't settled questions of their sentience. On the one hand, invertebrates lack a cortex, amygdala, as well as many of the other major brain structures routinely implicated in human emotion. And unsurprisingly, their nervous systems are quite minimalist compared to ours: we have roughly a hundred thousand bee brains worth of neurons in our heads. On the other hand, some invertebrates, including insects, do possess the rudiments of our stress response system. So the question is still on the table: do they experience emotion in a way that we would recognize, or just react to the world with a set of glorified reflexes?

—Jason Castro, "Do Bees Have Feelings?" *Scientific American*

> Bambi's mother, shot. Nemo's mother, eaten by a barracuda. Lilo's mother, killed in a car crash. Koda's mother in *Brother Bear*, speared. Po's mother in *Kung Fu Panda 2*, done in by a power-crazed peacock. Ariel's mother in the third *Little Mermaid*, crushed by a pirate ship. Human baby's mother in *Ice Age*, chased by a saber-toothed tiger over a waterfall. . . . The mothers in these movies are either gone or useless. And the father figures? To die for!
>
> —Sarah Boxer, "Why Are All the Cartoon Mothers Dead?" *The Atlantic*

2. Working with another student in your class, find examples from two or three different fields of academic arguments that strike you as being well written and effective. Spend some time looking closely at them. Do they exemplify the key features of academic arguments discussed in this chapter? What other features do they use? How are they organized? What kind of tone do the writers use? What use do they make of visuals? Draw up a brief report on your findings (a list will do), and bring it to class for discussion.

3. Read the following three paragraphs, and then list changes that the writer might make to convert them into an academic argument:

> The book—the physical paper book—is being circled by a shoal of sharks, with sales down 9 percent this year alone. It's being chewed by the e-book. It's being gored by the death of the book-shop and the library. And most importantly, the mental space it occupied is being eroded by the thousand Weapons of Mass Distraction that surround us all. It's hard to admit, but we all sense it: it is becoming almost physically harder to read books.
>
> In his gorgeous little book *The Lost Art of Reading—Why Books Matter in a Distracted Time*, the critic David Ulin admits to a strange feeling. All his life, he had taken reading as for granted as eating—but then, a few years ago, he "became aware, in an apartment full of books, that I could no longer find within myself the quiet necessary to read." He would sit down to do it at night, as he always had, and read a few paragraphs, then find his mind was wandering, imploring him to check his email, or Twitter, or Facebook. "What I'm struggling with," he writes, "is the encroachment of the buzz, the sense that there's something out there that merits my attention."
>
> I think most of us have this sense today, if we are honest. If you read a book with your laptop thrumming on the other side of the room, it can be like trying to read in the middle of a party, where

everyone is shouting to each other. To read, you need to slow down. You need mental silence except for the words. That's getting harder to find.

—Johann Hari, "How to Survive the Age of Distraction"

4.   Choose two pieces of your college writing, and examine them closely. Are they examples of strong academic writing? How do they use the key features that this chapter identifies as characteristic of academic arguments? How do they use and document sources? What kind of tone do you establish in each? After studying the examples in this chapter, what might you change about these pieces of writing, and why?

5.   Go to a blog that you follow, or check out one on the *Huffington Post* or *Ricochet*. Spend some time reading the articles or postings on the blog, and look for ones that you think are the best written and the most interesting. What features or characteristics of academic argument do they use, and which ones do they avoid?

Two Sample Academic Arguments

Where the Wild Things Should Be: Healing Nature Deficit Disorder through the Schoolyard

CHARLOTTE GEAGHAN-BREINER

The developed world deprives children of a basic and inalienable right: unstructured outdoor play. Children today have substantially less access to nature, less free range, and less time for independent play than previous generations had. Experts in a wide variety of fields cite the rise of technology, urbanization, parental over-scheduling, fears of stranger-danger, and increased traffic as culprits. In 2005 journalist Richard Louv articulated the causes and consequences of children's alienation from nature, dubbing it "nature deficit disorder." Louv is not alone in claiming that the widening divide between children and nature has distressing health repercussions, from obesity and attention disorders to depression and decreased cognitive functioning. The dialogue surrounding nature deficit disorder deserves the attention and action of educators, health professionals, parents, developers, environmentalists, and conservationists alike.

The most practical solution to this staggering rift between children and nature involves the schoolyard. The schoolyard habitat

---

Charlotte Geaghan-Breiner wrote this academic argument for her first-year writing class at Stanford University.

Margin notes:

Title begins with a reference many readers will recognize (Sendak) and then points to the direction the argument will take.

Background information introduces a claim that states an effect and traces it back to its various causes.

Considerable evidence supports the claim.

Presents a solution to the problem and foreshadows full thesis.

movement, which promotes the "greening" of school grounds, is quickly gaining international recognition and legitimacy. A host of organizations, including the National Wildlife Federation, the American Forest Foundation, and the Council for Environmental Education, as well as their international counterparts, have committed themselves to this cause. However, while many recognize the need for "greened school grounds," not many describe such landscapes beyond using adjectives such as "lush," "green," and "natural." The literature thus lacks a coherent research-based proposal that both asserts the power of "natural" school grounds *and* delineates what such grounds might look like.

> The author identifies a weakness in the proposed solution.

My research strives to fill in this gap. I advocate for the schoolyard as the perfect place to address nature deficit disorder, demonstrate the benefits of greened schoolyards, and establish the tenets of natural schoolyard design in order to further the movement and inspire future action.

> Ending paragraph of the introduction presents the full thesis and outlines the entire essay.

Asphalt Deserts: The State of the Schoolyard Today

> Author uses subheads to help guide readers through the argument.

As a formative geography of childhood, the schoolyard serves as the perfect place to address nature deficit disorder. Historian Peter Stearns argues that modern childhood was transformed when schooling replaced work as the child's main social function (1041). In this contemporary context, the schoolyard emerges as a critical setting for children's learning and play. Furthermore, as parental traffic and safety concerns increasingly constrain children's

> Explains why it's valuable to focus on the schoolyard

free range outside of school, the schoolyard remains a safe haven, a protected outdoor space just for children.

Despite the schoolyard's major significance in children's lives, the vast majority of schoolyards fail to meet children's needs. An outdated theoretical framework is partially to blame. In his 1890 *Principles of Psychology*, psychologist Herbert Spencer championed the "surplus energy theory": play's primary function, according to Spencer, was to burn off extra energy (White). Play, however, contributes to the social, cognitive, emotional, and physical growth of the child (Hart 136); "[l]etting off steam" is only one of play's myriad functions. Spencer's theory thus constitutes a serious oversimplification, but it still continues to inform the design of children's play areas.

Most US playgrounds conform to an equipment-based model constructed implicitly on Spencer's surplus energy theory (Frost and Klein 2). The sports fields, asphalt courts, swing sets, and jungle gyms common to schoolyards relegate nature to the sidelines and prioritize gross motor play at the expense of dramatic play or exploration. An eight-year-old in England says it best: "The space outside feels boring. There's nothing to do. You get bored with just a square of tarmac" (Titman 42). Such an environment does not afford children the chance to graduate to new, more complex challenges as they develop. While play equipment still deserves a spot in the schoolyard, equipment-*dominated* playscapes leave the growing child bereft of stimulating interactions with the environment.

Quotations by children provide evidence to support the claim and bring in a personal touch. Note that the writer is following MLA style for in-text citations.

Fig. 1: Addison Elementary in Palo Alto, CA, conforms to the traditional playground model, dominated by synthetic landcover and equipment.

Photo by Charlotte Geaghan-Breiner

Note that the figure is introduced in the text and has a caption.

Also to blame for the failure of school grounds to meet children's needs are educators' and developers' adult-centric aims. Most urban schoolyards are sterile environments with low biodiversity (see fig. 1). While concrete, asphalt, and synthetic turf may be easier to maintain and supervise, they exacerbate the "extinction of experience," a term that Pyle has used to describe the disappearance of children's embodied, intuitive experiences in nature. Asphalt deserts are major instigators of this "cycle of impoverishment" (Pyle 312). Loss of biodiversity begets environmental apathy, which in turn allows the process of extinction to persist. Furthermore, adults' preference for manicured, landscaped grounds does little to enhance children's creative outdoor play. Instead of rich, stimulating play environments for children, such highly ordered schoolyards are constructed with adults' convenience in mind.

Presents reasons why schoolyards continue to be poorly designed

The Greener, the Better: The Benefits of Greened School Grounds

Author cites research that discusses the health benefits of interacting with nature.

A great body of research documents the physiological, cognitive, psychological, and social benefits of contact with nature. Health experts champion outdoor play as an antidote to two major trends in children of the developed world: the Attention Deficit Disorder and obesity epidemics. A 2001 study by Taylor, Kuo, and Sullivan indicates that green play settings decrease the severity of symptoms in children with ADD. They also combat inactivity in children by diversifying the "play repertoire" and providing for a wider range of physical activity than traditional playgrounds. In the war against childhood obesity, health advocates must add the natural schoolyard to their arsenal.

The schoolyard also has the ability to influence the way children play. Instead of being prescribed a play structure with a clear purpose (e.g., a swing set), children in natural schoolyards must discover the affordances of their environment—they must imagine what could be. In general, children exhibit more prosocial behavior and higher levels of inclusion in the natural schoolyard (Dyment 31). A 2006 questionnaire-based study of a greening initiative in Toronto found that the naturalization of the school grounds yielded a decrease in aggressive actions and disciplinary problems and a corresponding increase in civility and cooperation (Dyment 28). The greened schoolyard offers benefits beyond physical and mental health; it shapes the character and quality of children's play interactions.

Social benefits of interacting with nature

The schoolyard also has the potential to shape the relationship between children and the natural world. In the essay "Eden in a Vacant Lot," Pyle laments the loss of vacant lots and undeveloped spaces in which children can play and develop intimacy with the land. However, Pyle overlooks the geography of schoolyards, which can serve as enclaves of nature in an increasingly urbanized and developed world. Research has shown that school ground naturalization fosters nature literacy and intimacy just as Pyle's vacant lots do. For instance, a school ground greening program in Toronto dramatically enhanced children's environmental awareness, sense of stewardship, and curiosity about their local ecosystem (Dyment 37). When integrated with nature, the schoolyard can mitigate the effects of nature deficit disorder and reawaken children's innate biophilia, or love of nature.

Biophilic Design: Establishing the Tenets of Natural Schoolyard Design

The need for naturalized schoolyards is urgent. But how might theory actually translate into reality? Here I will propose four principles of biophilic schoolyard design, or landscaping that aims to integrate nature and natural systems into the man-made geography of the schoolyard.

The author establishes four guidelines for redesigning schoolyards.

The first is biodiversity. Schools should strive to incorporate a wide range of greenery and wildlife on their grounds (see fig. 2). Native plants should figure prominently so as to inspire children's interest in their local habitats. Inclusion of wildlife in school grounds can foster meaningful interactions with other species. Certain plants and flowers, for example, attract birds, butterflies, and other insects; aquatic areas can house fish, frogs, tadpoles, and pond bugs. School pets and small-scale farms also serve to teach children important lessons about responsibility, respect, and compassion for animals. Biodiversity, the most vital feature of biophilic design, transforms former "asphalt deserts" into realms teeming with life.

Fig. 2: A seating area at Ohlone School in Palo Alto, CA, features a healthy range of plant species.

Photo by Charlotte Geaghan-Breiner

The second principle that schoolyard designers should keep in mind is sensory stimulation. The greater the degree of sensory richness in an environment, the more opportunities it affords the child to imagine, learn, and discover. School grounds should feature a range of colors, textures, sounds, fragrances, and in the case of the garden, tastes. Such sensory diversity almost always accompanies natural environments, unlike concrete, which affords comparatively little sensory stimulation.

Diversity of topography constitutes another dimension of a greened schoolyard (Fjortoft and Sageie 83). The best school grounds afford children a range of places to climb, tunnel, frolic, and sit. Natural elements function as "play equipment": children can sit on stumps, jump over logs, swing on trees, roll down grassy mounds, and climb on boulders. The playscape should also offer nooks and crannies for children to seek shelter and refuge. While asphalt lots and play structures are still fun for children, they should not dominate the school grounds (see fig. 3).

A figure illustrates a specific point about play structures.

Fig. 3: Peninsula School in Menlo Park, CA, has integrated traditional equipment, such as a playhouse and slide, into the natural setting.

Photo by Charlotte Geaghan-Breiner

Last but not least, naturalized schoolyards must embody the theory of loose parts proposed by architect Simon Nicholson. "In any environment," he writes, "both the degree of inventiveness and the possibility of discovery are directly proportional to the number and kinds of variables in it" (qtd. in Louv 87). Loose parts—sand, water, leaves, nuts, seeds, rocks, and sticks—are abundant in the natural world. The detachability of loose parts makes them ideal for children's construction projects. While some might worry about the possible hazards of loose parts, conventional play equipment is far from safe: more than 200,000 of children's emergency room visits every year in the United States are linked to these built structures (Frost 217). When integrated into the schoolyard through naturalization, loose parts offer the child the chance to gain ever-increasing mastery of the environment.

The four tenets proposed provide a concrete basis for the application of biophilic design to the schoolyard. Such design also requires a frame-shift away from adult preferences for well-manicured grounds and towards children's needs for wilder spaces that can be constructed, manipulated, and changed through play (Lester and Maudsley 67; White and Stoecklin). Schoolyards designed according to the precepts of biodiversity, sensory stimulation, diversity of topography, and loose parts will go a long way in healing the rift between children and nature, a rift that adult-centric design only widens.

Grounds for Change

In conclusion, I have shown that natural schoolyard design can heal nature deficit disorder by restoring free outdoor play to children's lives in the developed world. Successful biophilic schoolyards challenge the conventional notion that natural and man-made landscapes are mutually exclusive. Human-designed environments, and especially those for children, should strive to integrate nature into the landscape. All schools should be designed with the four tenets of natural schoolyard design in mind.

Author restates her claim.

Though such sweeping change may seem impractical given limitations on school budgets, greening initiatives that use natural elements, minimal equipment, and volunteer work can be remarkably cost-effective. Peninsula School in Menlo Park, California, has minimized maintenance costs through the inclusion of hardy native species; it is essentially "designed for neglect" (Dyment 44). Gardens and small-scale school farms can also become their own source of funding, as they have for Ohlone Elementary School in Palo Alto, California. Ultimately, the cognitive, psychological, physiological, and social benefits of natural school grounds are priceless. In the words of author Richard Louv, "School isn't supposed to be a polite form of incarceration, but a portal to the wider world" (Louv 226). With this in mind, let the schoolyard restore to children their exquisite intimacy with nature: their inheritance, their right.

Offers examples of successful biophilic schoolyard design

WORKS CITED

Dyment, Janet. "Gaining Ground: The Power and Potential of School Ground Greening in the Toronto District School Board." *Evergreen*, 2006, www.evergreen.ca/downloads/pdfs/Gaining-Ground.pdf.

Fjortoft, Ingunn, and Jostein Sageie. "The Natural Environment as a Playground for Children." *Landscape and Urban Planning*, vol. 48, no. 2, Winter 2001, pp. 83–97.

Frost, Joe L. *Play and Playscapes*. Delmar, 1992.

Frost, Joe L., and Barry L. Klein. *Children's Play and Playgrounds*. Allyn and Bacon, 1979.

Hart, Roger. "Containing Children: Some Lessons on Planning for Play from New York City." *Environment and Urbanization*, vol. 14, no. 2, October 2002, pp. 135–48, eau.sagepub.com/content/14/2/135.full.pdf.

Lester, Stuart, and Martin Maudsley. *Play, Naturally: A Review of Children's Natural Play*. Play England, National Children's Bureau, 2007.

Louv, Richard. *Last Child in the Woods: Saving Our Children from Nature-Deficit Disorder*. Algonquin of Chapel Hill, 2005.

Nicholson, S. "How Not to Cheat Children: The Theory of Loose Parts." *Landscape Architecture*, vol. 62, October 1971, pp. 30–35.

Pyle, Robert M. "Eden in a Vacant Lot: Special Places, Species, and Kids in the Neighborhood of Life." *Children and Nature: Psychological, Sociocultural, and*

Evolutionary Investigations, edited by Peter H. Kahn and Stephen R. Kellert, MIT Press, 2002, pp. 305–27.

Stearns, Peter N. "Conclusion: Change, Globalization and Childhood." *Journal of Social History*, vol. 38, no. 4, 2005, pp. 1041–46.

Taylor, Andrea F., et al. "Coping with ADD: The Surprising Connection to Green Play Settings." *Environment and Behavior*, vol. 33, no. 1, 2001, pp. 54–77.

Titman, Wendy. *Special Places; Special People: The Hidden Curriculum of Schoolgrounds*. World Wide Fund for Nature, 1994, files. eric.ed.gov/fulltext/ED430384.pdf.

White, Randy. "Young Children's Relationship with Nature: Its Importance to Children's Development & the Earth's Future." *Taproot*, vol. 16, no. 2, Fall/Winter 2006, *White Hutchinson Leisure and Learning Group*, www.whitehutchinson.com/children/ articles/childrennature.shtml.

White, Randy, and Vicki Stoecklin. "Children's Outdoor Play & Learning Environments: Returning to Nature." *Early Childhood News*, Mar. 1998, *White Hutchinson Leisure and Learning Group*, www.whitehutchinson.com/children/ articles/outdoor.shtml.

White, Randy, and Vicki Stoecklin. "Children's Outdoor Play & Learning Environments: Returning to Nature." *Early Childhood News* Mar. 1998. *White Hutchinson Leisure and Learning Group*. Web. 28 May 2012.

China: The Prizes and Pitfalls of Progress

LAN XUE

GrAI/Shutterstock

Abstract

Pushes to globalize science must not threaten local innovations in developing countries, argues Lan Xue.

Developing countries such as China and India have emerged both as significant players in the production of high-tech products and as important contributors to the production of ideas and global knowledge. China's rapid ascent as a broker rather than simply a consumer of ideas and innovation has made those in the "developed" world anxious. A 2007 report by UK think tank Demos says that "U.S. and European pre-eminence in science-based innovation cannot be taken for granted. The centre of gravity for innovation is starting to shift from west to east."[1]

This article was written by Lan Xue, a faculty member in the School of Public Policy and Management and the director of the China Institute for Science and Technology Policy, both at Tsinghua University in Beijing, China. It was published in the online edition of *Nature* in July 2008.

But the rapid increase in research and development spending in China—of the order of 20% per year since 1999—does not guarantee a place as an innovation leader. Participation in global science in developing countries such as China is certainly good news for the global scientific community. It offers new opportunities for collaboration, fresh perspectives, and a new market for ideas. It also presents serious challenges for the management of innovation in those countries. A major discovery in the lab does not guarantee a star product in the market. And for a country in development, the application of knowledge in productive activities and the related social transformations are probably more important than the production of the knowledge itself. By gumming the works in information dissemination, by misplacing priorities, and by disavowing research that, although valuable, doesn't fit the tenets of modern Western science, developing countries may falter in their efforts to become innovation leaders.

Vicious Circle

China's scientific publications (measured by articles recorded in the Web of Science) in 1994 were around 10,000, accounting for a little more than 1% of the world total. By 2006, the publications from China rose to more than 70,000, increasing sevenfold in 12 years and accounting for almost 6% of the world total (see graph, next page). In certain technical areas, the growth has been more dramatic. China has been among the leading countries in nanotechnology research, for example, producing a volume of publications second only to that of the United States.

The publish-or-perish mentality that has arisen in China, with its focus on Western journals, has unintended implications that threaten to obviate the roughly 8,000 national scientific journals published in Chinese. Scientists in developing countries such as China and India pride themselves on publishing articles in journals listed in the Science Citation Index (SCI) and the Social Science Citation Index (SSCI) lists. In some top-tier research institutions in China, SCI journals have become the required outlet for research.

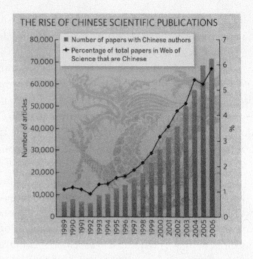

THE RISE OF CHINESE SCIENTIFIC PUBLICATIONS

Nature Publishing Group. Illustration by D. Parkins.

A biologist who recently returned to China from the United States was told by her colleague at the research institute in the prestigious Chinese Academy of Sciences (CAS) that publications in Chinese journals don't really count toward tenure or promotion. Moreover, the institute values only those SCI journals with high impact factors. Unfortunately, the overwhelming majority of the journals in SCI and SSCI lists are published in developed countries in English or other European languages. The language requirement and the high costs of these journals mean that few researchers in China will have regular access to the content. Thus as China spends more and publishes more, the results will become harder to find for Chinese users. This trend could have a devastating impact on the local scientific publications and hurt China's ability to apply newly developed knowledge in an economically useful way.

Several members of the CAS expressed their concerns on this issue recently at the 14th CAS conference in Beijing. According to Molin Ge, a theoretical physicist at the Chern Institute of Mathematics, Nankai University, Tianjin, as more high-quality submissions are sent to overseas journals, the quality of submissions to local Chinese journals declines, which lowers the impact of the local Chinese journals. This becomes a vicious circle because the lower the impact, the less likely these local journals are to get high-quality submissions.[2]

Setting Agendas

Research priorities in developing countries may be very different from those in developed nations, but as science becomes more globalized, so too do priorities. At the national level, developing countries' research priorities increasingly resemble those of the developed nations, partly as a result of international competitive pressures. For example, after the United States announced its National Nanotechnology Initiative (NNI) in 2001, Japan and nations in Europe followed suit, as did South Korea, China, India, and Singapore. According to a 2004 report by the European Union,[3] public investment in nanotechnology had increased from €400 million (U.S. $630 million) in 1997 to more than €3 billion in 2004.

Part of the pressure to jump on the international bandwagon comes from researchers themselves. Scientists in the developing world maintain communications with those elsewhere. It is only natural that they want to share the attention that their colleagues in the developed Western world and Japan are receiving by pursuing the same hot topics. The research is exciting, fast-moving, and often easier to publish. At the same time, there are many other crucial challenges to be met in developing countries. For example, public health, water and food security, and environmental protection all beg for attention and resources. If people perceive these research areas as less intellectually challenging and rewarding, the issues will fail to receive the resources, support, and recognition they require. Without better agenda-setting practices, the scientific community will continue to face stinging criticism. It can send a satellite to Mars but not solve the most basic problems that threaten millions of lives in the developing world.

The introduction of Western scientific ideals to the developing world can generate an environment that is hostile to the indigenous research that prima facie does not fit those ideals. The confrontation between Western medicine and traditional Chinese medicine dates back to the early days of the twentieth century when Western medicine was first introduced in China. The debate reached a peak last year when a famous actress, Xiaoxu Chen, died from breast cancer. She allegedly insisted on treatment by Chinese traditional medicine, raising the hackles of some who claimed it to be worthless. Many Chinese still support traditional medicine and say that the dominance of Western medicine risks endangering China's scientific and cultural legacy.

A similar row erupted around earthquake prediction. In the 1960s and 1970s, China set up a network of popular earthquake-prediction stations, using simple instruments and local knowledge. For the most part, the network was decommissioned as China built the modern earthquake-monitoring system run by the China Earthquake Administration. When the system failed to predict the recent Sichuan earthquake, several people claimed that non-mainstream approaches had predicted its imminence. Scientists in the agency have tended to brush off such unofficial and individual predictions. To many this seems arrogant and bureaucratic.

It would be foolish and impossible to stop the globalization of science. There are tremendous benefits to science enterprises in different countries being integrated into a global whole. One should never think of turning back the clock. At the same time, it is possible to take some practical steps to minimize the harmful effects of this trend on local innovation.

Prioritizing for the People

First of all, there is a need to re-examine the governance of global science in recognition of the changing international geography of science. Many international norms and standards should be more open and accommodating to the changing environment in developing countries. For example, there is a need to re-evaluate the SCI and SSCI list of journals to include quality journals in the developing countries. In the long run, the relevant scientific community could also think about establishing an international panel to make decisions on the selection of journals for these indices, given their important influence. The recent move by Thomson Reuters, the parent company of ISI, to expand its coverage of the SCI list by adding 700 regional academic journals is a step in the right direction.[4]

English has become the de facto global language of science. Developing countries should invest in public institutions to provide translation services so that global scientific progress can be disseminated quickly. Developing countries can learn from Japan, a world leader in collecting scientific information and making it available to the public in the local language. At the same time, there should also be international institutions to provide similar services to the global science community so that "results and the knowledge generated through research should be freely accessible to all," as advocated by Nobel Laureates John Sulston and Joseph Stiglitz.[5]

When setting agendas, governments in developing countries must be careful in allocating their resources for science to achieve a balance between following the science frontier globally and addressing crucial domestic needs. A balance should also be struck between generating knowledge and disseminating and using knowledge. In addition, the global science community has a responsibility to help those developing countries that do not have adequate resources to solve problems themselves.

Finally, special efforts should be made to differentiate between pseudoscience and genuine scientific research. For the latter, one should tolerate or even encourage such indigenous research efforts in developing countries even if they do not fit the recognized international science paradigm. After all, the real advantage of a globalized scientific enterprise is not just doing the same research at a global scale, but doing new and exciting research in an enriched fashion.

Notes

1. Charles Leadbeater and James Wilsdon, *The Atlas of Ideas: How Asian Innovation Can Benefit Us All* (Demos, 2007).

2. Y. Xie et al., "Good Submissions Went Overseas—Chinese S&T Journals Could Not Keep Up with Their Overseas Peers," *Chinese Youth Daily*, June 25, 2008.

3. http://ec.europa.eu/nanotechnology/pdf/nano_com_en_new.pdf

4. http://scientific.thomsonreuters.com/press/2008/8455931/

5. Joseph Stiglitz and John Sulston, "Science is Being Held Back by Outdated Laws," *The Times*, July 5, 2008.

21

Finding Evidence

Research and Arguments

Left to right: © Wavebreakmedia, Ltd./age fotostock; www.CartoonStock.com;
© Zoonar M Kang/age fotostock

In making and supporting claims for academic arguments, writers use all kinds of evidence: data from journal articles; scholarly books; records from archives; blogs, wikis, social media sites, and other digital sources; personal observations and fieldwork; surveys; and even DNA. But such evidence doesn't exist in a vacuum. Instead, the quality of evidence—how and when it was collected, by whom, and for what purposes—may become part of the argument itself. Evidence may be persuasive in one time and place but not in another; it may convince one kind of audience but not another; it may work with one type of argument but not with the kind you are writing. The point is that finding "good" evidence for a research project is rarely a simple matter.

Considering the Rhetorical Situation

To be most persuasive, evidence should match the time and place in which you make your argument—that is to say, your rhetorical situation. For example, arguing that government officials in the twenty-first century should use the same policies to deal with economic troubles that were employed in the middle of the twentieth might not be convincing on its own. After all, almost every aspect of the world economy has changed in the past fifty years. In the same way, a writer may achieve excellent results by citing a detailed survey of local teenagers as evidence for education reform in her small rural hometown, but she may have less success using the same evidence to argue for similar reforms in a large inner-city community.

College writers also need to consider the fields that they're working in. In disciplines such as experimental psychology or economics, **quantitative data**—the sort that can be observed and counted—may be the best evidence. In many historical, literary, or philosophical studies, however, the same kind of data may be less appropriate or persuasive, or even impossible

to come by. As you become more familiar with a discipline, you'll gain a sense of what it takes to support a claim. The following questions will help you understand the rhetorical situation of a particular field:

- What kinds of data are preferred as evidence? How are such data gathered and presented?

- How are definitions, causal analyses, evaluations, analogies, and examples used as evidence?

- How does the field use firsthand and secondhand sources as evidence? What kinds of data are favored?

- How are statistics or other numerical information used and presented as evidence? Are tables, charts, or graphs commonly used? How much weight do they carry?

- What or who counts as an authority in this field? How are the credentials of authorities established?

- What weight do writers in the field give to **precedence**—that is, to examples of similar actions or decisions made in the past?

- Is personal experience allowed as evidence? When?

- How are quotations used as part of evidence?

- How are still or moving images or sound(s) used as part of evidence, and how closely are they related to the verbal parts of the argument being presented?

As these questions suggest, evidence may not always travel well from one field to another. Nor does it always travel easily from culture to culture. Differing notions of evidence can lead to arguments that go nowhere fast. For instance, when Italian journalist Oriana Fallaci interviewed Ayatollah Khomeini, Iran's supreme leader, in 1979, she argued in a way that's common in North American and Western European cultures: she presented claims that she considered to be adequately backed up with facts ("Iran denies freedom to people. . . . Many people have been put in prison and even executed, just for speaking out in opposition"). In response, Khomeini relied on very different kinds of evidence—analogies ("Just as a finger with gangrene should be cut off so that it will not destroy the whole body, so should people who corrupt others be pulled out like weeds so they will not infect the whole field") and, above all, the authority of the Qur'an. Partly because of these differing beliefs about what counts as evidence, the interview ended unsuccessfully.

The need for evidence depends a lot on the rhetorical situation.

© Mick Stevens/The New Yorker Collection/The Cartoon Bank

CULTURAL CONTEXTS FOR ARGUMENT

The Rhetorical Situation

To take another example, a *Harvard Business Review* blog post from December 4, 2013, on "How to Argue across Cultures" recounts the story of a Western businessperson who was selling bicycles produced in China to a buyer in Germany. When the business owner went to pick up the bicycles, he noticed that they rattled. In considering how to bring up this defect with the Chinese supplier, the businessperson could have confronted him directly, relying on physical evidence to support his claim. He rejected this form of evidence, however, because he knew that such a confrontation would result in loss of face for the supplier and very likely lead to an undesirable outcome. So instead, he suggested that he and the Chinese supplier take a couple of bikes out for a ride, during which the bikes rattled away. At the end of the ride, the Western businessperson quietly mentioned that he "thought his bike had rattled" and then departed, leaving the Chinese supplier to consider his subtle presentation of evidence. And it worked: when the Germans received the bicycle delivery, the rattle had been repaired.

It's always good to remember, then, that when arguing across cultural divides, whether international or more local, you need to think carefully about how you're accustomed to using evidence — and about what counts as evidence to other people (without surrendering your own intellectual principles).

Using Data and Evidence from Research Sources

The evidence you will use in most academic arguments—books, articles, videos, documents, photographs and other images—will likely come from sources you locate in libraries, in databases, or online. How well you can navigate these complex territories will determine the success of many of your academic and professional projects. Research suggests that most students overestimate their ability to manage these tools and, perhaps more important, don't seek the help they need to find the best materials for their projects. We can't cover all the nuances of doing academic research here, but we can at least point you in the right directions.

Explore library resources: printed works and databases. Your college library has printed materials (books, periodicals, reference works) as well as terminals that provide access to its electronic catalogs, other libraries' catalogs via the Internet, and numerous proprietary databases (such as *Academic Search Complete, Academic OneFile, JSTOR*) not available publicly on the Web. Crucially, libraries also have librarians whose job it is to guide you through these resources, help you identify reputable materials, and show you how to search for materials efficiently. The best way to begin a serious academic argument then is often with a trip to the library or a discussion with your professor or librarian. Also be certain that you know your way around the library. If not, ask the staff there to help you locate the following tools: general and specialized encyclopedias; biographical resources; almanacs, yearbooks, and atlases; book and periodical indexes; specialized indexes and abstracts; the circulation computer or library catalog; special collections; audio, video, and art collections; and the interlibrary loan office.

At the outset of a project, determine what kinds of sources you will need to support your project. (You might also review your assignment to see whether you're required to consult different kinds of sources.) If you'll use print sources, find out whether they're readily available in your library or whether you must make special arrangements (such as an interlibrary loan) to acquire them. For example, your argument for a senior thesis might benefit from material available mostly in old newspapers and magazines: access to them might require time and ingenuity. If you need to locate other nonprint sources (such as audiotapes, videotapes, artwork, or photos), find out where those are kept and whether you need special permission to examine them.

Most academic resources, however, will be on the shelves or available electronically through databases. Here's when it's important to understand the distinction between library databases and the Internet/Web. Your library's computers hold important resources that aren't on the Web or aren't available to you except through the library's system. The most important of these resources is the library's catalog of its holdings (mostly books), but college libraries also pay to subscribe to *scholarly databases*—for example, guides to journal and magazine articles, the *Academic Search Complete* database (which holds the largest collection of multidisciplinary journals), the *LexisNexis* database of news stories and legal cases, and compilations of statistics—that you can use for free.

You should consult these electronic sources through your college library, perhaps even before turning to the Web. But using these professional databases isn't always easy or intuitive, even when you can reach them on your own computer. You likely need to learn how to focus and narrow your searches (by date, field, types of material, and so on) so that you don't generate unmanageable lists of irrelevant items. That's when librarians or your instructor can help, so ask them for assistance. They expect your questions.

For example, librarians can draw your attention to the distinction between subject headings and keywords. The Library of Congress Subject Headings (LCSH) are standardized words and phrases that are used to classify the subject matter of books and articles. Library catalogs and databases usually use the LCSH headings to index their contents by author, title, publication date, and subject headings. When you do a subject search of the library's catalog, you need to use the exact wording of the LCSH headings. On the other hand, searches with *keywords* use the computer's ability to look for any term in any field of the electronic record. So keyword searching is less restrictive, but you'll have to think hard about your search terms to get usable results and to learn how to limit or expand your search.

Determine, too, early on, how current your sources need to be. If you must investigate the latest findings about, say, a new treatment for malaria, check very recent periodicals, medical journals, and the Web. If you want broader, more detailed coverage and background information, look for scholarly books. If your argument deals with a specific time period, newspapers, magazines, and books written during that period may be your best assets.

How many sources should you consult for an academic argument? Expect to look over many more sources than you'll end up using, and be sure to cover all major perspectives on your subject. Read enough sources to feel comfortable discussing it with someone with more knowledge than you. You don't have to be an expert, but your readers should sense that you are well informed.

Explore online resources. Chances are your first instinct when you need to find information is to do a quick keyword search on the Web, which in many instances will take you to a source in *Wikipedia,* the free encyclopedia launched by Jimmy Wales in 2001. For years, many teachers and institutions argued that the information on Wikipedia was suspect and could not be used as a reliable source. Times have changed, however, and many serious research efforts now include a stop at Wikipedia. As always, however, let the buyer beware: you need to verify the credibility of all of your sources! If you intend to support a serious academic argument, remember to approach the Web carefully and professionally.

Like the catalogs and databases in your college library, the Internet offers two ways to search for sources related to an argument—one using subject categories and one using keywords. A subject directory organized by categories (such as you might find at About.com) allows you to choose a broad category like "entertainment" or "science," and then click on increasingly narrow categories like "movies" or "astronomy," and then "thrillers" or "the solar system," until you reach a point where you're given a list of Web sites or the opportunity to do a keyword search.

With the second kind of Internet search option, a search engine, you start right off with a keyword search—filling in a blank, for example, on Google's homepage. Because the Internet contains vastly more material than even the largest library catalog or database, exploring it with a search engine requires careful choices and combinations of keywords. For an argument about the fate of the antihero in contemporary films, for example, you might find that *film* and *hero* produce far too many possible matches, or hits. You might further narrow the search by adding a third keyword— say, *American* or *current.* In doing such searches, you'll need to observe the search logic that is followed by a particular database. Using *and* between keywords (*movies and heroes*) usually indicates that both terms must appear in a file for it to be called up. Using *or* between keywords usually instructs the computer to locate every file in which either one word or the other shows up, and using *not* tells the computer to exclude files containing a particular word from the search results (*movies not heroes*).

More crucial with a tool like Google is to discover how the resources of the site itself can refine your choice or direct you to works better suited to academic argument. When you search for any term, you can click "Advanced Search" at the bottom of the results page and bring up a full screen of options to narrow your search in important ways.

But that's not the end of your choices. With an *academic* argument, you might want to explore your topic in either Google Books or Google Scholar. Both resources send you to the level of materials you might need for a term paper or professional project. And Google offers other options as well: it can direct you to images, photographs, blogs, and so on. The lesson is simple. If your current Web searches typically involve no more than using the first box that a search engine offers, you aren't close to using all the power available to you. Explore that tool you use all the time and see what it can really do.

search.com

Advanced Search

include **all** of these words:	
include this **exact phrase**:	
include **at least one** of these words:	
exclude these words:	
language:	any language
file type:	any format
last updated:	anytime
limit domain to:	
that link to:	
related to:	

Cancel   Search

Most search engines offer many kinds of research tools like this "Advanced Search" page from search.com. Explore them from the "More" and "Even More" menus on search pages.

SEARCHING ONLINE OR IN DATABASES

- Don't rely on simple Web searches only.

- Find library databases targeted to your subject.

- Use advanced search techniques to focus your search.

- Learn the difference between *subject heading* and *keyword* searches.

- Understand the differences between academic and popular sources.

- Admit when you don't know how to find material — you won't be alone!

- *Routinely* ask for help from librarians and instructors.

Collecting Data on Your Own

Not all your supporting materials for an academic argument must come from print or online sources. You can present research that you have carried out or been closely involved with; this kind of research usually requires that you collect and examine data. Here, we discuss the kinds of firsthand research that student writers do most often.

Perform experiments. Academic arguments can be supported by evidence you gather through experiments. In the sciences, data from experiments conducted under rigorously controlled conditions is highly valued. For other kinds of writing, more informal experiments may be acceptable, especially if they're intended to provide only part of the support for an argument.

If you want to argue, for instance, that the recipes in *Bon Appétit* magazine are impossibly tedious to follow and take far more time than the average person wishes to spend preparing food, you might ask five or six people to conduct an experiment—following two recipes from a recent issue and recording and timing every step. The evidence that you gather from this informal experiment could provide some concrete support—by way of specific examples—for your contention.

But such experiments should be taken with a grain of salt (maybe organic in this case). They may not be effective with certain audiences. And if your experiments can easily be attacked as skewed or sloppily done ("The people you asked to make these recipes couldn't cook a Pop-Tart"), then they may do more harm than good.

Make observations. "What," you may wonder, "could be easier than observing something?" You just choose a subject, look at it closely, and record what you see and hear. But trained observers say that recording an observation accurately requires intense concentration and mental agility. If observing were easy, all eyewitnesses would provide reliable stories. Yet experience shows that when several people observe the same phenomenon, they generally offer different, sometimes even contradictory, accounts of those observations.

Before you begin an observation yourself, decide exactly what you want to find out, and anticipate what you're likely to see. Do you want to observe an action that is repeated by many people—perhaps how people behave at the checkout line in a grocery store? Or maybe you want to study a sequence of actions—for instance, the stages involved in student registration, which you want to argue is far too complicated. Or maybe you are motivated to examine the interactions of a notoriously contentious campus group. Once you have a clear sense of what you'll analyze and what questions you'll try to answer through the observation, use the following guidelines to achieve the best results:

- Make sure that the observation relates directly to your claim.

- Brainstorm about what you're looking for, but don't be rigidly bound to your expectations.

- Develop an appropriate system for collecting data. Consider using a split notebook page or screen: on one side, record the minute details of your observations; on the other, record your thoughts or impressions.

- Be aware that the way you record data will affect the outcome, if only in respect to what you decide to include in your observational notes and what you leave out.

- Record the precise date, time, and place of the observation(s).

You may be asked to prepare systematic observations in various science courses, including anthropology or psychology, where you would follow a methodology and receive precise directions. But observation can play a role in other kinds of arguments and use various media: a photo essay, for example, might serve as an academic argument in some situations.

Conduct interviews. Some evidence is best obtained through direct interviews. If you can talk with an expert—in person, on the phone, or online—you might obtain information you couldn't have gotten through any other type of research. In addition to an expert opinion, you might ask for firsthand accounts, biographical information, or suggestions of other places to look or other people to consult. The following guidelines will help you conduct effective interviews:

- Determine the exact purpose of the interview, and be sure it's directly related to your claim.

- Set up the interview well in advance. Specify how long it'll take, and if you wish to record the session, ask permission to do so.

- Prepare a written list of both factual and open-ended questions. (Brainstorming with friends can help you come up with good questions.) Leave plenty of space for notes after each question. If the interview proceeds in a direction that you hadn't expected but that seems promising, don't feel that you have to cover every one of your questions.

- Record the subject's full name and title, as well as the date, time, and place of the interview.

- Be sure to thank those people whom you interview, either in person or with a follow-up letter or email message.

A serious interview can be eye-opening when the questions get a subject to reveal important experiences or demonstrate his or her knowledge or wisdom.

Use questionnaires to conduct surveys. Surveys usually require the use of questionnaires. Questions should be clear, easy to understand, and designed so that respondents' answers can be easily analyzed. Questions that ask respondents to say "yes" or "no" or to rank items on a scale (1 to 5, for example, or "most helpful" to "least helpful") are particularly easy to tabulate. Because tabulation can take time and effort, limit the number of questions you ask. Note also that people often resent being asked to answer more than about twenty questions, especially online.

Here are some other guidelines to help you prepare for and carry out a survey:

- Ask your instructor if your college or university requires that you get approval from the local Institutional Review Board (IRB) to conduct survey research. Many schools waive this requirement if students are doing such research as part of a required course, but you should check to make sure. Securing IRB permission usually requires filling out a series of online forms, submitting all of your questions for approval, and asking those you are surveying to sign a consent form saying they agree to participate in the research.

- Write out your purpose in conducting the survey, and make sure that its results will be directly related to your purpose.

- Brainstorm potential questions to include in the survey, and ask how each relates to your purpose and claim.

- Figure out how many people you want to contact, what the demographics of your sample should be (for example, men in their twenties or an equal number of men and women), and how you plan to reach these people.

- Draft questions that are as free of bias as possible, making sure that each calls for a short, specific answer.

- Think about possible ways that respondents could misunderstand you or your questions, and revise with these points in mind.

- Test the questions on several people, and revise those questions that are ambiguous, hard to answer, or too time-consuming to answer.

- If your questionnaire is to be sent by mail or email or posted on the Web, draft a cover letter explaining your purpose and giving a clear deadline. For mail, provide an addressed, stamped return envelope.

- On the final draft of the questionnaire, leave plenty of space for answers.

- Proofread the final draft carefully. Typos will make a bad impression on those whose help you're seeking.

- After you've done your tabulations, set out your findings in clear and easily readable form, using a chart or spreadsheet if possible.

"*Next question: I believe that life is a constant striving for balance, requiring frequent tradeoffs between morality and necessity, within a cyclic pattern of joy and sadness, forging a trail of bittersweet memories until one slips, inevitably, into the jaws of death. Agree or disagree?*"

A key requirement of survey questions is that they be easy to understand.

© George Price/The New Yorker Collection/The Cartoon Ban

Wes Anderson, film's primary advocate of Twee, and *Moonrise Kingdom*

Indian Paintbrush/The Kobal Collection

Draw upon personal experience. Personal experience can serve as powerful evidence when it's appropriate to the subject, to your purpose, and to the audience. If it's your only evidence, however, personal experience usually won't be sufficient to carry the argument. Your experiences may be regarded as merely "anecdotal," which is to say possibly exceptional, unrepresentative, or even unreliable. Nevertheless, personal experience can be effective for drawing in listeners or readers, as James Parker does in the following example. His full article goes on to argue that—in spite of his personal experience with it—the "Twee revolution" has some good things going for it, including an "actual moral application":

> Eight years ago or so, the alternative paper I was working for sent me out to review a couple of folk-noise-psych-indie-beardie-weirdie bands. I had a dreadful night. The bands were bad enough— "fumbling," I scratched in my notebook, "infantile"—but what really did me in was the audience. Instead of baying for the blood of these lightweights . . . the gathered young people—behatted, bebearded, besmiling—obliged them with patters of validating applause. I had seen it before, this fond curiosity, this acclamation of the undercooked, but never so much of it in one place: the whole event seemed to exult in its own half-bakedness. *Be as crap as you like* was the message to the performers. *The crapper, the better. We're here for you.* I tottered home, wrote a homicidally nasty nervous breakdown of a review, and decided I should take myself out of circulation for a while. No more live reviews until I calmed down. A wave of Twee—as I now realize—had just broken over my head.
>
> —James Parker, *The Atlantic,* July/August 2014, p. 36

RESPOND

1. The following is a list of general topic ideas from the Yahoo! Directory's "Issues and Causes" page. Narrow one or two of the items down to a more specific subject by using research tools in the library or online such as scholarly books, journal articles, encyclopedias, magazine pieces, and/or informational Web sites. Be prepared to explain how the particular research resources influenced your choice of a more specific subject within the general subject area. Also consider what you might have to do to turn your specific subject into a full-blown topic proposal for a research paper assignment.

Age discrimination	Poverty
Child soldiers	Racial profiling
Climate change	Solar power
Corporal punishment	Sustainable agriculture
Drinking age	Tax reform
Educational equity	Urban sprawl
Immigration reform	Video games
Media ethics and accountability	Violence in the NFL
Military use of drones	Whistleblowing
Pornography	Zoos

2. Go to your library's online catalog page and locate its list of research databases. You may find them presented in various ways: by subject, by field, by academic major, by type—even alphabetically. Try to identify three or four databases that might be helpful to you either generally in college or when working on a specific project, perhaps one you identified in the previous exercise. Then explore the library catalog to see how much you can learn about each of these resources: What fields do they report on? What kinds of data do they offer? How do they present the content of their materials (by abstract, by full text)? What years do they cover? What search strategies do they support (keyword, advanced search)? To find such information, you might look for a help menu or an "About" link on the catalog or database homepages. Write a one-paragraph description of each database you explore and, if possible, share your findings via a class discussion board, blog, or wiki.

3. What counts as evidence depends in large part on the rhetorical situation. One audience might find personal testimony compelling in a given case, whereas another might require data that only experimental studies can provide. Imagine that you want to argue that advertisements should not include demeaning representations of chimpanzees and that the use of primates in advertising should be banned. You're encouraged to find out that a number of companies such as Honda and Puma have already agreed to such a ban, so you decide to present your argument to other companies' CEOs and advertising officials. What kind of evidence would be most compelling to this group? How would you rethink your use of evidence if you were writing for the campus newspaper, for middle-schoolers, or for animal-rights group members? What can you learn about what sort of evidence each of these groups might value—and why?

4. Finding evidence for an argument is often a discovery process. Sometimes you're concerned not only with digging up support for an already established claim but also with creating and revising tentative claims. Surveys and interviews can help you figure out what to argue, as well as provide evidence for a claim.

    Interview a classmate with the goal of writing a brief proposal argument about the career that he/she should pursue. The claim should be something like *My classmate should be doing X five years from now.* Limit yourself to ten questions. Write them ahead of time, and don't deviate from them. Record the results of the interview (written notes are fine; you don't need to tape the interview). Then interview another classmate with the same goal in mind. Ask the same first question, but this time let the answer dictate the next nine questions. You still get only ten questions.

    Which interview gave you more information? Which one helped you learn more about your classmate's goals? Which one better helped you develop claims about his/her future?

22

Evaluating Sources

Research and Arguments

Chapter 22, "Evaluating Sources," from *Everything's an Argument*, Seventh Edition, by Andrea A. Lunsford and John J. Ruszkiewicz, pp. 427–435 (Chapter 19). Copyright © 2016 by Bedford/St. Martin's.

Left to right: © Bartomeu Amengual/age fotostock; © Terry Harris/Alamy;
© Zoonar/pzAxe/age fotostock

As many examples in this text have shown, the effectiveness of an argument often depends on the quality of the sources that support or prove it. You'll need to carefully evaluate and assess all your sources, including those that you gather in libraries, from other print sources, in online searches, or in your own field research.

Remember that different sources can contribute in different ways to your work. In most cases, you'll be looking for reliable sources that provide accurate information or that clearly and persuasively express opinions that might serve as evidence for a case you're making. At other times, you may be seeking material that expresses ideas or attitudes—how people are thinking and feeling at a given time. You might need to use a graphic image, a sample of avant-garde music, or a controversial YouTube clip that doesn't fit neatly into categories such as "reliable" or "accurate" yet is central to your argument. With any and all such sources and evidence, your goals are to be as knowledgeable about them and as responsible in their use as you can be and to share honestly what you learn about them with readers.

"I'm *not* being a tattle-tale! —
I'm being a reliable source!"

Might a tattle-tale ever be a reliable source?

www.Cartoonstock.com

No writer wants to be naïve in the use of source material, especially since most of the evidence that is used in arguments on public issues—even material from influential and well-known sources—comes with considerable baggage. Scientists and humanists alike have axes to grind, corporations have products to sell, politicians have issues to promote, journalists have reputations to make, publishers and media companies have readers, listeners, viewers, and advertisers to attract and to avoid offending. All of these groups produce and use information to their own benefit, and it's not (usually) a bad thing that they do so. You just have to be aware that when you take information from a given source, it will almost inevitably carry with it at least some of the preferences, assumptions, and biases—conscious or not—of the people who produce and disseminate it. Teachers and librarians are not exempted from this caution: even when we make every effort to be clear and comprehensive in reporting information, we cannot possibly see that information from every single angle. So even the most honest and open observer can deliver only a partial account of an event.

To correct for these biases, draw on as many reliable sources as you can handle when you're preparing to write. You shouldn't assume that all arguments are equally good or that all the sides in a controversy can be supported by the same weight of evidence and good reasons. But you want to avoid choosing sources so selectively that you miss essential issues and perspectives. That's easy to do when you read only sources that agree with you or when the sources that you read all seem to carry the same message. In addition, make sure that you read each source thoroughly enough that you understand its overall points: national research conducted for the Citation Project indicates that student writers often draw from the first paragraph or page of a source and then simply drop it, without seeing what the rest of the source has to say about the topic at hand.

When might a blogger actually be a reliable source—and how would you know?

© Adam Zyglis/Cagel Cartoons, Inc.

Especially when writing on political subjects, be aware that the sources you're reading or citing almost always support particular beliefs and goals. That fact has been made apparent in recent years by bloggers—from all parts of the political spectrum—who put the traditional news media under daily scrutiny, exposing errors, biases, and omissions. Even so, these political bloggers (mostly amateur journalists, although many are professionals in their own fields) have their own agendas and so must be read with caution themselves.

Assessing Print Sources

Since you want information to be reliable and persuasive, it pays to evaluate each potential source thoroughly. The following principles can help you evaluate print sources:

- **Relevance.** Begin by asking what a particular source will add to your argument and how closely the source is related to your argumentative claim. For a book, the table of contents and the index may help you decide. For an article, look for an abstract that summarizes its content. If you can't think of a good reason for using the source, set it aside. You can almost certainly find something better.

- **Credentials of the author.** Sometimes the author's credentials are set forth in an article, in a book, or on a Web site, so be sure to look for them. Is the author an expert on the topic? To find out, you can gather information about the person on the Internet using a search engine like Yahoo! or Ask.com. Another way to learn about the credibility of an author is to search Google Groups for postings that mention the author or to check the Citation Index to find out how others refer to this author. If you see your source cited by other sources you're using, look at how they cite it and what they say about it, which could provide clues to the author's credibility.

- **Stance of the author.** What's the author's position on the issue(s) involved, and how does this stance influence the information in the source? Does the author's stance support or challenge your own views?

- **Credentials of the publisher or sponsor.** If your source is from a newspaper, is it a major one (such as the *Wall Street Journal* or the *Washington Post*) that has historical credentials in reporting, or is it a tabloid? Is it a popular magazine like *O: The Oprah Magazine* or a journal sponsored by a professional group, such as the *Journal of the American Medical Association*? If your source is a book, is the publisher one you recognize or that has its own Web site? When you don't know the reputation of a source, ask several people with more expertise: a librarian, an instructor, or a professional in the field.

- **Stance of the publisher or sponsor.** Sometimes this stance will be obvious: a magazine called *Save the Planet!* will take a pro-environmental position, whereas one called *America First!* will probably take a conservative stance. But other times, you need to read carefully between the lines to identify particular positions and see how the stance affects the message the source presents. Start by asking what the source's goals are: what does the publisher or sponsoring group want to make happen?

- **Currency.** Check the date of publication of every book and article. Recent sources are often more useful than older ones, particularly in the sciences. However, in some fields (such as history and literature), the most authoritative works may well be the older ones.

- **Accuracy.** Check to see whether the author cites any sources for the information or opinions in the article and, if so, how credible and current they are.

- **Level of specialization.** General sources can be helpful as you begin your research, but later in the project you may need the authority or currency of more specialized sources. Keep in mind that highly specialized works on your topic may be difficult for your audience to understand.

- **Audience.** Was the source written for a general readership? For specialists? For advocates or opponents?

 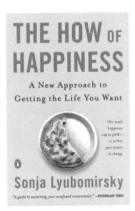

Note the differences between the cover of the *Journal of Abnormal Psychology* and *The How of Happiness*, a book about psychology.

- **Length.** Is the source long enough to provide adequate details in support of your claim?

- **Availability.** Do you have access to the source? If it isn't readily accessible, your time might be better spent looking elsewhere.

- **Omissions.** What's missing or omitted from the source? Might such exclusions affect whether or how you can use the source as evidence?

Assessing Electronic Sources

You'll probably find working with digital media both exciting and frustrating, for even though these tools (the Web, social networks, Twitter, and so on) are enormously useful, they offer information of widely varying quality—and mountains and mountains of it. Because Web sources are mostly open and unregulated, careful researchers look for corroboration before accepting evidence they find online, especially if it comes from a site whose sponsor's identity is unclear.

Every man [and woman] should have a built-in automatic crap detector operating inside him.
—Ernest Hemingway, during a 1954 interview with Robert Manning

Alfred Eisenstadt/The Life Picture Collection/Getty Images

Practicing Crap Detection

In such an environment, you must be the judge of the accuracy and trustworthiness of particular electronic sources. This is a problem all researchers face, and one that led media critic Howard Rheingold to develop a system for detecting "crap," that is, "information tainted by ignorance, inept communication, or deliberate deception." To avoid such "crap," Rheingold recommends a method of triangulation, which means finding three separate credible online sources that corroborate the point you want to make. But how do you ensure that these sources are credible? One tip Rheingold gives is to use sites like FactCheck.org to verify information, or to use the search term "whois" to find out about the author or sponsor of a site. Try googling Martin Luther King Jr., he says, and somewhere in the top ten "hits" you'll see something called "Martin Luther King, Jr.—a True Historical Examination," which sounds like it should be credible. Check by typing "whois" and the URL of the True Historical Examination, however, and you will find that it is sponsored by a group called Stormfront. Check out *that* site and you'll find that it is a white supremacist group. Hardly a fair, unbiased, and credible source.

In making judgments about online sources, then, you need to be especially mindful and to rely on the same criteria and careful thinking that you use to assess print sources. In addition, you may find the following questions helpful in evaluating online sources:

- Who has posted the document or message or created the site/medium? An individual? An interest group? A company? A government agency? For Web sites, does the URL offer any clues? Note especially the final suffix in a domain name—.*com* (commercial), .*org* (nonprofit organization), .*edu* (educational institution), .*gov* (government agency), .*mil* (military), or .*net* (network). Also note the geographical domains that indicate country of origin—as in .*ca* (Canada) or .*ar* (Argentina). Click on some links of a Web site to see if they lead to legitimate and helpful sources or organizations.

- What can you determine about the credibility of the author or sponsor? Can the information in the document or site be verified in other sources? How accurate and complete is it? On a blog, for example, look for a link that identifies the creator of the site (some blogs are managed by multiple authors).

- Who can be held accountable for the information in the document or site? How well and thoroughly does it credit its own sources? On a wiki, for example, check its editorial policies: who can add to or edit its materials?

- How current is the document or site? Be especially cautious of undated materials. Most reliable sites are refreshed or edited regularly and should list the date.

- What perspectives are represented? If only one perspective is represented, how can you balance or expand this point of view? Is it a straightforward presentation, or could it be a parody or satire?

What are the kinds and levels of information available on these Web sites—a commercial site about the TV show Stormchasers and a federal site on tornadoes and severe weather?

Left: Discovery Communications, Inc.; right: NOAA

Assessing Field Research

If you've conducted experiments, surveys, interviews, observations, or any other field research in developing and supporting an argument, make sure to review your results with a critical eye. The following questions can help you evaluate your own field research:

- Have you rechecked all data and all conclusions to make sure they're accurate and warranted?

- Have you identified the exact time, place, and participants in all your field research?

- Have you made clear what part you played in the research and how, if at all, your role could have influenced the results or findings?

- If your research involved other people, have you gotten their permission to use their words or other materials in your argument? Have you asked whether you can use their names or whether the names should be kept confidential?

- If your research involved interviews, have you thanked the person or persons you interviewed and asked them to verify the words you have attributed to them?

RESPOND

1. The chapter claims that "most of the evidence that is used in arguments on public issues . . . comes with considerable baggage" (p. 540). Find an article in a journal, newspaper, or magazine that uses evidence to support a claim of some public interest. It might be a piece about new treatments for malaria, Internet privacy, dietary recommendations for schoolchildren, proposals for air-quality regulation, the rise in numbers of campus sexual assaults, and so on. Identify several specific pieces of evidence, information, or data presented in the article and then evaluate the degree to which you would accept, trust, or believe those statements. Be prepared to explain specifically why you would be inclined to trust or mistrust any claims based on the data.

2. Check out Goodreads (you can set up an account for free) and see what people there are recommending—or search for "common reading programs" or "common reading lists." Then choose one of the recommended books, preferably a work of nonfiction, and analyze it by using as many of the principles of evaluation for printed books listed in this chapter as you can without actually reading the book: Who is the author, and what are his/her credentials? Who is the publisher, and what is its reputation? What can you find out about the book's relevance and popularity: why might the book be on the list? Who is the primary audience for the book? How lengthy is it? How difficult? Finally, consider how likely it is that the book you have selected would be used in an academic paper. If you do choose a work of fiction, might the work be studied in a literature course?

3. Choose a news or information Web site that you visit routinely. Then, using the guidelines discussed in this chapter, spend some time evaluating its credibility. You might begin by comparing it with Google News or Arts & Letters Daily, two sites that have a reputation for being reliable.

23

Using Sources

Research and Arguments

Chapter 23, "Using Sources," from *Everything's an Argument*, Seventh Edition, by Andrea A. Lunsford and John J. Ruszkiewicz, pp. 436–454 (Chapter 20). Copyright © 2016 by Bedford/St. Martin's.

Left to right: © imageBROKER/age fotostock; kstudija/Shutterstock; Paul Faith/PA Wire
URN:9724483 (Press Association via AP Images)

You may gather an impressive amount of evidence on your topic—from firsthand interviews, from careful observations, and from intensive library and online research. But until that evidence is thoroughly understood and then woven into the fabric of your own argument, it's just a stack of details. You still have to turn that data into credible information that will be persuasive to your intended audiences.

Practicing Infotention

Today it's a truism to say that we are all drowning in information, that it is pouring out at us like water from a never-ending fire hose. Such a situation has its advantages: it's never been easier to locate information on any imaginable topic. But it also has distinct disadvantages: how do you identify useful and credible sources among the millions available to you, and how do you use them well once you've found them? We addressed the first of these questions in Chapter 21, "Finding Evidence." But finding good sources is only the first step. Experts on technology and information like professors Richard Lanham and Howard Rheingold point to the next challenge: managing *attention*. Lanham points out that our age of information calls on us to resist the allure of every single thing vying for our attention and to discriminate among what deserves notice and what doesn't. Building on this insight, Rheingold has coined the term "infotention," which he says "is a word I came up with to describe a mind-machine combination of brain-powered attention skills and computer-powered information filters" (Howard Rheingold, "Infotention," http://www.rheingold.com).

Practicing infotention calls for synthesizing and thinking critically about the enormous amount of information available to us from the "collective intelligence" of the Web. And while some of us can learn to be mindful while multitasking (a fighter pilot is an example Rheingold gives of those

who must learn to do so), most of us are not good at it and need to train ourselves, literally, to pay attention to attention (and intention as well), to be aware of what we are doing and thinking, to take a deep breath and notice where we are directing our focus. In short, writers today need to learn to focus their attention, especially online, and learn to avoid distractions. So just how do you put all these skills together to practice infotention?

Building a Critical Mass

Throughout the chapters in Part 3, "Research and Arguments," we've stressed the need to discover as much evidence as possible in support of your claim and to read and understand it as thoroughly as you can. If you can find only one or two pieces of evidence—only one or two reasons or illustrations to back up your thesis—then you may be on unsteady ground. Although there's no definite way of saying just how much evidence is enough, you should build toward a critical mass by having several pieces of evidence all pulling in the direction of your claim. Begin by putting Rheingold's triangulation into practice: find at least three credible sources that support your point.

© Cog Design, Ltd.

And remember that **circumstantial evidence** (that is, indirect evidence that *suggests* that something occurred but doesn't prove it directly) may not be enough if it is the only evidence that you have. In the infamous case of Jack the Ripper, the murderer who plagued London's East End in 1888, nothing but circumstantial evidence ever surfaced and hence no one was charged with or convicted of the crimes. In 2007, however, amateur detective Russell Edwards bought a shawl at auction—a shawl found at one of the murder sites. After consulting with a number of scientific experts and using DNA evidence, Edwards identified Jack the Ripper as Aaron Kosminski, who eventually died in an asylum.

If your evidence for a claim relies solely on circumstantial evidence, on personal experience, or on one major example, you should extend your search for additional sources and good reasons to back up your claim—or modify the argument. Your initial position may simply have been wrong.

Synthesizing Information

As you gather information, you must find a way to make all the facts, ideas, points of view, and quotations you have encountered work with and for you. The process involves not only reading information and recording data carefully (paying "infotention"), but also pondering and synthesizing it—that is, figuring out how the sources you've examined come together to support your specific claims. Synthesis, a form of critical thinking highly valued by business, industry, and other institutions—especially those that reward innovation and creative thinking—is hard work. It almost always involves immersing yourself in your information or data until it feels familiar and natural to you.

At that point, you can begin to look for patterns, themes, and commonalities or striking differences among your sources. Many students use highlighters to help with this process: mark in blue all the parts of sources that mention point A; mark in green those that have to do with issue B; and so on. You are looking for connections among your sources, bringing together what they have to say about your topic in ways you can organize to help support the claim you are making.

You typically begin this process by paraphrasing or summarizing sources so that you understand exactly what they offer and which ideas are essential to your project. You also decide which, if any, sources offer materials you want to quote directly or reproduce (such as an important graph or table). Then you work to introduce such borrowed materials so that readers grasp their significance, and organize them to highlight important relationships. Throughout this review process, use "infotention" strategies by asking questions such as the following:

• Which sources help to set the context for your argument? In particular, which items present new information or give audiences an incentive for reading your work?

- Which items provide background information that is essential for anyone trying to understand your argument?

- Which items help to define, clarify, or explain key concepts of your case? How can these sources be presented or sequenced so that readers appreciate your claims as valid or, at a minimum, reasonable?

- Which of your sources might be used to illustrate technical or difficult aspects of your subject? Would it be best to summarize such technical information to make it more accessible, or would direct quotations be more authoritative and convincing?

- Which sources (or passages within sources) furnish the best support or evidence for each claim or sub-claim within your argument? Now is the time to group these together so you can decide how to arrange them most effectively.

- Which materials do the best job outlining conflicts or offering counterarguments to claims within a project? Which sources might help you address any important objections or rebuttals?

Remember that yours should be the dominant and controlling voice in an argument. You are like the conductor of an orchestra, calling upon separate instruments to work together to create a rich and coherent sound. The least effective academic papers are those that mechanically walk through a string of sources—often just one item per paragraph—without ever getting all these authorities to talk to each other or with the author. Such papers go through the motions but don't get anywhere. You can do better.

Paraphrasing Sources You Will Use Extensively

In a **paraphrase**, you put an author's ideas—including major and minor points—into your own words and sentence structures, following the order the author has given them in the original piece. You usually paraphrase sources that you expect to use heavily in a project. But if you compose your notes well, you may be able to use much of the paraphrased material directly in your paper (with proper citation) because all of the language is your own. A competent paraphrase proves you have read material or data carefully: you demonstrate not only that you know what a source contains but also that you appreciate what it means. There's an important difference.

Here are guidelines to help you paraphrase accurately and effectively in an academic argument:

- Identify the source of the paraphrase, and comment on its significance or the authority of its author.

- Respect your sources. When paraphrasing an entire work or any lengthy section of it, cover all its main points and any essential details, following the same order the author uses. If you distort the shape of the material, your notes will be less valuable, especially if you return to them later.

*"Who is the fairest one of all,
and state your sources!"*

Backing up your claims with well-chosen sources makes almost any argument more credible.

© Ed Fisher/The New Yorker Collection/The Cartoon Bank

- If you're paraphrasing material that extends over more than one page in the original source, note the placement of page breaks since it is highly likely that you will use only part of the paraphrase in your argument. You will need the page number to cite the specific page of material you want to cite.

- Make sure that the paraphrase is in your own words and sentence structures. If you want to include especially memorable or powerful language from the original source, enclose it in quotation marks. (See "Using Quotations Selectively and Strategically" on p. 558.)

- Keep your own comments, elaborations, or reactions separate from the paraphrase itself. Your report on the source should be clear, objective, and free of connotative language.

- Collect all the information necessary to create an in-text citation as well as an item in your works cited list or references list. For online materials, be sure you know how to recover the source later.

- Label the paraphrase with a note suggesting where and how you intend to use it in your argument.

- Recheck to make sure that the words and sentence structures are your own and that they express the author's meaning accurately.

Here is a passage from linguist David Crystal's book *Language Play*, followed by a student's paraphrase of the passage.

> Language play, the arguments suggest, will help the development of pronunciation ability through its focus on the properties of sounds and sound contrasts, such as rhyming. Playing with word endings and decoding the syntax of riddles will help the acquisition of grammar. Readiness to play with words and names, to exchange puns and to engage in nonsense talk, promotes links with semantic development. The kinds of dialogue interaction illustrated above are likely to have consequences for the development of conversational skills. And language play, by its nature, also contributes greatly to what in recent years has been called metalinguistic awareness, which is turning out to be of critical importance to the development of language skills in general and literacy skills in particular (180).

Paraphrase of the Passage from Crystal's Book

In *Language Play*, David Crystal argues that playing with language—creating rhymes, figuring out riddles, making puns, playing with names, using inverted words, and so on—helps children figure out a great deal, from the basics of pronunciation and grammar to how to carry on a conversation. This kind of play allows children to understand the overall concept of how language works, a concept that is key to learning to use—and read—language effectively (180).

Summarizing Sources

Unlike a paraphrase, a **summary** records just the gist of a source or a key idea—that is, only enough information to identify a point you want to emphasize. Once again, this much-shortened version of a source puts any borrowed ideas into your own words. At the research stage, summaries help you identify key points you want to make and, just as important, provide a record of what you have read. In a project itself, a summary helps readers understand the sources you are using.

Here are some guidelines to help you prepare accurate and helpful summaries:

- Identify the thesis or main point in a source and make it the heart of your summary. In a few detailed phrases or sentences, explain to yourself (and readers) what the source accomplishes.

- If your summary includes a comment on the source (as it might in the summaries used for annotated bibliographies), be sure that you won't later confuse your comments with what the source itself asserts.

- When using a summary in an argument, identify the source, state its point, and add your own comments about why the material is significant for the argument that you're making.

- Include just enough information to recount the main points you want to cite. A summary is usually much shorter than the original. When you need more information or specific details, you can return to the source itself or prepare a paraphrase.

- Use your own words in a summary and keep the language objective and denotative. If you include any language from the original source, enclose it in quotation marks.

- Collect all the information necessary to create an in-text citation as well as an item in your works cited list or references list. For online sources without page numbers, record the paragraph, screen, or section number(s) if available.

- Label the summary with a note that suggests where and how you intend to use it in your argument.

- Recheck the summary to make sure that you've captured the author's meaning accurately and that the wording is entirely your own.

Following is a summary of the David Crystal passage:

> In *Language Play*, David Crystal argues that playing with language helps children figure out how language works, a concept that is key to learning to use—and read—language effectively (180).

Notice that the summary is shorter than the paraphrase shown on p. 556.

Using Quotations Selectively and Strategically

To support your argumentative claims, you'll want to quote (that is, to reproduce an author's precise words) in at least three kinds of situations:

1. when the wording expresses a point so well that you cannot improve it or shorten it without weakening it,

2. when the author is a respected authority whose opinion supports your own ideas powerfully, and/or

3. when an author or authority challenges or seriously disagrees with others in the field.

Consider, too, that charts, graphs, and images may also function like direct quotations, providing convincing evidence for your academic argument.

In an argument, quotations from respected authorities will establish your ethos as someone who has sought out experts in the field. Just as important sometimes, direct quotations (such as a memorable phrase in your introduction or a detailed eyewitness account) may capture your readers' attention. Finally, carefully chosen quotations can broaden the appeal of your argument by drawing on emotion as well as logic, appealing to the reader's mind and heart. A student who is writing on the ethical issues of bullfighting, for example, might introduce an argument that bullfighting is not a sport by quoting Ernest Hemingway's comment that "the formal bull-fight is a tragedy, not a sport, and the bull is certain to be killed" and then accompany the quotation with an image such as the one on the next page.

The following guidelines can help you quote sources accurately and effectively:

*   Quote or reproduce materials that readers will find especially convincing, purposeful, and interesting. You should have a specific reason for every quotation.

A tragedy, not a sport?

Juan Castillo/AFP/Getty Images

- Don't forget the double quotation marks [" "] that must surround a direct quotation in American usage. If there's a quote within a quote, it is surrounded by a pair of single quotation marks [' ']. British usage does just the opposite, and foreign languages often handle direct quotations much differently.

- When using a quotation in your argument, introduce its author(s) and follow the quotation with commentary of your own that points out its significance.

- Keep quoted material relatively brief. Quote only as much of a passage as is necessary to make your point while still accurately representing what the source actually said.

- If the quotation extends over more than one page in the original source, note the placement of page breaks in case you decide to use only part of the quotation in your argument.

- In your notes, label a quotation you intend to use with a note that tells you where you think you'll use it.

- Make sure you have all the information necessary to create an in-text citation as well as an item in your works cited list or references list.

- Copy quotations carefully, reproducing the punctuation, capitalization, and spelling exactly as they are in the original. If possible, copy the quotation from a reliable text and paste it directly into your project.

- Make sure that quoted phrases, sentences, or passages fit smoothly into your own language. Consider where to begin the quotation to make it work effectively within its surroundings or modify the words you write to work with the quoted material.

- Use square brackets if you introduce words of your own into the quotation or make changes to it ("And [more] brain research isn't going to define further the matter of 'mind'").

- Use ellipsis marks if you omit material ("And brain research isn't going to define . . . the matter of 'mind'").

- If you're quoting a short passage (four lines or less in MLA style; forty words or less in APA style), it should be worked into your text, enclosed by quotation marks. Longer quotations should be set off from the regular text. Begin such a quotation on a new line, indenting every line a half inch or five to seven spaces. Set-off quotations do not need to be enclosed in quotation marks.

- Never distort your sources or present them out of context when you quote from them. Misusing sources is a major offense in academic arguments.

Framing Materials You Borrow with Signal Words and Introductions

Because source materials are crucial to the success of arguments, you need to introduce borrowed words and ideas carefully to your readers. Doing so usually calls for using a signal phrase of some kind in the sentence to introduce or frame the source. Often, a signal phrase will precede a quotation. But you need such a marker whenever you introduce borrowed material, as in the following examples:

> **According to noted primatologist Jane Goodall**, the more we learn about the nature of nonhuman animals, the more ethical questions we face about their use in the service of humans.

> The more we learn about the nature of nonhuman animals, the more ethical questions we face about their use in the service of humans, **according to noted primatologist Jane Goodall**.

The more we learn about the nature of nonhuman animals, **according to noted primatologist Jane Goodall**, the more ethical questions we face about their use in the service of humans.

In each of these sentences, the signal phrase tells readers that you're drawing on the work of a person named Jane Goodall and that this person is a "noted primatologist."

Now look at an example that uses a quotation from a source in more than one sentence:

In *Job Shift*, consultant William **Bridges worries about** "dejobbing and about what a future shaped by it is going to be like." Even more worrisome, **Bridges argues**, is the possibility that "the sense of craft and of professional vocation . . . will break down under the need to earn a fee" (228).

The signal verbs *worries* and *argues* add a sense of urgency to the message Bridges offers. They also suggest that the writer either agrees with—or is neutral about—Bridges's points. Other signal verbs can have a more negative slant, indicating that the point being introduced by the quotation is open to debate and that others (including the writer) might disagree with it. If the writer of the passage above had said, for instance, that Bridges *unreasonably contends* or that he *fantasizes,* these signal verbs would carry quite different connotations from those associated with *argues.*

In some cases, a signal verb may require more complex phrasing to get the writer's full meaning across:

Bridges recognizes the dangers of changes in work yet refuses to be overcome by them: "The real issue is not how to stop the change but how to provide the necessary knowledge and skills to equip people to operate successfully in this New World" (229).

As these examples illustrate, the signal verb is important because it allows you to characterize the author's or source's viewpoint as well as your own—so choose these verbs with care.

Some Frequently Used Signal Verbs

acknowledges	claims	emphasizes	remarks
admits	concludes	expresses	replies
advises	concurs	hypothesizes	reports
agrees	confirms	interprets	responds
allows	criticizes	lists	reveals
argues	declares	objects	states
asserts	disagrees	observes	suggests
believes	discusses	offers	thinks
charges	disputes	opposes	writes

Note that in APA style, these signal verbs should be in a past tense: *Blau (1992) claimed; Clark (2001) has concluded.*

Using Sources to Clarify and Support Your Own Argument

The best academic arguments often have the flavor of a hearty but focused intellectual conversation. Scholars and scientists create this impression by handling research materials strategically and selectively. Here's how some college writers use sources to achieve their own specific goals within an academic argument.

Establish context. Taylor Pearson, whose essay "Why You Should Fear Your Toaster More Than Nuclear Power" appears in Chapter 15, sets the context for his argument in the first two sentences, in which he cites a newspaper source ("Japan Nuclear Disaster Tops Scale") as representative of "headlines everywhere" warning of nuclear crises and the danger of existing nuclear plants. Assuming that these sentences will remind readers of other warnings and hence indicate that this is a highly fraught argument with high emotional stakes, Pearson connects those fears to his own argument by shifting, in the third sentence, into a direct rebuttal of the sources (such fears are "nothing more than media sensationalism") before stating his thesis: "We need nuclear energy. It's clean, it's efficient, it's economic, and it's probably the only thing that will enable us to quickly phase out fossil fuels." It will be up to Pearson in the rest of the essay to explain how, even in a context of public fear, his thesis is defensible:

> For the past month or so, headlines everywhere have been warning us of the horrible crises caused by the damaged Japanese nuclear reactors. Titles like "Japan Nuclear Disaster Tops Scale" have fueled

a new wave of protests against anything nuclear—namely, the construction of new nuclear plants or even the continued operation of existing plants. However, all this reignited fear of nuclear energy is nothing more than media sensationalism. We need nuclear energy. It's clean, it's efficient, it's economic, and it's probably the only thing that will enable us to quickly phase out fossil fuels.

When using Web sources such as blogs, take special care to check authors' backgrounds and credentials.

© Roz Chast/The New Yorker Collection/The Cartoon Bank

Review the literature on a subject. You will often need to tell readers what authorities have already written about your topic, thus connecting them to your own argument. So, in a paper on the effectiveness of peer editing, Susan Wilcox does a very brief "review of the literature" on her subject, pointing to three authorities who support using the method in writing courses. She quotes from the authors and also puts some of their ideas in her own words:

> Bostock cites one advantage of peer review as "giving a sense of ownership of the assessment process" (1). **Topping expands** this view, stating that "peer assessment also involves increased time on task: thinking, comparing, contrasting, and communicating" (254). The extra time spent thinking over the assignment, especially in terms of helping someone else, can draw in the reviewer and lend greater importance to taking the process seriously,

especially since the reviewer knows that the classmate is relying on his advice. This also adds an extra layer of accountability for the student; his hard work—or lack thereof—will be seen by peers, not just the instructor. **Cassidy notes**, "[S]tudents work harder with the knowledge that they will be assessed by their peers" (509): perhaps the knowledge that peer review is coming leads to a better-quality draft to begin with.

The paragraph is straightforward and useful, giving readers an efficient overview of the subject. If they want more information, they can find it by consulting Wilcox's works cited page.

Introduce a term or define a concept. Quite often in an academic argument, you may need to define a term or explain a concept. Relying on a source may make your job easier *and* enhance your credibility. That is what Laura Pena achieves in the following paragraph, drawing upon two authorities to explain what teachers mean by a "rubric" when it comes to grading student work:

> To understand the controversy surrounding rubrics, it is best to know what a rubric is. According to **Heidi Andrade, a professor at SUNY-Albany,** a rubric can be defined as "a document that lists criteria and describes varying levels of quality, from excellent to poor, for a specific assignment" ("Self-Assessment" 61). Traditionally, rubrics have been used primarily as grading and evaluation tools (**Kohn 12**), meaning that a rubric was not used until after students handed their papers in to their teacher. The teacher would then use a rubric to evaluate the students' papers according to the criteria listed on the rubric.

Note that the first source provides the core definition while information from the second offers a detail important to understanding when and how rubrics are used—a major issue in Pena's paper. Her selection of sources here serves her thesis while also providing readers with necessary information.

Present technical material. Sources can be especially helpful, too, when material becomes technical or difficult to understand. Writing on your own, you might lack the confidence to handle the complexities of some subjects. While you should challenge yourself to learn a subject well enough to explain it in your own words, there will be times when a quotation from an expert serves both you and your readers. Here is Natalie San Luis dealing with some of the technical differences between mainstream and Black English:

The grammatical rules of mainstream English are more concrete than those of Black English; high school students can't check out an MLA handbook on Ebonics from their school library. As with all dialects, though, there are certain characteristics of the language that most Black English scholars agree upon. According to Samy Alim, author of *Roc the Mic Right,* these characteristics are the "[h]abitual *be* [which] indicates actions that are continuing or ongoing. . . . Copula absence. . . . Stressed *been*. . . . *Gon* [indicating] the future tense. . . . *They* for possessive. . . . Postvocalic *-r*. . . . [and] *Ank* and *ang* for 'ink' and 'ing'" (115). Other scholars have identified "[a]bsence of third-person singular present-tense *s*. . . . Absence of possessive *'s*," repetition of pronouns, and double negatives (Rickford 111-24).

Note that using ellipses enables San Luis to cover a great deal of ground. Readers not familiar with linguistic terms may have trouble following the quotation, but remember that academic arguments often address audiences comfortable with some degree of complexity.

Develop or support a claim. Even academic audiences expect to be convinced, and one of the most important strategies for a writer is to use sources to amplify or support a claim.

Here is Manasi Deshpande, whose proposal argument appears in Chapter 19 (pp. 467–76), making the following claim: "Although the University has made a concerted and continuing effort to improve access, students and faculty with physical disabilities still suffer from discriminatory hardship, unequal opportunity to succeed, and lack of independence." See how she weaves sources together in the following paragraph to help support that claim:

The current state of campus accessibility leaves substantial room for improvement. There are approximately 150 academic and administrative buildings on campus (Grant). Eduardo Gardea, intern architect at the Physical Plant, estimates that only about nineteen buildings comply fully with the Americans with Disabilities Act (ADA). According to Penny Seay, PhD, director of the Center for Disability Studies at UT Austin, the ADA in theory "requires every building on campus to be accessible."

Highlight differences or counterarguments. The sources you encounter in developing a project won't always agree with each other or you. In academic arguments, you don't want to hide such differences, but instead

point them out honestly and let readers make judgments based upon actual claims. Here is a paragraph in which Laura Pena again presents two views on the use of rubrics as grading tools:

> Some **naysayers, such as Alfie Kohn**, assert that "any form of assessment that encourages students to keep asking, 'How am I doing?' is likely to change how they look at themselves and what they're learning, usually for the worse." Kohn cites a study that found that students who pay too much attention to the quality of their performance are more likely to chalk up the outcome of an assignment to factors beyond their control, such as innate ability, and are also more likely to give up quickly in the face of a difficult task (14). **However, Ross and Rolheiser** have found that when students are taught how to properly implement self-assessment tools in the writing process, they are more likely to put more effort and persistence into completing a difficult assignment and may develop higher self-confidence in their writing ability (sec. 2). Building self-confidence in elementary-age writers can be extremely helpful when they tackle more complicated writing endeavors in the future.

In describing Kohn as a "naysayer," Pena may tip her hand and lose some degree of objectivity. But her thesis has already signaled her support for rubrics as a grading tool, so academic readers will probably not find the connotations of the term inappropriate.

These examples suggest only a few of the ways that sources, either summarized or quoted directly, can be incorporated into an academic argument to support or enhance a writer's goals. Like these writers, you should think of sources as your copartners in developing and expressing ideas. But you are still in charge.

Avoiding "Patchwriting"

When using sources in an argument, writers—and especially those new to research-based writing—may be tempted to do what Professor Rebecca Moore Howard terms "**patchwriting**": stitching together material from Web or other sources without properly paraphrasing or summarizing and with little or no documentation. Here, for example, is a patchwork paragraph about the dangers wind turbines pose to wildlife:

Scientists are discovering that technology with low carbon impact does not mean low environmental or social impacts. That is the case especially with wind turbines, whose long, massive fiberglass blades have been chopping up tens of thousands of birds that fly into them, including golden eagles, red-tailed hawks, burrowing owls, and other raptors in California. Turbines are also killing bats in great numbers. The 420 wind turbines now in use across Pennsylvania killed more than 10,000 bats last year—mostly in the late summer months, according to the State Game Commission. That's an average of 25 bats per turbine per year, and the Nature Conservancy predicts as many as 2,900 turbines will be set up across the state by 2030. It's not the spinning blades that kill the bats; instead, their lungs effectively blow up from the rapid pressure drop that occurs as air flows over the turbine blades. But there's hope we may figure out solutions to these problems because, since we haven't had too many wind turbines heretofore in the country, we are learning how to manage this new technology as we go.

The paragraph reads well and is full of details. But it would be considered plagiarized (see Chapter 24) because it fails to identify its sources and because most of the material has simply been lifted directly from the Web. How much is actually copied? We've highlighted the borrowed material:

Scientists are discovering that technology with **low carbon** impact does not mean low environmental or social impacts. That is the case especially with wind turbines, whose **long, massive fiberglass** blades have been chopping up tens of thousands of birds that fly into them, including golden eagles, red-tailed hawks, burrowing owls, and other raptors in **California.** Turbines are also killing bats in great numbers. **The 420 wind turbines now in use across Pennsylvania killed more than 10,000 bats last year—mostly in the late summer months, according to the State Game Commission. That's an average of 25 bats per turbine per year, and the Nature Conservancy predicts as many as 2,900 turbines will be set up across the state by 2030.** It's not the spinning blades that kill the bats; instead, their lungs **effectively blow up from the rapid pressure drop that occurs as air flows over the turbine blades.** But there's hope we may figure out solutions to these problems because, since we haven't had too many wind turbines heretofore in the country, we are learning how to manage this new technology as we go.

But here's the point: an academic writer who has gone to the trouble of finding so much information will gain more credit and credibility just by properly identifying, paraphrasing, and quoting the sources used. The resulting paragraph is actually more impressive because it demonstrates how much reading and synthesizing the writer has actually done:

> Scientists like **George Ledec** of the World Bank are discovering that technology with low carbon impact "does not mean low environmental or social impacts" (**Tracy**). That is the case especially with wind turbines. Their massive blades spinning to create pollution-free electricity are also killing thousands of valuable birds of prey, including eagles, hawks, and owls in California (**Rittier**). Turbines are also killing bats in great numbers (**Thibodeaux**). The *Pittsburgh Post-Gazette* reports that 10,000 bats a year are killed by the 420 turbines currently in Pennsylvania. According to the state game commissioner, "That's an average of 25 bats per turbine per year, and the Nature Conservancy predicts as many as 2,900 turbines will be set up across the state by 2030" (**Schwartzel**). It's not the spinning blades that kill the animals; instead, *Discovery-News* explains, "the bats' lungs effectively blow up from the rapid pressure drop that occurs as air flows over the turbine blades" (**Marshall**). But there's hope that scientists can develop turbines less dangerous to animals of all kinds. "We haven't had too many wind turbines heretofore in the country," **David Cottingham** of the Fish and Wildlife Service points out, "so we are learning about it as we go" (**Tracy**).

Works Cited

Marshall, Jessica. "Wind Turbines Kill Bats without Impact." *Discovery News,* 25 Aug. 2008, news.discovery.com/20111112-turbinebats/.

Rittier, John. "Wind Turbines Taking Toll on Birds of Prey." *USA Today,* 4 Jan. 2005, usatoday30.usatoday.com/news/nation/2005-01-04-wind-mills-usat_x.htm.

Schwartzel, Erich. "Pa. Wind Turbines Deadly to Bats, Costly to Farmers." *Post-Gazette.com,* 17 July 2011, www.post-gazette.com/business/business-news/2011/07/17/Pa-wind-turbines-deadly-to-bats-costly-to-farmers/stories/201107170197.

Thibodeaux, Julie. "Bats Getting Caught in Texas Wind Turbines." *PegasusNews*.com, 9 Nov. 2011, www.pegasusnews.com/2011/11/09/bats-getting-caught-in-texas-wind-turbines/.

Tracy, Ryan. "Wildlife Slows Wind Power." The Wall Street Journal, 10 Dec. 2011, www.wsj.com/articles/SB10001424052970203501304577088593307132850.

RESPOND

1. Select one of the essays from Chapters 15–20. Following the guidelines in this chapter, write a paraphrase of the essay that you might use subsequently in an academic argument. Be careful to describe the essay accurately and to note on what pages specific ideas or claims are located. The language of the paraphrase should be entirely your own—though you may include direct quotations of phrases, sentences, or longer passages you would likely use in a paper. Be sure these quotations are introduced and cited in your paraphrase: *Pearson claims that nuclear power is safe, even asserting that "your toaster is far more likely to kill you than any nuclear power plant" (322)*. When you are done, trade your paraphrase with a partner to get feedback on its clarity and accuracy.

2. Summarize three readings or fairly lengthy passages from Parts 1–3 of this book, following the guidelines in this chapter. Open the item with a correct MLA or APA citation for the piece (see Chapter 25). Then provide the summary itself. Follow up with a one- or two-sentence evaluation of the work describing its potential value as a source in an academic argument. In effect, you will be preparing three items that might appear in an annotated bibliography. Here's an example:

   Pearson, Taylor. "Why You Should Fear Your Toaster More Than Nuclear Power." *Everything's an Argument*, by Andrea A. Lunsford and John J. Ruszkiewicz, 7th ed., Bedford/St. Martin's, 2016, pp. 322–27. Argues that since the dangers of nuclear power (death, radiation, waste) are actually less than those of energy sources we rely on today, nuclear plants represent the only practical way to generate the power we need and still reduce greenhouse gases. The journalistic piece provides many interesting facts about nuclear energy, but is informally documented and so does not identify its sources in detail or include a bibliography.

3. Working with a partner, agree upon an essay that you will both read from Chapters 15–20, examining it as a potential source for a research argument. As you read it, choose about a half-dozen words,

phrases, or short passages that you would likely quote if you used the essay in a paper and attach a frame or signal phrase to each quotation. Then compare the passages you selected to quote with those your partner culled from the same essay. How do your choices of quoted material create an image or ethos for the original author that differs from the one your partner has created? How do the signal phrases shape a reader's sense of the author's position? Which set of quotations best represents the author's argument? Why?

4. Select one of the essays from Chapters 15–20 to examine the different ways an author uses source materials to support claims. Begin by highlighting the signal phrases you find attached to borrowed ideas or direct quotations. How well do they introduce or frame this material? Then categorize the various ways the author actually uses particular sources. For example, look for sources that provide context for the topic, review the scholarly literature, define key concepts or terms, explain technical details, furnish evidence, or lay out contrary opinions. When you are done, write a paragraph assessing the author's handling of sources in the piece. Are the borrowed materials integrated well with the author's own thoughts? Do the sources represent an effective synthesis of ideas?

Plagiarism and Academic Integrity

Research and Arguments

Chapter 24, "Plagiarism and Academic Integrity," from *Everything's an Argument*, Seventh Edition,
by Andrea A. Lunsford and John J. Ruszkiewicz, pp. 455–464 (Chapter 21).
Copyright © 2016 by Bedford/St. Martin's.

Left to right: © imagineasia/age fotostock; Jutta Kuss/Getty Images; Dimitri Otis/Getty Images

In many ways, "nothing new under the sun" is more than just a cliché. Most of what you think or write is built on what you've previously read or experienced or learned from others. Luckily, you'll seldom be called on to list every influence on your life. But you do have responsibilities in school and professional situations to acknowledge any intellectual property you've made use of when you create arguments of your own. If you don't, you may be accused of **plagiarism**—claiming as your own the words, research, or creative work of others.

What is intellectual property? It's complicated. But, for academic arguments in Western culture, it is the *expression* of ideas you find in works produced by others that you then use to advance and support your own claims. You have to document not only when you use or reproduce someone's exact words, images, music, or other creations (in whole or in part), but also when you borrow the framework others use to put ideas together in original or creative ways. Needless to say, intellectual property rights have always been contentious, but never more so than today, when new media make it remarkably easy to duplicate and share all sorts of materials. Accustomed to uploading and downloading files, cutting and pasting passages, you may be comfortable working with texts day-to-day in ways that are considered inappropriate, or even dishonest, in school. You may, for example, have patched together sources without putting them in your own words or documenting them fully, practices that will often be seen as plagiarism (see p. 566).

Pet Hate # 561 - Copyright Thieves

But surely if something's on the web you can copy it - right?

Not necessarily.

The FBI has warned consumers for decades about the penalties for violating copyright. Your school no doubt has its own policies for handling such violations, including plagiarism.

www.cartoonsbysheila.com

So it is essential that you read and understand any policies on academic integrity that your school has set down. In particular, pay attention to how those policies define, prosecute, and punish cheating, plagiarism, and collusion. Some institutions recognize a difference between intentional and unintentional plagiarism, but you don't want the honesty of anything you write to be questioned. You need to learn the rules and understand that the penalties for plagiarism are severe not only for students but for professional writers as well.

But don't panic! Many student writers today are so confused or worried about plagiarism that they shy away from using sources—or end up with a citation for almost every sentence in an essay. There's no reason to go to such extremes. As a conscientious researcher and writer, you simply need to give your best effort in letting readers know what sources you have used. Being careful in such matters will have a big payoff: when you give full credit to your sources, you enhance your ethos in academic arguments—which is why "Academic Integrity" appears in this chapter's title. Audiences will applaud you for saying thanks to those who've helped you. Crediting your sources also proves that you have done your homework: you demonstrate that you understand what others have written about the topic and encourage others to join the intellectual conversation. Finally, citing sources reminds you to think critically about how to use the evidence you've collected. Is it timely and reliable? Have you referenced authorities in a biased or overly selective way? Have you double-checked all quotations and paraphrases? Thinking through such questions helps to guarantee the integrity of your academic work.

DOONESBURY   BY GARRY TRUDEAU

A Doonesbury cartoon on intellectual property pokes fun at best-selling historian and presidential biographer Stephen Ambrose, who was found to have plagiarized passages from at least twelve authors in at least six of his books—and in his doctoral dissertation.

Giving Credit

The basic principles for documenting materials are relatively simple. Give credit to all source materials you borrow by following these three steps: (1) placing quotation marks around any words you quote directly, (2) citing your sources according to the documentation style you're using, and (3) identifying all the sources you have cited in a list of references or works cited. Materials to be cited in an academic argument include all of the following:

- direct quotations
- facts that are not widely known
- arguable statements
- judgments, opinions, and claims that have been made by others
- images, statistics, charts, tables, graphs, or other illustrations that appear in any source
- collaboration—that is, the help provided by friends, colleagues, instructors, supervisors, or others

However, three important types of evidence or source material do not need to be acknowledged or documented. They are the following:

1. Common knowledge, which is a specific piece of information most readers in your intended audience will know (that Barack Obama won the 2012 presidential election, for instance)

2. Facts available from a wide variety of sources (that the Japanese bombed Pearl Harbor on December 7, 1941, for example). If, for instance, you search for a piece of information and find the same information on hundreds of different reputable Web sites, you can be pretty sure it is common knowledge.

3. Your own findings from field research (observations, interviews, experiments, or surveys you have conducted), which should be clearly presented as your own

For the actual forms to use when documenting sources, see Chapter 25.

Of course, the devil is in the details. For instance, you may be accused of plagiarism in situations like the following:

- if you don't indicate clearly the source of an idea you obviously didn't come up with on your own
- if you use a paraphrase that's too close to the original wording or sentence structure of your source material (*even* if you cite the source)
- if you leave out the parenthetical in-text reference for a quotation (*even* if you include the quotation marks themselves)

And the accusation can be made even if you didn't intend to plagiarize.

But what about all the sampling and mashups you see all the time online and in popular culture? And don't some artistic and scholarly works come close to being "mashups"? Yes and no. It's certainly fair to say, for example, that Shakespeare's plays "mash up" a lot of material from *Holinshed's Chronicles*, which he used without acknowledgment. But it's also true that Shakespeare's works are "transformative"—that is, they are made new by Shakespeare's art. Current copyright law protects such works that qualify as transformative and exempts them from copyright violations. But the issues swirling around the debate over sampling, mashups, and other uses of prior materials are far from clear, and far from over. Perhaps Jeff Shaw (in a posting that asks, "Is Mashup Music Protected by Fair Use?") sums up the current situation best:

> Lest we forget, the purpose of copyright law is to help content creators and to enhance creative expression. Fair use is an important step toward those ends, and further legislative work could solidify the step forward that fair use represents.
>
> —Jeff Shaw, "Is Mashup Music Protected by Fair Use?"

Getting Permission for and Using Copyrighted Internet Sources

When you gather information from Internet sources and use it in your own work, it's subject to the same rules that govern information gathered from other types of sources.

A growing number of online works, including books, photographs, music, and video, are published under the Creative Commons license, which often eliminates the need to request permission. These works—marked with a Creative Commons license—are made available to the public under this alternative to copyright, which grants permission to reuse or remix work under certain terms if credit is given to the work's creator.

Even if the material does not include a copyright notice or symbol ("©
2016 by Andrea A. Lunsford and John J. Ruszkiewicz," for example), it's
likely to be protected by copyright laws, and you may need to request
permission to use part or all of it. "Fair use" legal precedents allow writers
to quote brief passages from published works without permission from the
copyright holder if the use is for educational or personal, noncommercial
reasons and if full credit is given to the source. For blog postings or any
serious professional uses (especially online), however, you should ask permission of the copyright holder before you include any of his/her ideas,
text, or images in your own argument.

If you do need to make a request for permission, here is an example:

From: sanchez.32@stanford.edu
To: litman@mindspring.com
CC: lunsford.2@stanford.edu
Subject: Request for permission

Dear Professor Litman:

I am writing to request permission to quote from your essay
"Copyright, Owners' Rights and Users' Privileges on the Internet: Implied Licenses, Caching, Linking, Fair Use, and Sign-on
Licenses." I want to quote some of your work as part of an article
I am writing for the *Stanford Daily* to explain the complex debates
over ownership on the Internet and to argue that students at my
school should be participating in these debates. I will give full
credit to you and will cite the URL where I first found your work
(msen.com/litman/dayton.htm).

Thank you very much for considering my request.

Raul Sanchez

Acknowledging Your Sources Accurately and Appropriately

While artists, lawyers, and institutions like the film and music industries
sort out fair use laws, the bottom line in your academic work is clear: document sources accurately and fully and do not be careless about this very
important procedure.

Here, for example, is the first paragraph from a print essay by Russell Platt published in the *Nation*:

> Classical music in America, we are frequently told, is in its death throes: its orchestras bled dry by expensive guest soloists and greedy musicians' unions, its media presence shrinking, its prestige diminished, its educational role ignored, its big record labels dying out or merging into faceless corporate entities. We seem to have too many well-trained musicians in need of work, too many good composers going without commissions, too many concerts to offer an already satiated public.
>
> —Russell Platt, "New World Symphony"

To cite this passage correctly in MLA documentation style, you could quote directly from it, using both quotation marks and some form of note identifying the author or source. Either of the following versions would be acceptable:

> Russell Platt has doubts about claims that classical music is "in its death throes: its orchestras bled dry by expensive guest soloists and greedy musicians unions" ("New World").

> But is classical music in the United States really "in its death throes," as some critics of the music scene suggest (Platt)?

You might also paraphrase Platt's paragraph, putting his ideas entirely in your own words but still giving him due credit by ending your remarks with a simple in-text note:

> A familiar story told by critics is that classical music faces a bleak future in the United States, with grasping soloists and unions bankrupting orchestras and classical works vanishing from radio and television, school curricula, and the labels of recording conglomerates. The public may not be willing to support all the talented musicians and composers we have today (Platt).

All of these sentences with citations would be keyed to a works cited entry at the end of the paper that would look like the following in MLA style:

Platt, Russell. "New World Symphony." *The Nation*, 3 Oct. 2005, www. thenation.com/article/new-world-symphony/.

How might a citation go wrong? As we indicated, omitting either the quotation marks around a borrowed passage or an acknowledgment of the source is grounds for complaint. Neither of the following sentences provides enough information for a correct citation:

> But is classical music in the United States really in its death throes, as some critics of the music scene suggest, with its prestige diminished, its educational role ignored, and its big record labels dying (Platt)?

> But is classical music in the United States really in "its death throes," as some critics of the music scene suggest, with "its prestige diminished, its educational role ignored, [and] its big record labels dying"?

Just as faulty is a paraphrase such as the following, which borrows the words or ideas of the source too closely. It represents plagiarism, despite the fact that it identifies the source from which almost all the ideas—and a good many words—are borrowed:

> In "New World Symphony," Russell Platt observes that classical music is thought by many to be in bad shape in America. Its orchestras are being sucked dry by costly guest artists and insatiable unionized musicians, while its place on TV and radio is shrinking. The problem may be that we have too many well-trained musicians who need employment, too many good composers going without jobs, too many concerts for a public that prefers *The Real Housewives of Atlanta*.

Even the fresh idea not taken from Platt at the end of the paragraph doesn't alter the fact that the paraphrase is mostly a mix of Platt's original words, lightly stirred.

Acknowledging Collaboration

Writers generally acknowledge all participants in collaborative projects at the beginning of the presentation, report, or essay. In print texts, the acknowledgment is often placed in a footnote or brief prefatory note.

The eighth edition of the *MLA Handbook* (2016) calls attention to the shifting landscape of collaborative work, noting that:

Today academic work can take many forms other than the research paper. Scholars produce presentations, videos, and interactive Web projects, among other kinds of work...but the aims will remain the same: providing the information that enables a curious reader, viewer, or other user to track down your sources and giving credit to those whose work influenced yours.

RESPOND

1. Define *plagiarism* in your own terms, making your definition as clear and explicit as possible. Then compare your definition with those of two or three other classmates, and write a brief report on the similarities and differences you noted in the definitions. You might research terms such as *plagiarism, academic honesty,* and *academic integrity* on the Web. Also be certain to check how your own school defines the words.

2. Spend fifteen or twenty minutes jotting down your ideas about intellectual property and plagiarism. Where do you stand, for example, on the issue of music file sharing? On downloading movies free of charge? Do you think these forms of intellectual property should be protected under copyright law? How do you define your own intellectual property, and in what ways and under what conditions are you willing to share it? Finally, come up with your own definition of *academic integrity.*

3. Not everyone agrees that intellectual material is property that should be protected. The slogan "information wants to be free" has been showing up in popular magazines and on the Internet for a long time, often with a call to readers to take action against protection such as data encryption and further extension of copyright.

   Using a Web search engine, look for pages where the phrase "free information" appears. Find several sites that make arguments in favor of free information, and analyze them in terms of their rhetorical appeals. What claims do the authors make? How do they appeal to their audience? What's the site's ethos, and how is it created? After you've read some arguments in favor of free information, return to this chapter's arguments about intellectual property. Which arguments do you find most persuasive? Why?

4. Although this book is concerned principally with ideas and their written expression, other forms of intellectual property are also legally protected. For example, scientific and technological developments are protectable under patent law, which differs in some significant ways from copyright law.

Find the standards for protection under U.S. copyright law and U.S. patent law. You might begin by visiting the U.S. copyright Web site (copyright.gov). Then imagine that you're the president of a small high-tech corporation and are trying to inform your employees of the legal protections available to them and their work. Write a paragraph or two explaining the differences between copyright and patent, and suggest a policy that balances employees' rights to intellectual property with the business's needs to develop new products.

25

Documenting Sources

Research and Arguments

Chapter 25, "Documenting Sources," from *Everything's an Argument*, Seventh Edition, by Andrea A. Lunsford and John J. Ruszkiewicz, pp. 465–504 (Chapter 22). Copyright © 2016 by Bedford/St. Martin's.

Left to right: Seregram/Shutterstock; © Zero Creatives/Image/age fotostock; Iculig/Shutterstock

What does documenting sources have to do with argument? First, the sources that a writer chooses form part of any argument, showing that he/ she has done some research, knows what others have said about the topic, and understands how to use these items as support for a claim. Similarly, the list of works cited or references makes a statement, saying, "Look at how thoroughly this essay has been researched" or "Note how up-to-date I am!"

Writers working in digital spaces sometimes simply add hotlinks so that their readers can find their sources. If you are writing a multimodal essay that will appear on the Web, such links will be appreciated. But for now, college assignments generally call for full documentation rather than simply a link. You'll find the information you need to create in-text citations and works cited/references lists in this chapter.

Documentation styles vary from discipline to discipline, with one format favored in the social sciences and another in the natural sciences, for example. Your instructor will probably assign a documentation style for you to follow. If not, you can use one of the two covered in this chapter. But note that even the choice of documentation style makes an argument in a subtle way. You'll note in the instructions that follow, for example, that the Modern Language Association (MLA) style requires putting the date of publication of a print source at or near the end of a works cited list entry, whereas the American Psychological Association (APA) style places that date near the beginning of a references list citation. Such positioning suggests that in MLA style, the author and title are of greater importance than the date for humanities scholars, while APA puts a priority on the date— and timeliness—of sources. Pay attention to such fine points of documentation style, always asking what these choices suggest about the values of scholars and researchers who use a particular system of documentation.

MLA Style

Widely used in the humanities, MLA style is fully described in the *MLA Handbook* (8th edition, 2016). In this discussion, we provide guidelines drawn from the *MLA Handbook* for in-text citations, notes, and entries in the list of works cited.

In-Text Citations

MLA style calls for in-text citations in the body of an argument to document sources of quotations, paraphrases, summaries, and so on. For in-text citations, use a signal phrase to introduce the material, often with the author's name (*As Geneva Smitherman explains, . . .*). Keep an in-text citation short, but include enough information for readers to locate the source in the list of works cited. Place the parenthetical citation as near to the relevant material as possible without disrupting the flow of the sentence, as in the following examples.

1. Author Named in a Signal Phrase

   Ordinarily, use the author's name in a signal phrase to introduce the material, and cite the page number(s) in parentheses.

   Ravitch chronicles how the focus in education reform has shifted toward privatizing school management rather than toward improving curriculum, teacher training, or funding (36).

2. Author Named in Parentheses

   When you don't mention the author in a signal phrase, include the author's last name before the page number(s) in the parentheses.

   Oil from shale in the western states, if it could be extracted, would be equivalent to six hundred billion barrels, more than all the crude so far produced in the world (McPhee 413).

3. Two Authors

   Use all authors' last names.

   Gortner and Nicolson maintain that "opinion leaders" influence other people in an organization because they are respected, not because they hold high positions (175).

4. Three or More Authors

When there are three or more authors, brevity (and the MLA) suggests you use the first author's name with et al. (in regular type, not italicized).

Similarly, as Goldberger et al. note, their new book builds on their collaborative experiences to inform their description of how women develop cognitively (xii).

5. Organization as Author

Give the full name of a corporate author if it's brief or a shortened form if it's long.

Many global economists assert that the term "developing countries" is no longer a useful designation, as it ignores such countries' rapid economic growth (Gates Foundation 112).

6. Unknown Author

Use the full title of the work if it's brief or a shortened form if it's long.

"Hype," by one analysis, is "an artificially engendered atmosphere of hysteria" ("Today's Marketplace" 51).

7. Author of Two or More Works

When you use two or more works by the same author, include the title of the work or a shortened version of it in the citation.

Gardner presents readers with their own silliness through his description of a "pointless, ridiculous monster, crouched in the shadows, stinking of dead men, murdered children, and martyred cows" (*Grendel* 2).

8. Authors with the Same Last Name

When you use works by two or more authors with the same last name, include each author's first initial in the in-text citation.

Public health officials agree that the potential environmental risk caused by indoor residual spraying is far lower than the potential risk of death caused by malaria-carrying mosquitoes (S. Dillon 76).

9. Multivolume Work

Note the volume number first and then the page number(s), with a colon and one space between them.

Aristotle's "On Plants" is now available in a new translation edited by Barnes (2: 1252).

10. Literary Work

Because literary works are often available in many different editions, you need to include enough information for readers to locate the passage in any edition. For a prose work such as a novel or play, first cite the page number from the edition you used, followed by a semicolon; then indicate the part or chapter number (114; ch. 3) or act or scene in a play (42; sc. 2).

In Ben Jonson's *Volpone,* the miserly title character addresses his treasure as "dear saint" and "the best of things" (1447; act 1).

For a poem, cite the stanza and line numbers. If the poem has only line numbers, use the word *line(s)* in the first reference (lines 33–34) and the number(s) alone in subsequent references.

On dying, Whitman speculates, "All that goes onward and outward, nothing collapses, / And to die is different from what any one supposed, and luckier" (6.129–30).

For a verse play, omit the page number, and give only the act, scene, and line numbers, separated by periods.

Before he takes his own life, Othello says he is "one that loved not wisely but too well" (5.2.348).

As *Macbeth* begins, the witches greet Banquo as "Lesser than Macbeth, and greater" (1.3.65).

11. Works in an Anthology

For an essay, short story, or other short work within an anthology, use the name of the author of the work, not the editor of the anthology; but use the page number(s) from the anthology.

In the end, if the black artist accepts any duties at all, that duty is to express the beauty of blackness (Hughes 1271).

12. Sacred Text

To cite a sacred text, such as the Qur'an or the Bible, give the title of the edition you used, the book, and the chapter and verse (or their equivalent), separated by a period. In your text, spell out the names of books. In a parenthetical reference, use an abbreviation for books with names of five or more letters (for example, *Gen.* for Genesis).

He ignored the admonition "Pride goes before destruction, and a haughty spirit before a fall" (*New Oxford Annotated Bible*, Prov. 16.18).

13. Indirect Source

Use the abbreviation *qtd. in* to indicate that what you're quoting or paraphrasing is quoted (as part of a conversation, interview, letter, or excerpt) in the source you're using.

As Catherine Belsey states, "to speak is to have access to the language which defines, delimits and locates power" (qtd. in Bartels 453).

14. Two or More Sources in the Same Citation

Separate the information for each source with a semicolon.

Adefunmi was able to patch up the subsequent holes left in worship by substituting various Yoruba, Dahomean, or Fon customs made available to him through research (Brandon 115–17; Hunt 27).

15. Entire Work or One-Page Article

Include the citation in the text without any page numbers or parentheses.

Kazuo Ishiguro's dystopian novel *Never Let Me Go* explores questions of identity and authenticity.

16. Nonprint or Electronic Source

Give enough information in a signal phrase or parenthetical citation for readers to locate the source in the list of works cited. Usually give the author or title under which you list the source. If the work isn't numbered by page but has numbered sections, parts, or paragraphs, include the name and number(s) of the section(s) you're citing. (For paragraphs, use the abbreviation *par.* or *pars.*; for section, use *sec.*; for part, use *pt.*)

In his film version of *Hamlet*, Zeffirelli highlights the sexual tension between the prince and his mother.

Zora Neale Hurston is one of the great anthropologists of the twentieth century, according to Kip Hinton (par. 2).

Describing children's language acquisition, Pinker explains that "what's innate about language is just a way of paying attention to parental speech" (qtd. in Johnson, sec. 1).

17. Visual Included in the Text

Number all figures (photos, drawings, cartoons, maps, graphs, and charts) and tables separately.

This trend is illustrated in a chart distributed by the College Board as part of its 2014 analysis of aggregate SAT data (see fig. 1).

Include a caption with enough information about the source to direct readers to the works cited entry. (For an example of an image that a student created, see the sample page from an MLA-style essay on p. 605 in this chapter.)

Explanatory and Bibliographic Notes

We recommend using explanatory notes for information or commentary that doesn't readily fit into your text but is needed for clarification, further explanation, or justification. In addition, bibliographic notes will allow you to cite several sources for one point and to offer thanks to, information about, or evaluation of a source. Use a superscript number in your text at the end of a sentence to refer readers to the notes, which usually appear as endnotes (with the heading *Notes,* not underlined or italicized) on a separate page before the list of works cited. Indent the first line of each note five spaces, and double-space all entries.

Text with Superscript Indicating a Note

Stewart emphasizes the existence of social contacts in Hawthorne's life so that the audience will accept a different Hawthorne, one more attuned to modern times than the figure in Woodberry.[3]

Note

[3] Woodberry does, however, show that Hawthorne was often unsociable. He emphasizes the seclusion of Hawthorne's mother, who separated herself from her family after the death of her husband, often even taking meals alone (28). Woodberry seems to imply that Mrs. Hawthorne's isolation rubbed off on her son.

List of Works Cited

A list of works cited is an alphabetical listing of the sources you cite in your essay. The list appears on a separate page at the end of your argument, after any notes, with the heading *Works Cited* centered an inch from the top of the page; don't underline or italicize it or enclose it in quotation marks. Double-space between the heading and the first entry, and double-space the entire list. (If you're asked to list everything you've read as background—not just the sources you cite—call the list *Works Consulted*.) The first line of each entry should align on the left; subsequent lines indent one-half inch or five spaces. See p. 606 for a sample works cited page.

Print Books
The basic information for a book includes four elements:

- the author's name, last name first (for a book with multiple authors, only the first author's name is inverted)

- the title and subtitle, italicized

- the publication information, including the publisher's name (such as Harvard UP) followed by a comma, and the publication date

1. One Author

    Larsen, Erik. *Dead Wake: The Last Crossing of the Lusitania*. Crown Publishers, 2015.

2. Two or More Authors

    Jacobson, Sid, and Ernie Colón. *The 9/11 Report: A Graphic Adaptation*. Farrar, Straus, and Giroux, 2006.

3. Organization as Author

    American Horticultural Society. *The Fully Illustrated Plant-by-Plant Manual of Practical Techniques*. DK, 1999.

4. Unknown Author

    National Geographic Atlas of the World. National Geographic, 2004.

5. Two or More Books by the Same Author

    List the works alphabetically by title. Use three hyphens for the author's name for the second and subsequent works by that author.

    Lorde, Audre. *A Burst of Light*. Firebrand Books, 1988.

    ---. *Sister Outsider*. Crossings Press, 1984.

6. Editor

    Rorty, Amelie Oksenberg, editor. *Essays on Aristotle's Poetics*. Princeton UP, 1992.

7. **Author and Editor**
    Shakespeare, William. *The Tempest*. Edited by Frank Kermode, Routledge, 1994.

8. **Selection in an Anthology or Chapter in an Edited Book**
    List the author(s) of the selection or chapter; its title; the title of the book in which the selection or chapter appears; *Ed.* and the name(s) of the editor(s); the publication information; and the inclusive page numbers of the selection or chapter.

    Brown, Paul. "'This thing of darkness I acknowledge mine': *The Tempest* and the Discourse of Colonialism." *Political Shakespeare: Essays in Cultural Materialism*, edited by Jonathan Dollimore and Alan Sinfield, Cornell UP, 1985, pp. 48–71.

9. **Two or More Works from the Same Anthology**
    Include the anthology itself in the list of works cited.

    Gates, Henry Louis, Jr., and Nellie McKay, editors. *The Norton Anthology of African American Literature*, Norton, 1997.

    Then list each selection separately by its author and title, followed by a cross-reference to the anthology.

    Karenga, Maulana. "Black Art: Mute Matter Given Force and Function." Gates and McKay 1973–77.

    Neal, Larry. "The Black Arts Movement." Gates and McKay 1960–72.

10. **Translation**
    Hietamies, Laila. *Red Moon over White Sea*. Trans. Borje Vahamaki. Beaverton: Aspasia, 2000. Print.

11. **Edition Other Than the First**
    Lunsford, Andrea A., John J. Ruszkiewicz, and Keith Walters. *Everything's an Argument with Readings*. 7th ed. Boston: Bedford, 2016. Print.

12. **Graphic Narrative**
    If the words and images are created by the same person, cite a graphic narrative just as you would a book (see item 1 on p. 591).

    Bechdel, Alison. *Are You My Mother?* New York: Houghton Mifflin Harcourt, 2012. Print.

If the work is a collaboration, indicate the author or illustrator who is most important to your research before the title. Then list other contributors in order of their appearance on the title page. Label each person's contribution to the work.

Stavans, Ilan, writer. *Latino USA: A Cartoon History.* Illus. Lalo Arcaraz. New York: Basic, 2000. Print.

13. One Volume of a Multivolume Work

Byron, Lord George. *Byron's Letters and Journals.* Ed. Leslie A. Marchand. Vol. 2. London: Murray, 1973. Print. 12 vols.

14. Two or More Volumes of a Multivolume Work

Byron, Lord George. *Byron's Letters and Journals.* Ed. Leslie A. Marchand. 12 vols. London: Murray, 1973–82. Print.

15. Preface, Foreword, Introduction, or Afterword

Kean, Thomas H., and Lee H. Hamilton. Foreword. *The 9/11 Report: A Graphic Adaptation.* By Sid Jacobson and Ernie Colón. New York: Hill, 2006. ix–x. Print.

16. Article in a Reference Work

Robinson, Lisa Clayton. "Harlem Writers Guild." *Africana: The Encyclopedia of the African and African American Experience,* 2nd ed., Oxford UP, 2005.

17. Book That Is Part of a Series

Include the title and number of the series after the publication information.

Moss, Beverly J. *A Community Text Arises.* Hampton, 2003. Language and Social Processes Ser. 8.

18. Republication

Trilling, Lionel. *The Liberal Imagination.* 1950. Introduction by Louis Menand, New York Review of Books, 2008.

19. Government Document

Canada, Minister of Aboriginal Affairs and Northern Development. *2015–16 Report on Plans and Priorities.* Minister of Public Works and Government Services Canada, 2015.

20. Pamphlet

    The Legendary Sleepy Hollow Cemetery. Friends of Sleepy Hollow
        Cemetery, 2008.

21. Published Proceedings of a Conference

    Meisner, Marx S., et al., editors. *Communication for the Commons:
        Revisiting Participation and Environment.* Proceedings of Twelfth
        Biennial Conference on Communication and the Environment,
        6–11 June 2015, Swedish U of Agricultural Sciences, Interna-
        tional Environmental Communication Association, 2015.

22. Title within a Title

    Shanahan, Timothy. *Philosophy and* Blade Runner. Palgrave Macmil-
        lan, 2014.

Print Periodicals

The basic entry for a periodical includes three elements:

- the author's name, last name first, followed by a period

- the article title, in quotation marks, followed by a period

- the publication information, including the periodical title (italicized),
  the volume and issue numbers (if any, not italicized), the date of publication, and the page number(s), all followed by commas, with a period
  at the end of the page numbers

For works with multiple authors, only the first author's name is inverted.
Note that the period following the article title goes inside the closing quotation mark.

23. Article in a Print Journal

    Give the issue number, if available.

    Matchie, Thomas. "Law versus Love in *The Round House.*" *Midwest
        Quarterly,* vol. 56, no. 4, Summer 2015, pp. 353–64.

    Fuqua, Amy. "'The Furrow of His Brow': Providence and Pragmatism
        in Toni Morrison's *Paradise.*" *Midwest Quarterly*, vol. 54, no. 1,
        Autumn 2012, pp. 38–52.

24. Article That Skips Pages

    Seabrook, John. "Renaissance Pears." *The New Yorker,* 5 Sept. 2005,
        pp. 102+.

25. Article in a Print Monthly Magazine

Kunzig, Robert. "The Will to Change." *National Geographic*, Nov. 2015, pp. 32–63.

26. Article in a Print Weekly Magazine

Grossman, Lev. "A Star Is Born." *Time*, 2 Nov. 2015, pp. 30–39.

27. Article in a Print Newspaper

Bray, Hiawatha. "As Toys Get Smarter, Privacy Issues Emerge." *The Boston Globe,* 10 Dec. 2015, p. C1.

28. Editorial or Letter to the Editor

Posner, Alan. "Colin Powell's Regret." *The New York Times,* 9 Sept. 2005, p. A20.

29. Unsigned Article

"Court Rejects the Sale of Medical Marijuana." *The New York Times,* 26 Feb. 1998, late ed., p. A21.

30. Review

Walton, James. "Noble, Embattled Souls." Review of *The Bone Clocks* and *Slade House*, by David Mitchell, *The New York Review of Books*, 3 Dec. 2015, pp. 55–58.

Digital Sources

Most of the following models are based on the MLA's guidelines for citing electronic sources in the *MLA Handbook* (8th edition, 2016), as well as on up-to-date information available at its Web site (mla.org). The MLA advocates the use of URLs but prefers a Digital Object Indicator (DOI) where available. A DOI is a unique number assigned to a selection, and does not change regardless of where the item is located online. The basic MLA entry for most electronic sources should include the following elements:

- name of the author, editor, or compiler

- title of the work, document, or posting

- publication information (volume, issue, year or date). List page numbers (or *n. pag.*, not italicized, if none are listed).

- name of database, italicized

- DOI or URL

31. Document from a Web Site

Begin with the author, if known, followed by the title of the work, title of the Web site, publisher or sponsor (if it is notably different from the title of the Web site), date of publication or last update, and the Digital Object Identifier or URL. If no publication or update date is available, please include a date of access at the end.

"Social and Historical Context: Vitality." *Arapesh Grammar and Digital Language Archive Project*, Institute for Advanced Technology in the Humanities, www.arapesh.org/socio_historical_context_vitality.php. Accessed 22 Mar. 2016.

32. Entire Web Site

Include the name of the person or group who created the site, if relevant; the title of the site, italicized; the publisher or sponsor of the site; the date of publication or last update; and the URL.

Railton, Stephen. *Mark Twain in His Times*. Stephen Railton / U of Virginia Library, 2012, twain.lib.virginia.edu/.

Halsall, Paul, editor. *Internet Modern History Sourcebook*. Fordham U, 4 Nov. 2011, legacy.fordham.edu/halsall/index.asp.

33. Course, Department, or Personal Web Site

For a course Web site, include the instructor's name; the title of the site, italicized; a description of the site (such as *Course home page*, *Department home page*, or *Home page*—not italicized); the sponsor of the site (academic department and institution); dates of the course or last update to the page; and the URL. Note that the MLA spells home page as two separate words. For an academic department, list the name of the department; a description; the academic institution; the date the page was last updated; and the URL.

Film Studies. Department home page. *Wayne State University, College of Liberal Arts and Sciences*, 2016, clas.wayne.edu/FilmStudies/.

Masiello, Regina. 355:101: Expository Writing. *Rutgers School of Arts and Sciences*, 2016, wp.rutgers.edu/courses/55-355101.

34. Online Book

Cite an online book as you would a print book. After the print publication information (if any), give the title of the Web site or database in which the book appears, italicized; and the DOI or URL.

Riis, Jacob A. *How the Other Half Lives: Studies among the Tenements of New York.* Edited by David Phillips, Scribner's, 1890. *The Authentic History Center,* www.authentichistory.com/1898-1913/2-progressivism/2-riis/.

Treat a poem, essay, or other short work within an online book as you would a part of a print book. After the print publication information (if any), give the title of the Web site or database, italicized; and the DOI or URL.

Milton, John. *Paradise Lost: Book I. Poetry Foundation,* 2014, www.poetryfoundation.org/poem/174987.

35. Article in a Journal on the Web

For an article in an online journal, cite the same information that you would for a print journal. Then add the DOI or URL.

Bryson, Devin. "The Rise of a New Senegalese Cultural Philosophy?" *African Studies Quarterly,* vol. 14, no. 3, Mar. 2014, pp. 33–56, asq.africa.ufl.edu/files/Volume-14-Issue-3-Bryson.pdf.

36. Article in a Magazine or Newspaper on the Web

For an article in an online magazine or newspaper, cite the author; the title of the article, in quotation marks; the name of the magazine or newspaper, italicized; the date of publication; and the URL of the page you accessed.

Leonard, Andrew. "The Surveillance State High School." *Salon,* 27 Nov. 2012, www.salon.com/2012/11/27/the_surveillance_state_high_school/.

Crowell, Maddy. "How Computers Are Getting Better at Detecting Liars." *The Christian Science Monitor,* 12 Dec. 2015, www.csmonitor.com/Science/Science-Notebook/2015/1212/How-computers-are-getting-better-at-detecting-liars.

37. Entry in a Web Reference Work

Cite the entry as you would an entry from a print reference work (see item 16). Follow with the name of the Web site, the date of publication, and the URL of the site you accessed.

Durante, Amy M. "Finn Mac Cumhail." *Encyclopedia Mythica,* 17 Apr. 2011, www.pantheon.org/articles/f/finn_mac_cumhail.html.

38. Post or Comment on a Web Site

Begin with the author's name; the title of the posting, in quotation marks (if there is no title, use the description *Weblog post* or *Weblog comment*, not italicized); the name of the blog, italicized; the sponsor of the blog; the date of the most recent update; and the URL of the page you accessed.

mitchellfreedman. Comment on "*Cloud Atlas's* Theory of Everything," by Emily Eakin. *NYR Daily*, NYREV, 3 Nov. 2012, www.nybooks.com/daily/2012/11/02/ken-wilber-cloud-atlas/.

39. Entry in a Wiki

Since wikis are collectively edited, do not include an author. Treat a wiki as you would a work from a Web site (see item 31). Include the title of the entry; the name of the wiki, italicized; the date of the latest update; and the URL of the page you accessed.

House Music." *Wikipedia*, 16 Nov. 2015, en.wikipedia.org/wiki/ House_music.

40. Posting on a Social Networking Site

To cite a posting on Facebook or another social networking site, include the writer's name, a description of the posting, the date of the posting, and the URL of the page you accessed.

Bedford English. "Stacey Cochran explores Reflective Writing in the classroom and as a writer: http://ow.ly/YkjVB." *Facebook*, 15 Feb. 2016, www.facebook.com/BedfordEnglish/ posts/10153415001259607.

41. Email or Message on a Social Networking Site

Include the writer's name; the subject line, in quotation marks (for email); *Received by* (not italicized or in quotation marks) followed by the recipient's name; and the date of the message. You do not need to include the medium, but may if you are concerned there will be confusion.

Thornbrugh, Caitlin. "Coates Lecture." Received by Rita Anderson, 20 Oct. 2015.

42. Tweet

Include the writer's real name, if known, with the user name (if different) in parentheses. If you don't know the real name, give just the user name. Include the entire tweet, in quotation marks. Include the publisher (Twitter) in italics, follow by the date and time of the message and the URL.

Curiosity Rover. "Can you see me waving? How to spot #Mars in the night sky: https://youtu.be/hv8hVvJlcJQ." *Twitter*, 5 Nov. 2015, 11:00 a.m., twitter.com/marscuriosity/status/672859022911889408.

43. Work from an Online Database or a Subscription Service

For a work from an online database, list the author's name; the title of the work, in quotation marks; any print publication information; the name of the database, italicized; and the DOI or URL.

Goldsmith, Oliver. *The Vicar of Wakefield: A Tale*. Philadelphia, 1801. *America's Historical Imprints*, infoweb.newsbank.com.ezproxy.bpl.org/.

For a work from an online service to which your library subscribes, include the same information as for an online database. After the information about the work, give the name of the database, italicized; and the DOI or URL.

Coles, Kimberly Anne. "The Matter of Belief in John Donne's Holy Sonnets." *Renaissance Quarterly*, vol. 68, no. 3, Fall 2015, pp. 899–931. JSTOR, doi:10.1086/683855.

"The Road toward Peace." *The New York Times*, 15 Feb. 1945, p. 18. Editorial. *ProQuest Historical Newspapers: The New York Times*, search.proquest.com/hnpnewyorktimes.

44. Computer Software or Video Game

Include the title, italicized; the version number (if given); and publication information. If you are citing material downloaded from a Web site, include the title and version number (if given), but instead of publication information, add the publisher or sponsor of the Web site; the date of publication; and the URL.

Edgeworld. Atom Entertainment, 1 May 2012, www.kabam.com/games/edgeworld.

Words with Friends. Version 5.84. Zynga, 2013.

Other Sources (Including Online Versions)

45. Unpublished Dissertation

Abbas, Megan Brankley. "Knowing Islam: The Entangled History of Western Academia and Modern Islamic Thought." Dissertation, Princeton U, 2015.

46. Published Dissertation

Kidd, Celeste. *Rational Approaches to Learning and Development.* Dissertation, U of Rochester, 2013.

47. Article from a Microform

Sharpe, Lora. "A Quilter's Tribute." *The Boston Globe,* 25 Mar. 1989, p. 13. Microform. *NewsBank*: Social Relations 12, 1989, fiche 6, grids B4–6.

48. Personal, Published, or Broadcast Interview

For a personal interview, list the name of the person interviewed, the label *Personal interview* (not italicized), and the date of the interview.

Ashdown, Audrey. Personal interview, 1 Jan. 2015.

For a published interview, list the name of the person interviewed and the title (if any), or if there is no title, use the label *Interview by [interviewer's name]* (not italicized); then add the publication information, including the URL if there is one.

Weddington, Sarah. "Sarah Weddington: Still Arguing for *Roe.*" Interview by Michele Kort, *Ms.,* Winter 2013, pp. 32–35.

Jaffrey, Madhur. "Madhur Jaffrey on How Indian Cuisine Won Western Taste Buds." Interview by Shadrach Kabango, *Q,* CBC Radio, 29 Oct. 2015, www.cbc.ca/1.3292918.

For a broadcast interview, list the name of the person interviewed, the label *Interview* (not italicized), and the name of the interviewer (if relevant); then list information about the program, the date of the interview, and the URL, if applicable.

Fairey, Shepard. "Spreading the Hope: Street Artist Shepard Fairey." Interview by Terry Gross, *Fresh Air,* National Public Radio, WBUR, Boston, 20 Jan. 2009.

Putin, Vladimir. Interview by Charlie Rose. *Charlie Rose: The Week,* PBS, 19 June 2015.

49. Letter

Treat a published letter like a work in an anthology, but include the date of the letter.

> Jacobs, Harriet. "To Amy Post." 4 Apr. 1853. *Incidents in the Life of a Slave Girl*, edited by Jean Fagan Yellin, Harvard UP, 1987, pp. 234–35.

50. Film

For films, ordinarily begin with the title, followed by the director and major performers. If your essay or project focuses on a major person related to the film, such as the director, you can begin with that name or names, followed by the title and performers.

> *Birdman* or (*The Unexpected Virtue of Ignorance*). Directed by Alejandro González Iñárritu, performances by Michael Keaton, Emma Stone, Zach Galifianakis, Edward Norton, and Naomi Watts, Fox Searchlight, 2014.

> Scott, Ridley, director. *The Martian*. Performances by Matt Damon, Jessica Chastain, Kristen Wiig, and Kate Mara, Twentieth Century Fox, 2015.

51. Television or Radio Program

> "Free Speech on College Campuses." *Washington Journal*, narrated by Peter Slen, C-SPAN, 27 Nov. 2015.

> "Take a Giant Step." *Prairie Home Companion*, narrated by Garrison Keillor, American Public Media, 27 Feb. 2016, prairiehome.publicradio.org/listen/full/?name=phc/2016/02/27/phc_20160227_128.

52. Online Video Clip

Cite a short online video as you would a work from a Web site (see item 31).

> Nayar, Vineet. "Employees First, Customers Second." *YouTube*, 9 June 2015, www.youtube.com/watch?v=cCdu67s_C5E.

53. Sound Recording

> Blige, Mary J. "Don't Mind." *Life II: The Journey Continues (Act 1)*, Geffen, 2011.

54. Work of Art or Photograph

List the artist or photographer; the work's title, italicized; and the date of composition. Then cite the name of the museum or other location and the city.

Bradford, Mark. *Let's Walk to the Middle of the Ocean*. 2015, Museum of Modern Art, New York.

Feinstein, Harold. *Hangin' Out, Sharing a Public Bench, NYC*. 1948, Panopticon Gallery, Boston.

To cite a reproduction in a book, add the publication information.

O'Keeffe, Georgia. *Black and Purple Petunias*. 1925, private collection. *Two Lives: A Conversation in Paintings and Photographs*, edited by Alexandra Arrowsmith and Thomas West, HarperCollins, 1992, p. 67.

To cite artwork found online, add the title of the database or Web site, italicized; and the URL of the site you accessed.

Clough, Charles. *January Twenty-First*. 1988–89, Joslyn Art Museum, Omaha, www.joslyn.org/collections-and-exhibitions/permanent-collections/modern-and-contemporary/charles-clough-january-twenty-first/.

55. Lecture or Speech

Smith, Anna Deavere. "On the Road: A Search for American Character." National Endowment for the Humanities, John F. Kennedy Center for the Performing Arts, Washington, 6 Apr. 2015. Address.

56. Performance

The Draft. By Peter Snoad, directed by Diego Arciniegas, Hibernian Hall, Boston, 10 Sept. 2015.

57. Map or Chart

"Map of Sudan." *Global Citizen*, Citizens for Global Solutions, 2011, globalsolutions.org/blog/bashir#.VthzNMfi_FI.

58. Cartoon

Zyglis, Adam. "City of Light." *Buffalo News*, 8 Nov. 2015, adamzyglis.buffalonews.com/2015/11/08/city-of-light/. Cartoon.

59. Advertisement

Banana Republic. *Wired,* Sept. 2009, p. 13. Advertisement.

On p. 604, note the formatting of the first page of a sample essay written in MLA style. On p. 606, you'll find a sample works cited page written for the same student essay.

Sample First Page for an Essay in MLA Style

Author name and page number in upper right corner of each page

Emily Lesk
Professor Arraéz
Electric Rhetoric
15 November 2014

Name, instructor, course, date aligned at left

Title centered

Red, White, and Everywhere

America, I have a confession to make: I don't drink Coke. But don't call me a hypocrite just because I am still the proud owner of a bright red shirt that advertises it. Just call me an American. Even before setting foot in Israel three years ago, I knew exactly where I could find one. The tiny T-shirt shop in the central block of Jerusalem's Ben Yehuda Street did offer other designs, but the one with a bright white "Drink Coca-Cola Classic" written in Hebrew cursive across the chest was what drew in most of the dollar-carrying tourists.

Figure number and caption noting the source of the photo

Fig. 1. *Hebrew Coca-Cola T-shirt*. Personal photograph. Despite my dislike for the beverage, I bought this Coca-Cola T-shirt in Israel.

While waiting almost twenty minutes for my shirt (depicted in fig. 1), I watched nearly every customer ahead of me ask for "the Coke shirt, *todah rabah* [thank you very much]."

At the time, I never thought it strange that I wanted one, too. After having absorbed sixteen years of Coca-Cola propaganda through everything from NBC's Saturday morning cartoon lineup to the concession stand at Camden Yards (the Baltimore Orioles' ballpark), I associated the shirt with singing along to the "Just for the Taste of It" jingle and with America's favorite pastime, not with a brown fizzy beverage I refused to consume.

Heading centered

Works Cited

Coca-Cola Santa pin. Personal photograph by the author, 9 Nov. 2008.

"The Fabulous Fifties." *Beverage Industry,* vol. 87, no. 6, 1996, p. 16. *General OneFile,* go.galegroup.com/.

"Fifty Years of Coca-Cola Television Advertisements." *American Memory.* Motion Picture, Broadcasting and Recorded Sound Division, Library of Congress, memory.loc.gov/ammem/ ccmphtml/colahome.html. Accessed 5 Nov. 2014.

"Haddon Sundblom and Coca-Cola." *Thehistoryofchristmas.com,* 10 Holidays, 2004, www.thehistoryofchristmas.com/ sc/coca_cola.htm.

Hebrew Coca-Cola T-shirt. Personal photograph by the author, 8 Nov. 2014.

Ikuta, Yasutoshi, editor. *'50s American Magazine Ads.* Graphic-Sha, 1987.

Pendergrast, Mark. *For God, Country, and Coca-Cola: The Definitive History of the Great American Soft Drink and the Company That Makes It.* 2nd ed., Basic Books, 2000.

Subsequent lines of each entry indented

List is alphabetized by authors' last names (or by title when there is no author)

APA Style

The *Publication Manual of the American Psychological Association* (6th edition, 2010) provides comprehensive advice to student and professional writers in the social sciences. Here we draw on the *Publication Manual's* guidelines to provide an overview of APA style for in-text citations, content notes, and entries in the list of references.

In-Text Citations

APA style calls for in-text citations in the body of an argument to document sources of quotations, paraphrases, summaries, and so on. These in-text citations correspond to full bibliographic entries in the list of references at the end of the text.

1. **Author Named in a Signal Phrase**

   Generally, give the author's name in a signal phrase to introduce the cited material, using the past tense for the signal verb. Place the date, in parentheses, immediately after the author's name. For a quotation, the page number, preceded by *p.* (not italicized), appears in parentheses after the quotation. For electronic texts or other works without page numbers, paragraph numbers may be used instead, preceded by the abbreviation *para.* For a long, set-off quotation, position the page reference in parentheses one space after the punctuation at the end of the quotation.

   According to Brandon (1993), Adefunmi opposed all forms of racism and believed that black nationalism should not be a destructive force (p. 29).

   As Johnson (2005) demonstrated, contemporary television dramas such as *ER* and *Lost* are not only more complex than earlier programs but "possess a quality that can only be described as subtlety and discretion" (p. 83).

2. **Author Named in Parentheses**

   When you don't mention the author in a signal phrase, give the name and the date, separated by a comma, in parentheses at the end of the cited material.

   The Sopranos has achieved a much wider viewing audience than ever expected, spawning a cookbook and several serious scholarly studies (Franklin, 2002).

3. Two Authors

Use both names in all citations. Use *and* in a signal phrase, but use an ampersand (&) in parentheses.

Associated with purity and wisdom, Obatala is the creator of human beings, whom he is said to have formed out of clay (Edwards & Mason, 1985).

4. Three to Five Authors

List all the authors' names for the first reference. In subsequent references, use just the first author's name followed by *et al.* (in regular type, not underlined or italicized).

Lenhoff, Wang, Greenberg, and Bellugi (1997) cited tests that indicate that segments of the left brain hemisphere are not affected by Williams syndrome, whereas the right hemisphere is significantly affected (p. 1641).

Shackelford (1999) drew on the study by Lenhoff et al. (1997).

5. Six or More Authors

Use only the first author's name and *et al.* (in regular type, not underlined or italicized) in every citation, including the first.

As Flower et al. (2003) demonstrated, reading and writing involve both cognitive and social processes.

6. Organization as Author

If the name of an organization or a corporation is long, spell it out the first time, followed by an abbreviation in brackets. In later citations, use the abbreviation only.

First Citation   (Federal Bureau of Investigation [FBI], 2002)

Subsequent Citations (FBI, 2002)

7. Unknown Author

Use the title or its first few words in a signal phrase or in parentheses. (In the example below, a book's title is italicized.)

The school profiles for the county substantiate this trend (*Guide to secondary schools*, 2003).

8. Authors with the Same Last Name

If your list of references includes works by different authors with the same last name, include the authors' initials in each citation.

G. Jones (1998) conducted the groundbreaking study of retroviruses, whereas P. Jones (2000) replicated the initial trials two years later.

9. Two or More Sources in the Same Citation

List sources by the same author chronologically by publication year. List sources by different authors in alphabetical order by the authors' last names, separated by semicolons.

While traditional forms of argument are warlike and agonistic, alternative models do exist (Foss & Foss, 1997; Makau, 1999).

10. Specific Parts of a Source

Use abbreviations (*p.*, *pt.*, and so on) in a parenthetical citation to name the part of a work you're citing. However, *chapter* is not abbreviated.

Pinker (2003) argued that his research yielded the opposite results (p. 6).

Pinker (2003) argued that his research yielded the opposite results (Chapter 6).

11. Online Document

To cite a source found on the Internet, use the author's name and date as you would for a print source, and indicate the chapter or figure of the document, as appropriate. If the source's publication date is unknown, use *n.d.* ("no date"). To document a quotation, include paragraph numbers if page numbers are unavailable. If an online document has no page or paragraph numbers, provide the heading of the section and the number of the paragraph that follows.

Werbach (2002) argued convincingly that "despite the best efforts of legislators, lawyers, and computer programmers, spam has won. Spam is killing email" (p. 1).

12. Email and Other Personal Communication

Cite any personal letters, email messages, electronic postings, telephone conversations, or personal interviews by giving the person's initial(s) and last name, the identification, and the date. Do not list email in the references list, and note that APA style uses a hyphen in the word *e-mail*.

E. Ashdown (personal communication, March 9, 2015) supported these claims.

Content Notes

The APA recommends using content notes for material that will expand or supplement your argument but otherwise would interrupt the text. Indicate such notes in your text by inserting superscript numerals. Type the notes themselves either at the bottom of the page or on a separate page headed *Footnotes* (not italicized or in quotation marks), centered at the top of the page. Double-space all entries. Indent the first line of each note one-half inch or five spaces, and begin subsequent lines at the left margin.

Text with Superscript Indicating a Note

Data related to children's preferences in books were instrumental in designing the questionnaire.[1]

Note

[1]Rudine Sims Bishop and members of the Reading Readiness Research Group provided helpful data.

List of References

The alphabetical list of sources cited in your text is called *References*. (If your instructor asks you to list everything you've read as background—not just the sources you cite—call the list *Bibliography*.) The list of references appears on a separate page or pages at the end of your paper, with the heading *References* (not underlined, italicized, or in quotation marks) centered one inch from the top of the page. Double-space after the heading, and begin your first entry. Double-space the entire list. For print sources, APA style specifies the treatment and placement of four basic elements: author, publication date, title, and publication information. Each element is followed by a period.

- **Author:** List all authors with last name first, and use only initials for first and middle names. Separate the names of multiple authors with commas, and use an ampersand (&) before the last author's name.

- **Publication date:** Enclose the publication date in parentheses. Use only the year for books and journals; use the year, a comma, and the month or month and day for magazines and newspapers. Do not abbreviate the month. If a date is not given, put *n.d.* ("no date," not italicized) in the parentheses. Put a period after the parentheses.

- **Title:** Italicize titles and subtitles of books and periodicals. Do not enclose titles of articles in quotation marks. For books and articles, capitalize only the first word of the title and subtitle and any proper nouns or proper adjectives; also capitalize the first word following a colon. Capitalize all major words in the title of a periodical.

- **Publication information:** For a book published in the United States, list the city of publication and state abbreviation. For books published outside the United States, identify the city and country. Provide the publisher's name, dropping *Inc.*, *Co.*, or *Publishers*. If the state is already included within the publisher's name, do not include the postal abbreviation for the state. For a periodical, follow the periodical title with a comma, the volume number (italicized), the issue number (if provided) in parentheses and followed by a comma, and the inclusive page numbers of the article. For newspaper articles and for articles or chapters in books, include the abbreviation *p.* ("page") or *pp.* ("pages").

The following APA style examples appear in a "hanging indent" format, in which the first line aligns on the left and the subsequent lines indent one-half inch or five spaces.

Print Books

1. One Author
   Fraser, S. (2015). *The age of acquiescence: The life and death of American resistance to organized wealth and power.* New York, NY: Little, Brown.

2. Two or More Authors
   Steininger, M., Newell, J. D., & Garcia, L. (1984). *Ethical issues in psychology.* Homewood, IL: Dow Jones-Irwin.

3. Organization as Author
   Use the word *Author* (not italicized) as the publisher when the organization is both the author and the publisher.

   Linguistics Society of America. (2002). *Guidelines for using sign language interpreters.* Washington, DC: Author.

4. Unknown Author
   National Geographic atlas of the world. (2010). Washington, DC: National Geographic Society.

5. Book Prepared by an Editor
   Hardy, H. H. (Ed.). (1998). *The proper study of mankind.* New York, NY: Farrar, Straus.

6. Selection in a Book with an Editor

    Villanueva, V. (1999). An introduction to social scientific discussions on class. In A. Shepard, J. McMillan, & G. Tate (Eds.), *Coming to class: Pedagogy and the social class of teachers* (pp. 262–277). Portsmouth, NH: Heinemann.

7. Translation

    Pérez-Reverte, A. (2002). *The nautical chart* (M. S. Peden, Trans.). New York, NY: Harvest. (Original work published 2000)

8. Edition Other Than the First

    Bok, D. (2015). *Higher education in America* (Rev. ed.). Princeton, NJ: Princeton University Press.

9. One Volume of a Multivolume Work

    Will, J. S. (1921). *Protestantism in France* (Vol. 2). Toronto, Canada: University of Toronto Press.

10. Article in a Reference Work

    Chernow, B., & Vattasi, G. (Eds.). (1993). Psychomimetic drug. In *The Columbia encyclopedia* (5th ed., p. 2238). New York, NY: Columbia University Press.

    If no author is listed, begin with the article title, followed by the year, and the rest of the citation as shown here.

11. Republication

    Sharp, C. (1978). *History of Hartlepool.* Hartlepool, United Kingdom: Hartlepool Borough Council. (Original work published 1816)

12. Graphic Narrative

    If the words and images are created by the same person, cite a graphic narrative just as you would a book with one author (see item 1 on p. 611).

    Bechdel, A. (2012). *Are you my mother?* New York, NY: Houghton Mifflin Harcourt.

    If the work is a collaboration, indicate the author or illustrator who is most important to your research, followed by other contributors in order of their appearance on the title page. Label each person's contribution to the work.

    Stavans, I. (Writer), & Arcaraz, L. (Illustrator). (2000). *Latino USA: A cartoon history.* New York, NY: Basic.

13. Government Document

> U.S. Bureau of the Census. (2001). *Survey of women-owned business enterprises.* Washington, DC: Government Printing Office.

14. Two or More Works by the Same Author

List the works in chronological order of publication. Repeat the author's name in each entry.

> Lowin, S. (2006). *The making of a forefather: Abraham in Islamic and Jewish exegetical narratives.* Leiden, The Netherlands: Brill.

> Lowin, S. (2013). *Arabic and Hebrew love poems in Al-Andalus.* New York, NY: Routledge.

Print Periodicals

15. Article in a Journal Paginated by Volume

> Bowen, L. M. (2011). Resisting age bias in digital literacy research. *College Composition and Communication, 62,* 586–607.

16. Article in a Journal Paginated by Issue

> Carr, S. (2002). The circulation of Blair's Lectures. *Rhetoric Society Quarterly, 32*(4), 75–104.

17. Article in a Monthly Magazine

> Baker, C. (2008, September). Master of the universe. *Wired, 16*(9), 134–141.

18. Article in a Newspaper

> Nagourney, A. (2002, December 16). Gore rules out running in '04. *The New York Times,* pp. A1, A8.

19. Letter to the Editor or Editorial

> Erbeta, R. (2008, December). Swiftboating George [Letter to the editor]. *Smithsonian, 39*(9), 10.

20. Unsigned Article

> Guidelines issued on assisted suicide. (1998, March 4). *The New York Times,* p. A15.

21. Review

> Avalona, A. (2008, August). [Review of the book *Weaving women's lives: Three generations in a Navajo family,* by L. Lamphere]. *New Mexico, 86*(8), 40.

22. **Published Interview**

Shor, I. (1997). [Interview with A. Greenbaum]. *Writing on the Edge,*
8(2), 7–20.

23. **Two or More Works by the Same Author in the Same Year**

List two or more works by the same author published in the same year
alphabetically by title (excluding *A*, *An*, or *The*), and place lowercase
letters (*a*, *b*, etc.) after the dates.

Murray, F. B. (1983a). Equilibration as cognitive conflict. *Develop-*
mental Review, 3, 54–61.

Murray, F. B. (1983b). Learning and development through social
interaction. In L. Liben (Ed.), *Piaget and the foundations of*
knowledge (pp. 176–201). Hillsdale, NJ: Erlbaum.

Digital Sources

The following models are based on the APA's *Publication Manual* (6th edition). A change for handling electronic sources involves the use of a digital
object identifier (DOI) when available (instead of a URL) to locate an
electronic source. The DOI is a unique number assigned to an electronic
text (article, book, or other item) and intended to give reliable access to it.
A second change is that a date of retrieval is no longer necessary unless a
source changes very frequently. The basic APA entry for most electronic
sources should include the following elements:

- name of the author, editor, or compiler

- date of electronic publication or most recent update

- title of the work, document, or posting

- publication information, including the title, volume or issue number,
  and page numbers

- the DOI (digital object identifier) of the document, if one is available

- a URL, only if a DOI is not available, with no angle brackets and no
  closing punctuation

24. **Web Site**

To cite a whole site, give the address in a parenthetical reference. To
cite a document from a Web site, include information as you would

for a print document, followed by a note on its retrieval. Provide a date of retrieval only if the information is likely to change frequently.

American Psychological Association. (2013). Making stepfamilies work. Retrieved from http://www.apa.org/helpcenter/stepfamily. aspx

Mullins, B. (1995). Introduction to Robert Hass. Readings in contemporary poetry at Dia Center for the Arts. Retrieved from http://www.diacenter.org/prg/poetry/95_96/intrhass.html

25. Article from a Periodical on the Web
For an article you read online, provide either the URL of the periodical's homepage, preceded by Retrieved from (not italicized) or a DOI.

Haines, R. (2015, February 27). The problem with separate toys for boys and girls. *The Boston Globe. Retrieved from* http://www. bostonglobe.com

Lambert, N. M., Graham, S. M., & Fincham, F. D. (2009). A prototype analysis of gratitude: Varieties of gratitude experiences. *Personality and Social Psychology Bulletin, 35*, 1193–1207. doi:10.1177/0146167209338071

26. Article or Abstract from a Database
For an article you find on a database, provide a DOI if one is available. If the online article does not have a DOI, locate the homepage for the journal in which the article appears and provide that URL. You need not identify the database you have used.

Strully, K. (2014). Racially and ethnically diverse schools and adolescent romantic relationships. *American Journal of Sociology, 120*(3), 750–757. doi:10.1086/679190

Hayhoe, G. (2001). The long and winding road: Technology's future. *Technical Communication, 48*(2), 133–145. Retrieved from techcomm.stc.org

27. Software or Computer Program
OS X Lion (Version 10.7) [Computer operating system]. (2011). Cupertino, CA: Apple.

28. Online Government Document
Cite an online government document as you would a printed government work, adding the URL. Note that the APA spells website as one word.

Finn, J. D. (1998, April). *Class size and students at risk: What is known? What is next?* Retrieved from United States Department of Education website: http://www.ed.gov/pubs/ClassSize/title.htmlhtml

29. **Entry in a Web Reference Work**

    Cite the entry as you would an entry from a print reference work (see item 10). Follow with the date of publication, the name of the Web site, and the URL.

    Tour de France. (2006). In *Encyclopaedia Britannica Online*. Retrieved from http://www.britannica.com/EBchecked/topic/600732/Tour-de-France

30. **Posting or Comment on a Web Site**

    Begin with the author's name; the date of the most recent update; the title of the posting (if there is no title, use the description *Blog post* or *Blog comment*, not italicized); the name of the blog, italicized, and the URL.

    Marcotte, A. (2012). Rights without perfection. *Pandagon*. Retrieved from http://www.rawstory.com/rs/2010/05/pandagon-rights_without_perfection/

31. **Entry in a Wiki**

    Since wikis are collectively edited, do not include an author. Include the title of the entry; the date of the latest update; the name of the wiki, italicized; and the URL of the source.

    Fédération Internationale de Football Association. (2014). In *Wikipedia*. Retrieved May 11, 2014 from http://en.wikipedia.org/wiki/FIFA

32. **Posting on a Social Networking Site**

    To cite a posting on Facebook or another social networking site, include the writer's name, the date of the post, a description of the item in brackets, and the URL of the source.

    Ferguson, S. (2014, March 6). Status update [Facebook post]. Retrieved from https://www.facebook.com/sarah.ferguson?fref=nf

33. **Posting on a Public Facebook Page**

    When citing a posting on a public Facebook page or another social networking site that is visible to anyone, include the writer's name as it appears in the post. Give a few words from the post, and add an identifying label. Include the date you retrieved the post and the URL for the public page. Do not include a page on the list of references if your readers will not be able to access the source; instead, cite it as a personal communication in the text.

American Psychological Association (2014, April 24). Why do many people do their best thinking while walking? [Facebook post]. Retrieved April 24, 2014, from https://www.facebook.com/AmericanPsychologicalAssociation

34. Tweet

Include the writer's Twitter handle; the date of the tweet; the entire text of the tweet with no end punctuation, followed by *Tweet* in brackets; the words *Retrieved from*; and the full Twitter account URL with no end punctuation.

Aalrhetorician. (2014, August 27). Just read (again) about demise of the apostrophe. Argument getting a bit old [Tweet]. Retrieved from https://twitter.com/aalrhetorician

35. Newsgroup Posting

Include the author's name, the date and subject line of the posting, and the name of the newsgroup.

Wittenberg, E. (2001, July 11). Gender and the Internet [Msg 4]. Retrieved from news://comp.edu.composition

36. Email Message or Synchronous Communication

Because the APA stresses that any sources cited in your list of references must be retrievable by your readers, you shouldn't include entries for email messages or synchronous communications (MOOs, MUDs); instead, cite these sources in your text as forms of personal communication (see item 12 on p. 609). And remember that you shouldn't quote from other people's email without asking their permission to do so.

Other Sources

37. Technical or Research Reports and Working Papers

Kinley-Horn and Associates. (2011). *ADOT bicycle safety action plan* (Working Paper No. 3). Phoenix: Arizona Department of Transportation.

38. Unpublished Paper Presented at a Meeting or Symposium

Welch, K. (2002, March). *Electric rhetoric and screen literacy*. Paper presented at the meeting of the Conference on College Composition and Communication, Chicago, IL.

39. Unpublished Dissertation

Seward, D. E. (2008). *Civil voice in Elizabethan parliamentary oratory: The rhetoric and composition of speeches delivered at Westminster in 1566* (Unpublished doctoral dissertation). University of Texas at Austin, Austin, TX.

40. Poster Session

Mensching, G. (2002, May). *A simple, effective one-shot for disinterested students*. Poster session presented at the National LOEX Library Instruction Conference, Ann Arbor, MI.

41. Motion Picture, Video, or DVD

Bigelow, K. (Director). (2009). *The hurt locker* [Motion picture]. United States: Summit Entertainment.

42. Television Program, Single Episode

Burnett, A. (Writer), & Attias, D. (Director). (2014, March 26). The deal [Television series episode]. In J. Weisberg (Executive producer), *The Americans*. Los Angeles, CA: DreamWorks Television.

43. Online Video Clip

Weber, J. (2012). *As we sow, part I: Where are the farmers?* [Video file]. Retrieved from http://www.youtube.com/watch?v=_cdcDpM-f6qE

44. Sound Recording

Begin with the writer's name, followed by the date of copyright. Give the recording date at the end of the entry (in parentheses, after the period) if it's different from the copyright date.

Ivey, A., Jr., & Sall, R. (1995). Rollin' with my homies [Recorded by Coolio]. On *Clueless* [CD]. Hollywood, CA: Capitol Records.

Sample Title Page for an Essay in APA Style

Running Head: MOOD MUSIC   1

Running head (fifty characters or fewer) appears flush left on first line of title page

Page number appears flush right on first line of every page

Mood Music: Music Preference and
the Risk for Depression and Suicide
in Adolescents

Tawnya Redding

Oregon State University

Title, name, and affiliation centered and double-spaced

Author Note

This paper was prepared for Psychology
480, taught by Professor Ede.

Sample First Text Page for an Essay in APA Style

Full title centered

Mood Music: Music Preference and the Risk
for Depression and Suicide in Adolescents

Paragraphs indented

Music is a significant part of American culture. Since the explosion of rock and roll in the 1950s, there has been a concern for the effects that music may have on listeners, and especially on young people. The genres most likely to come under suspicion in recent decades have included heavy metal, country, and blues. These genres have been suspected of having adverse effects on the mood and behavior of young listeners. But can music really alter the disposition and create self-destructive behaviors in listeners? And if so, which genres and aspects of those genres are responsible? The following review of the literature will establish the correlation between potentially problematic genres of music such as heavy metal and country and depression and suicide risk. First, correlational studies concerning music preference and suicide risk will be discussed, followed by a discussion of the literature concerning the possible reasons for this link. Finally, studies concerning the effects of music on mood will be discussed.

Despite the link between genres such as heavy metal and country and suicide risk, previous research has been unable to establish the causal nature of this link.

The Correlation Between Music and Depression and Suicide Risk

A large portion of studies over the past two decades have focused on heavy metal and country music as the main genre culprits associated with youth suicidality and depression (Lacourse, Claes, & Villeneuve, 2001; Scheel & Westefeld, 1999; Stack & Gundlach, 1992). Stack and Gundlach (1992) examined the radio airtime devoted to country music in 49 metropolitan areas and found that the

Boldface headings help organize review

Parenthetical references follow APA style

Sample References List for an Essay in APA Style

References begin on new page

Heading is centered

References

Baker, F., & Bor, W. (2008). Can music preference indicate mental health status in young people? *Australasian Psychiatry, 16*(4), 284–288. Retrieved from http://www3.interscience.wiley.com/journal/118565538/home

George, D., Stickle, K., Rachid, F., & Wopnford, A. (2007). The association between types of music enjoyed and cognitive, behavioral, and personality factors of those who listen. *Psychomusicology, 19*(2), 32–56.

Lacourse, E., Claes, M., & Villeneuve, M. (2001). Heavy metal music and adolescent suicidal risk. *Journal of Youth and Adolescence, 30*(3), 321–332.

Lai, Y. (1999). Effects of music listening on depressed women in Taiwan. *Issues in Mental Health Nursing, 20,* 229–246. doi:10.1080/016128499248637

Martin, G., Clark, M., & Pearce, C. (1993). Adolescent suicide: Music preference as an indicator of vulnerability. *Journal of the American Academy of Child and Adolescent Psychiatry, 32,* 530–535.

Scheel, K., & Westefeld, J. (1999). Heavy metal music and adolescent suicidality: An empirical investigation. *Adolescence, 34*(134), 253–273.

RESPOND

1. The MLA and APA styles differ in several important ways, both for in-text citations and for lists of sources. You've probably noticed a few: the APA uses lowercase letters for most words in titles and lists the publication date right after the author's name, whereas the MLA capitalizes most words and puts the publication date at the end of the works cited entry. More interesting than the details, though, is the reasoning behind the differences. Placing the publication date near the front of a citation, for instance, reveals a special concern for that information in the APA style. Similarly, the MLA's decision to capitalize titles isn't arbitrary: that style is preferred in the humanities for a reason. Working in a group, find as many consistent differences between the MLA and APA styles as you can. Then, for each difference, speculate about the reasons these groups organize or present information in that way. The MLA and APA style manuals themselves may be of help. You might also begin by determining which academic disciplines subscribe to the APA style and which to the MLA.

2. Working with another person in your class, look for examples of the following sources: an article in a journal, a book, a film, a song, and a TV show. Then make a references page or works cited list (five entries in all), using either MLA or APA style.

Acknowledgements

Doug Bandow. "A New Military Draft Would Revive a Very Bad Old Idea" from *Forbes*, July 16, 2012, copyright © 2012 by Forbes LLC. All rights reserved. Used by permission and protected by the Copyright Laws of the United States. The printing, copying, redistribution, or retransmission of this Content without express written permission is prohibited.

Sara Barbour. From "Kindle vs. Books: The Dead Trees Society," first published in the *Los Angeles Times,* June 17, 2011. Reprinted by permission of the author.

David Brooks. "It's Not about You" from the *New York Times*, May 31, 2011. Copyright © 2011 by The New York Times. All rights reserved. Used by permission and protected by the Copyright Laws of the United States. The printing, copying, redistribution, or retransmission of this Content without express written permission is prohibited.

Edye Deloch-Hughes. From "So God Made a Black Farmer Too," reprinted by permission of the author. http://eldhughes.com/2013/02/05/so-god-made-a-farmer-dodge-ram/

Roger Ebert. From a review of Toy Story (1995). Used by permission of Ebert Digital, LLC.

Neil Irwin. "What the Numbers Show about N.F.L. Player Arrests" from the *New York Times*, September 13, 2014. Copyright © 2014 by The New York Times. All rights reserved. Used by permission and protected by the Copyright Laws of the United States. The printing, copying, redistribution, or retransmission of this Content without express written permission is prohibited.

Raven Jiang. "Dota 2: The Face of Professional Gaming" from the *Stanford Daily*, August 5, 2014, is reprinted by permission of the *Stanford Daily* and Raven Jiang.

Joyce Xinran Liu. "Friending: The Changing Definition of Friendship in the Social Media Era" by Joyce Xinran Liu, from *Vitamin IMC*, March 6, 2014. Reprinted by permission of the author.

Walter Russell Mead. From "It All Begins with Football," first published in the *American Interest*, December 4, 2011. Reprinted by permission of the author.

Trade
Excerpts

bell hooks
Claudia Rankine
Susan Sontag
Naomi Klein
Colin Beavan
Bill McKibben
Andrew Helfer

27

Refusing to Be a Victim

Accountability and Responsibility

bell hooks

When *Feminist Theory: From Margin to Center* was published in 1984, I urged women engaged in feminist movement to beware of embracing a mantle of victimization in our quest to draw public attention to the need to end sexism and sexist exploitation and oppression. Critiquing a vision of sisterhood rooted in "shared victimization" I encouraged women to bond on the basis of political solidarity. It seemed ironic to me that white women who talked the most about being victims as I wrote then "were more privileged and powerful than the vast majority of women in our society." And if shared victimhood was the reason to be feminist then women who were empowered, who were not victims, would not embrace feminism. My repudiation of the victim identity emerged out of my awareness of the way in which thinking of oneself as a victim could be disempowering and disenabling.

Coming to womanhood in the segregated South, I had never heard black women talk about themselves as victims. Facing hardship, the ravages of economic lack and deprivation, the cruel injustice of racial apartheid, I lived in a world where women gained strength by sharing knowledge and resources, not by bonding on the basis of being victims. Despite the incredible pain of living in racial apartheid, southern black people did not speak about ourselves as victims even when we were downtrodden. We identified ourselves more by the experience of resistance and triumph than by the nature of our victimization. It was a given that life was hard, that there was suffering. It was by facing that suffering with grace and dignity that one experienced transformation. During civil rights struggle, when we joined hands to sing "we shall overcome," we were empowered by a vision of fulfillment, of victory. Much of the awareness that I brought to feminist struggle about the danger of identifying with victimhood was knowledge that came from the oppositional life practices of black folks in the segregated South. When I cautioned women involved in feminist movement to beware of embracing a victim identity, I was confident that black people active in liberation struggle already possessed this awareness. And yet by the end of the eighties black folks were more and more talking about victimhood, claiming a victim identity. Suddenly, individual black critics were raising a public voice cautioning black folks about the danger of embracing victimhood. One such thinker was Shelby Steele. His essays *The Content of Our Character* were published with a cover heading that stated he was presenting "a new vision of race in America." This vision was simple. It called for a repudiation of the rhetoric of victimhood.

Most black Americans were in agreement with Steele's assertion that to claim victimhood in an absolutist way was dangerously disempowering. However, his demand that we repudiate a victim identity was undermined by his insistence that racist aggression was no longer a threat to the well-being of black folks. This line of argument seemed to be opportunistically directed at white readers; it was such an utterly unsubstantiated claim. Practically all African Americans experience some degree of racist harassment in this society, however relative, on a daily basis. Steele's will to deny this reality was linked to his refusal to call attention to the ways white Americans are responsible for perpetuating and maintaining white supremacy. By not calling attention to white accountability, he implied that black folks must assume sole responsibility for the task of ending racism, of repudiating the victim identity. This seemed ironic given the reality that it was precisely the collective white repudiation of militant black resistance to racism that lay the groundwork for an emphasis on victimhood.

The word "victim" does not appear in the vast majority of resistance writing from the civil rights era. Yet as early as 1965 Martin Luther King Jr. was sharing the insight that the demand for a "realization of equality" was not being heard by whites. In *Where Do We Go from Here* King identified a growing feeling of disempowerment signaled by white backlash against the gains of the civil rights movement:

> The Negroes of America had taken the president, the press and the pulpit at their word when they spoke in broad terms of freedom and justice. But the absence of brutality and unregenerate evil is not the presence of justice. To stay murder is not the same thing as to ordain brotherhood. The word was broken, and the free-running expectations of the Negro crashed into the stone walls of white resistance. The result was havoc. Negroes felt cheated, especially in the North, while many whites felt that the Negroes had gained so much it was virtually impudent and greedy to ask for more so soon.

Militant resistance to white supremacy frightened white Americans, even those liberals and radicals who were committed to the struggle to end racial discrimination. There was a great difference between a civil rights struggle that worked primarily to end discrimination and radical commitment to black self-determination. Ironically, many whites who had struggled side by side with black folks responded positively to images of black victimization. Many whites testified that they looked upon the suffering of black people in the segregated South and were moved to work for change. The image of blacks as victims had an accepted place in the consciousness of

every white person; it was the image of black folks as equals, as self-determining that had no place—that could evoke no sympathetic response. In complicity with the nation-state, all white Americans responded to black militancy by passively accepting the disruption of militant black organizations and the slaughter of black leaders.

In the wake of militant calls for black self-determination, privileged-class white women, many of whom had been active in civil rights struggle, began to organize women's liberation movement. Drawing on the rhetoric of black freedom struggle, these groups of women (not all of whom were white and privileged) found that it was useful to embrace a victim identity. Without witnessing the assassination of any of the leaders of feminist movement, without any police brutality, without a mass movement for social justice, white women were able to collectively redress wrongs enacted by a system of gender discrimination. The rhetoric of victimhood worked for white women. In the wake of feminist movement white women were suddenly receiving gains in the workforce. They were primary recipients of rewards from affirmative action. By the eighties white women had made greater gains in the short space of ten years than black women *and* men had made over decades of struggle. Those black males who were convinced that patriarchy should have allowed them to gain greater rights than white women were the most angered by the way the struggle for women's liberation was actually most successful when the focus was on gaining greater access to mainstream, traditionally white male-dominated spheres of power. This rage did not keep black males from deploying a similar rhetoric in the competition for favors and reparations from the white male power structure. White women active in contemporary feminist movement often behaved as did their nineteenth-century counterparts who when struggling for the vote were quite willing to evoke white supremacy as that structure of bonding that should lead white men to give them rights and privileges before extending them to black males.

When the rare white woman feminist of the early seventies wrote about racial hierarchy she usually did so to draw attention to her closeness to the white male power structure, to show the way she had been wronged. In 1970 Shulamith Firestone published *The Dialectic of Sex: The Case for Feminist Revolution* in which she argued that "racism is sexism extended"—that "racism is a sexual phenomenon." Drawing on Freudian paradigms, Firestone, like other white women during this time, saw race relations solely in terms of hierarchical relations within the white nuclear family. Firestone unabashedly wrote:

The white man is father, the woman wife-and-mother, her status dependent on his; the blacks, like children, are his property, their physical differentiation branding them the subservient class, in the same way that children form so easily a distinguishable, servile class vis-à-vis adults. This power hierarchy created the psychology of racism, just as, in the nuclear family, it creates the psychology of sexism.

The flaw in Firestone's analysis was her refusal to see the way in which patriarchal thinking mediates racism to disrupt the model she outlines. Since at the time of her writing, black folks were indeed no longer property of white men but rather dependents, it would have been more accurate to see white women and black men as siblings engaged in a rivalry for the attention of the father, to consider the absence of the "mother" in patriarchal formations of power hierarchy. Certainly, black male and white female responses to the early stages of contemporary feminism made it clear that they saw themselves as rivals, competing to be included within the white male power structure. Black women were indeed outside the loop.

Just when black women active in feminist movement, like myself, were demanding that there be a re-visioning of feminist theory and practice that would repudiate the centrality of a focus on victimization, black males were appropriating the rhetoric of victimization to turn the spotlight back on themselves. Careful reading of the literature of black civil rights and black power struggle makes it clear that the emphasis in those movements was solidly on the gaining of rights and privileges for men—just as the early literature of feminist movement focused exclusively on calling attention to the needs of white women. To some extent the white dominated women's movement shifted the public gaze away from black men and focused it on individual white women who wanted equality with men of their class. Jockeying for white male attention, black male leaders emphasized victimization, particularly the pain they suffered as a result of white racist aggression. Like their white female counterparts, they deployed a rhetoric of victimization because it was less threatening to white males. To name white males as all-powerful victimizers was to pay homage to their power, to see them as possessing the cure for all that ails.

As the rhetoric of victimization became more commonplace, it appeared to be an accurate description of the state of black America after the powerful forces of white supremacy had suppressed militant resistance. Despair and feelings of hopelessness are central to the formation of a psychology of victimization. The assassination of revolutionary black male political leaders naturally created a climate of loss and chaos that was ripe for the

growth of feelings of disempowerment. Suddenly a spirit of resistance that had been grounded in an oppositional belief that white power was limited, that it could be challenged and transformed, had dissipated. In its place was a rhetoric that represented that structure as all-powerful, unchanging.

The black church has always been a place in the United States where African Americans have learned oppositional ways of thinking that enhance our capacity to survive and flourish. Black liberation theology always intervened in any tendency to elevate humans to the status of all-powerful beings. This insistence on the limitations of humans was crucial for black people suffering at the hands of white oppressors and/or exploiters. The assumption that their power was limited, subject to forces beyond control, even a belief in the miraculous, was an empowering worldview running counter to the teachings of white colonizing forces. As religion becomes less central to the lives of contemporary African Americans, particularly to youth, those forms of oppositional thinking are not taught. Without alternative belief systems black folks embrace the values of the existing system, which daily reinforce learned helplessness. Mass media continually bombard us with images of African Americans which spread the message that we are hopeless, trapped, unable to change our circumstances in meaningful ways. No wonder then that a generation of black folks who learn much of their knowledge of race and struggles to end racism from movies and television see themselves as victims. Or that they see the only way out of being a victim is to assume the role of victimizer. While Shelby Steele chastised black folks for accepting the equation of blackness as victimization—"to be black is to be a victim; therefore, not to be a victim is not to be black"—he does not examine white investment in this equation. Yet those black folks who embrace victim identity do so because they find it mediates relations with whites, that it is easier to make appeals that call for sympathy rather than redress and reparations. As long as white Americans are more willing to extend concern and care to black folks who have a "victim-focused black identity," a shift in paradigms will not take place.

In order not to identify as victims, black folks must create ways to highlight issues of accountability that accurately address both the nature of our victimization within white supremacist capitalist patriarchy and the nature of our complicity. When individual black people project a victim identity because it brings their concerns into greater visibility, they are acting in complicity with an assaultive structure of racist domination in which they invest in the absence of agency. To name oneself a victim is to deny agency.

As long as white Americans have difficulty coping with the assertion of agency and self-determination by individual or collective groups of black folks, victimization will continue to be the location of visibility.

All marginal groups in this society who suffer grave injustices, who are victimized by institutionalized systems of domination (race, class, gender, etc.), are faced with the peculiar dilemma of developing strategies that draw attention to one's plight in such a way that will merit regard and consideration without reinscribing a paradigm of victimization. When African Americans locate our concerns about racism and white supremacy within a discourse that centers around victimization, we may gain the attention of whites while surrendering a focus on self-determination. It is no accident that the voice that speaks loudest against the evocation of a framework of victimization is most often the one that focuses on the need for racial separatism, for black folks to assume total responsibility for improving our lot. Both discourses are totalizing. A renewed organized struggle for black self-determination is needed to shift the focus from a framework of victimization to one of accountability. For it is that discourse that allows African Americans to recognize our complicity, our need for an ongoing process of decolonization and radical politicization, while remaining steadfastly clear about the primary role the vast majority of white Americans play in perpetuating and maintaining white supremacy. Indeed, the very white folks who see black folks as scamming to get something for nothing via a public discourse of victimhood tend to resist divesting of that racist socialization that makes them more comfortable with black folks who are wounded. White folks who want all black Americans to repudiate a victim-focused identity must be prepared to engage in a subject-to-subject encounter with black folks who are self-determining. To embrace this shift would be to open up to the very vision of full racial equality which King found so many white Americans could not imagine. Those white Americans who are eager to live in a society that promotes and rewards racial equality must be willing to surrender outmoded perceptions of black neediness that socialize them to feel comfortable with us only when they are in a superior, caretaking role. Until masses of white Americans confront their obsessive need for a black victim who lacks the agency to call for an accounting that would really demand a shift in the structure of this society, the rhetoric of victimization will continue to flourish.

Black Americans who exploit the rhetoric of victimization do so not only because it grants them moral authority but because it provides a platform from which demands can be made that are not mutual. If only white folks need to change then black folks are not required to undergo processes of radical politicization. Ironically, many African Americans feel more victimized (even though our ancestors certainly suffered harsher repression and injustice) because there has been an increased level of expectation. Those black folks raised in the segregated South who were taught to expect only exploitation at the hands of whites were not disappointed or psychologically crushed by forms of social exclusion and discrimination that were deemed minor. Nowadays, most black folks are taught by the rhetoric of liberal democracy, coming to us all from mass media, that they can expect to be treated equally. When this does not happen a disenabling sense of powerlessness and helplessness surfaces. That sense of victimization is linked to higher levels of expectation. Recently, I was giving a talk at Harvard University about black rage at white supremacy. I was saddened by the number of black female graduate students in the audience who spoke at great length about the terrible hardships they faced. Acutely aware of the myriad ways racial victimization articulates itself, they expressed a victim-focused identity. Yet their sense of victimization seemed to be totally out of proportion to a larger reality. They saw themselves as victims because they had imagined they would be treated as equals and when this did not happen they lacked the inner resources to confront and cope effectively. Contrary to Shelby Steele's assertion that black folks "claim more racial victimization than we have actually endured," the specific incidences they named documented actual victimization. However, their inability to respond to racist aggression with militant resistance seemed to intensify the feeling of victimization. One student described being in a class on feminist theory where my work was read. She found in that work a space of recognition and support. Yet the day it was discussed in class the white woman professor declared that no one was really moved by my work, that I was too negative. Unwilling to assert her agency, her engagement with the text, this young black woman felt both silenced and victimized. She felt like dropping out of graduate school. Had she resisted in this classroom setting, she would not have felt victimized. Instead she felt her blackness devalued even as she surrendered her personal agency and with it a sense of personal integrity. While militant response might not have gained her rewards, it would have preserved her sense of self. Teaching in privileged white institutions, I constantly encounter black students who feel victimized, who do not contextualize racist aggression so that they distinguish between the pain of being not invited to a party or left out of a discussion from severe economic deprivation, lack of access to basic skills and resources, etc.

To counter the fixation on a rhetoric of victimhood, black folks must engage in a discourse of self-determination. That discourse need not be rooted in separatist movement but can be part of an inclusive struggle to end racist domination. Progressive struggle to end white supremacy recognizes the political importance of accountability and does not embrace the rhetoric of victimhood even as it vigilantly calls attention to actual victimization.

28

"I" from Citizen: An American Lyric

Claudia Rankine

When you are alone and too tired even to turn on any of your devices, you let yourself linger in a past stacked among your pillows. Usually you are nestled under blankets and the house is empty. Sometimes the moon is missing and beyond the windows the low, gray ceiling seems approachable. Its dark light dims in degrees depending on the density of clouds and you fall back into that which gets reconstructed as metaphor.

The route is often associative. You smell good. You are twelve attending Sts. Philip and James School on White Plains Road and the girl sitting in the seat behind asks you to lean to the right during exams so she can copy what you have written. Sister Evelyn is in the habit of taping the 100s and the failing grades to the coat closet doors. The girl is Catholic with waist-length brown hair. You can't remember her name: Mary? Catherine?

You never really speak except for the time she makes her request and later when she tells you you smell good and have features more like a white person. You assume she thinks she is thanking you for letting her cheat and feels better cheating from an almost white person.

Sister Evelyn never figures out your arrangement perhaps because you never turn around to copy Mary Catherine's answers. Sister Evelyn must think these two girls think a lot alike or she cares less about cheating and more about humiliation or she never actually saw you sitting there.

Certain moments send adrenaline to the heart, dry out the tongue, and clog the lungs. Like thunder they drown you in sound, no, like lightning they strike you across the larynx. Cough. After it happened I was at a loss for words. Haven't you said this yourself? Haven't you said this to a close friend who early in your friendship, when distracted, would call you by the name of her black housekeeper? You assumed you two were the only black people in her life. Eventually she stopped doing this, though she never acknowledged her slippage. And you never called her on it (why not?) and yet, you don't forget. If this were a domestic tragedy, and it might well be, this would be your fatal flaw—your memory, vessel of your feelings. Do you feel hurt because it's the "all black people look the same" moment, or because you are being confused with another after being so close to this other?

An unsettled feeling keeps the body front and center. The wrong words enter your day like a bad egg in your mouth and puke runs down your blouse, a dampness drawing your stomach in toward your rib cage. When you look around only you remain. Your own disgust at what you smell, what you feel, doesn't bring you to your feet, not right away, because gathering energy has become its own task, needing its own argument. You are reminded of a conversation you had recently, comparing the merits of sentences constructed implicitly with "yes, and" rather than "yes, but." You and your friend decided that "yes, and" attested to a life with no turn-off, no alternative routes: you pull yourself to standing, soon enough the blouse is rinsed, it's another week, the blouse is beneath your sweater, against your skin, and you smell good.

The rain this morning pours from the gutters and everywhere else it is lost in the trees. You need your glasses to single out what you know is there because doubt is inexorable; you put on your glasses. The trees, their bark, their leaves, even the dead ones, are more vibrant wet. Yes, and it's raining. Each moment is like this—before it can be known, categorized as similar to another thing and dismissed, it has to be experienced, it has to be seen. What did he just say? Did she really just say that? Did I hear what I think I heard? Did that just come out of my mouth, his mouth, your mouth? The moment stinks. Still you want to stop looking at the trees. You want to walk out and stand among them. And as light as the rain seems, it still rains down on you.

You are in the dark, in the car, watching the black-tarred street being swallowed by speed; he tells you his dean is making him hire a person of color when there are so many great writers out there.

You think maybe this is an experiment and you are being tested or retroactively insulted or you have done something that communicates this is an okay conversation to be having.

Why do you feel comfortable saying this to me? You wish the light would turn red or a police siren would go off so you could slam on the brakes, slam into the car ahead of you, fly forward so quickly both your faces would suddenly be exposed to the wind.

As usual you drive straight through the moment with the expected backing off of what was previously said. It is not only that confrontation is headache-producing; it is also that you have a destination that doesn't include acting like this moment isn't inhabitable, hasn't happened before, and the before isn't part of the now as the night darkens and the time shortens between where we are and where we are going.

When you arrive in your driveway and turn off the car, you remain behind the wheel another ten minutes. You fear the night is being locked in and coded on a cellular level and want time to function as a power wash. Sitting there staring at the closed garage door you are reminded that a

friend once told you there exists the medical term—John Henryism—for people exposed to stresses stemming from racism. They achieve themselves to death trying to dodge the buildup of erasure. Sherman James, the researcher who came up with the term, claimed the physiological costs were high. You hope by sitting in silence you are bucking the trend.

Because of your elite status from a year's worth of travel, you have already settled into your window seat on United Airlines, when the girl and her mother arrive at your row. The girl, looking over at you, tells her mother, these are our seats, but this is not what I expected. The mother's response is barely audible—I see, she says. I'll sit in the middle.

A woman you do not know wants to join you for lunch. You are visiting her campus. In the cafe you both order the Caesar salad. This overlap is not the beginning of anything because she immediately points out that she, her father, her grandfather, and you, all attended the same college. She wanted her son to go there as well, but because of affirmative action or minority something—she is not sure what they are calling it these days and weren't they supposed to get rid of it?—her son wasn't accepted. You are not sure if you are meant to apologize for this failure of your alma mater's legacy program; instead you ask where he ended up. The prestigious school she mentions doesn't seem to assuage her irritation. This exchange, in effect, ends your lunch. The salads arrive.

A friend argues that Americans battle between the "historical self" and the "self self." By this she means you mostly interact as friends with mutual interest and, for the most part, compatible personalities; however, sometimes your historical selves, her white self and your black self, or your white self and her black self, arrive with the full force of your American positioning. Then you are standing face-to-face in seconds that wipe the affable smiles right from your mouths. What did you say? Instantaneously your attachment seems fragile, tenuous, subject to any transgression of your historical self. And though your joined personal histories are supposed to save you from misunderstandings, they usually cause you to understand all too well what is meant.

You and your partner go to see the film *The House We Live In*. You ask a friend to pick up your child from school. On your way home your phone rings. Your neighbor tells you he is standing at his window watching a menacing black guy casing both your homes. The guy is walking back and forth talking to himself and seems disturbed.

You tell your neighbor that your friend, whom he has met, is babysitting. He says, no, it's not him. He's met your friend and this isn't that nice young man. Anyway, he wants you to know, he's called the police.

Your partner calls your friend and asks him if there's a guy walking back and forth in front of your home. Your friend says that if anyone were outside he would see him because he is standing outside. You hear the sirens through the speakerphone.

Your friend is speaking to your neighbor when you arrive home. The four police cars are gone. Your neighbor has apologized to your friend and is now apologizing to you. Feeling somewhat responsible for the actions of your neighbor, you clumsily tell your friend that the next time he wants to talk on the phone he should just go in the backyard. He looks at you a long minute before saying he can speak on the phone wherever he wants. Yes, of course, you say. Yes, of course.

When the stranger asks, Why do you care? you just stand there staring at him. He has just referred to the boisterous teenagers in Starbucks as niggers. Hey, I am standing right here, you responded, not necessarily expecting him to turn to you.

He is holding the lidded paper cup in one hand and a small paper bag in the other. They are just being kids. Come on, no need to get all KKK on them, you say.

Now there you go, he responds.

The people around you have turned away from their screens. The teenagers are on pause. There I go? you ask, feeling irritation begin to rain down. Yes, and something about hearing yourself repeating this stranger's accusation in a voice usually reserved for your partner makes you smile.

A man knocked over her son in the subway. You feel your own body wince. He's okay, but the son of a bitch kept walking. She says she grabbed the stranger's arm and told him to apologize: I told him to look at the boy and apologize. Yes, and you want it to stop, you want the child pushed to the ground to be seen, to be helped to his feet, to be brushed off by the person that did not see him, has never seen him, has perhaps never seen anyone who is not a reflection of himself.

The beautiful thing is that a group of men began to stand behind me like a fleet of bodyguards, she says, like newly found uncles and brothers.

The new therapist specializes in trauma counseling. You have only ever spoken on the phone. Her house has a side gate that leads to a back entrance she uses for patients. You walk down a path bordered on both sides with deer grass and rosemary to the gate, which turns out to be locked.

At the front door the bell is a small round disc that you press firmly. When the door finally opens, the woman standing there yells, at the top of her lungs, Get away from my house! What are you doing in my yard?

It's as if a wounded Doberman pinscher or a German shepherd has gained the power of speech. And though you back up a few steps, you manage to tell her you have an appointment. You have an appointment? she spits back. Then she pauses. Everything pauses. Oh, she says, followed by, oh, yes, that's right. I am sorry.

I am so sorry, so, so sorry.

29

Selections from "AIDS and Its Metaphors"

Susan Sontag

Selections from *AIDS and Its Metaphors*

Susan Sontag

Copyright © 1988, 1989 by Susan Sontag

1

Two diseases have been spectacularly, and similarly, encumbered by the trappings of metaphor: tuberculosis and cancer.

The fantasies inspired by TB in the last century, by cancer now, are responses to a disease thought to be intractable and capricious—that is, a disease not understood—in an era in which medicine's central premise is that all diseases can be cured. Such a disease is, by definition, mysterious. For as long as its cause was not understood and the ministrations of doctors remained so ineffective, TB was thought to be an insidious, implacable theft of a life. Now it is cancer's turn to be the disease that doesn't knock before it enters, cancer that fills the role of an illness experienced as a ruthless, secret invasion—a role it will keep until, one day, its etiology becomes as clear and its treatment as effective as those of TB have become.

Although the way in which disease mystifies is set against a backdrop of new expectations, the disease itself (once TB, cancer today) arouses thoroughly old fashioned kinds of dread. Any disease that is treated as a mystery and acutely enough feared will be felt to be morally, if not literally, contagious. Thus, a surprisingly large number of people with cancer find themselves being shunned by relatives and friends and are the object of practices of decontamination by members of their household, as if cancer, like TB, were an infectious disease. Contact with someone afflicted with a disease regarded as a mysterious malevolency inevitably feels like a trespass; worse, like the violation of a taboo. The very names of such diseases are felt to have a magic power. In Stendhal's *Armance* (1827), the hero's mother refuses to say "tuberculosis," for fear that pronouncing the word will hasten the course of her son's malady. And Karl Menninger has observed (in *The Vital Balance*) that "the very word 'cancer' is said to kill some patients who would not have succumbed (so quickly) to the malignancy from which they suffer." This observation is offered in support of anti-intellectual pieties and a facile compassion all too triumphant in contemporary medicine and psychiatry. "Patients who consult us because of their suffering and their distress and their disability," he continues, "have every right to resent being plastered with a damning index tab." Dr. Menninger recommends that physicians generally abandon "names" and "labels" ("our function is to help these people, not to further afflict them")—which would mean, in effect, increasing secretiveness and medical paternalism. It is not naming as such that is pejorative or damning, but the name "cancer." As long as a particular disease is treated as an evil, invincible predator, not just a disease, most people with cancer will indeed be demoralized by learning what disease they have. The solution is hardly to stop telling cancer patients the truth, but to rectify the conception of the disease, to de-mythicize it.

When, not so many decades ago, learning that one had TB was tantamount to hearing a sentence of death—as today, in the popular imagination, cancer equals death—it was common to conceal the identity of their disease from tuberculars and, after they died, from their children. Even with patients informed about their disease, doctors and family were reluctant to talk freely. "Verbally I don't learn anything definite," Kafka wrote to a friend in April 1924 from the sanatorium where he died two months later, "since in discussing tuberculosis... everybody drops into a shy, evasive, glassy-eyed manner of speech." Conventions of concealment with cancer are even more strenuous. In France and Italy it is still the rule for doctors to communicate a cancer diagnosis to the patient's family but not to the patient; doctors consider that the truth will be intolerable to all but exceptionally mature and intelligent patients. (A leading French oncologist has told me that fewer than a tenth of his patients know they have cancer.) In America—in part because of the doctors' fear of malpractice suits—there is now much more candor with patients, but the country's largest cancer hospital mails routine communications and bills to outpatients in envelopes that do not reveal the sender, on the assumption that the illness may be a secret from their families. Since getting cancer can be a scandal that jeopardizes one's love life, one's chance of promotion, even one's job, patients who know what they have tend to be extremely prudish, if not outright secretive, about their disease. And a federal law, the 1966 Freedom of Information Act, cites "treatment for cancer" in a clause exempting from disclosure matters whose disclosure "would be an unwarranted invasion of personal privacy." It is the only disease mentioned.

All this lying to and by cancer patients is a measure of how much harder it has become in advanced industrial societies to come to terms with death. As death is now an offensively meaningless event, so that disease widely considered a synonym for death is experienced as something to hide. The policy of equivocating about the nature of their disease with cancer patients reflects the conviction that dying people are best spared the news that they are dying, and that the good death is the sudden one, best of all if it happens while we're unconscious or asleep. Yet the modern denial of death does not explain the extent of the lying and the wish to be lied to; it does not touch the deepest dread. Someone who has had a coronary is at least as likely to die of another one within a few years as someone with cancer is likely to die soon from cancer. But no one thinks of concealing the truth from a cardiac patient: there is nothing shameful about a heart

attack. Cancer patients are lied to, not just because the disease is (or is thought to be) a death sentence, but because it is felt to be obscene—in the original meaning of that word: ill-omened, abominable, repugnant to the senses. Cardiac disease implies a weakness, trouble, failure that is mechanical; there is no disgrace, nothing of the taboo that once surrounded people afflicted with TB and still surrounds those who have cancer. The metaphors attached to TB and to cancer imply living processes of a particularly resonant and horrid kind.

2

Throughout most of their history, the metaphoric uses of TB and cancer crisscross and overlap. The *Oxford English Dictionary* records "consumption" in use as a synonym for pulmonary tuberculosis as early as 1398.[1] (John of Trevisa: "Whan the blode is made thynne, soo folowyth consumpcyon and wastyng.") But the pre-modern understanding of cancer also invokes the notion of consumption. The OED gives as the early figurative definition of cancer: "Anything that frets, corrodes, corrupts, or consumes slowly and secretly." (Thomas Paynell in 1528: "A canker is a melancolye impostume, eatynge partes of the bodye.") The earliest literal definition of cancer is a growth, lump, or protuberance, and the disease's name—from the Greek *karkínos* and the Latin *cancer*, both meaning crab—was inspired, according to Galen, by the resemblance of an external tumor's swollen veins to a crab's legs; not, as many people think, because a metastatic disease crawls or creeps like a crab. But etymology indicates that tuberculosis was also once considered a type of abnormal extrusion: the word tuberculosis—from the Latin *tuberculum*, the diminutive of *tuber*, bump, swelling—means a morbid swelling, protuberance, projection, or growth.[2] Rudolf Virchow, who founded the science of cellular pathology in the 1850s, thought of the tubercle as a tumor.

Thus, from late antiquity until quite recently, tuberculosis was—typologically—cancer. And cancer was described, like TB, as a process in which the body was consumed. The modern conceptions of the two diseases could

---

1   Godefroy's *Dictionnaire de l'ancienne langue française* cites Bernard de Gordon's *Pratiqum* (1495): "*Tisis, c'est ung ulcere du polmon qui consume tout le corp.*"

2   The same etymology is given in the standard French dictionaries. "*La tùbercule*" was introduced in the sixteenth century by Ambroise Paré from the Latin *tùberculum*, meaning "*petite bosse*" (little lump). In Diderot's *Encyclopédie*, the entry on tuberculosis (1765) cites the definition given by the English physician Richard Morton in his *Phthisiologia* (1689): "*des petits tumeurs qui paraissent sur la surface du corps.*" In French, all tiny surface tumors were once called "*tubercules*"; the word became limited to what we identify as TB only after Koch's discovery of the tubercle bacillus.

not be set until the advent of cellular pathology. Only with the microscope was it possible to grasp the distinctiveness of cancer, as a type of cellular activity, and to understand that the disease did not always take the form of an external or even palpable tumor. (Before the mid-nineteenth century, nobody could have identified leukemia as a form of cancer.) And it was not possible definitively to separate cancer from TB until after 1882, when tuberculosis was discovered to be a bacterial infection. Such advances in medical thinking enabled the leading metaphors of the two diseases to become truly distinct and, for the most part, contrasting. The modern fantasy about cancer could then begin to take shape—a fantasy which from the 1920s on would inherit most of the problems dramatized by the fantasies about TB, but with the two diseases and their symptoms conceived in quite different, almost opposing, ways.

TB is understood as a disease of one organ, the lungs, while cancer is understood as a disease that can turn up in any organ and whose outreach is the whole body.

TB is understood as a disease of extreme contrasts: white pallor and red flush, hyperactivity alternating with languidness. The spasmodic course of the disease is illustrated by what is thought of as the prototypical TB symptom, coughing. The sufferer is wracked by coughs, then sinks back, recovers breath, breathes normally; then coughs again. Cancer is a disease of growth (sometimes visible; more characteristically, inside), of abnormal, ultimately lethal growth that is measured, incessant, steady. Although there may be periods in which tumor growth is arrested (remissions), cancer produces no contrasts like the oxymorons of behavior—febrile activity, passionate resignation—thought to be typical of TB. The tubercular is pallid some of the time; the pallor of the cancer patient is unchanging.

TB makes the body transparent. The X-rays which are the standard diagnostic tool permit one, often for the first time, to see one's insides—to become transparent to oneself. While TB is understood to be, from early on, rich in visible symptoms (progressive emaciation, coughing, languidness, fever), and can be suddenly and dramatically revealed (the blood on the handkerchief), in cancer the main symptoms are thought to be, characteristically, invisible—until the last stage, when it is too late. The disease, often discovered by chance or through a routine medical checkup, can be far advanced without exhibiting any appreciable symptoms. One has an opaque body that must be taken to a specialist to find out if it contains cancer. What the patient cannot perceive, the specialist will determine by analyzing tissues taken from the body. TB patients may see their X-rays or

even possess them: the patients at the sanatorium in *The Magic Mountain* carry theirs around in their breast pockets. Cancer patients don't look at their biopsies.

TB was—still is—thought to produce spells of euphoria, increased appetite, exacerbated sexual desire. Part of the regimen for patients in *The Magic Mountain* is a second breakfast, eaten with gusto. Cancer is thought to cripple vitality, make eating an ordeal, deaden desire. Having TB was imagined to be an aphrodisiac, and to confer extraordinary powers of seduction. Cancer is considered to be de-sexualizing. But it is characteristic of TB that many of its symptoms are deceptive—liveliness that comes from enervation, rosy cheeks that look like a sign of health but come from fever—and an upsurge of vitality may be a sign of approaching death. (Such gushes of energy will generally be self-destructive, and may be destructive of others: recall the Old West legend of Doc Holliday, the tubercular gunfighter released from moral restraints by the ravages of his disease.) Cancer has only true symptoms.

TB is disintegration, febrilization, dematerialization; it is a disease of liquids—the body turning to phlegm and mucus and sputum and, finally, blood—and of air, of the need for better air. Cancer is degeneration, the body tissues turning to something hard. Alice James, writing in her journal a year before she died from cancer in 1892, speaks of "this unholy granite substance in my breast." But this lump is alive, a fetus with its own will. Novalis, in an entry written around 1798 for his encyclopedia project, defines cancer, along with gangrene, as "full-fledged *parasites*—they grow, are engendered, engender, have their structure, secrete, eat." Cancer is a demonic pregnancy. St. Jerome must have been thinking of a cancer when he wrote: "The one there with his swollen belly is pregnant with his own death" ("*Alius tumenti aqualiculo mortem parturit*"). Though the course of both diseases is emaciating, losing weight from TB is understood very differently from losing weight from cancer. In TB, the person is "consumed," burned up. In cancer, the patient is "invaded" by alien cells, which multiply, causing an atrophy or blockage of bodily functions. The cancer patient "shrivels" (Alice James's word) or "shrinks" (Wilhelm Reich's word).

TB is a disease of time; it speeds up life, highlights it, spiritualizes it. In both English and French, consumption "gallops." Cancer has stages rather than gaits; it is (eventually) "terminal." Cancer works slowly, insidiously: the standard euphemism in obituaries is that someone has "died after a long illness." Every characterization of cancer describes it as slow, and so it was first used metaphorically. "The word of hem crepith as a kankir,"

Wyclif wrote in 1382 (translating a phrase in II Timothy 2:17); and among the earliest figurative uses of cancer are as a metaphor for "idleness" and "sloth."[3] Metaphorically, cancer is not so much a disease of time as a disease or pathology of space. Its principal metaphors refer to topography (cancer "spreads" or "proliferates" or is "diffused"; tumors are surgically "excised"), and its most dreaded consequence, short of death, is the mutilation or amputation of part of the body.

TB is often imagined as a disease of poverty and deprivation—of thin garments, thin bodies, unheated rooms, poor hygiene, inadequate food. The poverty may not be as literal as Mimi's garret in *La Boheme*; the tubercular Marguerite Gautier in *La Dame aux camélias* lives in luxury, but inside she is a waif. In contrast, cancer is a disease of middle-class life, a disease associated with affluence, with excess. Rich countries have the highest cancer rates, and the rising incidence of the disease is seen as resulting, in part, from a diet rich in fat and proteins and from the toxic effluvia of the industrial economy that creates affluence. The treatment of TB is identified with the stimulation of appetite, cancer treatment with nausea and the loss of appetite. The undernourished nourishing themselves—alas, to no avail. The overnourished, unable to eat.

The TB patient was thought to be helped, even cured, by a change in environment. There was a notion that TB was a wet disease, a disease of humid and dank cities. The inside of the body became damp ("moisture in the lungs" was a favored locution) and had to be dried out. Doctors advised travel to high, dry places—the mountains, the desert. But no change of surroundings is thought to help the cancer patient. The fight is all inside one's own body. It may be, is increasingly thought to be, something in the environment that has caused the cancer. But once cancer is present, it cannot be reversed or diminished by a move to a better (that is, less carcinogenic) environment.

TB is thought to be relatively painless. Cancer is thought to be, invariably, excruciatingly painful. TB is thought to provide an easy death, while cancer is the spectacularly wretched one. For over a hundred years TB remained the preferred way of giving death a meaning—an edifying, refined disease. Nineteenth-century literature is stocked with descriptions of

---

3   As cited in the OED, which gives as an early figurative use of "canker": "that pestilent and most infectious canker, idlenesse"—T. Palfreyman, 1564. And of "cancer" (which replaced "canker" around 1700): "Sloth is a Cancer, eating up that Time Princes should cultivate for Things sublime"—Edmund Ken, 1711.

almost symptomless, unfrightened, beatific deaths from TB, particularly of young people, such as Little Eva in *Uncle Tom's Cabin* and Dombey's son Paul in *Dombey and Son* and Smike in *Nicholas Nickleby*, where Dickens described TB as the "dread disease" which "refines" death

> of its grosser aspect in which the struggle between soul and body is so gradual, quiet, and solemn, and the result so sure, that day by day, and grain by grain, the mortal part wastes and withers away, so that the spirit grows light and sanguine with its lightening load . . . .[4]

---

4   Nearly a century later, in his edition of Katherine Mansfield's posthumously published *Journal*, John Middleton Murry uses similar language to describe Mansfield on the last day of her life. "I have never seen, nor shall I ever see, any one so beautiful as she was on that day; it was as though the exquisite perfection which was always hers had taken possession of her completely. To use her own words, the last grain of 'sediment,' the last 'traces of earthly degradation,' were departed forever. But she had lost her life to save it."

30

Democracy in Shackles

Who benefits from free trade?

Naomi Klein

"Democracy in Shackles," from
Fences and Windows: Dispatches From the Front Lines of the Globalization Debate

Naomi Klein

Copyright © 2002 by Naomi Klein

During the April 2001 Summit of the Americas in Quebec City, U.S. President George W. Bush proclaimed that the proposed Free Trade Area of the Americas (FTAA) would help usher in "a hemisphere of liberty." Explicitly linking globalization and democracy, Bush argued that "people who operate in open economies eventually demand more open societies."

Does globalization really foster democracy? It depends on the kind of globalization we create. The current system simply outsources decision making to opaque and nonrepresentative institutions, but there are other choices available. At home and on the world stage, democracy is a choice, one that demands constant vigilance and renewal.

President Bush seems to have a different vision. Like so many defenders of the current global economic model, he argues that democracy is not so much an active choice as a trickle-down effect of economic growth: free markets create free peoples. Would that democracy really were such a laissez-faire matter. Unfortunately, investors have proven themselves all too willing to support oppressive monarchies like Saudi Arabia's, or Communist authoritarianism in China, as long as these regimes crack open markets to foreign companies. In the race for cheap labour and precious natural resources, pro-democracy movements are often trampled.

Sure, capitalism thrives in representative democracies that embrace pro-market policies such as privatization and deregulation. But what about when citizens make democratic choices that aren't so popular with foreign investors? What happens when they decide to nationalize the phone company, for instance, or to exert greater control over their oil and mineral wealth? The bodies tell the story.

When Guatemala's democratically elected government introduced sweeping land ownership reforms in the 1950s, breaking up the monopoly held by the U.S's United Fruit Company, the country was bombed and the government ousted. At the time, the U.S. claimed it was an inside job, but nine years later, president Dwight D. Eisenhower reflected that, "We had to get rid of a Communist government that had taken over." When General Suharto staged his bloody coup in Indonesia in 1965, he did so with co-operation from the United States and Europe. Roland Challis, the BBC's Southeast Asia correspondent at the time, maintains that "getting British companies and the World Bank back in there was part of the deal." Similarly, it was "free market" forces in the United States that instigated the military overthrow of democratically elected Chilean President

Salvador Allende in 1973, eventually leading to his death. (At the time, Henry Kissinger famously commented that a country shouldn't be allowed to "go Communist due to the irresponsibility of its own people.")

The current open talk in Washington about the need to unseat Venezuelan president Hugo Chavez shows that this deadly logic didn't die with the Cold War. But these days, the free market's interference with democracy usually takes subtler forms. It's a directive from the International Monetary Fund requiring governments to introduce user fees in health care, or to slash billions from public services, or to privatize a water system. It's a plan cooked up by the World Bank to erect a massive dam, implemented without consulting the communities displaced by the project, ones whose way of life will disappear. It's a World Bank report calling for more "flexibility" in the labour market of a heavily indebted country—including restrictions on collective bargaining—in order to attract foreign investors. (If they resist and defend themselves, they may well find themselves classified as terrorists, and all means to suppress them will become permissible.)

And sometimes the interference is a complaint to the World Trade Organization that public ownership of a national postal service "discriminates" against a foreign courier company. It's a trade war waged against countries that decide, democratically, to ban hormone-treated beef or to provide free AIDS drugs to their citizens. It's the incessant clamouring for tax cuts from business lobbies in every country, based on the ever-present threat that capital will flee if we don't grant the corporations' up-to-the-minute wish list. Whatever the methods employed, "free markets" rarely stand by and tolerate truly free peoples.

When we talk about the relationship between globalization and democracy, we need to look not only at whether nations have won the right to cast ballots every four or five years but also at whether citizens still consider those ballots meaningful. We must look not only for the presence of electoral democracy but also examine the day-to-day quality and depth of those liberties. Hundreds of thousands take to the streets outside trade meetings not because they oppose trade itself but because the very real need for jobs and investment is systematically being used to undermine all our democracies. The unacceptable trade is the one that erodes sovereign rights in exchange for foreign investment. What I dislike most about the trickle-down democracy argument is the dishonour it pays to all the people who fought, and fight still, for genuine democratic change in their countries, whether for the right to vote, or to have access to land, or to

form unions. Democracy isn't the work of the market's invisible hand; it is the work of real hands. It is often stated, for instance, that the North American Free Trade Agreement is bringing democracy to Mexico. In fact, workers, students, indigenous groups and radical intellectuals are the ones slowly forcing democratic reforms on Mexico's intransigent elite. NAFTA, by widening the gap between rich and poor, makes their struggle more militant, and more difficult.

In the place of such messy, disruptive, real-world democratic movements, President Bush offers a calm, soothing lullaby: just relax and wait for your rights to come to you. But contrary to this lethargic vision of trickle-down democracy, globalization in its current form doesn't bring liberty. Neither does the free market or the ready availability of Big Macs. Real democracy—true decision-making power in the people's hands—is always demanded, never granted.

31

If Only Pizza Didn't Come on Paper Plates

Colin Beavan

"If Only Pizza Didn't Come on Paper Plates," from *No Impact Man*

Colin Beavan

Copyright © 2009 by Colin Beavan

Early on, when we were dating, Michelle made me her "signature" dish, spaghetti carbonara. Candles cast a warm glow. She set the table beautifully. She placed before me a dish of undercooked, nearly crunchy pasta, piled on top of a runny puddle of heavy cream.

"Delicious," I said dutifully.

"I think I forgot to put something in," Michelle said.

"The eggs?" I ventured.

Michelle blushed. "I don't actually cook," she said.

"It's delicious," I insisted.

When the No Impact project started, as a matter of simple self-preservation, we never even discussed the possibility of Michelle taking charge of grocery shopping and cooking. What I would have to come to terms with, if we were to eliminate our appalling twenty-gallon-a day waste habit, was an end to takeout and its assortment of disposable plastic tubs. I would have to make a new habit of—God help me—grocery shopping and cooking. Me. Myself. I. By which I mean: not Michelle.

"Besides, it's your project," Michelle would, fairly, point out. Or, as she liked to note to friends: "One fun thing about No Impact has been watching my husband transform himself into a 1950s housewife."

A Provençal housewife. For my initiatory jaunt into the world of fresh-food shopping, as an ideal I had in mind what I'd seen in the markets of the little villages of rural France, and even in the small shops that line the high streets of the residential neighborhoods of Paris. Fresh goods laid out on wooden tables. Not a morsel packed in containers, cardboard boxes, or aluminum foil wrappers. At worst, a baker in a red-and-white apron might twist a fresh little quiche into a piece of waxed paper with a flourish.

> In Paris, I once saw a woman make a carrier out of the hem of her skirt.

Baguettes stick out of chic ladies' reusable shopping bags protected by not so much as a piece of cling film. Heads of lettuce, salamis, and peaches balance precarious in bicycle baskets. There is no plastic or paper to peel off the food once it's home. There is no packaging. And if you don't have your own reusable shopping bag, if you should suggest that a throwaway plastic bag might be supplied, the clerk scowls and tsks and offers to let you reuse a cardboard box from that morning's deliveries.

In Paris, I once saw a woman, who had purchased some food items during an obviously unplanned shopping trip, make a carrier out of the hem of her dress, carefully calculating, as she walked home, the balance between dropping her vegetables and showing everyone her underwear. I'd seen Parisians carrying their groceries in canvas bags, backpacks, wicker baskets, or those bags made from netting—*les filets*, as the French call them—that scrunch into a ball in your pocket but then, voilà, can carry home your family's dinner.

So as I was preparing to venture into the world of grocery shopping and cooking in order to stop making trash, expunging disposable bags from my world became my first obsession. I should be like the French, I thought, which was fine with me, because the French are cool.

And for starters, what I needed to be truly environmental, I decided, was to buy myself a French net bag.

Wasn't anybody who cared about the planet at all already carrying canvas shopping bags? Not if they were anything like I was. Certainly, in periodic blusters of goodwill toward all creatures, I had *bought* canvas bags, but they now lay crumpled and completely forgotten at the back of some closet.

My goal now was not just to own an alternative to the throwaway bag, but to actually use one—all the time, no exceptions. As Environmentalism 101 as this sounds, it's a good benchmark for how far behind the touchdown line I had started, and, symbolically, how far behind the United States lags when it comes to cleaning up its environmental act. China, South Africa, Ireland, Bangledesh, Taiwan, Uganda, and Tanzania had already taxed or restricted plastic bags into virtual extinction.

This was an easy entrée for a neophyte like me just making his first steps into environmental living. It was merely the opening salvo in my brewing jihad against the disposable plastic crap that filled my trash bags.

And it was a simple test, like the cloths I'd been carrying around as handkerchiefs, of my hypothesis that eliminating the colossal waste from our lives, responsible for so much of the damage we do to our planetary habitat, does not entail depriving ourselves but just changing some

no-longer-functional habits. After all, who would suggest that to do without plastic bags is to be deprived? Who could possibly argue that using plastic bags makes us happier?

Every year, we junk some 4 to 5 trillion plastic bags worldwide, according to the Worldwatch Institute. Around the globe, plastic bags, used for a matter of minutes and then thrown away, leave stores and markets in quantities hundreds of times greater than any other piece of merchandise. They are the world's most ubiquitous consumer item and, not coincidentally, its most pervasive throwaway product.

We recycle plastic bags at a rate of less than 1 percent, and thrownaway bags formed some 4 million tons of municiple waste in the United States in 2006. They poison our air when burned in incinerators, or leach nasty chemicals in our landfills for hundreds of year. And thanks to their light-weight aerodynamics, the wind carries an estimated 1 percent of plastic bags out of trash depositories. These renegade bags end up billowing from trees, hanging from fences, or, worst of all, floating in the ocean.

In 1988, across a span of just two weeks, fifteen leatherback turtles, an endangered species, washed up dead on the beaches of Long Island. Alarmed by the deaths, marine biologists performed autopsies. They discovered that eleven of the fifteen dead turtles had ingested plastic bags that blocked their stomach openings. Leatherback turtles, you see, have the unfortunate twin qualities of a taste for jellyfish and bad eyesight. To these nearly blind turtles, it seems, a submerged plastic bag looks simply delicious.

The crazy thing is that the bags, which are designed to be thrown away, are made out of a material that is designed to last forever. They are far from the only plastic-containing disposables: think of razors, eating utensils, toothbrushes, water bottles, coffee cups, pens, combs, and on and on. Because plastic is so durable, all these things persist for hundreds of years. As a result, there are 46,000 pieces of plastic floating in every square mile of ocean, according to the United Nations Environment Program.

A thousand miles off the coast of California, in the middle of the Pacific Ocean, there is a swirling soup of floating trash twice the size of the continental United States. The "garbage patch," as it's called, contains six times as much plastic, by weight, as bio-matter. Way out there in the Pacific Ocean, a thousand miles from the nearest human, plankton, jellyfish, and fish are outnumbered (by weight) six to one by plastic bags, water bottles, and other throwaway plastic tchotchkes.

In the North Pacific alone, an estimated 100,000 sea turtles and sea mammals, a million seabirds, and countless fish starve to death each year after plastic blocks their digestive tracks. A recent study on Sand Island, in the northwestern Hawaiian chain, showed that 97 percent of Laysan albatross chicks had ingested plastic picked up by their parents from the ocean surface and mistakenly fed to them as food.

Meanwhile, those floating plastic discards that don't choke marine animals slowly break down in the salt and sunlight until they are suspended in the water like microscopic Christmas-tree bobbles. The plankton-eaters devour them, then the big fish eat the little fish, and then guess who eats the big fish? The sushi restaurants that make dinners for us grown-ups and the fish-stick factories that make school lunches for our kids. What starts at the bottom of the food chain inevitably ends up at the top.

It turns out that each of us has, in our body, detectable amounts of up to one hundred industrial chemicals nobody had even heard of fifty years ago. Many of these chemicals come from the production and use of the same disposable plastic crap that fills my garbage bags. Bisphenol-A, for example, a compound used in the liners of food cans and to make disposable water bottles and other hard plastics, is a known hormone disrupter that raises the risk of certain cancers, hampers fertility, and may contribute to childhood behavioral problems such as hyperactivity.

> To those nearly blind turtles, it seems, a submerged plastic bag looks simply delicious.

You are what you eat, they say, and it's not just the turtles who are ingesting the plastic crap we throw away. What happens to the wildlife on this planet is an early warning sign of what's happening to us.

The way my culture lives its life, I can't help wondering: Really? Are plastic bags (and paper bags, which aren't any better for the environment) something for which we are willing to threaten the planetary habitat we all depend upon for our health, happiness, and security?

On balance, if we have to choose—and I think we kind of do—would we rather have a planet overflowing with plastic bags and all the rest of the disposable plastic crap, or would we rather have sea turtles and chemical-free children?

It is with a fixation not so much on saving turtles, I have to admit, as on getting myself a couple of those cool French net shopping bags that, in the

middle of a late-November afternoon, with what I think is plenty of time to spare, I venture out into the world to gather food for our first non-trash-generating meal.

I call Michelle and give her the choice between omelettes and tofu scramble for dinner. In the spirit of a true eco-wannabe, she chooses tofu scramble. I head, first, to the nearby Whole Foods on Union Square.

Down in the store's lower level, I explain very carefully to a shop clerk what I am looking for—and it's not tofu. "You know," I say, "those bags that kind of look like fishing net but they have handles."

The clerk doesn't follow.

I start to explain again.

The clerk stops me.

No, he says. Whatever it is I'm after, Whole Foods doesn't have it. They carry black, canvas-type bags made out of recycled plastic. "But, no, nothing made out of, um, fishnets."

I go to Bed, Bath & Beyond. Nope. I go to the Container Store. Nope. I try Home Depot. Nope. I walk up Sixth Avenue and down Broadway, explaining to every shopkeeper who will listen all about the net bags they use in France. But, no.

Suddenly it's 5:00 p.m. I have to pick up Isabella from Peggy, our child-carer. The ample couple of hours I'd allowed for shopping is up. Once home, I look out of my ninth-floor window, down at the trees, and see three plastic bags tangled in the branches. I look around the apartment and see that it is virtually littered with bags I could have used to go shopping—including the ones at the back of the closet I'd bought in my last blush of eco-consciousness.

Michelle gets home from work. "Is dinner almost ready?"

I give her a dejected look. I have no tofu, and there will be no tofu scramble. Yet again we Google the number for the Big Enchilada. Yet again we order takeout. Yet again our trash is filled with plastic tubs.

Since the tubs will persist for a thousand years, I realize, I could put a note in one in the hope that it might be found by my grandchildren's grandchildren's grandchildren's grandchildren. Here's what the note would say: "Dear kids. Sorry about the turtles."

If the goal is to keep empty the garbage bags that used to be filled with take-out containers, filling a grocery cart with plastic-wrapped veggies, cardboard-boxed pasta, yogurt in tubs, and eggs in cartons won't do the trick. Prepackaged grocery-store food is out. By the time I wake up first thing the next morning and make shopping for food—and only shopping for food—the priority of the day, I've realized that loose produce and unpackaged food sold from bulk bins are my holy grail.

So I grabbed my long-neglected reusable bags and walked over to the Integral Yoga grocery score, where I'd had my plastic-or-paper-bag ordeal. Integral Yoga Natural foods, as it is called in full, is run by the acolytes of someone called Sri Swami Sarchidananda. They sell an extensive selection of unpackaged food that you scoop into containers with little shovels. The Swami, I suppose, preached the importance of bulk bins.

The problem, though, when you're faced with bins full of everything from pasta and rice to seaweed and raisins, is that you still have to find a way to carry the food home. You can't just stuff your pockets with brown rice. Normal people—those who aren't making their life's work out of not making trash—tear off plastic bags from rolls hanging by the bins. But with last night's take-out enchilada slip, I'd hit a bottom with my turtle choking, and starting today I had very proudly thought of a better solution.

Back at home, I had gathered a bunch of empty glass jars out of our cupboards and stuffed them in the canvas bags I'd finally rescued from the back of the closet. I lugged the jars with me to Integral Yoga with the intention of putting my pasta and my rice and coffee and freshly ground-up peanut butter in them. I had even weighed the jars, so I knew how much the cashier should subtract after I'd filled them with commodities.

So, I arrive at Integral Yoga, scoop various grocery needs into jars, and am feeling very proud of myself. I'd found my place. I'd arrived at my new eco-home. I'd discovered my family's new nutritional center of gravity.

With filled-up jars, I get in line to pay. My turn comes and I put my jars on the counter and smile at the young woman behind the cash register. I look forward expectantly to her recognition of my eco-effort and her smile of encouragement.

"What's all this?" she asks, looking at the jars.

I explain about the jars and not using plastic bags and I point to the weights I'd written on masking tape stuck to the lids and she calls the manager to figure out how to do the subtraction. I'm growing anxious about the line

of customers behind me yet looking forward to the cashier telling me how great I am for not using plastic bags.

But she doesn't.

You know what she does instead?

She sighs.

Then she looks at me. Then she looks at the jars. Then she looks at me again. Then, you know what she does? She rolls her eyes.

Since deciding to loosely model my life, for a year, on the smidgeon I'd heard about the wood-harvesting philosophy of the Menominee tribe, I've idealized them in my mind. They've become my symbol of good living, of living happily, taking from the planet what it can sustainably offer and not taking what it can't.

> Do the Menominee suffer crises of confidence? Because I am hitting my first.

Today, though, I want to know: Do the Menominee suffer crises of confidence? Because I am hitting my first.

The Menominee's philosophy, as McDonough and Braungart put it in *Cradle to Cradle*, demanded that they never took more lumber than the forest could sustainably offer them. But what about years of hunger or drought? What about years when wood prices fell so low that they couldn't meet the needs of their children? What about years when they were just overwhelmed by wanting and desire and craving?

I mean, it's been a couple of weeks now since the Integral Yoga cashier scowled at me; and, in truth, I've made a lot of progress.

We've stopped eating takeout in plastic tubs. Canceled our newspaper subscriptions. Avoided buying anything in packaging. Put our names on the do-not-send-me-catalogs-and-junk-mail lists. Begun taking clothes to the tailor for repair instead of throwing them out. Taken our own reusable containers to take-out places when we just couldn't get ourselves to cook. Replaced paper towels with rags made from discarded clothes. Collected used printer paper from my publisher and used the other side to write on. Kept cloth handy to wrap things in, use as a napkin, and dry our hands on when we're out of the house.

Further: We've carried reusable cups everywhere. Accepted that we can't have coffee if we forget our cups. Turned a nose up at bottled water by using our cups for tap water, too. Replaced throwaway produces, like Bic pens and Gillette razors, with reusable versions (think straight razor and fountain pen). Celebrated the diminishing of our waistlines, since we're pretty much off packaged cans of Pringles, not to mention Ben & Jerry's Chubby Hubby.

I'd even proved my environmental bona fides by having an argument with Michelle about whether she would make the switch from throwaway tampons to those reusable menstrual cups made from medical-grade silicon. I lost (but I'd wear her down eventually).

None of these steps was too unpleasant at all. I'd even found little pull-string organic muslin bags so light that you don't have to subtract their weight when you fill them with pasta from the bulk bin and put them on the scale at Integral Yoga. Even my old nemesis, the cashier, is secretly starting to like me. My family's trashcan and even our recycling bin is yawningly empty. I've come to think I can do this. I've hit my stride. Or so I thought.

Although today, walking past a pizza place on Fourteenth Street, I find myself looking longingly in the window. Not hungrily. Longingly. It's just a hankering, really. And before this no-impact thing started, such a hankering would have had me marching straight through the door and up to the counter to chow down a slice on a now prohibited paper plate. Same if I wanted soda in a now-prohibited plastic bottle. Same, really, if I wanted just about anything.

But today I'm thinking maybe I'll cheat.

Living in New York City, I'd long felt that I could gratify my wants pretty much the moment I had them. No more. To avoid making trash, I've had to say no more than a few times in the last couple of weeks.

No to an everything bagel with scallion tofu wrapped in waxed paper from Bagel Bob's. No to a bottle of seltzer water. No to herbal tea in a paper cup from News Bar. No even to a tinfoil-wrapped Hershey's Kiss from the snack area at the Writers Room, where I go to work. No peanuts. No potato chips. No popcorn at the movies. Our entire universe, apparently, is individually wrapped. Unless you're willing to toss out that handful of barely used packaging within five minutes of getting it, without ever even using it, you're screwed.

"Good Lord, man," National Public Radio presenter Scott Simon would say to me during an interview for *Talk of the Nation*, "isn't the whole point of living in New York to enjoy the good life?"

"God, yes!" I would have shouted if he asked me today. I felt like I was making sacrifices for the sake of environmentally poor decisions that other people had made. There was no reason that pizza needed to be on a plate made from a dead tree. Couldn't the geniuses of our culture find an ecologically sensitive way to do these things? For now, I felt like I was the one paying for their bad systems.

It's true that I discovered Ronnybrook Farm, a dairy with a stand at the farmer's market that sells its milk in glass bottles that I can return for reuse. I love that I've found blocks of unpackaged tofu I can put in my own container, and egg farmers who take back and reuse their egg cartons. There are some small-scale systems that can be found that don't require resources to be wasted, and I feel really good about getting our groceries home and making our meals without making trash. And I dig the childishly naughty feeling I get that by doing all this I'm somehow being subversive and giving a finger to the Matrix.

But there comes a time when, hell, you just want a slice of pizza, even if "the man" hasn't thought to provide it in a sustainable way. What I've accomplished until now mostly has to do with investigating and planning—where to shop, what unpackaged product to buy. Passing up a slice of pizza (and the paper plate) would have more to do with accepting that, if I want to live sustainably, I can no longer have exactly what I want exactly when I want it. Because our systems are not designed to be sustainable, I had to swim against the cultural tide, and sometimes I got tired.

Self-restraint. Crap!

That's how I imagine the Menominee must have felt on so many occasions over their hundreds of years of managing their forests. There must have been many times when they wanted more but could not take it, many times when enough did not seem like enough. But how would they keep their lumber business if they cut too many trees down? How will I make discoveries in this experiment if every time I have a craving I cave in?

Today, again, since I have no way to avoid using a paper plate and napkin, I say no to the pizza. But I'm not happy.

I walk away down Fourteenth Street. Stopped at the red light on the corner of Third Avenue is a guy in a BMW. Anger washes over me. And self-righteousness. This idiot is guzzling oil and pumping carbon into the air in the middle of a city that has wonderful public transportation, my mind tells me. But I'm not mad so much as I'm envious. This guy gets to sit in his fancy car, listening to his Bose in car stereo while pretty girls crossing the street turn to look at him, and I'm stuck in my self-imposed year of not having a piece of pizza when I want one.

How do the Menominee-in-my-mind feel when they are exercising self-restraint but they see a company like Kimberly-Clark raking in millions by clear-cutting every tree in sight to make paper plates to put pizza on? Do the Menominee feel sorry for themselves? Do they have the feeling I do today—that everyone can have what they want but me? I doubt it. By now, I'm sure, they've learned that there is a strong payoff to living the way they do.

The Menominee know that in a hundred years they will have still more trees to cut down. With the Amazon rain forest losing 2,000 trees a minute, Kimberly-Clark and the rest of us very well may not. That's the sustainability payoff for the Menominee. My question is: Where's the sustainability payoff for me?

Michelle comes bursting through the door, carrying a big plastic cup filled with nuclear-purple goop.

"I have great news," she says, all smiles. "What?" I ask, eyeing her disallowed plastic cup.

"I've discovered the No Impact weight-loss diet."

The thing is, Michelle is one of those New York media-industry glam-girl fashionistas. It's who she is. For her, a great carefree night out consists of ten friends at Pastis, shouting over the dinner about clothes, then men, then diets, probably in that order. Michelle and her friends are like the spymasters of undiscovered designer-sample sales and the mad scientists of weight-loss schemes that will get them to fit into those clothes.

In the week before the No Impact project, in a panic about the coming year, she went on a clothes-shopping bender that reaped her two really nice pairs of leather boots and cost us the cashing-in of one small, unserviced 401(k). The No Impact project, in other words, doesn't come easily to her. But she's a sport. And she has an open mind about how it might turn out.

Anyway, her last high-tech weight-loss scheme involved payment of huge amounts of cash to a nutritionist and then a month spent eating space meals from little tinfoil packets to which you add water. As of today, apparently, it's juice fasting. She has just come home from a place on Third Avenue called Juiceteria. Her friend Tara told her about it.

"I know, I know. I got a disposable cup," Michelle says, "but I talked to the lady behind the counter and she supports our project.

She says I can bring my own reusable bottle or cup."

I force a smile.

The thing is, while my grandparents had their nice little retirement home in Westport, Massachusetts, Michelle's maternal grandparents did everything they could to get their children a better life than they themselves had on a farm in the Midwest. Their families had lived through the hardship of the Dust Bowl. They had eeked a living off the land. To Michelle's family, therefore, who had moved off the land and become rich, to buy what they wanted when they wanted it—like the juice—had become a sign of their overcoming difficulty. It was, in their way, even an expression of gratitude for their good fortune. This purchasing freedom was evidence of the family's hard work.

Is this expression of identity any less true or valuable or understandable than my own grandparents' insistence on thrift? No.

But the question remains: How do we reconcile such a way of life with the fact that the planer we depend upon for our health, happiness, and security is so depleted? The trick, in part, will be to make living sustainably as easy as falling off a log. We must find production processes, ways to generate energy, and manufacturing materials that do not damage our planet so substantially. Then Michelle can have her juice and affirm her family's success, too.

Meanwhile, our culture's whole way of operating is one huge juggernaut heading in a consume-every-resource direction. Somehow I'm supposed to persuade poor Michelle to live differently, to reject, in a way, the culture of her family. Is this right?

Besides which, I wonder: What's so great about trying to be right if it keeps you separate? What's so great about trying to be right if it makes you lonely?

The juice is Michelle's version of the French net bag. You try to go to the end of the consumerist universe but keep finding yourself back at its center, back in the old buy-something-to-fix-something, eat-to-lose-weight, consume-to-conserve trance that we're all stuck in. But, today, I just don't have the heart to say anything.

My thought process around this discouraging time:

1.   I worried that the whole pizza episode pointed to the larger fact that the human species may be called upon to exercise superhuman restraint when it comes to not using resources the planet cannot afford for us to use. "The problem with people like you is that you don't accept that people are basically selfish and they're never going to change," I'd get told more than a few times during the No Impact project. At this low point, when I still felt bitter about the things I could not have, and awful for denying Michelle the things she wanted, I thought maybe they were right. I began to worry again that people were just too selfish.

2.   But, for starters, the idea that people, including me, are driven first by selfishness goes against my whole worldview and my gut instinct. Most of us love our children and want to be polite to our neighbors. Most of us, unless we are hobbled by terrible living conditions or alcohol or drugs, would rather help than harm. Most of us, in our hearts, want peace and harmony for ourselves and for everyone else. Most of us believe that we should take good care of the planet. None of us actually *likes* trashing our resources.

3.   Besides, it's not an issue of whether we want things, it's an issue of how the system delivers the things we want. My desire for the pizza was not the problem. The fact that it came on a disposable paper plate was the problem. Our system makes it virtually impossible to get the things we want and need without leaving behind a trail of trash and pollution and greenhouse gases. Sit down at a fastfood restaurant, for example, and within moments the garbage surges at you. First comes the paper placemat and the paper napkin, then the straw, the straw wrapper, a throwaway glass bottle with your drink, a paper doily, a Styrofoam box, a little plastic cup for ketchup. "You're going to think this is weird," I must have said to a hundred servers, "but I'm on this

don't-make-trash kick. I brought my own cloth napkin. Would you mind terribly much putting this paper one back where you got it?"

4.   Just because trash crashes like a tidal wave through my life doesn't mean I made the tidal wave. Trash and pollution and greenhouse gases, therefore, are not a result of some total flaw in human nature.

5.   But when I started reading a little history, I learned that there were reasons why I felt so guilty and selfish. "People start pollution. People can stop it." Remember that message? It came from the Keep America Beautiful (KAB) campaign's public-service announcement, the one with the Native American who cries because of all the litter. Well, guess what? It turns out that KAB was established by the American Can Company and the Owens-Illinois Glass Company, the inventors of the throw-away, nonreturnable beverage can and bottle, respectively. They recruited fellow industrial polluters, from paper-cup manufacturers to oil companies, to help fund KAB and then use it to promote the idea that individuals rather than companies are responsible for litter and pollution. As Heather Rogers writes in her book about garbage, *Gone Tomorrow,* "KAB wanted to turn any stirrings of environmental awareness away from industry's massive and super toxic destruction of the natural world… singling out the real villain: the notorious 'litterbug.'" No wonder I feel so guilty.

> My desire for the pizza was not the problem. The fact that it came on a disposable paper plate was the problem.

6.   History also taught me that the United States has already proved that it's perfectly possible for a culture to operate without sending so much to landfills and incinerators, selfishness and altruism notwithstanding. Before 1900, most households didn't even have a trashcan. The rag-and-bone man came to your door and paid you to give him, among other things, your old clothes for paper-making, your meat bones for button-making, and your cooking grease for soap-making. What was left, you burned in your stove for heat. But this cultural ethic of reuse changed when, by way of example, button factories discovered it was cheaper and more efficient to get their bone from the conveyor-belt slaughterhouses, and paper producers discovered a way to make paper from trees

instead of from cloth. With industrialization, our materials economy stopped working in a circle that went from producer to consumer and back again, and instead became unidirectional—from producer to consumer to landfill and incinerator.

7.   To me, this proves again that making so much trash and pollution and greenhouses gases is not the result of our natures—selfish or otherwise—but simply of corporate habits our culture can no longer sustain. And if we changed once, from closed to open loop, I figured, we can just as easily change from open to closed loop. Germany, I discovered, already has a system called "extended producer responsibility," a policy that requires producers to be physically or financially responsible for their products, including the packaging, after their useful life. This take-back obligation gives producers an incentive to think of ways to make their products more reusable or recyclable so that fewer resources end up making a beeline for the landfill or incinerator.

8.   But after thinking all this through, my mood took a turn for the worse. I thought, Oh great, the problem is not selfish human nature; it's just our whole manufacturing and distribution system. Like that's going to be easier to fix. If I'm hoping for change, I might as well blow my head off.

9.   What was the point of this stupid No Impact project?

10.   Then, a regular reader of my blog, a woman who lives in India named Uma Padmanabhan, left behind this quote from the *Bhagavad Gita*, the epic Hindu poem: "To action alone hast thou a right and never at all to its fruits; let not the fruits of action be thy motive; neither let there be in thee any attachment to inaction." In other words, just do it!

11.   And a woman calling herself Jen from Brooklyn left on the blog the story of Nachshon, who was the first of the Israelites to enter the Red Sea when fleeing from Egypt. Nachshon, she wrote, was an ordinary guy, not a leader or anything like that. Nachshon didn't have the slightest idea how he was going to get across the Red Sea, but he marched on in just the same. All he had was courage and determination and maybe faith, and so he just did the only thing he could, which was to take each step as it came. He didn't know what would happen. The good news is, and maybe it will be the good news for all of us who try, that just as

he got to the point where the water came up to his nose, the Red Sea parted.

12.   I find myself reminded that the whole project is about not waiting around to see what might help. It is about stumbling forward and beginning to try to make a difference, rather than sitting around wondering if I can make a difference.

13.   So whether it's human nature or industrial systems that need to change, when it comes to saving the world, the real question is not whether I can make a difference. The real question is whether I am willing to try.

14.   Am I willing to try?

Here's a little thought experiment that keeps obsessing me.

We know that for all the material that ends up in our products, the manufacturing process has already trashed seventy times that much material. Do the math and that means that, of all the raw material taken from the earth to make consumer products, only 1.5 percent of it actually ends up in our hands. Meanwhile, 98.5 percent of what we suck out of the ground, the rivers, and the forests ends up being trucked straight to the landfill or the incinerator without it ever even being used by us.

Now, I'm no economist or production analyst, so I'm sure the situation isn't as perfectly straightforward as I'm about to make it sound, but from where I'm sitting, this means that of the water and air the manufacturing sector pollutes, of the forests it cuts down, of the natural habitats it destroys, of the greenhouse gases it creates, of the total environmental damage created by manufacturing, 98.5 percent results in nothing but industrial waste, producer trash that consumers never even see.

So here's my little thought experiment:

Suppose we, as a culture, ask the manufacturing people co reduce their waste by just 1.5 percent. "Hey, you guys," we could say, "just tone it down a little. Tell you what, though, you can still waste 97 percent of what you dig out of the planet. We just want you to reduce your waste by 1.5 percent." Personally, I don't feel that asking this of them would be too terribly harsh.

But here's the thing: if they wasted just that little bit less, then the amount of raw materials available to actually end up in products would jump from

1.5 percent (what's left behind by 98.5 percent waste) to 3 percent (what's left behind after reducing waste to 97 percent). That's huge. Because that's a doubling of the resources available to go in products, this would mean that, for manufacturing to get what it needs, it could chop down half as many trees, blow the tops off half as many mountains, pollute half as many rivers, and pump out half the greenhouse gases. And what would it take? Reducing their waste from 98.5 percent to 97 percent.

That doesn't sound like too much to ask, does it?

As I walked away from the pizza, I was feeling angry, as if everybody else were allowed to have what they want but not me. I suddenly felt like I was transported back to being the ten-year-old "have-not" of my seaside childhood town, where the motorboat and minibike of my classmate Skippy Manchester were mysteriously denied me.

But to suggest that that feeling derived from being the quasi-poor kid doesn't explain it, either.

Because Michelle, who grew up the child of millionaires, lived in the then-biggest house in Bismarck, North Dakota. She was, in fact, the Skippy Manchester of her town. But she tells me she spent half her time wishing she lived in a one-story ranch house like "normal" people, and the other half wishing she could drive around a family estate in a golf cart like her even richer, billionaire friends.

Michelle and I talk about this because the No Impact project forces us to come face-to-face with daily desires we're so unaccustomed to confronting. We talk about how the poor kid and the rich kid—me and her—both suffered the same amount of want and envy. We talk about how everybody, in any life situation, in any circumstances, at any time, seems to want something. We talk about how wanting is a kind of perpetual-motion machine that lives in our minds.

My attention now drawn to the fact, I see that when I get what I want, my want does not go away, it just turns to the next thing. In some ways, it's incorrect to say, "I want this" or "I want that." It's more correct to just say, "I want," in the same way as we say, "I ache." If I got the net bag, I would have just gone on to want something else. I wonder if, understanding that wanting is at the base of human experience and that it is not alleviated by fulfilling the capricious desire of the day, I might perhaps allow myself to get off the hamster wheel.

At the same time, Michelle and I noticed that what we wanted on the surface—the minibike or the "normal" ranch house—were just proxies for what we really wanted: to fit in. We wanted to be loved. We wanted not to feel what we imagined that everyone else didn't feel—insecurity. We wanted to feel accepted.

So, here' s the big question: If we want to demonstrate our membership in the human race, if we want to fit in, where on earth did the idea come from that we have to do it by having or aspiring to have exactly what everyone else has, by eating what everyone else ears, by drinking what everyone else drinks? People are such social animals, so much more than we realize. We'll do, or can be tricked into doing, almost anything for the promise of love.

"We're getting rid of the TV," Michelle announced when I came home one night. It had been a few weeks now that, by Michelle's original insistence, the TV had been unplugged. Our television, by the way, was this forty-six-inch-screen, rear-projection giant that took up much more living-room space than we could spare.

"Hold your horses," I said. "We may want it when the project is over."

"It's evil,' 'Michelle said. "It's never caused us anything but problems and I want it out of here."

What she was saying was true. Michelle had developed, by her own admission, a little bit of an addiction to reality television. We had fought about it. I felt it got in the way of our relationship—something to do with her preferring to watch *The Bachelor* than to talk to me. And Isabella, in the week or two before the project began, had actually said, in her squeaky going-on-two-year-old voice, "I want *Bridezilla*, Mommy."

"When your kid asks for *Bridezilla*," Michelle said, "you know you're putting your viewing pleasure before your parenthood. Get rid of it. This is non-negotiable."

For the woman who had spent a small retirement fund on boots a few weeks earlier, this was quite the turnaround.

> Four weeks after the project began, we weren't just changing the way we lived; changing the way we lived was changing us.

I thought about it. I thought about the 2,000 to 5,000 advertisements people like Michelle and me see every day, depending on where you're getting your stats. I thought about how the consumption activist Annie Leonard said, in her video *Story of Stuff*, that "three thousand times a day, we're told that our hair is wrong, skin is wrong, clothes are wrong, our furniture is wrong, our cars are wrong, we are wrong but that it can be made right if we just go shopping." And I thought, No wonder I feel like a loser for no longer buying exactly what I want the moment I want it.

I'm trying to become a nonconsumer of planetary resources, and here in the middle of my house was this box whose purpose was to pump messages at me, telling me that unless I used more resources I was a loser. To be No Impact Man, it told me, was to be a loser. It told me that to put not making trash before having more stuff was to be a loser. Waking up to the fact that the TV was making me feel bad about my life—and making the project harder—was like discovering that the enemy was encamped in my living room.

Which clinched it. By Michelle's decree, we would be a no-TV family from here on in. Four weeks after the project began, we weren't just changing the way we lived; changing the way we lived was changing us. Michelle made arrangements to give the TV to a family who might otherwise buy a new one. Two huge 250-pound men marched into our living room, lifted up our forty-six-inch television, and carried it away.

32

Maybe We Should Call It Something Scarier

Bill McKibben

Maybe the problem is with the name. "Global warming" just doesn't sound that bad.

That's the only explanation I can think of for how unworried we are by the onset of the greenhouse effect.

The halfhearted set of measures announced by President Clinton aren't really designed to "combat" global warming; they're designed, eventually, to slow it down a tad. Under his plan, by 2010 or there abouts we will try to return to emitting no more carbon dioxide than we emitted in 1990—which was exactly the same promise President Bush made in Rio in 1992, except that Bush was ambitious enough to promise he'd do it by 2000. Even the Japanese, completely dependent on imported fuel, have called for tougher measures.

Contrast that nonchalance with the flurry of activity and interest surrounding that other weather menace, El Niño. We have national conferences, emergency plans, T-shirts, weathermen pointing transfixed at a map of the Pacific, showing the pool of warm water sneaking up on the California coast; we have contractors working around the clock to fix people's roofs, all before the first drop of torrential rain hits the subdivisions of Greater Los Angeles. It's enough to make Noah look like a carefree slacker.

And yet what is El Niño? It's a weather phenomenon that begins off the coast of South America with the appearance of warmer-than-expected water. It changes weather patterns in several parts of the globe for a year or two, and then switches, becoming a La Niña, a pool of cooler-than-expected water.

In other words, El Niño is like a temporary junior version of global warming: a small-scale greenhouse effect. If it worries you, then consider that within fifty years we will have a permanent, planetwide El Niño that does all the same things, just forever.

Already, in fact, we are seeing far more severe disruptions of the planet's climate than El Niño threatens. Warmer air means more evaporation and hence more rainfall—already, global warming has increased severe storms across our continent by 20 percent. Warmer air means changes in the seasons—already, global warming has moved winter around, bringing spring a week earlier to the northern hemisphere. New studies show widespread permafrost melting across the Arctic and rapid glacial melting everywhere from Montana to Patagonia. Global warming means nothing less than the most fundamental alteration of the planet's systems since the last ice age; El Niño is just a thirty-second trailer before the main feature, a feature that lasts into eternity, or at least until the next big asteroid slams into the earth.

And yet it doesn't bother us much, at least not compared with the possibility of economic disruption that effective controls might mean. Administration economists hand around reports showing that taxing carbon enough to reduce its emissions might reduce GNP 1 percent or 3 percent, as if that was a danger comparable to changing the planet's basic functioning. Even environmentalists don't give the White House enough grief to balance the lobbying from carmakers and utilities and coal miners.

So here's my plan. Let's give global warming a new, scarier name. *El Piquante Grande*, perhaps? Or *La Chaleur Enorme*. Do those sound malevolent enough? How about Hell on Earth? Maybe then it will start to sink in.

33

A New Leader

Andrew Helfer

CHAPTER NINE: *A NEW LEADER*

AN ACT OF VIOLENCE COMMITTED IN APRIL 1957, HOWEVER, DID BRING MALCOLM AND THE NATION OF ISLAM INTO THE NATIONAL SPOTLIGHT.

ONE VERSION OF THE STORY HAS IT THAT TWO WHITE POLICEMEN IN HARLEM SAVAGELY BEAT A DRUNK MAN.

ONE OBSERVER, AN NOI BROTHER NAMED JOHNSON X HINTON, WAS INCENSED.

JERKS. YOU'RE NOT IN ALABAMA—

DISGUSTED, HINTON TURNED TO LEAVE, UNAWARE THAT HE HAD SUCCEEDED IN REDIRECTING THE POLICEMEN'S RAGE.

NUGGGHHH!!

WHEN HINTON MANAGED TO GRAB THE FIRST COP'S NIGHTSTICK, BACKUP POLICEMEN SUDDENLY APPEARED ON THE SCENE.

OTHERS SAY THAT HINTON WAS IN A HARLEM PRECINCT JAIL CELL PRAYING WHEN THE NIGHTSTICKS CAME DOWN.

IN EITHER EVENT, WORD OF THE BRUTALITY QUICKLY SPREAD ACROSS HARLEM.

FURIOUS, RESIDENTS FLOCKED TO THE PRECINCT HOUSE TO DEMAND JUSTICE.

NOW IT WAS THE POLICE WHO WERE OUTNUMBERED.

IN A PANIC, SOME SAY, THE POLICE PHONED MALCOLM ASKING FOR HELP.

HOWEVER HE GOT THE NEWS, MALCOLM MOBILIZED THE NOI IMMEDIATELY AND WAS ON HIS WAY.

THE PARAMILITARY UNIT OF THE NOI KNOWN AS THE FRUIT OF ISLAM (FOI) ARRIVED, POSITIONING THEMSELVES TO MAINTAIN ORDER.

WHEN MALCOLM ARRIVED, HE WAS SHOCKED BY HINTON'S INJURIES.

"IT WAS ALL I COULD DO TO CONTAIN MYSELF," MALCOLM REMEMBERED. "HE WAS SEMICONSCIOUS. BLOOD BATHED HIS HEAD, FACE, AND SHOULDERS."

MALCOLM DEMANDED THAT BROTHER JOHNSON RECEIVE IMMEDIATE MEDICAL ATTENTION.

THE AMBULANCE ARRIVED, AND A CROWD OF MORE THAN 2,000 FOLLOWED IT TO THE HOSPITAL ON FOOT.

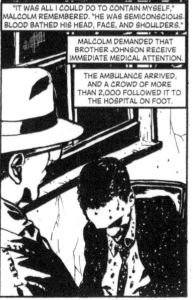

WHEN MALCOLM WAS SATISFIED THAT HINTON WOULD BE TAKEN CARE OF, HE STEPPED OUT OF THE HOSPITAL AND WAVED HIS HAND...

...AND THE FRUIT OF ISLAM PEACEFULLY DISPERSED THE CROWD.

POLICE INSPECTOR MAGOWAN OBSERVED MALCOLM'S POWERFUL ACT OF CROWD CONTROL WITH A MIXTURE OF IN AWE AND APPREHENSION.

NO MAN SHOULD HAVE THAT KIND OF POWER...

AMSTERDAM NEWS EDITOR JAMES HICKS ADDED:

WHAT HE *REALLY* MEANT IS THAT NO *BLACK* MAN SHOULD HAVE THAT KIND OF POWER.

WHATEVER THE EXACT EVENTS OF THAT DAY, WHAT IS CERTAIN IS THAT NOT ONLY HAD MALCOLM BECOME A HERO TO THE BLACK PEOPLE OF HARLEM...

...BUT HE AND THE NATION OF ISLAM HAD MADE THEIR FIRST STEP INTO THE CONSCIOUSNESS OF WHITE AMERICA.

MALCOLM'S INTENSE SCHEDULE LEFT HIM LITTLE PERSONAL TIME—BUT AS HIS PUBLIC STATURE SHOT UP, MALCOLM SEEMED DRIVEN TO PUT DOWN ROOTS AS WELL.

IN DECEMBER OF 1957, HE SOUGHT MUHAMMAD'S BLESSING TO MARRY COLLEGE-EDUCATED NOI SISTER BETTY X, FORMERLY BETTY SAUNDERS.

THE MESSENGER'S VERDICT: SISTER BETTY X WAS A FINE SISTER.

WITH MUHAMMAD'S BLESSING IN HAND, MALCOLM DROVE TO LANSING.

JUST OUTSIDE DETROIT, HE STOPPED AT A GAS STATION AND CALLED BETTY.

OH HELLO, BROTHER MINISTER.

LOOK, DO YOU WANT TO GET MARRIED?

THE MOST CALCULATING OF SPEAKERS, HE LATER CLAIMED HE DIDN'T KNOW WHAT HE WAS GOING TO SAY TO HER UNTIL HE SAID IT.

YES.

"JUST LIKE I KNEW SHE WOULD," MALCOLM ADMITTED.

WELL, I DON'T HAVE A WHOLE LOT OF TIME, YOU'D BETTER CATCH A PLANE TO DETROIT.

THEY WERE MARRIED IN LANSING TWO DAYS LATER, ON JANUARY 14, 1958. BY NOVEMBER, THE FIRST OF THEIR SIX DAUGHTERS WAS BORN.

IN JULY 1959, THE FIRST PART OF A FIVE-PART DOCUMENTARY SERIES HOSTED BY MIKE WALLACE WAS BROADCAST.

THE HATE THAT HATE PRODUCED

IT PURPORTED TO REVEAL THE TRUE HISTORY AND CURRENT STATE OF THE NOI.

ALTHOUGH THE SERIES WAS PRODUCED WITH THE FULL PARTICIPATION OF MALCOLM, MUHAMMAD, AND MANY MEMBERS OF THE NOI...

...AND NOTHING ANY NOI MEMBER SAID OR DID WAS PARTICULARLY THREATENING...

...THE DOCUMENTARY WAS EDITED IN SUCH A WAY THAT THE JUXTAPOSED IMAGES WERE OMINOUS.

AND IF THE IMAGES ALONE DIDN'T SCARE THE DAYLIGHTS OUT OF WHITE AMERICA...

...MIKE WALLACE'S NARRATION WOULD DO THE TRICK.

WHILE CITY OFFICIALS, STATE AGENCIES, WHITE LIBERALS, AND SOBER-MINDED NEGROES STAND IDLY BY, A GROUP OF NEGRO DISSENTERS ARE TAKING TO STREET-CORNER STEPLADDERS...

...CHURCH PULPITS, SPORTS ARENAS, AND BALLROOM PLATFORMS ACROSS THE NATION TO PREACH A GOSPEL OF HATE THAT WOULD SET OFF A FEDERAL INVESTIGATION IF IT WERE TO BE PREACHED BY SOUTHERN WHITES.

VIEWERS WERE LEFT WITH THE IMPRESSION THAT THE NOI WAS A CLEAR AND PRESENT THREAT TO AMERICA.

MALCOLM WAS MORE THAN HAPPY TO CONCUR. NEW RECRUITS POURED INTO THE NOI.

AFTER *THE HATE THAT HATE PRODUCED* APPEARED, THE NOI RECEIVED TWO TYPES OF CALLS.

THE FIRST WAS FOR INTERVIEWS WITH THE SHOCKING "ANGRY NEGROES." *LOOK, NEWSWEEK,* AND *TIME* DID FEATURE-LENGTH STORIES ABOUT LIFE IN THE NATION OF ISLAM.

WRITER/DIRECTOR/PHOTOGRAPHER GORDON PARKS'S PHOTO ESSAY ON "THE BLACK MUSLIMS" FOR *LIFE* MAGAZINE WAS AMONG THE MOST INFLUENTIAL.

WHILE WRITING A *READER'S DIGEST* PIECE, "MR. MUHAMMAD SPEAKS," ALEX HALEY MET MALCOLM X.

THEIR RELATIONSHIP WOULD GO FROM A CLASSIC *PLAYBOY* INTERVIEW TO *THE AUTOBIOGRAPHY OF MALCOLM X*, ONE OF THE BEST-SELLING AUTOBIOGRAPHIES OF ALL TIME.

THE SECOND TYPE OF CALL WAS THE ONE MADE TO EXPRESS HATE. *THE HATE THAT HATE PRODUCED* ANGERED MANY PEOPLE ACROSS THE COUNTRY WHO HAD SEEN IT...

...AND THEY FELT COMPELLED TO SHARE THE HATE THE PROGRAM PRODUCED.

IN THE SOUTH, A NEW FORM OF PROTEST—SIT-INS AT SEGREGATED LUNCHROOM COUNTERS—CAUGHT THE EYE OF THE SCLC. BUT SOME FELT IT MOVED TOO SLOWLY AND WAS NOT IN TOUCH WITH THE YOUNGER GENERATION OF BLACKS.

THESE CONCERNS LED TO THE CREATION OF THE STUDENT NONVIOLENT COORDINATING COMMITTEE (SNCC).

THE CONGRESS OF RACIAL EQUALITY (CORE), FOUNDED IN THE 1940S, ALSO EMBRACED GANDHI'S NONVIOLENT TACTICS.

TO DESEGREGATE THE SOUTH'S BUS LINES, CORE, WORKING WITH THE SNCC, FILLED BUSES WITH "FREEDOM RIDERS."

THE RIDERS WERE HARASSED AND BEATEN, ULTIMATELY REQUIRING THE ASSISTANCE OF THE FEDERAL GOVERNMENT.

ALTHOUGH BLACKS OUTNUMBERED WHITES IN MANY SOUTHERN DISTRICTS, FEW WERE REGISTERED TO VOTE.

IN MISSISSIPPI, ALABAMA, AND GEORGIA, CORE AND THE SNCC BEGAN MASSIVE VOTER REGISTRATION DRIVES.

BUT REGISTERING COULD BE DANGEROUS. MIDDLE-AGED FANNIE LOU HAMER WAS ONE OF MANY BLACKS BEATEN AND THROWN IN JAIL AFTER REGISTERING TO VOTE WITH THE SNCC'S SUPPORT.

IN JUNE 1963, NAACP MEMBER MEDGAR EVERS WAS SHOT IN HIS JACKSON, MISSISSIPPI, DRIVEWAY AS HE WALKED TO HIS HOME WITH AN ARMFUL OF "JIM CROW MUST GO" T-SHIRTS.

AND IN SEPTEMBER FOUR BLACK GIRLS WERE KILLED WHEN THE KU KLUX KLAN BOMBED THEIR CHURCH IN BIRMINGHAM, ALABAMA.

MALCOLM'S CONFRONTATIONAL APPROACH WAS NOW BEGINNING TO MAKE MORE SENSE TO YOUNG BLACKS THAN DR. KING'S POLICIES OF NONVIOLENCE.

IN THE SUMMER OF 1963, WHILE MILLIONS OF BLACKS JOINED KING FOR HIS MARCH ON WASHINGTON, MALCOLM WATCHED, EVEN THOUGH ELIJAH MUHAMMAD HAD FORBIDDEN IT.

MALCOLM, WHO WAS SERVING AS INTERIM MINISTER AT THE WASHINGTON, DC, MOSQUE AT THE TIME, LATER SARCASTICALLY NOTED THAT "WHILE KING WAS HAVING A DREAM, THE REST OF US NEGROES ARE HAVING A NIGHTMARE."

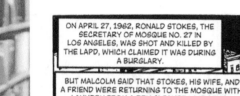

ON APRIL 27, 1962, RONALD STOKES, THE SECRETARY OF MOSQUE NO. 27 IN LOS ANGELES, WAS SHOT AND KILLED BY THE LAPD, WHICH CLAIMED IT WAS DURING A BURGLARY.

BUT MALCOLM SAID THAT STOKES, HIS WIFE, AND A FRIEND WERE RETURNING TO THE MOSQUE WITH LAUNDRY FROM A DRY CLEANER WHEN THEY WERE STOPPED BY TWO LAPD OFFICERS.

YOU GOT A LICENSE TO SELL CLOTHING?

LOOK, OFFICER— I'M NOT SELLING THESE CLOTHES, AND THEY WEREN'T STOLEN.

NO? I HEAR YOU GUYS ARE ALWAYS STEALING THINGS.

EXCUSE ME?

YEAH... STEALING FROM WHITE FOLKS.

WE HAVEN'T DONE ANYTHING.

THAT'S ALLOWED, RIGHT? STEALIN'? AS LONG AS THEY'RE WHITE.

AS HIS WIFE RACED BACK TO THE MOSQUE, STOKES TRIED TO HANDLE THE LAPD, BUT THE COP WAS LOOKING FOR TROUBLE.

LOOK, I KNOW YOU'RE ONLY DOING THIS BECAUSE WE'RE MUSLIMS...

...BUT IF YOU JUST CALM DOWN WE CAN—

STOP TALKING WITH YOUR HANDS! YOU PEOPLE'RE ALWAYS TALKING WITH YOUR HANDS!

SEE? MUCH BETTER!

ARRRRRR!!

MUHAMMAD SENT MALCOLM TO LOS ANGELES TO MINISTER AT THE VICTIM'S FUNERAL. MALCOLM HAD BEEN A CLOSE FRIEND OF STOKES; HIS MURDER HAD HIT HIM HARD. BUT HE WAS ALREADY THINKING ABOUT THE SERMON HE'D DELIVER—THERE WAS MUCH TO BE SAID.

MALCOLM FELT THAT AS PUBLIC AWARENESS OF THE NOI GREW, SO WOULD ACTS OF VIOLENCE AGAINST THEM. WHEN ATTACKED, THE NOI SHOULD RESPOND IN A LIKE MANNER.

THE POSSIBILITY OF NOI REPRISALS ALONE WOULD MAKE POTENTIAL AGGRESSORS THINK TWICE BEFORE ASSAULTING MUSLIMS.

MALCOLM DEFERRED TO MUHAMMAD'S WISHES, BUT REMAINED CONVINCED THAT THE NOI WOULD NEED TO CHANGE TO SURVIVE.

MUST GO

MUSLIMS GET OUT

U.S.A

NOI OUT

MERICA FOR ERICANS

NO NOI

BUT MUHAMMAD FORBID MALCOLM TO EXPRESS THIS OPINION, INSISTING THAT FURTHER VIOLENCE MUST BE AVOIDED.

NINE DAYS LATER, THE CORONER RULED STOKES'S DEATH A "JUSTIFIABLE HOMICIDE." STILL, NO RIOTS OR PROTESTS FOLLOWED.

FOR MANY NOI MEMBERS, THE ONLY CONSOLATION WAS MUHAMMAD'S NEWSPAPER COLUMN ON THE SUBJECT.

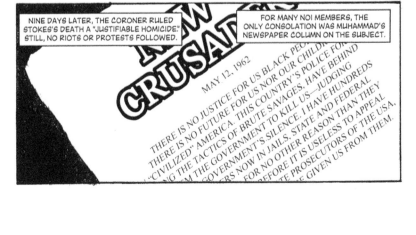

NEW CRUSADER

MAY 12, 1962

THERE IS NO JUSTICE FOR US BLACK PEO... THERE IS NO FUTURE FOR US NOR OUR CHILD... "CIVILIZED" AMERICA. THIS COUNTRY'S POLICE FO... ...G THE TACTICS OF BRUTE SAVAGES, HAVE BEHIND ...M THE GOVERNMENT TO KILL US—JUDGING ...GOVERNMENT'S SILENCE. I HAVE HUNDREDS ...RS NOW IN JAILS, STATE AND FEDERAL ...FOR NO OTHER REASON THAN THEY ...BEFORE IT IS USELESS TO APPEAL ...TE PROSECUTORS OF THE USA, ...E GIVEN US FROM THEM.

Reading Credits